Life is not perfect.
But there are perfect moments.

- C L Alexander

Everything I Miss At Home

C L Alexander

Order this book online at www.trafford.com
or email orders@trafford.com

Most Trafford titles are also available at major online book retailers.

Printed in the United States of America.

ISBN: 978-1-4269-7264-5 (sc)
ISBN: 978-1-4269-7265-2 (hc)
ISBN: 978-1-4269-7266-9 (e)

Library of Congress Control Number: 2011909983

Trafford rev. 06/28/2011

 www.trafford.com

North America & international
toll-free: 1 888 232 4444 (USA & Canada)
phone: 250 383 6864 ♦ fax: 812 355 4082

Acknowledgements

To God be the Glory. It is through his grace and mercy that I was able to write this book. I would like to thank my husband, Robert for giving me everything and never asking for anything in return. My children Ty and Tre are honestly my true blessings, in my life. To my mommy and daddy Betty and Andre I can't thank you enough for all you all have done for me. It is through you all that I've learned to appreciate life, love, and happiness. To my besties, Cheryl, Pootchie and Dawn. I celebrate and appreciate you girls for being more like my family than my friends. Thank you Tracy for taking the time to read over my manuscript. To the best brother in the world, Bishop James S McIntyre, for always reminding where I came from. I love you! And to anyone else I may have overlooked. I will catch you on the next novel.

1

The phone rang startlingly, just after Zoric's hand had awakened me to the tickling of his fingertips gliding up my thighs and finding their way to the tip of my mountain peaks. My senses were stirred even though I was near deep in a subconscious state of mind and longed for another three hours of sleep. My body began to tingle by his hard pressed lips easing around my sensitive spine.

The abrupt sound of the phone ringing again interrupted his seduction.

My hand extended from under the covers and touched the base of the phone. "Don't answer it," his warm breath whispered over my shoulder. "Let the voicemail get it. I want you now baby." Soft wet kisses followed those words down the center of my back.

I deliberated for a moment before I freed my hand from its base and turned over to welcome his strong tensed body over mine. His lips parted and we exchanged passion with each stroke of his tongue in my mouth. I crooned the sounds of pleasure, desiring, at that moment to want more... to feel more.

However, the phone rang again disturbing the rush of blood to every nerve cell in my body. I pulled my attention away from my longing to feel satisfied and thought about the fearful possibilities that waited on the other end of the phone. What if something happened to my brother? What if Tamra needed me? But that wouldn't be an emergency, necessarily because she always needed something. What if it's my mom? My body suddenly fell listless to his sensual caress. Instinctively, my hand rushed to answer the phone.

"Hello." I forced myself to utter, feeling like I'd just come up for air.

"Rocquelle. Are you awake?" It was the voice of my mother, sounding a bit frail.

"No," I lied, unsure of how to have answered that question. My eyes glared over at the alarm clock to capture 3:10 illuminating through the darkness. "Mom, are you okay? It's after three in the morning." I felt Zoric motion from under the covers and trailed around the bed and into the bathroom.

"Rocqui, I think I am quite aware of what time it is." She replied with much ornery in her voice. "It's just that... they got me laying up here in this hospital and you know I don't like sleeping anywhere besides my own bed."

Hearing only the word 'hospital' caused my chest to piercingly heave in and out. My limp body suddenly became stiff as I sat up in my bed. "You are in the hospital", I gasped fearfully?

"Yes, I'm in the hospital." Her words were casual, as if she spoke of the sun shining on a normal day. "I've been here for a couple of days, now. The doctor says she is just running some test, that's all," she replied nonchalantly.

Zoric entered from the bathroom, with all of his nakedness standing before me. I heard him mumble

"Who's that on the phone," before he retraced his steps back to his side of the bed and slid under the covers, to await for the phone call to end.

"What kind of test, mother? Is it the cancer? Has it come back? I thought you were in remission. You were doing fine." I kept trying to get a grip of what she was obviously reluctant to say by bombarding her with questions.

"I am feeling fine." Her words sounded definite. "I told the doctor just that, when she decided to admit me overnight in this room. She thinks it might just be the cancer again", she expressed lightly.

I was at a lost for words. The startling admittance of my mother having to battle breast cancer again had me paralyzed with fear.

"Rocqui, I don't want you to worry. I've fought this thing before and won and I will do it again. You just go back to sleep. I didn't mean to wake you."

"Mom, do you need me to come home?"

"No child. I don't need you to do anything. I will be just fine." I could tell she was easily becoming antsy with our conversation. "Listen, I'll call you tomorrow when I know more. Just go back to sleep."

"I love you Mom." Those were the last words I was able to release from my lips before she abruptly hung up the phone.

"Rocqui, what's wrong? What's the matter," I heard Zoric questioned from the background of my deep thoughts.

"I don't know," I finally brought myself to say, still staring off into the darkness trying to take in this sudden interruption of everything.

"But, I have to find out."

"Is your mother okay," he asked?

"I don't know... I don't think so."

Later that morning, I dialed Tamra's phone in Texas. "Did you know that mom was in the hospital?'

"What time is it?" Her voice sounded crackled and displaced.

I asked her again, ignoring the obvious grogginess in her voice. "Did you know that our mother was in the hospital?"

"Did you know that it is six in the morning, here in Texas and I'm still in the bed", she candidly responded, becoming more annoyed by my persistence?

"I'm sorry to have awakened you. But mom called me at three this morning and I haven't been able to sleep since." I was sitting from my desk from my home office staring down at Richmond's business district arising to the dawn of a new day. The traffic flow began to increase. Business suits and black pumps strutted down the sidewalks toting their brief cases over one arm while caring a cup of java in the other.

"Yeah... I knew. I'm surprised she called you, because she insisted that I wouldn't say anything."

"You got to be kidding me! Why wouldn't she want me to know? I'm her child too. I have the right to know what's going on with our mother," I pleaded frustratingly. "Now that I'm the last to know anything, could you please tell me what is exactly going on," I insisted?

Slowly, her words leaked from her mouth, with caution. "She had a mammogram that showed another lump in her breast a couple of weeks ago... And so her doctor asked her to come in for a biopsy to check to see if it is benign or malignant." Her voice began to sound weak and sorrowful. "She didn't want to tell you just yet because she wasn't certain and she knew that you would get all worked up and cause more worrying than necessary."

I was silent. All I could do was just breathe steadily.

"Rocqui? Rocqui... are you still there?

"I'm here," I answered softly, tightly gripping the phone like I was holding on to my mother's life.

"It's probably not that serious, Rocqui."

"It might not be, but something is not right. She sounded like she needed me. I've never heard her like this before. I was already planning to come down for her birthday next week. I'll just come there a few days earlier and stay a little longer just to make sure she is okay."

My phone beeped. It was my mother. "Hi mother. Are you still at the hospital," I asked with caution, fearing what the answer might be?

"No. I'm home. Your mother is still alive and breathing." She certainly sounded like she was full of herself this morning.

My eyes looked to the ceiling, as if it was the heaven above and thanked God. Sounding a bit relieved I implied, "You are sounding much livelier than earlier this morning."

"Oh child, I'm fine... At least I will be."

"What did the doctor say? Are you gonna be okay," I asked with the sound of hope spiraling through my words?

"I'm gonna be fine baby," she insisted.

The burden of anxiety was lifted off my shoulder and I exhaled. "It's not cancer that I should be worried about," I asked to make sure that I understood her correctly?

"Well, the biopsy revealed that cancerous cells are now present in my left breast. Apparently, it is malignant. But, I'm not worried. I fought it one time before and defeated it, I will do it again with the will of God on my side," she firmly stated, as if she knew this to be factual.

Baffled by total confusion, I asked "How can you sound so optimistic, mother?"

"Because... I'm alive today. I need not to worry about what tomorrow may bring. I've always told you too many times before that nothing is promised to you, not even tomorrow."

"Mom, do you want me to come home," I asked knowing that her answer would be no? But, I asked anyway to detect some type of neediness in her tone, so that I would know how serious this situation really was.

"Rocquelle." The sound of my birth name uttering from her breath confirms the matter to be as serious as I was beginning to think it was. "You don't have to drive all the way here to see about me. I'm fine." Surely, she sounded fine and rather convincing. But, at that point, I wasn't.

"I have a few things to finish up at the office this week. But you should expect to see me by Saturday. Okay Mother?"

She retreated with a simple, "okay". I ended my call with her and Tamra and got dressed to go to work.

The weeks exhausting long days ended with work still left undone piled upon my office desk. After endless hours of returning pertinent phone calls and meeting with lenders and lawyers over home mortgages, I had given up my relentless pursuit of perfection.

Friday night had arrived. I had to cancel Zoric and my dinner date at Ruth's Chris. At nine o'clock, my body still remained framed behind my desk. There was too much to do before I deserted my office space for two ineffective weeks, yet not enough time to do it all.

I was in the midst of solidarity. Everyone else had left there office space many hours ago. Finally I decided to vacate the building, myself. When I arrived home, Chee Chee faithful greeting trailed behind me up the stairs and into the room of my overly embellished systemized closet. I carefully studied my choice of outfits citing my mother's upcoming birthday... and a dress for Sunday. I knew she was going to want me to go to church, with her, even though I hadn't showcased my Sunday's best in a few shameful years. What shoes, which purse, and the right adorning accessories were all too many choices for my overworked mind.

The bright sunlight glaring through my window frame welcomed the dawn of a new day. I'd awaken to an empty space next to me. However, the presence of black socks and yesterday's underwear scattered across the bedroom floor offered comfort that he was home. And then I heard his voice. "Rocqui, breakfast is ready."

I turned toward the sound of his voice. "I'll be right down," I'd hope.

Every Saturday was like a routine for Zoric and me. There is breakfast. Nothing fancy...just croissant or muffins and always coffee.

The breakfast table serves as the meeting of our minds and exchange of our agendas that keep us atone to one another lives. Without it, the demands and work overload from our successful careers would probably make us near strangers.

After breakfast, our lives separated only to fulfill some unremitting prophecy of perfection. For Zoric, it's golf. For me, it's an early morning at the hair salon, only to return immediately to my office for continual work.

Later on, our day would reconvene with the two of us snuggling our bodies together on our favorite part of the sectional sofa, in anticipation of a good movie. His arm would gently wrap around my shoulder just long enough until I drifted off into a tiresome snore.

However, on this particular morning I didn't have time for breakfast. Zoric repeatedly called out to me to join him. Yet, the constant interruption of the phone ringing and trying to decide which outfits to pack hindered my efforts to join him at the breakfast table.

By the time I stumbled down the stairs, his golf club bag was parked at the front door. Chee Chee was wagging his fluffy tail while he fed from his kettle. And Zoric was clearing away his dishes, in the kitchen were I met him.

"There goes my beautiful raga muffin," Zoric spoke, as I made my final daunting appearance, with a scarf tied around my head, wearing a pair of unflattering pajama pants.

"That's exactly what I feel like right now."

"Coffee," he suggested handing me an already prepared mug?

"I wish I had time for coffee. I have so much stuff to do right now. I just wanted to come down and say bye before you left."

"Baby I think you overextend yourself sometimes. You don't have to leave today to go to Fayetteville. You could relax and spend the day with me. Then go to Fayetteville tomorrow."

"That sounds tempting, but, I feel like I should have been in Fayetteville yesterday. So, to me, I'm a day behind my life right now. But thanks anyway for the suggestion."

"Alright. Have it your way. Just make sure you take some time to relax when you get there."

"Okay. I will try to as much as I can."

We kissed and set a time to see each other before I headed to my mother's house at twelve.

Twelve o'clock on the dot had come and gone... and still no Zoric. The deli turkey and cheese spread over rye bread, I made for him, rested on the plate next to my car keys. The constant back and forth glances at my keys and at the sandwich made me anxious. Eventually, I became annoyed.

I grabbed my keys. The alarm was set and the garage door lifted as I stirred my wheels into reverse. I paused for a moment and gloated at the life that I had created for myself. Then, with a sense of hesitance, I shifted my gear into drive and prepared my mind for a return to a place that I once called home.

Welcome to Fayetteville NC... the home of the 82nd Airborne. Fort Bragg and Pope Air Force Base and the annual Dogwood Festival are all there is to this quaint southern town in the middle of nowhere. It's been three easily departing years, since my last return. It doesn't seem that long ago, but my absence seem to have serve Fayetteville well. My eyes were lost at the unexpected views of a multi-media complex and shopping malls. Acres and acres of trees have been cleared for land staking commercial development. What was once trailer lots and neglected estates have now become a prime source of real estate and luxury gated apartments.

A comfort suppressed my displacement when I turned left onto Murchinson Rd. Salem Baptist Church, my family church, was still in place, retraining its structural finishes of clay brick walls and towering white pillars that showcased its grandeur, since the days of all day Sunday praise and worship. And indirectly across from it was Suburban Mart, a convenient store where my sister, my brother and I, would carefully race across the street, after church for their five cent butter cookies and paper bag candy. At night, it transformed into a safe haven for drunks and hustlers, where they would toss their dimes and dice steadily against its side corner wall.

An unexpectant smile unfolded across my face over my moment of childhood nostalgia. Yet, I started to feel sad. Sad enough to bring tears to my eyes. Now my vision was a blur as I began to feel worried over the thought that the cancer, in which my mother had fought for many years had returned with a vengeance.

"Hey baby," The recognizable voice transmitted through my blue tooth and interrupted my moment of sorrow.

An uncontrollable smile unfolded across my lips. "Hi baby."

"I'm sorry I didn't make it home in time to see you off. Calvin and I were at the range and time kinda got the best of us."

"It's okay. You know I would have waited longer for you, but I was kinda anxious to get on the road."

"Are you home yet?"

In my mind, home is where I left four hours ago, in Richmond Va., where Zoric and I share the same address on a brand new condo, we just recently bought.

"I'm here in Fayetteville, but I haven't arrived at my mom's yet." I probably could have been there by now but the open interstate seem to have lead me into endless thoughts about seeing the strength and will in my mother become weaken by this ill-fated disease, once again and the anticipation of dealing with my older brother, whose life had only amounted to a quick dollar and a crack pipe. And lets not omit my little, grown married-ass sister who always, always needs me for everything.

"I miss you already." My thoughts drifted back to his strong shoulders, his yellowish-brown hue that stood 6ft tall, his ripened soft lips that I savored to taste and his round firm behind that I've always loved to hold when he was fully deep inside of me.

"I miss you too baby. I don't know how I'm gonna stand you being gone for two weekends. Even Chee Chee is missing you", he continued. "He has been wondering aimlessly up and down the stairs and sitting at the front door wagging his tail waiting for you to open the front door. I keep telling him you'll be back next weekend but he won't even listen to me. He just sits and barks at me like I did something to you."

Entertained by his story, I began to laugh... "I love you."

"I love you too. That's why we need to hurry and get married to make it official." The tentative date for our wedding is June 29th, of next year.

I have made many attempts to interview wedding planners over the past several weeks. However, I haven't made anything definite. Between the overwhelming stack of bridal magazines that are kept beside my bed and Zoric's ridiculous excitement over reality wedding TV shows, I have been left exhausted from making any wedding decisions.

Zoric is obviously more excited over getting married than I am. Raised in the 'hood of Akron Ohio, Zoric lived small, but dreamed big. His single-parented mother, Vanessa never held a salary income, just hourly wages, that barely afforded Zoric and his younger sister with enough to eat and minimum to wear. However, he was handsome, or just simply 'fine' as tagged by the women that encountered him.

The women at Virginia Commonwealth University, hopelessly, shared him as a prize. He arrogantly seduced their purses into providing him with diamond encrusted bracelets, every exclusive released pair of Jays' and Polo on his back. Everything he own was given to him. They loved him and sexed him and bought him. And he lusted in the temporary enjoyment that they gave him.

However, I was a different kind of woman than what he was use to. I wasn't in the business of buying a man. I was just as interested in the head on his shoulders as the other women were in the head that hung between his legs.

"I know baby. You know that there is nothing that I want more than to be Mrs. Huntington". That dream had to rest for now. I didn't know how to make Zoric understand the fear that now awakes me as I worriedly enter into the reality of my mother's ailment. "But, unfortunately that's not my biggest worry right now. I just need to know that she is okay, so that I will be."

"I understand. I'll be here, no matter what. I'm not going anywhere."

"Thank you. I promise at the first of the year, you and I are going to sit down and plan the perfect wedding anyone had ever seen."

"It doesn't have to be perfect as long as I'm marrying you."

I melted over his charm.

We said our 'goodbyes' and then suddenly, I had the urgency to use the bathroom. I was just minutes from the house I was raised in, yet I could no longer hold my pee. I pulled my recently purchased brand new black Lexus convertible, with the hard-top up, into same service station where my dad would fill his old white pick-up truck up with gas and I would always get a cherry cola slushy.

It is August. Even at night, the air is still very hot and humid. A few steps out of my car and I have already been bitten twice by mosquitoes that have stolen a taste of my honey tone skin around my bare ankles and up my thighs. After using the restroom, I glanced over at what appeared to be the same ole slushy machine that was here when I was a kid. Feeling tempted I walked over to the drink fountain and grabbed me a cup and filled up with blueberry. There were no cherry cola. The store's door chirped when I exited and I was well on my way to my mom's, sipping on my cool slushy.

Just a straight drive from the service station and then on my right, I turned into the entrance of the half brick wall that read 'The Gardens'... my ole neighborhood. The homes here have retained their middle class values from the days of my brother and sister and I, along with our friends, playing kickball or dodge ball, in the middle of the street. 'The Gardens' had always been well known, around town, as the predominant well-off African American neighborhood where professors at Fayetteville St University, retired military soldiers or Black and Decker power plants employees, like my father come to own their all brick split-level or ranch-style home.

After thirty years of loyal service, my father finally retired from Black and Decker only to die five years later from a sudden heart attack. I was a freshman at Howard University with my head in the clouds, feeling like the world was my footstool. Only for all my dreams and plans that I had with my father to be interrupted when

I received the call from my mother barely able to voice words that I never imagined that I would ever hear her say. "Your dad died." I denied that this was happening to me. Other people's daddy dies... not my daddy. He was supposed to walk me down the aisle one day. My children were gonna call him 'Pa Pa.'

During the long eight hour train ride home, I tried to imagine a world without my daddy. But, there was no image that I could retain. I held on to my hopes of this being a bad dream and that when I arrive back in Fayetteville, my daddy would be standing outside waiting patiently as the train pulls into the station. And I would spot him easily out of a crowd wearing his favorite weekend carpenter pants, and his wool flannel coat holding his pipe steadily to the right side of his mouth, and setting my eyes on his mouth barely parting into a smile upon seeing me step off the train.

It was the longest train ride of my life. When it finally arrived, there were no crowds and no sign of my daddy. From my window seat, there were just a few people, patiently waiting to board with their ticket in one hand and their bag in another; and my brother, Monty. He stood a tall resemblance of my father in his younger days wearing jeans and a grey hoodie. The emptiness that shadowed his face confirmed what I was refusing to believe. Suddenly, my stomach felt empty and my eyes were heavy with tears. My two overstuffed luggage felt weightless and the numbness in my legs made me stumble, a bit, while stepping off the train. I hurried into Monty's arms as if I needed him to catch me, because I was falling.

For a while, after my father's death, I could barely stand to look at myself in the mirror. It was easier for me to pretend that a part of me no longer existed, because he no longer did. Then one day, I stood at my bathroom sink and was washing my face when I caught a glimpse of myself in the mirror... and I saw my father. I saw his almond brown eyes and narrow pointy nose. I smiled at myself for the first time in a while. At another time, while I was getting dress, I slipped into a sexy sundress and twirled around in the mirror. My actions spun an immediate smile that evolved into laughter. I was overjoyed by the sight of my long slender legs, my father gave me. It was at that point that I was alright with the world, again.

My car eased into the driveway behind my mother's Camry. The headlights from my car must have detected to her that I had finally arrived. Before I could reach the doorsteps, she switched the front porch lights on and opened the door.

"Rocqui." Her face beamed with joy and she extended her petite frame around my towering body.

"Hi mom," I smiled back and locked my arms around her waist.

2

My mother and I lack any physical similarities. If we were to stand side by side, you would think that she created me strictly from a seed of my father and not of her own. She is not a big woman, just a curvaceous one. She is nothing over five feet tall, with shapely hips and plenty of backside. Upon meeting her, you would be greeted by her confidence and enduring smile. You would easily become captivated by her coffee brown eyes when they widen with joy and laughter. With the touch of her hands pressed firmly against my back, it felt like she was giving me air to breathe and I exhaled.

I followed her very old raggedy, yet precious house slippers swishing pass the off-limit living room leading into the kitchen. The smell of my father's stale tobacco from his hand carved pipe still lingered in the house, like his presence was still apart of our everyday lives. Family portraits, my sister's early days of cheerleading, Monty's little league photos and my infamous first grade missing front tooth pictures were all gracefully hung along the hall that led into the kitchen and den area.

"Are you hungry? I just finished cooking. You look like you could stand to gain a few pounds," she asked as if she was displeased with my size six figure. "Do you and that boy eat in Virginia," she continued to interrogate me in her motherly tone? I watched her walk over towards the stove and dipped a large serving spoon inside of one of her oversize pots.

"Of course we eat." I answered animatedly as I sat comfortably at the same kitchen table and in the same chair I'd always sat in since the days my feet dangled inches over the floor.

"I should have made you girls spend more time in the kitchen. That's what I should have done. I don't see how you and Tamra have been able to find men who are ok with you girls not being able to cook," she continued as she brought me my plate, loaded with baked macaroni and cheese, steamed cabbage, cornbread and fried pork chop.

In all the days of my mother and her sister's lives, they had found their sanctuary standing over a hot stove for hours to make sure the hungry souls and empty mouths of their families were fed. However, for my mother, raising three kids and rubbing my daddy's feet when they were tired did not fulfill every moment of her life. She took the interest of becoming a registered nurse and spent twelve hours of her days at the Medical Center. Where did she find the extra time for the church bake sale, while serving as president of the PTA at my school and making sure that my daddy's uniform for the week was starch and pressed, stumps me.

I can't stand in the kitchen long enough to boil an egg. Whereas I've been trained to keep a house clean, my overzealous drive and commitment to maintain a successful business had left little room for me to make that effort. I would probably be lost without the assistance of my three times a week cleaning lady. Remarkably, my eyes glare across the table and studied the face of a woman who is petite in stature, but larger than life. Intimidatingly, I wondered if I could be just as successful and perfect as I had known her life to be.

"Mom I can cook." I was obviously lying, but I wanted her to think that I was at least trying.

"Rocqui, you must have forgotten about that chicken you tried to fry when I was there visiting with you in Richmond."

My remembrance of the incident still flushed me with embarrassment. My mother had come to visit with me earlier this year, right after Zoric and I had announced our engagement. I really wanted to impress her. I thought if I showed her that I was trying to cook, then she would see that I moving in the steps towards being more like her.

"That chicken looked deliciously crispy and golden brown on the outside." She was holding back her humorous smile, but her tone comically increased as she continued to relay the story. "I thought you had really out done yourself. But as soon as I sunk my teeth in it... I thought that chicken was gonna holler and scream from the table, it was so alive." She enjoyed her comic relief, laughing hysterically, as I sat across from her with my face hidden behind my hands, in shame.

Her laughter toned down when she realized how increasingly sensitive I was becoming. "Oh baby. It's okay. As long as you and Zoric are happy, that's all that matters. If ordering out everyday works for you and him, then make it work."

I lowered my hands and released a deep sigh. She reached across the table for my hand and gripped it tightly. "You are wonderful at being you. You don't have to try to be me or anyone else."

"I feel like there is a lot I need to know before I'm married."

"What are you talking about girl?" She looked at me with strange eyes.

"You and daddy probably had one of the most amazing marriages known to mankind. I think there are very few people in this world that actually get marriage right. And you and daddy are obviously one of the ones who did."

Her forehead remained crinkled. "What is there to get right? All you need to know is that I loved him and he loved me. That's it. Everything else that we had to deal with fell within those boundaries. Anything else that fell outside of those lines was not love and it was not us."

"But, how did you guys make it look so easy?"

At that moment, her look became straight-faced. "There is nothing easy about marriage. But, what made the tough times worthwhile was that we were able to stand on the shoulders of God and rely on the trust that we held between us to keep us together. No matter what, at the end of the day, I trusted him enough to sleep at night and I never doubted that he didn't have my best interest at heart, no matter what he did."

The things she said did not have any significant meaning to me. I was anticipating that she would give me the secrets to a great marriage. Instead, I became bored by the conversation and began staring off at the outdated Coo Coo clock still hanging onto twenty-some odd years along that same spot, against the wall.

"What's the matter Rocqui? Are you having doubts about marrying Zoric?"

The sudden posing of that question rushed me with anxiety. Quickly, I defended, "Of course not. I love him."

She was obviously unconvinced by my answer for her to say, "You don't decide to marry someone based on the happiness of someone else's marriage. You and Zoric have got to figure out what makes you and him happy in order for it to work."

It often amazed me how a simple comment or question directed at my mother somehow always ends up smacking me directly in my face.

"Where's Monty," I began to wonder becoming aware of his absence? "I thought maybe he would have been here to welcome me home."

"Child, you know your brother. There is no telling where he could be", she answered worriless.

I probably passed him along Murchinson Rd, hemmed up in an alley with a crack pipe up to his mouth burning the tips of his fingers were my thoughts.

"Is he working anywhere," I continued to probe?

"He said that he is doing some construction work here and there. You know how funny construction work is though. You work one day and you may not work anymore that week if it rains." Her words sounded like she was covering up his shortcomings, as they always had.

"I hope he is helping out a bit around here. Is he giving you any money?"

"Look Rocqui, don't start worrying me about your brother. He is my son, and I will do whatever I need to do for my son, until I leave this earth." She left no room for an argument when she rose from the table, disturbingly and went downstairs into the family room.

My eyes narrowed, as my emotions were thrown back fifteen years ago. Here I was, once again, trying to comprehend my mother's overly protectiveness towards Monty. He could have created a bomb that devastatingly ended the entire world. Yet, she would have found a way to proudly speak of his profound accomplishment. I was her easiest child. Smart, ambitious and always followed the narrow path towards perfection. However, my mistakes could have never been so easily forgiven or forgotten like Monty's were.

I got up from the table, with my food barely eaten and went out onto the deck, to sit under the stars. Many hot long summer days were spent in this very setting. A bittersweet feeling came over me as I glance over our backyard where countless barbeques and family gatherings were held. The tall weeping willow tree that is deeply rooted in the center of the yard had been touched or tagged by every small hand in the neighborhood from the games of hide-n-go seek and to kickball.

The sight of the storage shed stirred up tender memories of my dad. The contents of it included his Saturday morning gardening tools. As a little girl, his early morning labor had my undivided attention. And I would sit, unarrested by the noise, the dirt and the grass flying everywhere, to watch him complete one task after another. He effortlessly made our lives complete. Looking up at the stars, I felt empty inside. And I began to miss him.

Then, I thought about my mother and how someday soon, her presence would become a memory to me too. I did not want moments, like this, to pass us by. Therefore, I swallowed my pride to change every thing that was wrong and make it right, and reminded myself that I was here to be there for her and not against her.

Moments later, she pulled the sliding door back to hand me the cordless phone. "Who is it," I asked as I reached for it?

"It's your sister," she answered before going back inside.

A smiled released my tensed worries. I needed her voice of laughter and her senseless humor, to comfort me. Even though Tamra had always tested the grounds which she walked on, she is, admittedly, my best friend. She was just 15 years old, when I woke up in the middle of the night to the sound of her bellowing out tears. When I came to her room door, I could see through the darkness, her silhouette balled up like she was in pain. It wasn't pain that she felt, but the fear and ailment of thinking that she was pregnant. Thank God, the nurse at the health clinic confirmed that she wasn't.

I, again stepped in at her rescue, when she kept rattling on about this group of girls that wanted to jump her. When I cornered these very same girls, after leaving a Friday night football game and questioned their intentions with my sister, they all adamantly disclosed that it was Tamra who started all the shit talking, which didn't surprise me too much.

Through it all, I always wanted and hoped for the best of her life. I was her biggest fan, yelling and wooing her name, when she strutted conceitedly, across the stage to receive her high school diploma. Holding on to my high hopes of her continuing her education, I was floored when she called me two years later, at the start of my graduate studies, to tell me she was marrying some G.I. from Fort Bragg.

My dreams of her becoming self-dependent were lost behind her disillusion of love. And after five years of her marital bliss, I still don't hide easily, my resentfulness of her running off to get married over a career.

"Hi Tamra."

"Hi Rocqui. What time did you finally arrive?"

"I'm not sure...probably around eight."

"How does mom look? Every time I try to talk to her about the cancer, she just brushes it off, like it's no big deal."

"I know. I really don't want to bring it just yet. Not until I find out more from her doctor. You know mom. She will only tell us what she wants us to know, when she wants us to know."

"I'm scared, Rocqui. I don't understand why this is happening all over again." Her voice began to tremble with sorrow.

"I know. I'm scared too. On my way here, I thought about our mother's birthday, next week. I'm really praying that this will not be our last time we get to celebrate it with her."

"Don't say that Rocqui. She is our mother. Mothers are not supposed to die until they are old and grey. Our Mother is not old. And she is certainly not grey," she asserted.

The corner of my mouth quirked upward. "She is gonna be okay. We have to give her all of our strength so that she will have the desire to fight this disease as long as she can. We've needed and depended on her all of our lives. Now, she needs and depends on us."

The thought of losing my mother, as I had already lost my dad allowed the tears to make a streamline down my face. I had to quickly change the subject, before she and I began crying a river. "How's Texas?"

"Texas is hot… and I'm bored and lonely without my love muffin."

"How much longer does he have in Iraq?

"Til whenever we find who the hell our government is looking for? This shit had been going on for so long I've forgotten why we are even involved in this mess in the first place?"

"Me too. You seem to be holding up okay without him though.

"That's because I've been more worried about mom than anything else right now."

"Have you bought your ticket yet to come here?"

"No…"

"What are you waiting for? I've discussed this with you before. You knew a while ago that we were both coming here to be with mom and that you needed to buy a plane ticket. What's the problem?"

"I thought I had the money for a ticket. But, I don't."

"What do you mean you thought? You either have it or you don't?"

"Well, I don't!"

"You are killing me. Don't you and Don or Darryl, or whatever his name is have some money saved up, in case of an emergency?"

"I know you know his name by now, so you can stop with your phony ignorance. And if we had money saved up, then you and I wouldn't be having this conversation. Now would we?"

Becoming increasingly irritated by that same excuse that I've heard a million and one times, I answered," How could you be broke, if you are the only one there to spend the money He is making? What you need to do is seriously, get a job, Tamra." I could hear myself yelling.

Defensively, she tossed back. "I don't need you to be my mother right now, Rocqui. I still have one, if you have forgotten. I'll get my own ticket. I don't need your help."

Guilt began to weigh in on my conscience. No matter how hard I try, 'no' is rarely an answer I've given to her whenever she calls me in need. And this was certainly not a time for lessons to be learn, especially when I needed her more now than she probably needed me. I altered my mood and told her I would search for a plane ticket tomorrow.

"I plan to return home Saturday. I will see you that Friday."

"What date is that Friday?"

"It is ..." scheming through my blackberry for the exact date "the 28th."

"Why? "It's not like you have so much to do," I added full of sarcasm in my tone.

"You don't know how much I have to do. I do have a life."

"Yeah, yeah," I responded, showing no interest in her justification of her so called life. "Just say 'thank you' would be fine," I concluded.

"Thank you, sis. If you're feeling really generous, could you make it First-Class. Cause I've never flown First-Class before," she boldly added.

"I think you've asked for enough already", I finalized. "I'm going to lie down for a little", I yawned. I will call you tomorrow."

After our conversation ended, I returned inside to notice my uneaten plate covered in aluminum foil placed next to the stove. I didn't bother to open it. Not much of an appetite stirred inside of me, now. My mother had darkened the house, except for the dim light that glowed over the stove and a soft light that seeped from the downstairs guest room.

I did not waste anymore time lingering downstairs dwelling on the time that had past by. Unhurriedly, I trekked my tiresome body up the curving stairway into the second floor bedrooms. I walked past my room that no longer housed my twin bed with matching dresser and mirror. Now, all that resonated of my past life here was a poster of Prince during his Purple Rain era. Monty and Tamra's room still remained identical to their childhood. Monty's collection of cars still neatly organized his desk, while Tamra's assortment of dolls and stuff animals covered her bed.

There was no disappointment that filled my thoughts over the disappearance of my room. I just understood the clearing of my memorabilia, now replace with storage containers and my mom's sewing machine desk, only to mean that my parents heard me loud and clear when I said, I would never return home to live once I moved far away.

After roaming around my mother's bedroom, I found myself standing inside her closet staring up at her collection of wigs sitting on Styrofoam heads. Emotionally, I thought back at the first time she was diagnosed with breast cancer. She had her through-the-week wig, her run-to-the-store wig and her Sunday wig. The other wigs that were apart of her collection were essentially for those days when she needed a boost of moral and to feel beautiful about herself again, when chemo took her natural hair away. As I stood in her closet, looking up at the aligned row of wigs, I became scared that we were going to have to go wig shopping again. I was going to have to pretend to be strong again, as I watched her try on several styles before she found the right one, even though I was an emotional wreck. Something in the pit of my stomach turned tightly.

Before I knew it, I found myself stretched out, under the covers of my mother's bed fast asleep. My nap would have turned into a long night's worth of rest if it wasn't for the sudden interruption caused by the glare of the bright ceiling light blaring down over my face. My eyes squinted to a narrow view of Monty standing over me extending his arms out for a hug.

"What's up sis", he greeted animatedly.

"Hey Monty." My body sprung up from its slumber to receive his embrace. Without a wasted breath, I quickly had to remember where my purse was. After a couple quick lessons of my money being stolen right out of my purse by Monty, I always have to think twice about where I could safely leave my purse whenever Monty was around. As long as I could keep his hands far out of my purse, I knew we could keep some of closeness we once shared when we were young.

As my arm gently fell from his tight shoulder, I eyed my Louis on my mother's dresser exactly where I had placed it before I went to bed. I was instantly relieved and ready to receive the love and attention from my admiring big brother.

"Why are you in the bed so early?"

"What are you talking about?" I looked over at the alarm clock and it read 12:06am. "It is late."

"It's just getting started. Come on, Rocqui. We need to go out and have some drinks or something."

As Monty sat on the edge of the bed my eyes were in full view of his shaven mustache and freshly groomed haircut. He was dressed in this orange-stripped short sleeve shirt and sagging blue jeans. His body flavored the scent of a designer's cologne. He looked like a man of substance, a man with a job and responsibilities rather than a dope feen that he had come to be. Optimistically, I thought maybe he was free from his addiction.

"How are you?" I asked him feeling quite unsure of how to word what I really was thinking.

"I'm good," he answered with confidence, the first time. However, when he repeated it, it sounded more like a self persuasion. "Come on and let's have some fun... It will be good for us. We have not hung out in a while."

"Where's mom," I asked realizing that she had not come to bed yet?

"She is downstairs in the guest bedroom. She sleeps down there sometimes when she doesn't feel like walking upstairs."

He obviously read the concern I now felt written across my face because he quickly added, "Mom has been sleeping in that room, long before she was even sick, Rocqui. The house is just too big for her."

That was true. The house is too big for her to live here by herself. Monty's insistent persuasion made me realize that we haven't been out together in a while. There was apart of me that was still hesitant about his invitation even though I rose up out of the bed and stood in the mirror to see how I looked. My shoulder length hair was tossed all over my head and my silk sundress I wore was draped in wrinkles.

He described the place as a casual bar for upscale adults. I wasn't quite sure to trust his use of adjectives, but I opened my suitcase and found a pair of khaki linen Bermuda shorts and low cut floral tank top, anyhow. After a quick shower, with my hair pulled back tight in bouncy ponytail and strappy stilettos, I was ready for a possible disappointment that I believed my brother was setting me up for.

3

My memories of downtown Fayetteville were only limited to circling around the Market House to find my way in and out of the traffic just to get from one end of town to the other. Downtown just didn't offer much attraction to us suburbanites. There were no skyscrapers, no quaint outdoor eating venues and no artistic sculptures to bring any appeal or attractiveness to the cities center. In addition, there were no exclusive shops to buy the latest wear, as offered by the development of malls. Just blocks and blocks of buildings, that seemed to have been around since the days of Jim Crow.

As we entered within the city limits, I took note of the ghostly bare dark streets. The presence of people seemed to have faded away with the sun. The Market House, which was once the site where slaves were sold, during the Antebellum, still was monumentally seated in the center of town. However, as we curved around the

South's unforgotten past, the city appeared to have been given a new existence.

Steadily cruising down Hay Street, the darken sky seemed to have lit up. Neon street lights spotlighted different phases of renovation and construction some buildings had undergone. There were side street iron benches, manicured shrubs growing out of huge black urns place along the brick sidewalks that had a stature as if they were always there. The narrow street was crowded with luxury sedans and SUVs parked along the curve side, while people, in their casual attire, filled the sidewalks with drinks in their hands and enthusiasm in their voices.

Georgia's was the name gleaming down below a mass crowd outside its entrance in Broadway lights. Monty pointed out that this was our destination. There were no parking available in the front of the building, so he directed me into a gravel parking lot adjacent to the old-world style brick building. Cars were steadily entering behind us, quickly feeling in the limited hidden spaces behind the building.

I looked over at Monty very amazed at his choice of this place.

"What," he said, reading the look of surprise across my face? "You thought I didn't have taste or something?"

"Well, I have to admit, I am a bit surprised."

"Look Rocqui, I know that you are all about class. I mean, I've been to some rough places, but I wouldn't take you there. Since you are always talking shit about 'the Ville' and how this is only a place for backyard country fun, I wanted to show you what you've been sleeping on."

Without any further exchanged of words, we got out of the car. I was very careful of how I stepped in my BCBG's stilettos over the gravel crunching under my freshly manicured toes. When we reached the front door entrance, we were greeted by a blond-haired white lady in a sexy low-cut black dress standing behind a podium. While she was ID'ing Monty and me, my eyes explored the black walls that shadowed the red carpeted stairway. There, a jazzy melody seduces your thoughts into to a smooth and mellow atmosphere. We followed the stairway into a softly lit loft that had a wall to wall bar, flat screen TVs flanked on every wall, and bistro tables with bar stools centered the floors. We settled ourselves by grabbing two seats at the bar. I ordered a red wine pinot and Monty requested a Corona.

"Do you like this sis?" The excitement in his voice screamed louder than the music that was blaring in our ears.

After a sip from my wine glass, I admitted, that I really did like the ambience of this place. The observance of professionals casually talking, laughing and drinking created a welcoming social atmosphere. This was something I've never experienced before at home.

Placing my attention back on Monty, I grabbed his hand and said "you really look good." In my mind, I was hoping his looks also meant that he was free from drugs and ready to start living a decent life.

His head shamefully dropped. "I'm trying Rocqui. I'm trying to do better. Especially for mom. I don't want her to keep seeing me like this. But, it's so hard, sometimes. I wish I could just say 'no'. But I don't know how.... Somehow, somewhere along the way, I fucked up. Right now, I am repaying for the mistakes I made in the past every single day. And sometimes it's a good fight and I win. And sometimes I lose." He had a boyish look; a face of innocence. I knew that look. I've seen how it erases any suspicion or doubt from my mother's mind about her son. For that instant, I was seduced by his vulnerability.

"Anyway, enough about me. I heard you and that dude Rick or somebody are getting married soon."

"Yes." I proudly showed him my three carat canary yellow diamond platinum ring. "*Zoric* and I haven't set a date just yet. I don't think I could handle a whole lot of things going on in my life, right now."

"I understand. Well, it looks like he does well for himself." He held my hand up to let the diamonds sparkle off the reflection of the dim lights. "I'm proud of you sis."

"Thank you Monty. I wouldn't have it any other way."

"I'm serious. I've always been proud of you. You've always been smart and driven to make things happen for you, the right way."

For a quick second, I forgot I was in a bar and without any hesitation, I hugged him tightly.

He took a long swig to finish off his beer and sat the empty bottle on the counter. "I feel like playing some pool." Don't you want to play some pool with your big brother?"

"No, I think I'm gonna order another drink and maybe I'll join you afterwards."

"That's cool. You wouldn't happen to have twenty five dollars on you. These cats up here won't even let you come close to the table unless you are pocking some dollars... I promise you I will give it right back to you after I win a couple of rounds."

I'm not sure if it was my second glass of wine or my confidence I was feeling towards him that enticed me to reach into my handbag and pulled twenty-five dollars out of my billfold. My eyes followed Monty as far as they could before he disappeared through the moving crowd of people. I pulled out my cell phone and was tempted to call Zoric. I was wishing he could be here and enjoy this vibe, but it was one-thirty in the morning. I knew he was home in bed cuddling between two pillows.

I nearly finished my second glass of wine before I became restless and wanted to wander off into Monty's existence. I grabbed my glass and threw my bag over my shoulder and walked pass a circle of acquaintances and followed the turn of the walls to the left. There, a Brunswick pool table was centered, surrounded by men with pool sticks in their hands along with a few women plotting their next strategy of the layout of high and low balls on the table. Monty stood at the other end of table, analyzing a player's move. His opponent, an older black guy with salt and pepper hair, aimed and missed his shot.

Monty was enthused by my sudden appearance standing at the opposite end of the table where he stood. His eyes immediately lit up. "Watch this sis. Watch me kick this old man's ass."

I nervously watched Monty extend his stick under his arm and bridge his aim with his right hand. With all his force, he sunk the eight ball into the corner pocket. Game Over.

"Give me my money, ole man", Monty belted out with laughter. He collected fifty dollars from him. A few onlookers handed him more twenty dollar bills into his hand.

"I told you sis. Here's your twenty five dollars back." He placed my money in my hand.

I felt a rush of excitement to see him win at something, again. It felt like he had just thrown the winning touchdown at the football game, back in high school when he was the quarterback. I was his number one fan and obviously still am today. "Monty I didn't know you had skills like that."

"There's a lot that you don't know about your brother", he proudly stated. "Hey, one of my boys supposed to be meeting me here. I'm gonna check downstairs to see if he is here. Are you gonna be okay"?

"Yes, Monty. I'm a big girl. I think I could manage without you for a few minutes."

"Ok. I'll be right back", he assured me. I turned and watched him until he was gone. I refocused my attention back to the pool table realizing that I was suddenly all alone. Just the pool table, some chairs and me. Trusting the words of my brother, I decided to sit on one the barstools, with my legs crossed and wait patiently for his return. I wanted another drink, but my two glasses had me comfortably tipsy. I'm not a drinker. Too many more glasses of wine would have made me drunk.

I was starting to feel awkward, however. The pool table was empty of stripes or solid balls. The pool sticks were strategically hung on the rack. The billiard light that hung from the ceiling bounced off the red cloth that covered the table. A look at my watch signaled that time was moving faster than Monty's return, so I began counting down my move to drive home without him.

I breathe a sigh of impatience and edge my butt off the seat of the chair. As my heels gently touched the floor, I bent over to grab my bag that I'd placed beside my chair. When I stood upwards, I raised to the sudden presence of a stranger...a handsome stranger, who was strikingly beautiful. I was startled, nonetheless captivated by his presence.

He had a bold jaw line and soft mysterious eyes. His face was neatly groomed with a beard that connected to his mustache. He looked strong, with hardened curves and jet black silky hair that tapered his hairline.

My brain searched recklessly for words to say but none spilled out of my mouth.

Very aware of my presence, he confidently spoke "Hi".

I was deliberately careful not to show any interest, by uttering a simple 'hi" in return.

The search for words did not come easy, when I tried to find something else to say. I wondered how obvious my attraction was to him. To distract myself away from him, I dug relentlessly for my keys buried deep within my handbag. Slowly, I pivoted my feet to remove myself from his seductive presence. However, before I made my full departure, he stated, "I hope you are not leaving because of me."

Timidly, I answered, "No. I was waiting on my brother. But it looks like something came up. I think I better go."

"Please don't go," he begged sweetly. "Maybe something did come up. Or maybe, he just needs a couple more minutes. Wouldn't you be disappointed if you missed him?"

There was something powerful about hearing a man say 'please'. I was immediately smitten. At that point, I might have been even more disappointed if Monty would have instantly showed up and interrupted this moment.

Feeling my nerves settling, I decided, "Well, maybe I should give him a few more minutes." My actual thought at that particular point was it didn't matter to me if Monty never showed up.

He smiled and revealed a perfect set of teeth even under the softly lit room.

"Would you like to play pool with me," he proposed, as he moved over towards the rack to grab a stick?

"I don't know how?"

"I could teach you," he offered, while grabbing two sticks as if he knew that I would agree.

Feeling totally out of my comfort zone, I don't know what possessed me to say 'yes', but I did. He handed me a pool stick and I studied his every move, while he effortlessly racked the balls up in a triangular shape.

"Now, I need you to break them."

"Oh no", I quickly rejected.

"I will help you," he assured me smilingly. Before I could further protest, he positioned his body behind me, extended his left arm over mine and gripped my wrist. His body was locked around me. My stance gave way to a comfort I held, as if he was guarding me. However, before I fell too deep under his submission, he gently pulled my arm back and relinquished a powerful forced that caused all of the balls to explode across the red velvet table.

Feeling increasingly at ease, I said "that was easy". "Now, are you going to do that every time it's my turn?"

He intensely answered as his eyes gazed deeply into mine, "for you...anything."

Every time he stood closely behind me to help me correctly hold the stick or to show me a perfect aim, his body encased mine, like a shield and I felt safe. With each physical contact, I inhaled his fresh scented cologne and pleasured the touch of his long soft hands over mine. He gave me fewer instructions, as my confidence grew stronger. At one point, he just repositioned the stick in my hand and I was able hit a ball in the side pocket all by myself. I so was excited that I rushed over and gave him a high five, like I had known him for years.

Laughter and conversation filled the time that we were together. By the time the game was over, most of the people had totally vacated the building, except for the bartenders and the manager.

"Thank you", I said accepting that our time together had come to an undesiring end.

"You are welcome..."

All that time we spent talking, and playing pool, a simple manner of introduction was overlooked by the both of us. "I'm Rocqui." I extended my hand out towards him.

"Rocqui, like Sylvester Stallone 'Rocky', he smirked.

I pulled back my hand quickly before he had the chance to shake it and said "No, Rocqui, like short for Rocquelle".

"I'm sorry. I think it's cute. I've never met a lady name Rocqui before. I'm Avery." Switching back to serious mode, he held his hand out for mine.

I slowly extended my hand to his. And he gently pulled it towards his lips and kissed it. I felt giddy.

"It was nice to meet you. Thank you for teaching me how to play pool." I turned to leave and placed my bag over my shoulders.

"It doesn't have to end now, does it? I mean I just met you and you just met me. Plus, all this pool playing has made me kinda hungry. I betcha you are a little hungry too," he cunningly implied.

"Excuse me," I replied in my 'sister girl' poise. "Are you implying that I look hungry?"

Once he had gotten over his laughter he added, "I'm sorry. You look nothing of hunger. Beautiful and stunning, yes. But not hungry," he coolly tried to fix. I felt kinda silly for hanging onto every word he said. But it sounded so good. "What I was really trying to say before I put my foot in my mouth was ask you if you would like to join me for breakfast. And you don't have to eat if you don't want to. I honestly would like to hang out with you some more."

Relax Rocqui, I told myself. You've dated men before. You have heard those very same words spoken to you before, in some kinda way. I was overly anxious to say, 'yes.' So, I said, "I may not look hungry, but I don't mind eating. What exactly did you have in mind?" I was totally interested in whatever proposal he had in mind.

"We could go to IHOP. It's not too far from here."

It had been so long since I had been to IHOP, I had to remember what type of food it served. I didn't even think IHOP still existed. Did I really want pancakes at two in the morning? And did it really matter? Quickly I answered to myself 'no', it really didn't. I subtly agreed.

When we existed the building, the entire block was left blank. The only mobilized vehicle that I saw out front was a sleek black two-wheeled customized motorized machine.

"Are you ready", he motioned? I trailed behind him closely inspecting this 'man versus machine'.

"You got to be kidding me" I said filled with fright.

"It won't hurt you. I got you."

He noted the apprehensiveness that rested along my face and attempted to bring some assurance to my full protection. "There are a few cars on the road at this time at night. Trust me," he pleaded. "I promise not to let anything happen to you. You could hold onto me as tight as you like", he flirted.

"Maybe I should take a taxi and meet you there."

"Or maybe you should trust me and know that I will protect you."

Hesitantly, I followed his lead and he placed his heavy black glossy helmet over my head. He went back inside only to momentarily return with another black helmet. Next, he straddled the bike with his body. The engine ignited with a roar. The throttle vibrated between my jumpy legs. Nervously, I imprinted my hands into his chest. My butt settled on the leather seat behind him. My thighs tightly locked around his legs.

Within seconds, we were piercing through the wind as it gusted against my face. The street felt like it belonged to us. There were a few sighted cars, just as he promised, that we zoomed passed. Nothing I'd ever experienced before felt so free and so dangerous, at the same time. I could have been Lois Lane and he, Superman, flying high above Metropolis.

IHOP was not as far as I wanted it to be. He could have driven me to New York and that probably would not have been long enough to fully enjoy the ride. There was something sexy about holding him tight and being exposed to the world. Yet, feeling protected and guarded by his body.

We arrived to a minimum crowd. We took our seats and ordered coffee, Belgium waffles and eggs. "I know IHOP is not the ideal place for a date, but it's the only spot that is open in this area, at this time of night," he apologetically implied.

"This is a date," I asked, trying to infer his intentions with me?

"It's not an 'official' date. Our official date is next Saturday at eight o'clock."

"And how do you know this and I don't."

"I don't either. I'm just playing off wishful intentions."

He had me stumped. "I guess you are the type of guy that has everything all figured out?"

"Not even a little bit. I am that guy who tries to figure things out, as I go."

"Have you figured me out, yet?"

"No. I don't think that I have to. I think that's why I'm so intrigued by you. I'm just curious to find out what's next."

"There is a possibility that there is no 'next'. This is probably all what needs to be between you and me."

"Wow. Just shoot a brother down for trying. It's not even Saturday yet. We haven't even gone out on our real date. I would like to do something special for you. At least let me show you more than IHOP."

My legs were still tingling from the motorcycle ride. What more did he need to show me. "What exactly do you like to do on a date," I wondered?

"I prefer a more intimate setting where maybe I could cook for my date rather than buying someone else's meal. But, that's only if I'm particularly interested."

"And what if you are not 'particularly' interested in someone?"

"Then I will bring them here to IHOP."

We laughed. The conversation between us was easy. It felt profoundly natural. There wasn't even the slight concern of food being stuck on my teeth or if I even appeared to look greedy when I tried to swallow a fork full of eggs. He gave me a sense that none of those things really mattered to him.

After eating, we furthered our journey on the motorcycle to an undisclosed location, crowded by tall trees and long dark side streets. I wanted to pretend like I knew him well enough to trust him. However, in reality sharing a couple of cups of coffee and laughing over rooty tooty fresh and fruity pancakes meant only that I knew him as well as the waitress that serve us.

Despite the fear that overcame me when we parked on a dirt secluded path, I felt protected. I tried nervously to remove the helmet off my head. For some reason, my persistent effort only made it harder and nearly impossible for it to slide off.

"Here, let me help you," he soothingly offered. As charmingly as he was, he gently slipped the helmet off my head. Once the restraint was freed from my shoulder, I easily looked around and noticed a red light blinking from the end of a long wide road. Then finally, with the yellow caution lights systematically aligned along the landing strip I knew exactly where I was. The airport. It was just seconds after my revelation that a huge seven, forty-seven lowered steadily above our heads and landed on the ground.

"That's incredible," I mumbled in awe.

"It is nice, isn't it?" Both of our eyes were fixated at the sight of the plane touching down from the sky.

"Why haven't I ever been here before?"

He turned and looked into my wondrous eyes. "Because this moment was created just for you and me." The setting was illustrated flawlessly for a perfect kiss. The stars flickered within the picturesque dark sky, while we rested high along a hill removed from the world below. Nonetheless, I was not easily giving of myself.

He leaned in for the awaiting kiss. But I gave him my cheeks instead. No stunning look was given and no question was asked. He comfortingly settled with his arms tightly around me, as my head pressed down into his chest.

When we returned back to Georgia's, the sun was beginning to appear. The early morning dew had settled on the ground and the neon lights had now faded. He drove up to the ghostly parking lot where my car was the only car that remained.

"Nice car. You think your brother ever came back?"

"I don't think he had any intentions on ever coming back."

"I'm sorry about that... On the other hand, when you see your brother, tell him, 'Thank You' for me?"

"Thank you for what?"

"Thank you for allowing me this opportunity to meet you... I had a nice time."

"So did I." I smiled and handed him back his helmet. He reached over and put his arms around my waist and I leaned over to allow his lips to gently press against my cheeks.

"Could I call you later?"

"Sure. I would like that. I guess it's Goodnight...or good morning I should say?"

"It's starting out to be that way." We both exchanged heart-felt smiles before departing our separate ways.

4

Several days had gone by and I haven't heard from Zoric. Not even a simple text had been delivered to my screen. I could not figure out if this sense of loneliness I now had stemmed from an absence of Zoric or was it arising from a desire to be with Avery.

The night with Avery was exciting and refreshing. Something about him made me feel free to live and breathe. I was tempted to want more. Yet, my phone had not rung from him either. For a moment I felt alone or maybe even bored and needed to be reminded of my rightful place. That place was the promise I made to marry Zoric. I needed to call him and hear his voice. I searched deep into my Bogetta hand bag for my blackberry and called him at work.

"Thanks for calling Merrill Lynch. How may I help you?"

"Zoric Huntington, please?"

"Just one moment." The melody of Boney James flowed through the phone, while I waited to hear Zoric's voice.

"This is Zoric Huntington," he answered in his professional manner.

The air I held in my chest finally expelled from my mouth. "Well, hello stranger."

"Hey beautiful. How are you?"

"Missing the man of my dreams. Do you still miss me?"

"Every awaking moment," he declared.

"It doesn't really feel that way. You haven't even called me in the last couple of days. Have you been too busy to call and say *Hello*?"

"I'm not going to lie. I've been very busy. Last night, I was up so late trying to finish up my quarterly report, that I fell asleep with my laptop on my lap on the sofa. But, none of that is excusable for me not calling you. I've missed you even more."

"Good. I was beginning to think I was the only one doing all the missing between us."

"Nah Baby. It's not just you. It's been hard coming home to an empty house. The first night I came home I just sat out in my car in the garage wondering what in the world was I gonna do when I got inside without you."

My heart melted. "I can't wait to see you again."

"Yeah. Me too. How's everything going with your family and your mom?"

"Everything is going okay for now. It had taken me a minute to absorb being home again, but things are fine." I was hoping my nonchalant manner would disguise the uneasiness that I was feeling. Yet, it didn't.

"What's the matter Rocqui, You don't sound like everything is okay?

"Nothings the matter. I just miss you... I miss my home. I miss my dog. I miss my life," I confessed of my self-pity.

"I know, baby. But, you could come home anytime you want. You know that"

"I know. But, I can't leave until I at least know that my mother's gonna be okay. It's just that it's a lot harder than I imagined it would be coming back here again. Richmond is only three hours away, yet if feels like worlds apart."

"It will always be like that when you go home. You have a very different life now. You are not the same person you once were when you lived there before. That's just the way it is. That is exactly how it feels for me whenever I go back to Akron."

"I guess you're right."

"I can't tell you how cold my feet have been without you."

"It's summertime. Your feet are cold like ice in the winter."

"That doesn't dismiss the fact that I still need to cuddle up to you."

His words filled my emptiness and I remembered why I loved him so. I decided not to drown him anymore in my pity and changed the mood of the conversation. "So... what do you have planned for the rest of the day?"

"I was about to head off to a conference meeting, which would probably take up the rest of my work day."

"I didn't mean to keep you away from your work."

"No, you didn't. I needed to hear your voice. I can't wait to see you, love.

"Me too. Don't work too hard. I don't want you too tired for me when I get there."

"I would never be too tired for you, my dear. Sweetheart, I'll call you tonight. I think they are waiting on me."

"Okay. Love you."

"Love you too."

I still love him the same as I did the first time I ever said it. Yet, I still looked down at my cell phone hoping that Avery would call. Even though he is not necessarily my type, he definitely leaves me something to think about. He is Ed Harley in a pair of rugged stone washed jeans. A bit rough, yet gentle. Smart but edgy. His welcoming eyes seem to see more than just a pretty face when he looks at me. His voice is intense and I am captivated by every word he says.

Zoric, on the other hand, is Gucci and Prada. More refined and polished. He is a man that had acquired a respectful level of power and prestige. Whether it's due to his striking good looks or his overridden confidence, he immediately commands attention whenever he enters a room. And I loved that about him.

I needed to shake off this feeling of confusion I was dwelling on. I decided to pull on my blue spandex and running bra and go running. I pranced downstairs, where my mother was resting on the sofa and told her I was headed out for a jog around the neighborhood.

The lyrics of Jill Scott, Kem, and Mary J. made my stride seem shorter than the two miles I ran. I had returned to the steps of mom's house, once again, breathing, sweaty and feeling liberated. My eyes were not troubled at the sight of my mother immobile, lying flatly in the same position she was in before I left.

"Ma, you must be really tired, taking a nap in the middle of the day," I observed from her body lying motionless on the sofa in the den as I walked into the kitchen to fill my bottle with ice and water.

I took a big gulp and stared at her strangely, noticing that my words had not provoked any gesture or movement.

"Ma," I cried out. "Are you okay?"

Still no response and no subtle movement from her body. Instinctively, I raced to her side, grabbing her hand and wept, "Mommy!

Slowly, her eyes prevailed as if she had just returned from a world outside her own. "Hi Baby," she spoke in a whisper, gently, stroking the strands of my hair. "I didn't mean to scare you. The constant intrusion of chemotherapy is supposed to help me sustain a longer life but all it does is steal moments of my life away. It makes me so tired and weak, sometimes.... But, I'm okay." With the touch of her fingers, caressing my cheeks, the tears that had filled my eyes, suddenly, were released and flooded down my face. She sat up and I was like a child, in her arms.

"Mom lets go somewhere" I proposed over my sniffles, trying to settle my sorrow.

"Where are we going to go?" She looked into my sadden face."

"Anywhere! We could go to Jamaica, the Bahamas! Or even to the beach", my words sung in pure desperation.

"Why... to hide from death? No, Baby, you can't hide from death. Death comes a stealing at any hour, any day and any occasion."

"I think you need a slight vacation? It's nothing for me to pick up the phone and book tickets. We could be on an airplane first thing in the morning."

"Baby, I haven't worked for five years. I think I have had my share of vacation. And plus, being home with you kids is all that matters to me now. Nothing else could make me happier." She sealed that with a kiss on my forehead and rose from the sofa. "Now come on and let's cook dinner."

"Well... if I can't take you on a vacation, could I at least take you out to dinner?" I was trying any means of desperation to escape from reality.

"What do you have in mind?"

"I don't know. Anywhere, besides the usual franchise restaurants. I don't want any Applebee's and TGIF's or anything like that."

"You want to go Georgia's?"

"I think that's where Monty took me the other night. Isn't that a bar?"

"Yes, but downstairs is a nice quaint restaurant. Your father and I use to go there a lot in our courting days." Her face lightened over her thoughts of memory lane with my dad. "That's when it was an old juke joint for beer and barbeque. I heard her son had taken over the business and turned it into an upscale restaurant."

"Okay. We could go there."

Still appearing a bit fatigue, she found a second wind and prepared for our dinner date. She wore a tailored pair of cream slacks and button up a sleeveless top. Her freshly brushed cropped hair radiated her grey tresses of 'wisdom', as she likes to say, along her cheek-bone. I threw on a floral haltered sundress, with thong sandals and allowed my shoulder length hair to loosely flow.

When we arrived, there were limited seating due to an unforeseen Sunday crowd. Our wait was just a few minutes before a caramel-skinned hostess in black slacks and a white blouse showed us to our table. The tall brick walls were structured under wood beam cathedral ceilings. The leather booths that lined the walls of restaurant where accented under soft pendant lights. The aisle tables had sconces to make each seat feel intimate and cozy. The fully extended bar allowed an open view into the kitchen. And a seat next to the window, gives you an illusion that you were in a major city, at a quick glance, through the wooden blinds.

After we settled ourselves and placed our order, we sipped on our glass of wine and talked about Zoric and my excitement over our future together. We discussed Tamra's upcoming arrival and how it's going to be like good and bad times all over again. I was at ease again to experience another moment of my mother's laughter and to be in the presence of her smile again.

"Has Monty called you?"

"I haven't heard from your brother since that night you and him went out. I don't know where he is."

"That worries me. It makes me scared to think he is back on streets again."

"It scares me too, Rocqui. But your brother is thirty-two years old. I don't understand him. I've given him the same life as you and Tamra and this is what he has chosen to do." She shakes her hand in disbelief. "I pray for my son every night in hopes that he would find his way."

The waiter arrived with our food. I ordered the lamb with gravy and mash potatoes. My mom ordered baked chicken with grilled vegetables.

"This looks amazing." I stated after the beautiful presentation of my food.

My mother agreed. "Yes, this is a long way from the fried chicken plates and chitterlings with a side order of collard greens me and your father use to get from here."

The juices from the lamb aroused my taste buds. I no longer wanted to talk. I just wanted to eat, until my belly had fattened.

The waitress returned to our table and presented my mother and me with chocolate a soufflé dessert. I thoughtfully replied, "That looks delicious. But I absolutely have no more room left for dessert."

She cunningly smiled. "This is on the house at the chef's request." And then walked away leaving us puzzled.

This is odd, I thought. My mother looked over at me strangely as well. Then we both agreed to taste a bite since everything else had been delicious.

Oh my gosh, I thought. This is sinful. I glimpsed at mother, who was motioning her mouth like she was making love to its decadent taste. I had never seen her so pleasured and satisfied by food before. I laughed out loud.

She justified "This is good girl. I don't know what you are laughing at".

"How are you lovely ladies enjoying your dinner," The sudden intrusion of a male's voice inquired? I looked up into Avery's eyes.

Startled by his unforeseen presence, my words stumbled when I tried to speak. "What are you doing here?"

"I'm fine, thank you. How are you?" He chuckled over my rudeness to respond to his question.

"I'm sorry." I tried to correct my bluntness. "I am fine. I am having dinner with my mother Jacqueline. Mom, this is Avery."

She extended her hand to his and he kissed it. "Nice meeting you she replied as she continued to indulge in her soufflé."

I pushed my dessert away from me and teasingly asked, "Are you following me?"

"From noticing you from the kitchen, I thought you were following me," he answered with a devilish smile.

Then I noticed his white chef's overcoat. "You work here?"

"Yes."

"Did you personally, cook our meal?"

"I did. Did you enjoy it?"

"It was wonderful." After the brief questioning and short answering, our eyes met and said things that our mouths could not say.

My mother interjected. "I don't know what this conversation is all about but I'm not going to sit here all night while you two gaze into each other eyes and try to read each other's mind."

Laughter.

"I have to finish up a few things," he implied looking back into the kitchen. Then he turned to me and asked, "Would you stay and wait for me? Just for a few minutes", he begged?

My mother abruptly answered for me, "yes" and "I'm going home."

"I can't stay and wait for you. I'm here with my mother and we are spending some time together", I apologetically replied.

"Rocqui, I don't need a baby-sitter. I'm going home. It is quite obvious to me that whatever you and this young man have to say needs to be said", my mother stated before getting up from the table.

"How am I going to get home," I asked aloud, without thinking?

"Child please! You have always been book smart, but common sense had always been your downfall. Now if I could have the keys, ma'am."

I handed her the keys like an obedient child and she shook Avery's hands again before leaving.

He sat in her seat across from me. "I've been thinking about you every since we met."

Not trusting if this was a typical line, I responded "I guess that's why I've been getting so many calls from you in the past few days."

"I've been kinda busy working here, unexpectedly... You look beautiful." His words felt honest and real.

He glanced at his watch. "We are closing in thirty minutes. I just need to finish up a few things... Please don't go." The longer he looked at me, the more vulnerable I became.

I convincingly answered 'I won't', before he rose from the table and

exited through the swinging black doors.

I knew that I should have left with my mother, but I chose to stay. I gotta to be crazy, I kept telling myself. I'm engaged. Avery's not even my type. He is a chef. Zoric is one of the top financial advisor's at Merrill Lynch. How much does a chef even make I recklessly entertained? But, he is obviously good at what he does, because my dinner was amazing. Calm yourself, Rocqui. It's not like I'm marrying the guy. He is just a friend, nothing else, nothing more. I'll just hang out with him just for tonight. Then, straightforwardly, I would confess that I'm involved with someone else. And we could be just friends is how I persuaded myself to naïvely believe.

The restaurant had emptied, leaving me and a wondrous mind, alone. Momentarily, the congenial waitress, who brought me the soufflé, approached me and said "Mr. A would like for you to join him in his office." She had a welcoming disposition and I rose from my table and followed her lead. "Did you enjoy the soufflé" she inquired?

"Yes" I casually responded.

"Yeah. Everybody loves it when Mr. A comes in to cook. It's not often that he does, but when he does the house is packed."

I was intrigued. "He is not the regular chef here?"

She stopped in her steps and protested my notion, "No! Mr. A owns this place."

I was dumbfounded. My perception of him had become disfigured. But before I could get anymore information from the waitress, we had arrived at his office. I stood parallel against the closed door and saw a different man keying in data on the computer than the one I thought I knew. My eyes traveled around the room studying his many awards of achievements and recognition hanging against the white walls. He continued to hide his eyes behind his monitor, as if my presence was without any bearing on his work.

"You are the owner of this place?"

He stopped and swiveled his chair to face me. His arms fell relaxingly behind his head as he leaned back in his black leather chair. "Yes."

"And you are Georgia's son, I assume?"

"Georgetta is her name. This was her restaurant. And yes, I am her son."

"Does that make you also the owner of the bar upstairs?"

"It does", he proudly answered.

I released a deep sigh, as if I had been holding my breath. "Is there anything else about you that I don't know?"

He rose from his chair and walked so close to me that I could inhale nothing but the air that he breathed. "I want you to know everything about me", he confirmed in a deep whisper.

His eyes looked through me tenderly and I felt naked. Our lips teasingly touched. I felt the gentleness of his tongue tasting my wet kisses, while my body was held firmly against the door. His hand softly stroked my face. I was helpless and stimulated. I tightly held onto his waist because I was overpowered by his touch.

The spell that I was under was suddenly interrupted by a startling knock at the door.

"Yes", he answered, without ever removing his eyes from me.

"Mr. A, I'm gone. I will see you tomorrow," the voice from the other side echoed.

A smiled unfolded across his face. "I guess we should go too", he softly whispered to me.

He walked back to his desk and shut down his computer. A flicker of the lights and we stood for a moment in darkness. He opened the door and held my hand as we found our way to the main door. The alarm was set and the building was secured.

I turned to look at the vacant street. "No motorcycle today", I jokingly asked?

"No motorcycle", he confirmed.

I was a bit disappointed, even though I was wearing an airy sundress. With our fingers intertwined, he led me to the back of the building and opened my door of his F150.

When he got inside, I could feel myself becoming nervously excited. The kiss back in the restaurant made me desire to feel more of his touch and to grind sensually to the rhythm of his drum. But, the weight of the diamond that I promised to uphold, felt heavy along my finger. I looked up at him and studied his face. I wanted him to see that I was engaged without me ever having to say it. I feared the words that I say would be too definite and final when I wasn't quite certain about anything at this particular point.

I spoke intently, "You are a man full of surprises."

"You mean the restaurant," he answered.

"Yes, the restaurant," I replied.

"I wasn't trying to hide it from you. I guess in the midst of us hanging out the other night, it just never came up," he nonchalantly conveyed.

Stealing a quick glance at my engagement ring, I knew exactly what he meant. Apart of me was hoping the conversation about this ring would not come up, either. Sooner or later, however, I knew neither one of us could be blind by what was obvious to see.

My nerves were becoming slowly at ease when I noticed his attention was distanced from me. He stared off into the darkness, through the windshield, as if he was seeing his life being replayed right before him. "I never thought that I would take over my mother's business," he finally spoke. "When I was a kid, my mom use to bring me to the restaurant and I would play and sometimes do homework in the dining area while she would cook and get things ready for the dinner or the late crowd. Eventually, I grew restless and couldn't sit still anymore and wounded up messing things up and getting in her way. She decided to put all of my energy to some use and made me stir a little this and rinse a little of that. As I grew older, standing in the kitchen became second nature. By the time I was sixteen, I was cooking full-time... even showing my mom a few tricks." He chuckled. "I shoulda went to college. But, I was so ready to get out of Fayetteville. I took a free ticket into the Army and gave up five years of my life, only to return right back to the 'the Ville.' It's funny sometimes, how you have your life all planned out how you want it to be, only for it to end up sometimes nothing like you expected."

"Are you happy owning the restaurant," I asked?

He hesitated for a second before answering, "Yeah I am. This is who I am." His hand gently caressed my fingers and stumbled on my engagement ring. He switched on the interior light and held my hand up high to study my ring. "It's beautiful. I guess this is who you really are, as well" he supposed before turning the light off.

"I wouldn't say that this is who I am. This ring is more of a symbol of who I will be."

"I see. And when is the wedding?"

I didn't feel a bit comfortable talking about my wedding to him. I started fidgeting with the hem of my blouse, to avoid direct eye contact with him. However, he asked a question that deserved some sort of an answer. And I gave him one. "The date suppose to be sometime in June. But, I haven't yet decided."

"You don't sound so happy about it. Are you...?"

"Am I what?"

"Are you happy?"

His quiz, ironically, caught me by surprise. I glanced down at my diamond like my answer was hidden inside the stone. I wanted to answer 'yes', but, somehow, 'yes' felt like it was stuck between 'no' and 'maybe'. There was something different about him asking me that made me hesitate for a moment before I nodded my head. After I said it, I felt like I had just walked into a brick wall.

His expression remained unreceptive to my answer. "Right." He let out a deep sigh before he began again. "I guess this means that we would not have that date this Saturday?"

I chuckled. "Yeah. At least, you had the chance to cook for me."

His voice became mellow and sincere. "Yes, I did. But that wasn't all I was looking forward to doing for you." He gently reached over and touched my hand and continued, "Have you ever met any one before and felt like you've known them forever?"

I could not believe he had just said what I had been thinking since I had met him. The similar thought excited me more than I had alluded to him. Subtly, I answered "yes".

"Being with you feels familiar to me. It feels like finding a missing shoe, if that makes any sense."

We both laughed. "And now Ima shoe," I implied.

"A beautiful shoe," he added to dress up his implication.

"Could I be a pair of Louboutin," I asked, being very specific about if I had to be a shoe, then I had to be the best designer shoe ever made?

"Yes. You can be a Louie, whatever his name is," he rushed to appease me in order to make his point. "I've been searching really hard to find this shoe. Sometimes, I would give up on finding it and just wear another one. Imagine me, the fool, going around with mismatch shoes on. I regretted it every single time. But, I had to wear something. And now finally I've found the right shoe," he continued with a smile. "I don't want to lose this shoe again.

The mood suddenly shifted away from comical shoe talk to seriousness. "I respect the fact that you are engaged. And I'm okay with accepting that you and I were just a chance meeting. Nothing more and nothing less. But I can't help to ask you one more time, while I have you here for another opportunity to see you again. Even if it means that I would have to sit far from you across a crowded room, just to have you in my presence. That would be enough to make a brother smile for days."

Immediately, I felt flattered and amused by his comparison. By continuing to listen to his persuasion, my defense was weakening and my engagement ring was slowly fading from the image of my mind.

His eyes gazed intensely through me, patiently waiting for a response. Little does he know that he had me when he referred to me as a beautiful shoe. But I guarded my honesty. Nervousness and fear stood in between my tempting desires I had towards him. Without any added pressure, he removed his dishearten stare away from my perplexed face and turned the key of the ignition. The sound of the engine humming kindled something inside of me and that finally compelled me to say, "Okay."

5

"Zory," a whiny voice persistently called out interrupting my concentrated thought.

Zoric and I met when we both attended VCU (Virginia Commonwealth University). I was at the beginning of my MBA and he was at the end of his Bachelor's in Banking and Finance. It was the start of the fall semester and I, just like many others crammed the campus bookstore in hopes of discovering every assigned textbook listed under a used price. No luck there. The Concept of Management book was priced at $200.00. The value must have reflected more of the books weight, because the text had me totally oblivious to the scene of laughter conversations and excitement that filled the walls of the store.

"Zory, I think you should get this one. This looks good on you," she sounded again in an irritating serenade. His name seemed to have rung out on every aisle I traveled down.

I was beginning to hate Zoric or 'Zory' as he was being called at that moment before I ever saw his face. My eyes never stirred away from the book to see who this gallant of a man was but his carelessness would surely defined our destiny to meet on that day.

Feeling hungry, 'cause I'd skipped lunch to waste my afternoon in the bookstore searching for $500 worth of books and tired because I had been busy all week moving into my newly purchased condo, I was impatiently anxious to leave. But, just as I was turning to walk toward the checkout counter, Zoric's fully erect body collided into mine causing all of my books to tumble to the floor between us.

We both dropped to our knees in a race to see who would be the first to pick them up. He respectfully apologized but I was more inspired by the sight of his hazel eyes. He looked dreamy. Damn near perfect for any woman who liked the good hair and the light-skinned type. His eyes gazed into me with a stare, as if I was something new to his liking, as well. But all that instantaneous attraction was cut short by the unwelcoming presence of his accompanying floozy, who, by no surprise, was white. My mind easily rested on any notion of this introduction becoming more than just an 'accident'.

After that day, I would see him occasionally, in passing around campus, sometimes alone, but often with another female fan hanging from his side, displaying no racial preference. Little did I know that in the upcoming weeks, our next encounter would mark the start of forever between us.

It was homecoming. Spirits were high and bodies were grinding as the speakers filled the room with reggae melodies. Ice chilling the glass of daiquiri that I sipped, made my fingertips a bit numb. My body stood in the path of the front door and I observed it slowly to reveal the arrival of Zoric. I instantly ignored his presence, only after I recognized that he was alone and continued to laugh and talk carelessly amongst my girlfriends. As the night grew old, his steps led to a path directly before me. Briefly, after an exchange of 'hi' he identified me as the 'the girl at the book store' and I played ignorant to his memory.

Just short of me finally telling him my name, he said to me as a matter of fact, "I'm gonna make you love me?"

As silly as I may have sounded, I asked him, "and how are you gonna do that?"

"Easily," he conceited.

Falling in love with him did come easily. His intelligence and wit got the best of my reservation I had towards him and I quickly became a fan, too. Romantic walks and long dreamy talks led to me wanting to have him for more than just one night.

My feelings towards him began to surface one particular day when he was a no-show from our usual lunch date. I waited patiently; then angrily. When I called, there was no answer. My thoughts were heavy and I felt paralyzed to do anything. Finally, with my mind made up I grabbed my keys with the intent on moving on with daily plans. Only to open the door and to my surprise, he was standing. Our lips locked. My legs wrapped around his waist, as he tightly held my thighs and carried me off to my bedroom. Our bodies grinded and pulsated until we lay helpless exhausted between the sheets.

Thirstiness overwhelmed me from all the moaning and groaning that just took place. I got up out of the bed and walked into the kitchen for some cold water. I reached for ice from the freezer and then poured a glass of Evian from the refrigerator. As I closed the top door, Zoric's yellowish hue appeared before me glowing like the sun, uninhibited by all that God gave him. He said "I love you." And without any hesitance in my voice I said "I love you too." We've lived together every since that moment.

The door bell rang. I paced my steps down the stairs and opened the door to welcome Avery inside. A slight chuckle escaped him immediately after settling his sights on my three inch heels. "You do love shoes. You may want to change those, though," he suggested.

Glancing down at my beautiful strappy sandals, I asked, "Why?"

"Because Celebration Station does not allow anyone to enter with shoes three inches or higher on their feet."

"Are you kidding me?"

"Yes. But, not about changing your shoes into something more comfortable."

"By the way, what is a Celebration Station? I've never heard of a place like that."

"It is a place of celebration and outdoor fun. I think you would enjoy it."

I returned upstairs to my mother's room and retrieved my sneakers from underneath the bed. As I tied my Air Shox, I questioned what in the world was I really doing. I wanted to believe that this was just innocent fun, even though I was starting to feel something much more peculiar. People get together all the time for fun, I tried to convince myself. But maybe he didn't understand that this would be only for fun and nothing serious.

I was thinking stupidly. Who was I kidding? I had decided that when I return down the stairs to where he stood, I will stop this foolishness. Any further relationship between us would end at the point of me saying goodbye to him, at my mother's front door.

However, my reasonable thoughts couldn't catch up to my irrational feelings fast enough. When I returned in full view of him standing casually in his cargo shorts and a loose fitting grey t-shirt and leather strapped flip-flops, he looked absolutely stunning. He embodied every man, I had ever known. His left muscular bicep exposed a tattoo of a green fire breathing dragon underneath his short sleeve that left me curious to want to explore more about him.

His unreserved presence was so casual and free that it made me feel unpretentious and uninhibited. I immediately felt as though I could be just as comfortable with him in high heels as I could be in flip flops or sneakers. No need to touch up my lips with a fresh coat of color or to smear on a layer of an illuminating shine. He had already made me feel pretty when he smiled at me upon my return.

All doubts and second thoughts I had, had been removed from my mind. I couldn't wait to get out the door fast enough to be with him.

The night had fallen on our joyous time together. Along our drive to this place, that I'm still not quite sure what it is, we stopped at the service station. He got out to fuel his truck as I patiently waited inside listening to music and gazing out the window.

Something familiar struck my eyes as I saw a figure that posed the embodiment of my brother. Reluctantly I decided that this guy that was the same towering stature and wearing the same clothes he wore the last time I saw him, could not be my brother. This guy was appeared dingy and his hair was matted and tangled. This guy was obviously homeless. My brother had a home.

This guy continued to address uncaringly every stranger for an easy nickel or dime. This couldn't be the same guy that was the star quarter back of his high school football team and had colleges at his mercy, guaranteeing him a full scholarship, if he would play for their team. This was not my brother.

I could no longer pretend that the truth did not exist before me. In slow motion, I eased out of the truck and guided towards the façade. He was consistent in his game of hustling. Talking fast, but not saying much of anything to store patrons as they entered and existed the parking lot. I stood closely in the background observing his scene of addiction being played out right before my eyes. Finally I called out, "Monty?"

His own name held no meaning to him. He proceeded in antagonizing a white male that arrived in a sleek black Porsche. Monty kept going on and on about the man's car, about how much it cost and with his magical towel that he held, he could make his rims sparkle like diamonds for a buck or two.

"Monty" I yelled again. This time, he turned around to where I was.

"Hey sis" he exclaimed, as he rushed up to me, to hug and grabbed me by my waist!

"What are you doing Monty" I worriedly asked.

"Rocqui." He eyeballed me like a lustful stranger. "If you were not my sister, I would be trying to holler at you, girl."

His dry chapped lips looked as if they thirst for water. He harbored this horrendous stench, like his new residence was a dumpster stationed outside a restaurant. Seeing him vulnerable and carrying out this reckless behavior made me sick beyond repulsion.

"What happen to you? I'm taking you home right now," I demanded as I grabbed him by his wrist to lead him toward the truck.

He insisted, yanking his arm away from my weak hold. "No sis. I'm not going home. I'm not going anywhere, until I'm ready….Now, if you really want to help me you could give me few dollars 'cause your brother ain't eaten in days" he added with humor.

"Why don't you come home so that you could get a hot meal, then", I insisted?

"I'm not coming home Rocquelle. If you want to help me, give me some damn money." I could see the desperation in his face.

Avery approached us and intervened. "Is everything okay?"

"What's up my man? Say, you wouldn't happen to have a few dollars on you would you" Monty asked in a jiveful manner?

"Avery, this is my brother... Monty."

Avery welcomingly shook Monty's hand and stated "Nice meeting you." He then turned to me, full of concern and asked, "Are you okay?"

I assured him that I was fine and he returned to the truck to wait for me. I refocused my attention back to Monty, who had now moved on to an approaching stranger to solicit money from them. "Monty, stop doing this to yourself. Please let me take you home", I begged.

"Not gonna happen, Rocqui. I will be fine. Tell mom I'm ok and don't wait up." he answered. Then he disappeared through a path that followed along the side of the store.

When I returned to the truck, I noticed the engine was turned off. And Avery sat patiently and quietly as if he knew that my mind had weighed heavy with contemplation.

I opened my mouth and allowed any words to fall. "It seemed like a long time ago, that we were all apart of a perfect family. My mom and dad cared financially and emotionally for us. Every summer we went on a family vacation. They supported and followed our dreams of what ever we wanted to become. But after my father died, everything seemed to unravel. My brother lost his football scholarship and my sister just stopped dreaming... I don't get it," I concluded helplessly shaking my head in disbelief.

"Sometimes, we try really hard controlling things that we have no control over. At some point in time, we have to know when to hold on and fight or just let go," he advised.

"I know. But, I just need to understand what went wrong. We were raised to be more than a street corner crack addict. It disgusts me to see all that my parents have sacrificed for us for him to end up this way."

"You have to be careful and not take on that burden. You can't change who you brother is, even though I'm sure you want to. Every man has to answer for himself, no matter who their parents are."

Even though he made perfect sense, my mood was still a bit distorted. The bright huge florescent sign that seem to hang from the sky only encouraged my aggravation. We had finally arrived at Celebration Station.

"Are you ready," he looked over at me and asked?

My fake smile silenced a 'yes' even though my mind echoed 'no'. Hand and hand we entered the double doors of gaming rings and jingles and children recklessly running to the counter with strings of tickets in their hand in exchange for prizes.

One quick glance at my exasperated face, he sensed my displeasure. Yet he seemed persistent in leading me into a night of fun. We walked out back were more adults merrily gathered around less chaos.

"Come on. Let's race some cars," he suggested. I followed him down the path of steps that led towards the track, playing along in his suspended adolescent behavior.

My chosen car was position two rows ahead of Avery. Comfortably secured in my seat, the lights switch to green and we were off. After one complete circle around the track, I was ahead of Avery and other mindless teenagers. A rush of adrenaline overshadowed any frustration or sadness I felt. By the time the stoplight reversed to red, I was not the winner, but I did, cheerfully, beat Avery. I jumped from the car and leaped into his arms for a victory kiss.

By the time we visited the miniature golf course, my emotions had revealed a more entertained and easily amused 'me.'

Hunger summoned us to the food court for pizza and coke. Like a teenage crush, we filled one side of the booth and his arm rested across my shoulders. His opened mouth lured me to feed him a slice of my pizza like we've been doing this forever.

By the time we left, my demeanor had become childlike as I merrily filled my mouth with pink cotton candy.

When we exited the parking lot, I was quite sure that our next stop would return me to my mother's house. But, instead of the turning signal signaling left, he turned right. I sat quietly, but puzzled as we cruised down Bragg Blvd. only to exit off into a newly constructed home site. He turned left into lighted stone sign that read Rolling Hills.

I reservingly asked, "Where are we going?"

"To my house", he nonchalantly replied. "I want you to meet my girl."

My girl as in 'my daughter', I nervously thought. I was a bit disturbed over the idea that he had a 'little girl' and that I was thrown into her exposure unprepared. With a serious face, I concerningly replied, "I don't think this a good idea."

"Why not? I figure since, I had to let her outside to relieve herself, I matters well see if she likes you or not."

"And if she doesn't like me?"

"She may bite," he jokingly insinuated with a sheepish grin.

I understood that his inferences were in regard to his dog. However, when he opened the front door of his newly built home, I did not expect a grey mane horse, to greet me at my thighs.

Nervously, I spoke "This is not a dog. This is half of a chariot." Fear had paralyzed all movement in my body.

He laughed uncontrollably. "This is Sasha. Sasha, this is Rocquelle."

"I'm not good on introductions with animals that are too big to be carried around in a purse."

"She would never hurt you. She is a good dog."

"I wouldn't know that because she keeps waging her long tongue at me."

"I'm sorry. She is not use to any other woman invading her domain. I will put her in the garage." He gestured for her to follow him and she immediately responded galloping her long hind legs beside him.

I released a cool sigh. "Is she safely stored away now?" My voice loudly traveled throughout the scarcely furnished 2-story house. "I mean, she is not capable of opening that door or anything, is she?"

He gracefully appeared back into the living room, where I stood nervously still. "I don't think I've taught her how to do that just yet." Gently grasping my hand, he led me into the kitchen.

His cherry cabinets, with brush nickel finishes flanked the walls of the kitchen. Over his island, hung three soft pendant lights. I was quite impressed with his decorative choices he had chosen to accent his home.

"Would you like something to drink," he asked as he stood parallel between the open double doors of his stainless steel refrigerator?

Modestly, I replied, "No. I'm good."

Closing the door, he turned towards me, "Would you like something to eat?"

I was beginning to feel like this was a series of unimportant questions, in which I responded indifferently each time. "No."

His steps moved closer into my personal space, until our bodies met. Before I allowed him to move any further into his game of trivia, I interjected, "Why did you really bring me here?"

Very forwardly, in a deep whisper, he answered, "To be with you."

My subtle smile was welcomed by a pleasurable taste of his soft full lips and the sweet caress of his tongue, sucking and kissing my neck, my shoulders, and the cleavage of my breasts.

His touch penetrated up and down my spine, evoking a feeling of sensation and sparked a rush of intensity throughout my body. He lifted me up and sat me on his island. My breasts were more accessible for his velvety tongue to wrap around my nipples. Each gentle pull from his lips, kindled a cry of pleasure and I moaned into ecstasy.

His face appeared mesmerized by my vulnerability. I was seduced under his spell. I wanted him and I desperately desired to   feel him inside of me. No words were necessary to interpret what we both obviously felt. I wanted him right then and right there. His hand reached for mine that led me up the darken stairs and into his bedroom. I sat nervous, yet anxious as hell, on the edge of his bed. Watching and taking note of his harden body, with all the right curves and muscles in all the right places, as he removed his shirt. It wasn't long before his hands were removing my sneakers and his fingers were unfastening my shorts.

Effortlessly, he slid my panties down my thighs and over my knees, until they drifted into mid air. A simple kiss on the lips was only the start of his mouth tasting all of my other body parts. His face got lost between my legs. And his lips pierced my inner core while his tongue tickled and teased all of the excitement within me. He was obviously gift in massaging, sucking and licking until my juices oozed from within. My hands uncontrollably grasp his head at the numbness of my feet and my body shivered helplessly until I cried out with pleasure. I lay their, faintly, glaring up at his trey ceiling, spellbound in pleasure. My mind and body felt opened and free. I felt for a moment like I was floating

He lengthen his naked body over mind and I felt his entrance into my canal. He filled my emptiness and I breathe deeply, excited by his penetration. My body quivered as his hands clasped my hips and I grooved harmoniously to his rhythm. What began as a delicate tempo, spiraled into pleasurable pain, with each throbbing thrust. Finally, he came...hard. I came too.

Again and again. He held me tightly until he yielded to his vulnerable state.

Our tired bodies settled side by side, with a few intermittencies of words and laughter, before falling into a deep slumber.

It was morning. The sunlight shining across my sleeping face did not interrupt my slumber. However, the open profile of white fangs and a long purplish tongue salivating within a nose reach of my delicate face did. I panicked. "Avery", I screamed!

Seconds later, he appeared instantly to rescue me from my foreseen danger. "I'm so sorry. Sasha, let's go," he commanded. She obediently responded to his command, kicking up her hind legs up as she galloped from the bedroom.

"I'm really sorry. I'd forgotten the room door was open", he consoled me with the touch of his hands gently caressing my naked body entangled in his sheet.

"I guess if she wanted to eat me, she would have done that while I was sleeping", I jokingly implied.

He laughed and then stated, "If she knew how good you tasted, maybe she would have."

Recollection of last night's sexual exposure forced a blushingly smile across my face. The smell of food being cooked invaded my senses and I suddenly felt hungry. "Are you cooking breakfast?"

"Yeah. My plan was to bring it to you in bed. That reminds me, I need to go and check on it."

"You don't have to bring it to me in bed," I modestly implied. "I'll just meet you downstairs after I get dress."

He left the room and I scuffled trying to find my panties and bra that were hidden between the sheets. I slipped my shorts on and pulled my blouse over my head. Before I had a chance to think about what to do with my morning breathe, he reappeared handing me an unopened toothbrush package. "I had to run out to the grocery store, this morning. I figured you would need this."

Surprisingly, I replied, "Thank you."

I entered into his kitchen, where two place settings were neatly arranged along the island next to one another. I took my seat in the barstool and he turned from the stove with a plate in his hand covered with a large omelet and two sausage links and toast. My mouth watered with anticipation of devouring every single crumb from my plate. We toast our wine glasses filled with mimosa and my taste buds escaped into heaven.

"If I keep hanging out with you, I'm gonna get fat," I implied after realizing how much I've eaten since I've been in his company.

"You would still be beautiful to me, no matter how round you become," he jokingly insinuated, while patting my butt on the stool.

"That would never be cute, no matter how many times you men tell that lie."

"You may be right. Some of us are very specific about what we want in a person. I, on the other hand, want something more than just a round ass and a big chest."

"Really? What do you want?" I was intrigued.

"I want you."

"I'm flattered. Maybe if I wasn't engaged and lived in Richmond that would sound appealing."

"If that was the case, then I don't think you and I would have ever had the chance to meet. Then it would be some round ass big chest woman sitting up here instead of you."

"I don't know what to say to that."

"I'm joking. That's not me. That's not even my type."

"What's your type?"

"I don't have a specific type. I've dated different women in the past. Most of them were basically good women, but not necessarily the right woman. Because I've never really thought about getting married before, I never singled out the 'wifey' type. I always assumed that if she is out there, I would automatically know. I wouldn't need a checklist to verify that. "

"Then how would you know if she is right for you."

"Because when she is not with me, I can't think, sleep or breathe without her."

"That's kinda deep. She sounds like she gotta be an amazing woman."

"Yes, she does... and she is. What about you? How do you know you've met the person that you want to spend the rest of your life with?"

"Unlike you, I have a checklist. And he must fulfill everything on that list, in order for him to be right for me."

"What's on the list?"

"Financial security, good looks and a good heart."

"That doesn't sound too bad. I thought maybe you were gonna say he has to make six hundred thousand dollars a year and drive a Land Rover or something like that."

"Well, all that sounds pretty darn good too."

"And what if someone else came along and gave you more."

"What could be more than that?"

"Happiness."

Trying to convince him and myself that my ideas are realistic, I adamantly stated, "I don't want you think that I'm being superficial or unrealistic. I think most people would be happy with money and good looks."

His expression appeared unconvinced, he simply replied, "It's quite obvious you already have those things. But does that make you happy?"

I didn't know what to think anymore. What happiness once meant no longer seems to hold any validity anymore. "Happiness comes in all various shapes and sizes, you know."

My eyes wondrously traveled around the kitchen carefully savoring one bite after the other as we loosely talk about life and other intriguing matters. However, the moment soon came interrupted, at the sight of 11:30, glowing from his microwave.

"Oh my gosh," I panicked, with my mouth full of food! "I supposed to have picked my sister up from the airport at ten o'clock." I paused for a brief second and then concluded, "I gotta go."

6

It wasn't long before Avery pulled up into my mother's driveway that a petite silhouette reflected through the glass storm door. I released an air of calmness and knew that it was no one other than, my baby sister, Tamra. My mind was distant from Avery as my eyes rested on her mirrored frame.

"What's the matter," Avery asked?

My throat felt dry. The voice that I sputtered sounded raspy and off-cord. "I don't know. I've been counting down the days to when my sister would finally arrive home. But, now that she is here, I feel awkward for her to see me getting out of a truck of someone other than the man I'm supposed to marry."

"Listen, you don't have to feel a certain way about yourself because of what you and I shared. Last night wasn't about just one night. I barely even know you... yet I want to spend every night with you" he profoundly stated. "That's just me."

Even though his words sounded sincere, I wasn't totally comfortable with myself over our sexual interlude from last night. I was a different woman last night when I was crooning his name in high octave. This other woman that now sat next to him in his truck had standards and respect for herself and would never cheat on someone she cares about.

"I know this may sound silly but, this...you and I thing is totally out of character for me," I plainly stated. "I've never had a one night stand before. Any guy that I've ever been with physically was because I was emotionally and mentally connected to them."

"Are you saying that this time, you were not emotionally and mentally connected? And that I am just a one time thing for you," he examined?

"No, no...that's not what I mean," I quickly tried to correct my choice of words.

Coolly he implied, "You don't have to explain. This is obviously not just about us. I won't ask or expect anything from you other than what you are willing to give me."

He was sweet and gentle in such ways that were only seen in movies or promised in love songs. His sweet scent still held in the clothes that I wore from last night. For a quick instance, I had forgotten all about the existence of Tamra. The awareness of her gazing at my subtle intentions through the storm door was a vague memory from what I was thinking, at that very moment.

My nerves were at ease, a bit, before I pulled the door handle to exit the truck. He leaned towards me and kissed my cheek. I stood stiffly watching his truck reverse out into the street and drive away.

My feet slowly paced along the curved walkway and up the steps. She steadily opened the door. Her face lit up with an ironic gesture of delight. "Hey slut", she greeted without any indifferences in her welcomingly manner.

I couldn't help but to chuckle, a bit. "Hey lil' girl", I replied through our exchange of hugs.

"Who's that guy?" Her interrogations followed me into the kitchen. "It's certainly not Zoric."

"He's just a friend," I casually answered, while pouring me a cup of coffee.

She settled down suspiciously next to me at the table and continued. "You know… I've always knew that you had a little hootchie in you. It's just sad that it took this long to bring it out of you. But, it's okay. We all have a little hootch in us," she intentionally implied.

"Spending sometime with a guy does not make me a hootchie."

"Oh really." She was ready for comeback with neck turning and twisting lips. "What does that make you, like a virgin?"

Becoming a bit disturbed by her continual insinuations, I interjected, "Would you shut up, please. Life is not all about sex."

"No it's not. But it certainly makes life a bit more exciting; especially if it's good sex. And I mean real good sex."

My tolerance for this conversation had peeked. I knew exactly what would change the direction of this dialogue. "Where is my eight hundred dollars that you borrowed from me last year and seemed to can't pay back?"

In a child-like manner, she whined, 'It's coming. I promise, Rocqui. I got you." Quick thinking to get my attention off of her accrued debt, she suggested, "From the looks of that brand new car, I know you are not in a rush for eight hundred little dollars."

"It does not matter if it is little or not, it's mine. And I want my money back," I insisted without a fold from my lips.

"Yes sis. I understand. You are feeling a little tense now. How about a quick spin around the block in your sexy new car to relax your mind?" Could you imagine how good I'd look riding around with the top down and the wind breezing threw my hair," she conceited?

I immediately knew that she was hinting to drive me car. I was not going to allow that to happen so quickly. Rather than entertaining her idea, I parted from the table and headed upstairs to change into some clean clothes, like I didn't catch her last words she was implying.

After a long hot shower, I returned down the stairs to join my mother and my sister at the table, conversing over their unfinished breakfast.

"You want some breakfast," my mother asked?

"Nope." My sister interjected. "I think she already ate ma", she delivered with a devilish grin on her face.

My eyes sneered in annoyance at Tamra's unsubtle insinuation.

"Mom, how would you like to celebrate your fifty-fifth birthday on Sunday," I asked, hoping that she would provide some clue, for a woman who seems to think she had everything.

"You girls know already not to make too much of a fuss over my birthday. Heck, everyday is a birthday, a holiday, a blessing, if you ask me," she firmly stated.

"Yeah but, I would like to do something special for you."

"My sisters have already planned something special for me."

"Like what?"

"We are all dressing up like rich white women, in our fancy dresses and adorning our heads with elaborate hats, to have brunch at the Rose Garden."

"That is it," Tamra's voice rose with disappointment. "You don't want a party, with big balloons and streamers decorated all over the place," she continued as if she had big plans?

"Do I look ten years old to you?"

"Well, I wasn't thinking of any balloons and whatnots. But, I did want to have a mini celebration of some sort. You are our mother," I inserted.

She looked interested in my proposal. "What do you have in mind?"

"Hmmm. I could make an appointment for the three of us to go to the spa, tomorrow. It would be like a pre-celebration, I guess. We could have an all girls day of being pampered."

"Now that sounds like a winner," she agreed.

I looked over at Tamra who was eyeing me like a dog that anxiously awaited a bone. "What are you looking at," I conceited?

"I was just wondering, does this all girl thing mean that my expenses would be covered too?"

"Doesn't it always mean that," I retorted.

My mother chuckled. It always made me feel special when I could simply make her laugh. So, I don't understand what prompted me to say this next thing that could wipe a smile off of a clown's face.

"I saw Monty last night," I announced.

"How is my brother, the crackhead, doing," Tamra, apathetically inquired?

Recalling the images of what I saw last night verses the man that I once knew, I regretfully affirmed, "not good. He was at this service station, hustling money off of people. He stinks. He looked like a man without a past and certainly no future."

My mother rose from the table in silenced. My eyes followed her as she placed her finished plate in the kitchen sink and looked aimlessly through the back window.

Tamra animatedly implied, "We should go and find him and bring him home. I'm sure it won't be hard. There is a crack house on every corner along 'the Mirk."

My mother broke her silence and candidly stated, "He'll come home when he's ready."

Tamra and I alarming eyes met simultaneously from across the table, without an exchange of words. We carefully understood that our mother's stern remark had finalized any further discussion she cared to listen to about our brother.

As Tamra washed the dishes, I remained at the table reading the newspaper, while my mother began cleaning downstairs. "Are you ready to go to the mall," Tamra asked?

I had suggested earlier to Tamra that we needed to go shopping to buy a gift for mom, for her birthday. Her readily acceptance reminded me that her idea of shopping had more to do with emptying my pocket at attempt to fill her closet. Hesitantly, I replied, "I guess."

After hours of credit card transactions, with me signing receipts and Tamra ecstatically grabbing the shopping bags, we settled at the food court, for lunch. Looking across from her was like looking into a younger face of my mother. A round nose and big brown eyes perfectly outfitted on her short and curvy body. Years of cheerleading and dance have kept her hips from spreading and her behind from widening, but it is inevitable that her body would embrace the same curves and thickness like all the Jones' women, on my mother side of the family.

When we were young, Monty and I use to convincingly taunt her with lies that she was adopted because she didn't embody our long and narrow frame, our lighter tinted skin, and our almond shaped eyes that we inherited from our father. Monty teasingly called her 'Three feet' because he'd convinced her that she would never grow any taller than three feet.

She hated the name. She despised the shortcomings of her height, but was left with little defense seemingly she was the youngest and the smallest of the family. However, she cleverly discovered her use of words to stand taller than the both of us, with her sassiness and sarcasm.

"So... who was that guy in the truck?" She revisited her morning inquisitions.

"You are really not gonna let that rest, are you?"

"Nope."

"He is really no one important," I tried to convincingly persuade her to believe, hoping that maybe it would be the end of the conversation.

Yet, it wasn't. She began to question me like she was a defense attorney. "Really! You are engaged to be married. And you've been here one week and slept with a NOBODY. I would say that he makes for somebody. And possibly somebody special from the look of your face earlier this morning when he dropped you off."

I couldn't believe that I was about to open my mouth up and discuss my sexual relations with Tamra, but something inside of me felt so good, I had to share. "You know what's really interesting is... last night was everything great sex should be. I found myself screaming 'no' when my body was yelling 'yes' at the same. I was amazing." The tightness in my cheek made me realized that I was blushing over my admittance.

"You came," she announced, like it was for all ears to hear!

"Shhh! Yes," I whispered, as my eyes swiftly moved around to the crowded food court, hoping no one heard our conversation.

"Tamra, as long as I been with Zoric and as much as I love him, he had never made me feel the way this man did in one night. I have never gotten this much excitement and fulfillment from any man before, like this."

"Well, I'm glad that you have finally joined the Orgasm Club. Some women never make it there no matter how long they have been out there trying."

"And you know what's really funny. I thought all that orgasm stuff was made up. But it is so real. Damn, it's so real!" I started getting horny reliving that experience all over again in my mind.

"Congratulations! Now what? Are you gonna let him screw your brains out some more while you are hear to? Now that you have had it, you can never go back to ordinary sex again. It would never be the same again."

"That's the worse part of it all. I know that I can't see him anymore. I'm engaged. Everything about last night was wrong between us. My life is already complicated."

"AND..." she probed for more information.

"Did you hear me say that I was engaged?"

"How much of that mattered last night when he was banging your head against the headboard?"

"You are absolutely crazy."

"Maybe I am crazy. Or maybe you are to think that this guy that you are never gonna see this guy again that just turned you out."

"I'm not turned out. And... I'm not changing my entire life for someone I've only known for a week. Zoric and I have been together for four years. We are perfect together."

"Perfect how, Rocqui? If you and Zoric are so perfect together, than how did last night happen?"

I felt stupid. Her wisdom caught me off guard. "Wow. Since when did you grow up and learned how to rationalize decisions as an adult?"

"Since I became an adult. Duh! Plus, Big Sis, I Am Married," she clarified! "And one thing that I have come to understand is that perfect does not exist in any relationship or marriage and definitely not yours. I don't care how many times you stand in front of the altar and rehearse those vows over and over again. It does not make do for perfection."

I wasn't convinced that she knew what she was talking about until she rambled on, "And I don't care how much you love someone... there are gonna be days when you wished that you never married them."

Her words filled my mind with deep thought and left little room for me to finish the rest of my chicken sandwich that I had bought from Chick Fillet.

The next day at Shalone's Day Spa, no one expected to hear the disturbance Tamra and I encountered.

"Aah...Ooh. That feels good. Oh yes! Oh yes! Right there," she moaned breathing heavily and deeply with each penetrating massage. If I didn't know my mother to be the sanctified God-fearing person that she is, I would have thought that the male masseuse was entering inside forbidden territory where no man has gone since the days of my father.

Tamra and I embarrassingly listened outside the closed door, snickering and often mortified by our mother's crooning of pleasure being administered to her.

"What is the matter with you girls," she asked, quickly assessing our strange behavior, once her session was complete?

"Ah..." I stammered, with widen eyes. "Just didn't think you would enjoy it that much."

"Well, gosh Rocqui. I am still alive. I do still enjoy being touch."

"Of course, Mom. We all do, right Rocqu?" Tamra wittingly added.

While the receptionist was totaling my bill, I had stolen a glimpse of my mother and my sister, who were sampling aroma therapy lotions and body oils. My eyes were fixed on my mother's glowing youthful beauty. Her brilliant smile symbolized joy and happiness that had pervaded her spirited life. Nothing in her actions or mannerism spoke of death or dying. That's when I rested on the notion that she was going to be okay. The cancer that had revisited my mother's body once again was only taking up temporary residency. She is a fighter. And she would win I reassuringly concluded.

"You paid this much money for the three of us", Tamra belted out leaning nosily over my shoulder, at my receipt.

Tamra's obvious indiscretion sparked my mother's interest in how much I spent on our day at the spa. She immediately took note of the total bill, herself. Her stare at me was me somewhat disapprovingly. "Rocqui, you didn't have to spend that much money on me. I would have been just as happy, if we would have stayed home and given each other pedicures and manicures."

"Honestly mother," Tamra jumped in, "If I was giving you a massage and you started moaning like you did earlier, I would have completely jumped out of my skin."

Laughter filled our voices as we got inside of my car to return home.

I don't know what sparked Tamra to interest me into making a homemade pizza with her. We both fumbled around the kitchen, like we knew what we were doing. She had slightly forgotten that she and I don't cook. The only time we ever stood in the kitchen simultaneously was to fill our plates with the food our mother had already prepared.

"Tamra how are we gonna unthaw the sausage in enough time to prepare the pizza?" I looked over the counter at all the ingredients we'd collected from the cabinets and the refrigerator. The Italian sausage placed next to the sealed content of pepperoni slices, looked harder than stone.

"Just put it in the microwave for three minutes," she instructed, as she steadily focused on chopping the onions.

"I didn't know you knew how to unthaw meat in the microwave."

"Do I look like an idiot to you? Every house in America has a microwave, including mine."

"They better. It holds good resale value. We are looking at an eighty percent return from well design kitchen."

"Who cares?"

"My bank account does."

Dismissing my sales jargon, she proceeded with, "Well, after you finish putting the sausage in the microwave, spread the tomato sauce over the dough. Then we can start layering it with cheese."

"Okay Chef Boyardee." I walked to over to the counter and began spooning the sauce in a circular motion over the flatten dough. I was getting into this groove of cooking until my cell phone unexpectantly chimed. I place the spoon to the side and found my phone inside my purse. It was a text from Avery. A pleasant smile spread across my face.

'What are you doing?'

I texted, *'Making Pizza'.*

'Sounds good. Would you like some ice cream to go with your pizza?'

'Ice cream?'

'Ice cream would be perfect on a particular hot day, like today.'

'Sounds tempting. What time did you have in mind?'

'I'm hoping that now would be good.'

'Now?'

'Yes. I went out for a ride and thought maybe you wanted to join me.'

My fingertips paused over the keys of my phone. I immediately began to deliberate, as I stood next to the microwave that was now beeping, repeatedly. The sausage had defrosted. Yet, all I could hear were my impending actions flustering my thoughts. He wasn't really outside in my mother's front yard, was he? That would be bold and spontaneous. Nevertheless, I was intrigued.

As I skirted passed Tamra, her words roped me around. "Rocqui, aren't you gonna get the sausage out of the microwave," she questioned?

I glanced at her anxiously and replied, "I'll get it in a minute." My feet nearly tumbled over one another trying to get to the front, before she found more words to say. The glass storm door didn't nearly come close to complimenting his handsome presence, as he poised himself calmly and coolly against his shiny sleek motorcycle...the very same motorcycle that gave me wings to fly the first night I met him.

I slowly stepped out onto the front porch, to draw myself nearer to him. Impulse drew me closer and closer. My heart pounded of excitement with each rapid beat. His tasty lips quirked into a tender smile, as his soft brown eyes held my elated gaze.

"Would you like to go for a ride with me," he asked smoothly?"

"For ice cream, right," I playfully added?

"Yeah. We could have that too," he charmingly whispered.

"I'll be right back."

"I'll be waiting."

I carefully disguised my anxious walk, as I returned back into the house for my purse.

"Thanks for helping with the pizza Rocqui," Tamra squealed, who had now resided on the sofa in front of television, after placing the pizza in the oven.

"Here." I tossed a couple of twenties at her. "This is for all of your work." I rushed out the door before she began with a list of questions.

Just as soon as my arms clenched his defined chest, we zoomed through the gentle breeze from a late summer day. The air felt good pushing against my body, as my hands firmly explored his chest. At one point, while we waited at a red light, he turned to me and said under his shielded face, "You like this, don't you?"

I blushingly nodded my heavy helmet and squeezed him even firmer to assure him so.

Everything felt good. The cooling sunset, the slight wind that blew through my hair and the ice cream that cooled my warm body with each slow lick from its cone. We sat on the patio outside of the *Ice Cream Shop*, gathered by a few others that craved some relief from the summer heat. I could feel his awed gaze trying to study my thoughts. Finally he said, "What are you thinking about?"

"I'm thinking..." I paused as I looked up at the skies. And then returned my dreamy eyes towards him, "how beautiful today is."

He nodded in agreement. Yet, his steady eyes still remained fixed on my face, while he carefully licked his ice cream. "What are you thinking," I returned?

"I was thinking", he slowly yet genuinely, replied..."if everyday with you is just as beautiful, as today."

I was speechless. He words sent a rush of warmth through my body. Right then and there, I wanted him to fill me. However, as I looked at him still swirling his tongue around his vanilla cone, he seemed to be in no hurry to leave.

"You know, there is a lot of trust that goes into letting someone ride you on the back of their motorcycle," I overtly mentioned.

"Are you saying that you trust me?"

"I might be saying that...or, I might be crazy."

He chuckled. "I'm glad that you trust me. You should know that I would never hurt you in any shape, form, or fashion." He words held truth through his promising eyes.

"I'm curious. Is this all that you do?"

'What do you mean?"

"I mean...when you are not at the restaurant, do you spend most of your days leisurely riding your bike and occasionally going out for ice cream and meeting new people?"

"I wish that's all I had time to do. But, that's not my reality, even by a little. Interestingly enough, this past week had been my first time that I've taking her out in over a month. I got my hands tied up in many different things, like the restaurant and 'the club' that I barely have time even for simple pleasures, like ice cream."

"And as far as meeting new people, I meet new people all the time...every day. But, I've never met anyone like you."

"I'm nothing special."

"I beg to differ with you on that."

I blushingly tried to hold back a smile. "How many chefs do you have in your restaurant?"

"I have four sous chefs."

"Why do you spend so much time cooking at the restaurant, yourself?"

"Because, it is what I love to do. I really can't see myself doing anything else that feels as natural to me as cooking does."

"What is your favorite thing to cook?"

"Hmm. I don't have one particular favorite dish. I just love cooking. Food brings people together. Every important moment in people lives are defined by the gathering of food. People connect, celebrate, and console one another through food. It gives me a pleasure to offer that moment of relief or comfort through my cooking. "

"I wish I could cook."

"Would you like for me to teach you?"

"No. I would just settle on the fact that cooking is not for me. But I like to eat, though," I playfully grinned.

"That helps me out in my business." He smiled.

"I tell you what I could do."

"What?"

"I could change a tire on a car," I proudly bragged.

"Really?" His face read the exact expression that I expected...total surprise.

"Yes. When I was fifteen, my daddy taught me how to change the tire on his old white pick-up truck. He said he wanted me to how to change a tire on a car so that I would never have to wait around for a man to do it for me."

"Wow. Such a profound statement from a man."

"I know. My dad was clever like that. The irony is instead of me not waiting for a man to change my tire, I now have to wait on a man to cook for me, I guess."

"That is ironic...and very funny. It would be very interesting to see you change a flat tire, however."

"Not as interesting as to see me standing in the kitchen, with an apron tied around me."

We both laughed.

"I like you. I like being with you," he admitted with all seriousness in his face. "I'm glad you are here with me."

I swallowed hard, before I gently spoke again. "So am I. This is nice. I feel myself getting too comfortable being around you though."

"That's not a bad thing."

"For you, maybe. But I'm just days away from returning to Richmond."

"I know."

I smiled. "You are not going make me leaving easy, are you?"

"No. Not when I want you to stay. But that's just me, even though it's not fair for me to say."

He gave me a look like maybe he had said too much. "The sun is about to set," he stated gazing up at the sky. "How bout we go for another ride?" He stood up and handed me the other helmet.

"Where to," I asked, sliding the black helmet over my head?

"Too a better view of the skyline." **Zoomed,** we sped at of the parking lot.

We traveled faster than the speed of light, down the All American freeway. By the time we reached his house, there was no picturesque view of the sun setting. Darkness had moved in. On the inside, the house remained exactly as I remembered it, open and empty. We both knew why we were there. And it didn't take us long to do what we came here to do.

My naked body lay blanketed between the plush fibers of his carpeted floor and his hard naked body. We tried to make it upstairs into the bedroom, but when our lips touched something bigger and deeper inside of us, overwhelmed our intention. Our craved bodies settled on the convenience of his living room floor. Shorts and pants had dropped down to our feet. Shirts became swiftly undone and drifted into the air that enveloped us. And shoes were intentionally tossed somewhere to the side to be careful they would not end up somewhere unpleasant. At some point during our sexual intertwine I think I even cried. He pleased me and touched me in places that I never knew I had feelings before.

"Am I too heavy on you," he whispered, as he gently stroked my cheek with the palm of his hand?

"You didn't seem to mind moments ago, to ask me that question," I playfully replied.

"You seem to have not mind moments ago, that I was heavy either. But, now I'm starting to notice your breathing becoming shorter and faster, as I lay here."

"That was before the blood stopped circulating in my body."

"Are you hungry? I can cook a quick meal and maybe we could watch a movie or something," he proposed.

"Eating sounds like a great idea right now. But, as much as I would like to, I can't stay here tonight," I regretfully felt the need to say.

"This is what it feels like to be used."

I chuckled. "No. Tomorrow is my mother's birthday. And it wouldn't seem right if I wasn't there first thing in the morning to wish her 'Happy Birthday.'

"That's understandable." He slowly raised his perfect well sculptured anatomy off of mind. But, not without giving me one last long wet kiss.

7

"**W**here were you all night?" My tired eyes ignored Tamra's immediate questioning, as I crossed her path trying to make my way into the bathroom.

I returned from out of the bathroom, after brushing my teeth and walked downstairs into the kitchen where I anticipated more grilling from her. "Where's mom?" I asked, staggering over to the coffee pot to empty the remaining sips into my cup.

"Mom left for church seven thirty this morning. She probably won't be back until late this afternoon."

"I'm sorry I missed her. I wanted to say 'Happy Birthday' to her before she left." I sat across from her at the kitchen table.

"Well, you are the one who decided to get your freak on all night. Where did you go anyway?"

"I went out for ice cream."

"Ice cream? Until two in the morning?"

"Sort of. We went for ice cream. And then we went back to his place. And then we went to his club for some drinks."

"We, as in you and that mystery guy?"

"Yeah, except he is not a mystery guy. His name is Avery."

"What did I tell you? I knew you were gonna go back to him. Once you reach that feeling, you can never go back to regular sex again. I'm willing to bet you that this time was probably better than the first time, wasn't it?"

"Shut up Tamra."

"I was teasing you before. But I think you really like this guy?"

I pondered the word 'like' in my mind, as if I never thought of fact that I actually might 'like' him. "I think I *might* like him, too. But, I have some questions about who this man really is."

"What do you mean?"

"I mean, he is either very cheap or very smart. On the couple of dates that we have been on, he has taken me to IHOP and out for ice cream...things like that. I don't have a problem with going to places like that. It's just that I've kinda grown accustom to fine dining and upscale settings, I guess."

"If ice cream and pancakes are all it takes to get into your panties, then I would be cheap too?"

"Why am I talking to you?" I snapped.

"Because I'm your sister. And I'm the only that cares to listen to you right now."

"Not if you're going to be a smartass every time I say something."

"Okay. I will behave. I promise." She raised her hand high enough as if she was making a pledge. "Maybe he knows that, already. Maybe he is giving you a taste of things in which you may have been missing."

"Maybe." Her answer drew a brief moment of silence between us. Until I added, "I just hope that everything that happens here stays here. If Zoric ever finds out..."

"Zoric who?"

"Stop playing with me Tamra."

"I was just wondering if you still knew who Zoric was."

"Yes. My fiancé."

"Girl, you better stop playing with that word. Every time you say, it sounds like it has been rehearsed."

"Look you can think whatever you like. But I will be leaving on Saturday for Richmond and returning to my normal life."

"Don't you mean your perfect life, as you often like to remind everyone? And speaking of perfect, why didn't your perfect fiancé come down here with you?"

"Zoric is a workaholic. He really doesn't visit too many places. He hardly even goes home to visit his family."

"Why?"

"He has his reasons, I guess. The last time Zoric and I went to visit his mom in Akron he acted like he was too good to ride down the same block where he was raised. I really didn't understand it. This guy was walking up along side of the car and Zoric quickly doubled locked the doors and sneered at him, like he was afraid that the guy was gonna rob us or something."

"If he lived in the hood like some of these places around here, I probably would have done the same thing."

"Tamra, no one should become too good in which they can't ever go home?"

"Isn't that what happened to you? You act like you are too good to come home. I mean it has been three years since you've been here."

"That is because you moved to a different state. I moved to another state. And Zoric has his own family, in which we visit once in a while. Besides, it's not like we haven't seen each other or spent every other holiday together."

"It doesn't matter where we live. There is no other place like home. You seemed to have forgotten that."

The last statement she made did not have me readily convinced that coming home was necessarily a good thing. She could tell that I wasn't easily sold. "Rocqui, don't you just miss mama's cooking and now being able to sit in the grown folks living room... a room in which we as children were never able to sit in?"

I began to chuckle.

"See we can go in there right now, with our shoes on and put our feet up on the coffee table."

A fear struck over me from that mere image. I implied seriously," I don't know what house you are talking. But walking over mama's plush carpet and putting your feet up on her expensive table will never happen in this house. In this house, you could be killed for that."

We both broke out into a harmonious laughter. "You maybe right. But it's still home. And that matters to me more than any other place on earth. I think while you are here, it would be a good time for you to reconnect with your family. It's good that you've put Zoric aside for a while."

"I have not put Zoric aside," I frankly stated.

I was sitting there before her at the breakfast table wondering why was I allowing her the opportunity to go on and on about my life as if she had some say in it. My facial expression read nothing. But she went steadily on like she had my best interest at heart. "Ima tell you what you need to do. This guy Avery, he apparently is good at what he does. Let him keep doing it."

"Let him keep doing what?"

"Stirring your pot. And then when you go back to Richmond you will be all relaxed and calmed. Zoric will not even recognize you, anymore."

I darned near looked at her crossed eyed. I could never fathom how she comes up with the craziest things to say. I had to laugh, even though I didn't want to. "I don't know really know what to say. Right now he seems to be a great guy. But, I'm not expecting anything else from him."

"Well anyone gotta be better than Zoric. Zoric is just someone good to look at...someone to brag to friends to say how 'fine' he is. That's all you can do with a man like Zoric."

Specifically, I reminded her, "Well, I'm gonna marry him."

"Good luck with that." Our conversation was quickly coming to an end with that response.

"You can be such an asshole sometimes, Tamra."

"The worlds finest," she smile cunningly.

It was much later than I had anticipated that my mother finally arrived home. She walked in wearing a bright tangerine-colored sheath dress. Her ivory wide rim hat elegantly canopied her head. "Well, hello ladies," she sung as she walked through the foyer and into the kitchen.

"Did you have fun," I asked, already detecting from her obvious smile that she did?

"Yes. I really did." She answered like apart of her was still there having a great time.

I trailed behind her entering into her bedroom. There, she was surprised by a huge gift basket of scented lotion and sprays that waited upon her bed. "Rocqui, you really didn't have to do this. You've done so much already." She walked over towards me and embraced me with a hug.

"I know. But you are my mother. And if I have it, I want to share it with you."

"That's all well and good. But, stop thinking money and things are the key to happiness. It shouldn't take that much to make someone happy. And it certainly doesn't for me."

I couldn't argue with her on that. I just settled comfortably upon her bed, as I watched her slip out her dress and slide her stockings down her thick legs to finally adorn herself in something more comfortable, like her housecoat. She finally relaxingly sat down next to me, like she needed to share her thoughts. "Tell me what's going on with you?"

"What do you mean," I nervously felt?

"I mean, you've been here for two weeks, met some guy that got you running up down the streets like you're behind is on fire."

"Mother," I frowned. I felt a bit embarrassed.

"Well, it's the truth. Have you forgotten that you are engaged? Aren't you supposedly getting married next year?"

"Yes."

"What are you doing? What is this rendezvous you've been taking up with this young man all about?"

"It's not about anything," I whined. "He is just a friend."

"Umm hmm. Are you gonna introduce Zoric to your new friend?"

"No," I sharply replied.

"Then, he is not just a friend. And you are kidding yourself if you think otherwise."

"I don't know what to do. I like him, but..."

"But? What do you mean but? Do you hear yourself? You've already said enough by saying 'I like him. I tell you what...you girls have gotten too big for your own britches. One man is not enough to have these days. Now you need two."

"Mom, I don't need two men. I just have one."

"I guess you are gonna keep lying to yourself until you figure it out, aren't you?"

"I don't need to figure anything out. I'm in love with Zoric."

"That sounds as convincing to me as seeing you get in and out that truck that boy drives." Mom always refer to any and every guy I've ever dated as 'that boy.'

The room became suddenly timidly silent after surviving a moment over my mother's beaten words. I can feel her eyes on me, even though I held my face down, staring through the floral print of my dress. "It's quite obvious that what you are doing has nothing to do with love," she added.

"I do love Zoric," I sulked.

"You don't need to convince me. This is between you, your fiancé and your new found 'friend'."

It wasn't too much longer after my mother's candid remarks that Tamra made her appearance and entered into the room. Tamra and my mother immediately relayed a few words leaving me totaling distant in my own world of thought. I was puzzled and confused. I always believed that I had everything, until the moment he (Avery) made me realize that I was without something.

He made things feel so right that it couldn't be wrong. But it was wrong. From the moment I allowed IHOP to become a place of convenience for us, I was wrong. I had allowed Avery to have me for more than a moment, even though I'd vowed that Zoric will have me forever. I understood that I needed to fix what was wrong and make it right. I just didn't know how to.

"Rocqui, tell mommy I probably got the worst whooping out of all us." Tamra held too much excitement in her voice. I probably was incoherent for about five minutes of their conversation.

"What," I muttered, returning back to reality?

"Rocqui, you hardly got any whipping," Tamra adamantly stated.

I shook off my previous thoughts and became atoned to my mother and sister's conversation. "That's not true. Monty and I use to get whippings every Monday and Friday. It was like mom was whipping us, just in case we got into trouble during the week. I would be like, 'mom, but I had a good week'. And she would be steady whipping our tails."

Laughter...

"But I do remember that one time Tamra, when you were trying smoke and you burned a hole in momma's sofa. You remember that mom?" I looked over at her smilingly nodding. "You let mom blame the incident on daddy thinking that his cigar was what caused it. Until, she accidentally knocked your purse off the counter, one day and a box of Newport's appeared on the floor. And you know who the first person she questioned, even after she seen the evidence from your purse...*Me*. Like I was somehow at fault for you smoking. I prayed for you that day. I couldn't stand to be in the house when she confronted you because I knew that she was going to kill you."

My mother had to brace herself over her laughter to say, "She shouldn't been smoking in the first place."

After a couple of weeks of visiting with my mother and my sister, Friday quickly arrived. My two week stay was coming to a subtle end. I needed to go home to Richmond to return to my business, my home and to Zoric. Even though, I unhappily desired to do so.

I began slowly and regrettably packing my suitcase for my early morning drive when Avery called.

"How are you," he softly spoke?

The sound of his voice comforted me like a cashmere sweater. I could have unreservingly expressed how happy I was to hear from him. Better yet, disclosed that I have been thinking about him every minute in a day. It would have all be true. However, at the break of dawn, I will return to the security and luxury of my life in Richmond; a life that has been perfectly rehearsed and organized, with little room for impromptu. I disconnected my mind from my emotions and responded, "I'm fine. I'm just finishing up packing for my trip home."

"I hope everything went well with your visit here?"

Dry and a bit detached, I answered, "Things went well. I had a nice visit. I realized that it has been a long time coming since I been here. I've missed being home."

"Probably just as much as I'm gonna miss you while you are away."

I pursed my lips. I held back my desire to admit that my feeling was mutual.

I breathe deeply, releasing an air of doubt. "Look Avery, the time I spent with you was nice... really nice between us. But, I don't know where this thing between us is going. I don't want to set up false expectations between us especially with my circumstance."

"I get that. It would be irrational for me to think that the few times we shared together, would change that. At the same time, I have to let you know that, how I feel about you. And if, by any chance, you will allow me any opportunity to be with you, I'm yours."

I was nearly floored...damn near wordless, over his candidness. Yet in still, I wasn't going to change everything I had and everything I'd worked for over a couple nights of mind-blowing sex. But, I undeniably, liked him. "Can we just be friends," I offered? It was an illusory proposal. I had no specific meaning of what 'friends' meant, under my statement. Yet, I couldn't just let go of him.

He patiently resigned in acceptance with, "Being friends is good," he easily agreed. "I hope you drive safely. Maybe our paths will cross again when you return," he added.

I held back a slight chuckled and sternly replied, "Maybe." I needed to, constantly, remind myself to distance my thoughts away from this moment.

The continual words that drifted between us felt dry and rehearsed. There was even a moment of awkward silence when we waited for one another to speak. Finally he initiated our exchange of goodbyes.

When I finally gave in to my tiresome body, my emotions were filled of Avery. I could still feel his arm wrapped around my body holding me and guarding me, like I belonged to him. And there was me, not wanting him to let me go. Those thoughts played in and out of my mind until I gave way to a peaceful slumber.

Six hours had passed. The streetlights still cast a shadow upon the black pavements, I discovered as I looked out my mother's window. I felt like I was only one in the world awake, along with the harmonizing crickets, loading my luggage and my mother's sour cream cake she'd baked for Zoric, into my car.

I looked in on Tamra, who was nestled in her old bed sound asleep. I creped downstairs to the guest room where my mother was asleep, but her eyelids parted at the sound of me opening her room door.

"You're leaving, sweetheart," her voice crackled when she spoke?

"Yes mom, I'm leaving. I'll be back on Wednesday to take you to the doctor."

"Did you get that sour cream cake off the stove?"

"Yes mom, I got the cake. Go back to sleep. I will call you when I arrive. I love you"

"I love you too. Drive safely."

8

The morning sun glazed across the Richmond skies as I entered into the city. All of a sudden, this nervous feeling, like a tinge of butterflies entered my stomach, just as I entered into Jackson Ward district... a few blocks away from home.

Once upon a time, 'The Ward' was a prominent spot of southern living for African Americans. It was known, after the Reconstruction era, as the 'Harlem of the South' destined to attract ambitious African Americans to its financial district, with hopes of making a dollar out of fifteen cents. Money moved from one hand of a black man to the other. And it was here, that Maggie L. Walker, the first woman ever, provided a financial institution for every nickel and dime they earned.

Today, the community is now divided by poverty and inner city violence on one side and preservation of its historical integrity on the other. Small businesses, quaint coffee shops and boutiques, as well as myself are apart of the growing wave of trendsetters, who are revitalizing the once forsaken cultural center of Richmond.

As I turned right onto E. Clay Street, I entered into an address where Richmond's most dignified and classy Black folks, once lived. Neighboring elegant Victorian style row homes with cast iron porches that lined the street complements my modern three-story brownstone that sits adjacent from them. Its gracious view projecting through my living room windows, showcase the wealth of its residents during a period when poverty was not spared by any man.

I had finally arrived home. I steered my car into the garage next to Zoric's Land Rover and entered through the lower leveled media room. Before I could drop my shoulder bag next to the mini bar, Chee Chee pranced down the stairs and greeted me with his jovial barking.

"Hey boy." I excitedly spoke, while picking her up in my arms. "You miss your mommy," I continued in a pampering voice?

Up the stairs we went, to the main level. I stood in the middle of my living room close to the exposed brick wall and made one complete circle. There were no stacked dirty dishes along the granite counters. The hardwood floors was free from dust and every decorative pillow was neatly fluffed and its place. It was clean and perfect, just as I left it. Chee Chee distracted me from my assessment with his continuous barking and energetic parading. Finally, I gave into his pessimism and followed him up to the third floor and into my bedroom.

My birdcage style canopy was neatly made with throw pillows centered on the jacquard aqua blue comforter. Zoric's prep for a day of golf was ironed and neatly draped across the bed. The sound of the water cascading from the shower, led me towards the bathroom. Slowly I widened the door and zoomed in on Zoric's flawless naked body reflecting through the tempered glass door. Remembering the echo sounding from my heels tapping against the floors, prompted me to loosen the strap from around my ankles, before making my entrance. With my feet exposed to the tiled floor, I tiptoed slowly inside to steal a touch of his wet soapy body while his thoughts were far from my sudden arrival.

"This better be my fiancée or you are in trouble," he stated unarrested by my touch.

"Well, this better be my man, or we are both are in trouble." I replied.

He slowly pivoted his body around. "Welcome home baby," he passionately said, as his kisses swallowed up my unremitting smile. His hands reached for my body and pulled me into the shower with him, fully clothed.

"Zoric, I screamed! "You got me all wet."

"That's exactly how I want you to be."

His lips remained gentle and soft as they covered my neckline, down to my breast. He helped me peel the wet clothes off of my body, creating a trail from the bathroom floor to the bedroom. Eventually we ended up in the bed, with our bodies bare and intertwined between the satin sheets, with nothing between us but sweat. I was, at least I thought I was, happy to see him and to feel him extended between my legs. However this place were he now deepen, felt like it was no longer his. His hands felt abrasive as they fondled against my smooth skin. The kisses that I once longed for have become rigid and unpleasureable. Every ooh and aah that echoed from my cords were empty noise. It was just over a week ago that I thought that Zoric was the only man that could love me… that was until Avery touched me.

Zoric had gone hours before I'd awaken from my nap. It was Saturday and Chee Chee needed to meet his usual scheduled Saturday grooming appointment, while I decided to head into work. I parked in front of my modest four-cornered building nestled between a shoe store and sub shop on Broad St, just walking distance from home.

The clear glass entrance door bear the business logo with my name as owner and broker scripted below. It reminds me every working day that I am 'The Boss', even if I'm not wearing high heels or a short skirt, like on this particular day.

"Hi Rocqui," my assistant Keisha cheerily welcomed me as I made my entrance through the front door. Her long, yet thick body was hidden behind the raised-front cherry oak desk, where she greeted clients as they entered into the building. Her bronze glow is a reflection of her Virginia heritage and possible ancestry blood line of a slave owner. She was wearing tailored khaki slacks with a matching blazer. Her hair looked freshly relaxed, as if she had spent most her Friday night at a crowded hair salon getting her usual Doobie style for her shoulder length hair.

I stumbled onto an introduction of Keisha just a few years ago when I was out showing a client a house in a new construction development. She was an assistant at the development, working inside one of the model homes. Her job was simple - taking names and asking potential clients to fill out survey cards as they toured the homes. However, she conveyed an instinctual desire to be more, in her mannerism.

When I sat across from her with my client and asked a couple of questions about the development, I was quite impressed with how professional and how informative she was of the real estate business.

Curiosity led me down a path of questions into her personal life. Like 'why wasn't she already an agent and what did she do before she took on this job. She admitted regretfully to have been misguided by love and was on her way to marrying someone who promised the world at her feet. However, when he found himself in a position to at least offer her half of the world in which she dreamed of, he passed her by and handed it off to another woman. - A white woman, at that.

She clearheadedly asserted that she was figuring out how to make ends meet for herself without depending on the financial financial resources from a man to live by. This was just a temporary stop to get her life going, she adamantly pointed out, even though the lucrative possibilities of the real estate business were certainly enticing her career interest.

I was profoundly impressed by her humbleness, yet her crafty sales-pitch to charm my client into buying one of the developer's spec homes. I vowed to her that day, that if she comes to work for me, as my assistant, that I would train her to become a realtor and assist her with paying for her real estate classes. She willingly accepted. I certainly didn't have a need for an assistant. My business was new. I was a one woman act. I could have easily continued to answer my calls, greet my own clients and set up appointments. However, there was an instant vibe between us that I perceived. A connection that I once shared with my sister before distance and her marriage divided our worlds apart... unless she needed some money or a new pair of shoes.

"Hey Keisha." The corner of my mouth quirked into a half smile, at the comforting sight of her.

"I didn't expect to see you today. I thought you weren't going to be in until Monday."

My fingers rested along her desk, as my mind dwindled on the real reason why I was here at work, after an extended three hour drive, on a Saturday. The truth of the matter was that the solitude of home was allowing too many opportunities for Avery to crowd my mind. And...I was starting to miss him. But that was too much information to share with Keisha, at this point. I modestly answered, "Yeah, I know. But I needed a head start on all the work I have to catch up on my desk, before Monday."

"How's everything back home in North Carolina?"

"Just as I left it three years ago," I vaguely implied trying not to go into too many details about my mother and my other situation, like Avery."

She took the hint not to ask any more questions beyond the answer I'd given her and stated, "Well, I've missed you."

"How have things been since I've been gone," I asked as I flipped through the mail she handed to me?

"It's been kinda steady. There had been a few potential clients, walk-ins… and I gave them your business card. But other than that, it's been quiet."

"Where's everyone today? Are you the only one in the office," I asked as I took a quick survey of the empty office desks that sat before me?

She gave me the 411 of my agents as she strolled next to me leading into my office. "Joddy is out showing a client a new home. She did not close the deal on that house in the Fan District. Something about the client didn't report all there loses to the bankers and they pulled the loan right from under her. Diane had two closing scheduled for the next month and a house in escrow. Bret is just Bret. Still walking around bitching worst than a female about everything."

She'd finally concluded with her summary on my employees, and departed back to her front desk. I sat comfortably behind my desk. Before picking up the receiver to check my messages, my wandering gaze noticed the five by nine picture frame of Zoric tightly gripping my waist and his head relaxingly holding over my shoulder. The smile that embraced my overly rapturous face at that moment seems like a lifetime ago. I shook my head in dismay, not willing to allow myself to become distracted by uncomfortable feelings and preceded with dialing my message code.

"You have fifteen messages," the automatic voice messenger responded. My first message was from Andrew Spencer, a white business lawyer and also my first and most loyal client.

"Hi Rocquelle. I love my house. Everything is great. But, I need a beach house. One of my colleagues just recently purchased a condo at Virginia Beach. And I can't let him out do me. Give me a call when you get in and let's see what's available." Hearing that message gave me a sense of relief, because I needed to keep my revenue flowing.

After deleting a couple phone solicitors and reminders of upcoming appointments, my attention was caught by Ray's voice.

"Hey Rocqui. Look, I need to meet up with you whenever you get a chance. I think I have another business opportunity you might be interested in and would like to share it with you. Give me a call as soon as possible, so that we could make it happen."

Ray Goodman is a man about business. He is always coming across the next best way to get rich. Fairly nice looking with a shiny bald-head, his solid build is coated in chocolate. He is always consciously dressed in a collard shirt and tie and tailored slacks. And his choice of cologne is well suiting for any and every occasion.

We met a few years back, at a convention for black entrepreneurs. The ballroom was filled with African Americans, young and old, in search of answers to owning apart of the American dream. He welcomed himself to a seat next to me and I overlooked his presence like many other strangers that joined me at a table. At this particular time, Ray own a small detailing shop, but was anxiously looking for ways to stretch his modest dollar. Without any formal introduction, he openly spilled his dreams of becoming rich and investing all his dollars in real estate, to any one who cared to listen. My attention was caught at that moment and I announced that I was in the last phase of starting my own real estate business.

Ray, without question, embodies the characteristics a 'good man'. He could have easily become someone that I would have been proud to bring home. And he didn't hold back any ideas he had conceived about the possibility of us becoming something more. That was before he was aware of the existence of Zoric in my life.

Zoric was my life, at that point and I quickly let him and anyone else be very aware of that fact. From that point on our relationship had evolved more into a brother-sister, in which he persists to romance me into some of his potential wealth opportunities.

Meeting with Ray on some 'golden opportunity' is not what I wanted out of my four days at home. But, hesitantly, I called him back.

"Hi Ray. This is Rocquelle."

Loudly, he greeted, "Rocqui, what's up girl? I thought you've moved away for good or something."

"No. I went home to my mom's to take care of some personal business."

"Everything's all good on the home front, I hope", he asked?

Not willing to open up about my life's interruptions, I stated, "Things could be better."

"Oh, ok. Tell me what do you think?"

"About what?"

"You obviously didn't listen to all of your messages... About the property on North 24th Street."

I was without a clue what Ray was referring to. But, I decided to proceed with entertaining the conversation anyhow. "Where is at on 24th Street?"

"It's located in Union Hill. Listen, how long are you gonna be in the office today?"

Before he got too excited I decided to raise the stop sign on his enthusiasm. "Ray. I'm not gonna spend the rest of my Saturday at work. Besides, I have not eaten yet."

"Good. Stay right were you are. I'm on my way. Better yet, meet me at Croakers and you can eat and listen, while I talk."

I was listening to a dial tone, before I even had the chance to contest the idea. I had mentally planned a brief meeting with my staff, this afternoon, by ordering in an afternoon lunch. Instead, Ray had swindled my plans into listening to him idealize over some big money making idea.

I informed Keisha that I would be out of the office the rest of the day and to inform my staff that on Monday I would hold a staff meeting. Twenty minutes later, I arrived at Croaker's, at the corner of E. Leigh and N. 2nd St. Ray was pulling up right behind me; punctual as expected.

We were seated in one of their mahogany wooden booths, sustained against the aged brick walls.

"Here's a picture of it." Ray handed me a photo of a decaying neglected 2-story single family home.

"What am I looking at Ray?" I asked not to be ignorant of the details of the picture, but to inquire about his intentions with this ramshackle property.

"Our next big investment," he excitedly answered!

"Our next investment?"

"Yeah. I want you to join in on this one with me. I need you Rocqui."

I already knew what he needed, but I dove in deeper with questions anyhow. "What do you need from me?"

"I need you to appraise the property, because I think it's overly price. And... I need your money."

Exactly what I thought he wanted when he answered. "How much Ray?"

"About... forty thousand."

I shouldn't have been shock just by the looks of the place. It certainly needed that and more. But, I wasn't expecting him to ask that much from me. "Ray, you have lost your mind. You are asking for money out of my business account."

"Rocqui, do you know from this property alone, you could gross at least a hundred thousand dollars. I'm thinking we could take this house and flip it into a multi-family unit."

I was overwhelmed in deep thought over this proposition. It was more thought and money then what I wanted to give.

"Rocqui", he continued with his oration of persuasion, "if anyone could make this happen, you can."

"It sounds like a great plan. Let me think it over, Ray. And before I leave for Fayetteville on Tuesday, I'll let you know."

My plate of curry shrimp had finally arrived. Ray ordered a crabcake sandwich.

Before he dug into his sandwich, he continued with his questioning. "You're talking about Fayetteville, NC?"

"Yeah," I answered, as I tried to swallow my shrimp from my fork. "Why you ask?"

"Man... There is a lot of money in real estate down there. I was just in Raleigh a few weeks ago with my Boy. Real estate is booming down there with old and new property."

I was listening with one ear trying to concentrate on enjoying my food.

"Rocqui, what you need to do is get your real estate license in NC and set up shop down there."

"I don't live there, Ray. I live here."

"Well, I'm just telling you. With me, we could rake up millions, easily."

I stopped in the middle of my chewing and pondered the idea for a short second. The only way millions could ever be raked up easily is by winning the lottery. Otherwise, you gonna be putting in a lot of work just to make even a few thousands to happen. Then, I continued to eat and finish off my lunch date, with Ray.

Later that night, Zoric and I found our old forsaken spot snuggled under one another's arms, along the buttery soft L-shaped sofa. We were intensely engaged in viewing this movie projecting from our wall mounted flat screen TV when I noticed Chee Chee racing back and forth towards the garage door. His repetitive nature signaled that one of us needed to get up and walk him outside to relieve himself.

Zoric looked at me with eyes that told me, he wasn't volunteering. "What baby... It's your turned," he answered noticing that my intentional stare at him, automatically volunteered him for the job.

Impatiently, I rose from my comfy spot and went upstairs to the kitchen to retrieve his leash.

As I reached across the counter to grab my keys, I noticed my cell phone light was beaming. I opened it to read a text message from Avery. 'Friend .' I immediately smiled from its intent. Not too many minutes pass that I don't think of him. The hours in my day felt too long without being able to see him or touch him, now that I have met him.

I discretely texted him back, 'Hi Friend '. While I was on my long walk with Chee Chee freely roaming about, we talked.

"After I realized that you were gone, I found myself driving along town like I was looking for you."

"If you would have driven a few miles further, you probably would have found me."

"I did have that thought."

"When I was taking my bags out the trunk of my car, I came across the tennis ball that you autographed for me."

"That's what happens when your game is not on the same level as your talk."

"Well, you only won because you cheated on that last point."

"To be real honest with you, I came into this with the idea that I was gonna let you win. But, then that incredible backhand came out of nowhere. I said game on."

"I told you that you don't know who you are messing with."

"You're right. And I can't wait to find out more."

"I had a great time with you. By the time I make it back to Fayetteville, you would probably find someone else to play tennis with."

"Even though, it's quite obvious that I can't have you doesn't mean that I'm not gonna stop trying."

Time kinda passed me by as I stood like a shadow along the dark street. Chee Chee had already taken care of his business and waited for me patiently at the door until I recovered from my stirred emotions.

When I opened the door, I was startled from Zoric's voice. "I'm glad you are okay. I was about to come outside and look for you."

"Oh, yeah. I'm fine."

I was staring at the red stop lights from the car in front of me. My cell phone vibrated against my keys in my purse. I would have ignored the buzzing sound, but its jagged shifting made my keys rattle every time it went off. I caught Zoric's curious eyes, staring down at my purse that sat in my lap. "Aren't you gonna answer it?"

Nervously, I didn't want to. However, now that my cell phone had his attention, I was given no other choice. We were on our way over to Calvin's house, one of Zoric's closest friends, for an intimate casual dinner.

Zoric was driving, while I sat on the passenger side and dwelled on thoughts of my family, in Fayetteville. A wave of emotions surfaced in and out of my mind.

Returning to a place that I once knew had opened old wombs. In addition, my short visit had now seemed to have created new ones that I now had to bare.

I steadily unsnapped my small purse and retrieved my glowing phone. I could sense before I'd even revealed my phone that it would be a text from Avery. And I was absolutely right. It read, This is just a 'friendly' reminder that I was thinking about you . I suddenly gasped over the rush of anxiety that overwhelmed me.

"Who was that," Zoric questioned noticing my startled gaze?

"Um"... I stammered.... "That was Tamra," I quickly thought. "She was just texting me to tell me that she cooked dinner tonight, that's all," still feeling a bit stiff.

"From the look on your face, did she burn the house down while doing so," he continued to question?

As my heart began to settle into a regular beat, I continued on with this act. "Nah. She said that it turned out good."

"Oh." Finally, his curiosity rested.

Even though, I convincingly told myself that I would just let the memories of Avery just fade away, I didn't. There have been a couple of nights, in which, I was absolutely lonely. I needed to hear a voice and some form of communication of understanding, none in which Zoric was available to give me at that time. Work had been his driving force for a lot of tiresome and late nights. Furthermore, even when he was physically available, I often felt like he was unemotionally there.

To make matters even more tempting, I missed Avery with each increasing moment. Secretly, during long walks with Chee Chee, at my office, or even sometimes when I was upstairs and Zoric was downstairs, we have talked. Sometimes, even eye-chatted. All the secrecy and mistrust had only created an even further displacement for me in my relationship with Zoric.

However, never had he or I boldly transmitted messages while I was in the company of Zoric. It immediately made me uneasy. Even after we arrived at Calvin and Ciantra's place, I kept thinking that I needed to get a better handle of this situation, than what I have allowed.

"What up Bro," Calvin readily greeted Zoric hand to hand, as he opened the front door of his and his fiancé Ciantra's home.

"I can't call it", Zoric jivefully exchanged.

"Hi Rocqui. Looking beautiful as ever," Calvin complimented me, before we all moved forward into the open living room and kitchen area. Calvin is slightly shorter than Zoric and me, but stood tall on his words and his confidence. Zoric and Calvin were the only two African American men offered a managerial position, when they were first hired, at Merrill Lynch. As a result their bond, extended beyond the doors of their office.

They golf together, hang out together and are planning to marry their prospective brides in the upcoming year. As far as my efforts made, I've patiently flipped through a few bridal magazines here and there and made visits to a few potential reception sites. Ciantra, on the other hand had already ordered her wedding gown, put down the deposit at the Embassy suite for the reception and began a rigorous exercise plan to become the skinniest bride, she can imagine.

"Well, hello stranger," rang from Ciantra's voice when she noticed my appearance in the living room. She waltzed from out of the kitchen, sporting a freshly cut evenly shape bob and a slimmer physique. Graciously, she embraced with me with a warm hug.

"Hi Ciantra," I replied smilingly, as I stood back and noticed she dropped a couple of dress sizes since the last time I saw her. "Girl, that diet plan is really working for you. You look beautiful," I acknowledged.

"Do I really," she marveled? She did a quick three hundred, sixty degree twirl, showcasing her new figure, with us all circled around her like spectators. "See honey, I told you my diet is working," she remarked to Calvin, before playfully elbowing him in his side.

"Baby, I didn't say it wasn't working. I just said that you looked fine without all of this dieting. I don't understand why women want to waste a lot of money and time just on that one day," he rebutted.

"Well, at least your woman is making strive. My baby is still stuck at just thumbing through magazine pages," Zoric added, while holding tight to my waist.

"What's up Rocqui? That ring that my man bought you isn't big enough for your exclusive taste?" Before I could respond, Calvin continued to ramble on, as he normally does.

"I told Zoric he should have gotten that five carat emerald cut ring. But, no... he was convinced that the princess cut was what you wanted," Calvin animatedly entertained.

Calvin is one of those people that had to have been ugly growing up. You can tell because, hidden underneath the expensive suits and well groomed face still lies a hint of ugliness within him. His skin tone was of a dusty brownish color and he had big bug eyes. His overbearing personality only makes his absence of good looks worse as he constantly reminds us of how loud and obnoxious he can be. I often wondered was he that kid that was always picked on and ran home crying with a snotty nose.

"I'm happy with the ring Zoric bought me," I chimed in.

"You should be. It's like you and Ciantra basically picked out the rings for us. Telling us which jewelry store to go to and be certain to ask for Braaaddd? I felt gay walking up in there and asking for Brad? Who the hell is Brad, I had to ask myself?"

Everyone was sitting in the living room laughing entertainingly except for me. Calvin's voice was starting to irritate me. Or was it all this talk about getting married.

"I never met a jeweler name Brad. That must have been some of Ciantra's doing," I returned with a serious face.

"Yeah, man. I didn't buy Rocqui's ring from a dude named Brad," Zoric interrupted. "As a matter of fact, I wasn't even with you when I bought her ring."

"I tell you what. Brad and even Ciantra, for that matter, will never get that much money from me ever again." His words were final. And I was relieved that he finally took a minute to shut up.

"Have you set a date yet Rocqui," Ciantra, inquired as she leaned closer towards me to talk privately? At that point, Zoric and Calvin held their own dialogue.

"I'm working on it. I've had some unexpectant issues to come up. But, as soon as my life begins to fall into place, I will." My words felt convincing enough for her to reply, "Ok." I wasn't at all interested in having a conversation about getting married. Therefore, I hope my nonchalant mannerism didn't come off offensive towards her.

Ciantra, I believe had dreamt of being married every since her childhood days of playing mommy and daddy. Yet, her relationship with Calvin had never been as quite of a fairy tale that she'd imagine. He had cheated on her. She had busted his windows out of his Mercedes. He had shoved her forcefully into a wall. She had him arrested only to bail him out five hours later. He had threatened to leave her. She had begged him to come back. Nevertheless, throughout it all, she had insisted still on marrying this man. That's their answer to love. Taking each other through hell only to pretend like nothing happen the following day.

As we began to move into the dining area to prepare for dinner, Calvin warned, "Now, I told Ciantra that she better not cook no low fat, salt free food for me. I don't care what kind of diet she's on. I need food with some taste," He adamantly added.

"Oh, be quiet", she gently silenced him. "I cooked lemon bake chicken...with all the fat and salt that Calvin likes," she entertainingly added.

Dinner was comfortably entertaining. There were a couple of times when Calvin put his foot in his mouth. Yet, no one seemed to really care, but me. We all talked and laughed like married folks. It was then, that I reminded myself that I am going to marry Zoric. I needed to start behaving so. I came to the final conclusion, at the table, while everyone talked over my deep thoughts, that I would finally end this so-called 'friendship' with Avery.

When, Zoric and I finally arrived home, I waited until Zoric went into our bathroom and quickly escaped downstairs to the kitchen with my cell phone in my hand. The only lights that shone through the darkness were the streetlights from outside our living room windows. I text him, as quickly as my trembling fingers would allow me, *'Avery, this is the end of us, even as friends. I've recommitted to my relationship with Zoric and prefer that the distance that is between us remains that way.'* Before I could rethink my brash decision, I quickly pressed send on my phone. I tiptoed back upstairs into my bed, just before Zoric emerged out of the bathroom.

"Guess what I'm gonna do on Tuesday," I stated to Zoric, happy for the first time to be in the right place with the right man.

"What," he asked, before crawling into his side of the bed?

I turned and gazed at him, filled with honesty in my heart and declared, "I'm gonna go with Ciantra tomorrow and shop for a bridal gown."

His eyes widened with excitement to my sudden plan. "Thank you, baby" he gladly uttered. "You don't know how happy that has made me to hear you say that." He felt my forehead with a short kiss.

9

The next morning, I felt like singing, 'stand by your man.' Zoric is my man and I was more determined than ever to let the world know it. The renewal spirit of love that I was feeling was evident in the way I slid my panties up my thighs this morning. It was in the way I gently stroked the brush along my hair and it was in the way I strutted my stuff down the busy downtown sidewalk streets as if all eyes were on me. I was anxious and on my way to meet Matt Hunter, one of Bank of America's loan managers for lunch to discuss a business plan. But, then immediately following, I was going to walk, just a few blocks away to Zoric's office for a surprise visit.

Matt Hunter had already arrived at the understated crowded Magnolia's Wine Bar and Bistro, when I walked in. He blended right into the scene of corporate America... white male, over thirty, wearing a trendy tailored shirt and tie, with a black leather tote waiting by his side.

His eyes studied behind the Wall Street journal, as I eagerly settled into the chair across from him, at the table. I ordered a white wine spritzer, from the waiter as I build up my nervous effort to present my idea to him

"You're early," I noted subtly.

"Or maybe, you're late," he replied, finally removing the newsprint from his face.

I checked my watch and saw that it was one o'clock, the exact time that I had agreed to meet him at the popular wine spot. Punctual as usual, I confirmed. Yet, it was no surprise to me for Matt to have responded with mockery.

When I first began my career in real estate, there was a lot that I needed to know, if I wanted to properly represent my clients. I had little knowledge and experience on the various types of loans that lenders offered. I sought the advice from a mortgage consultant. Through an open conversation I was having with a few associates, someone offered me Matt Hunter's business card. 'The best in the business', I was informed. I naturally assumed that the acclaim was something commonly spoken about one white man to another.

But, that didn't hinder me from calling him on the phone and setting up an appointment to meet with him. When his secretary led me inside his large window cornered office to await his arrival, I was immediately impressed by his award- winning plaques and outstanding certificates displayed against his walls. However, after waiting thirty minutes longer beyond my valuable time had allowed, I quickly created a premature dislike for him.

Who does he think he is I began to combat? I have clients to meet and money to make, just like he does. I'm gonna give this inconsiderate, self-interested son of a.... And then, in he waltzed through his office door, with softly tinted pale skin all tucked in a well tailored suit and spike blond hair. He settled at his desk casually as

I waited a moment for his introduction. Yet, when there wasn't one, I spoke first.

"Hi, I'm Rocquelle Johnson of Dream House Realty," I politely stood and extended my hand before him.

His strikingly green eyes looked straight through me, without exchanging a handshake or even an apology. "What can I do for you," he blatantly asked? I've already understood that I would have to prove myself to be twice as smart and twice as intelligent because I was a black woman. Yet, I was new to the game of business and hadn't yet found my force to be reckoned. I wasn't like Zoric, just yet. He could swag into any room and immediately command attention from anyone, respectfully. I'm not quite sure if it is because he is a man and men naturally create a sense of comradely amongst themselves. Or, maybe it is because his lighter complexion was often equivocal to their tanned skin that immediately placed him on equal playing fields. But, I've never known him to have to justify being smart and being black in this world of business, as I've had to. Whatever the stereotypical or racial factor that exists in America's ideology about blacks and women, Zoric had certainly found his place. And I deeply respected him for it... even envied him, slightly.

I continued humbly and honesty with my proposal. "I was hoping that I can be of some service to you, in exchange of some service you could offer me." His uninterested glare had fallen into a few files that laid on his desk. However, I pressed forward, shifting uncomfortably in my seat. "I need a mortgage consultant to help me expand the knowledge of my business. And I was hoping with some guidance from you, you can teach me about various loans so that, maybe, I can help inform my clients about different loan opportunities that may be available for them to purchase their new home. In exchange for your help, I will refer your service to them, as their mortgage loaner," I concluded, without any continual signs of interest from him, whatsoever.

A few quiet moments passed, as I watched him become self absorbed into the files on his desk, while I starred impatiently at him. Then finally, "Mr. Hunter, I don't know if you realize if or not, but I've been sitting here in your office for over forty minutes, apparently wasting my time," I assertively stated, with the strap of the briefcase thrown over my shoulder.

When he still refused to utter a response, I rose from my seat and began to walk towards the door. "Miss Johnson," he delicately spoke. "I get new loan applicants everyday. As a matter of fact, while you were making your speech I was just reviewing one. What makes you think that you can help me?"

I pivoted on the heel of my shoe towards him and sharply replied, "Because Mr. Hunter, you and I are in the business to make money. The more money we make, the better our business. Therefore, if you're not interested in the proposal I'm offering, I will offer my business elsewhere."

In slow motion it appeared, he rose his towering body from behind his high back leather chair and cautiously walked up to me with his hand hanging out front of me. "Forgive me for my lateness. I was caught up in a meeting, earlier."

I felt doubtful of shaking his hand at first, until I saw his eyes filled with sincerity. My hand met his and we returned to our seats, while we created a collaborative plan to make money.

"Let's talk about how we can make ourselves more money," he gladly stated.

That was two years ago that we formed a slight partnership. Today, I sat before him asking a little bit more from him.

"Matt, all I am saying is that a lot of people want to buy homes but struggle with affording a down payment for a home. Through this seminar that I'm trying to get underway I can educate potential homeowners and offer them a small percentage towards their down payment." I argued, while Matt piercingly studied my intentions.

"Who are you…John Rockefeller's great granddaughter? Where did get money like that to just give away," he condescendingly questioned?

"It's not my money. It's federal grant money that I was awarded to assist people with buying their first home."

"What do you want me to do, Rocquelle," he apathetically replied?

"The program won't be federally funded unless I have a Mortgage Lender advising the program."

"These people that you are referring to are often on the borderline of having bad credit anyhow. These programs often set this unrealistic dream that they can afford a home when in reality, they can't. I'm telling you Rocqui, you should just stick with your rich clients, as you have in the past and settle less on people with issues of credit and money."

"I totally disagree with you. I think everyone, regardless of their credit, desire to own a home. But, some just don't have the resources available for them to make it happen. I don't think its fair for the world to stop for the wealthy and not offer something back for those who are trying. I believe through this program that I am sponsoring I can at least assist those that truly desire a home through financial assistance geared towards a down payments or closing costs."

"Rocquelle, the reason why they can't afford a down payment is because realistically they can't afford a house." He plainly stated.

I had to relax my tense shoulders and breathe deeply. Softly and slowly I continued. "All I am asking is if you will help me organize this program to educate people on the home buying process. I believe that through this mortgage program, it will at least empower people to make smarter choices, so that they can have better credit and be better suited to buy a home."

"Look, it's not that I'm not interested in what you are saying. But I have a million other things to do, right now."

"Like what, going to Georgetown for the weekend where you could hobnob with your Ivy League colleagues over golf and tea?"

"No," he stated quite frankly. "What I was going to say is I can't directly be involved in this but I have a few associates, in training in which I could easily persuade to me involved. How does that sound?"

It sounded fabulous. Yet I simply uttered, "Wonderful" with a graceful smile.

"Is Zoric participating in the Bank of America golf challenge this year," he asked edging a competitive spirit?"

"Ah, I think so. He and Calvin have been spending many Saturdays practicing their forward swing."

"This year, I look forward to bringing the trophy back to my office. Every since Zoric has joined the competition, my other trophies have become lonely," he added with a cunning smile.

"I'm on my way to his office right now," I stated smiling back. "I will be sure to tell him."

After my lunch with Matt, I was happy and excited, that I could have skipped two blocks to Zoric's office. But, instead I floated through the busy sidewalks, alongside the cities skyline. I could feel myself giving off a subtle glow, even though the sun beamed brightly through the skies.

I didn't realize how hard I smiled until my reflection stood in front of me through the metal elevator doors inside Zoric's office building. There I was, a bit surprised at myself. I couldn't remember the last time the thought of Zoric succumbed me with such immediate joy and happiness.

The elevator steadily rose midway into the skies, until I arrived on the seventeenth floor. I took in an air of joy, as the doors pulled apart to welcome me into the path that led to Zoric's office.

I audaciously strutted passed the arena of cubicles where tensed faces and persuasive voices tried to lock in consumer's loose dollars to secure their futures, before reaching Abby's desk. However, Abby, Zoric's secretary was not there even though his door was partly ajar. Voices and laughter exchanged inside his office walls. I slowly moved toward the door, unsure to make an abrupt appearance or not. I felt compelled to wait for Abby's return to announce my arrival. He could have been in the middle of an important meeting, I considered. However, when I heard intimate chuckling belting from an obvious female voice, I poke my head through the opening of the door and announced my arrival.

"Hi honey," I spoke. My eyes quickly zoomed in on him leisurely leaning against the front of his desk, while a pair of short-skirted long legs, angled around a chair, in front of him.

The air in the room suddenly felt thick and awkward. "Hey babe," Zoric stammered to say when his eyes immediately met mine. "Come in," he anxiously hurried me holding his arms out to welcome me with a hug.

My eyes scanted over the top of the woman's golden tresses as I moved passed the chair she was sitting in and locked my arms around Zoric. "I hope I wasn't interrupting anything," I courteously stated, even though that was my full intention.

"Oh no, love. We were just finishing up here." I breathed in his nervous air.

I heard her say, "We can continue this another time," in a soft conspicuous manner.

I turned toward this unfamiliar voice, but she was gone. It was like she had suddenly disappeared, without me ever getting a glimpse of her face. "Who is that," I questioned, with raise eyebrows?

"Oh, that's no one," he instantly dismissed. "Wow. What a surprise you are today!" His arms finally released my body and led me behind his desk where I settled down on his lap. His tight face relaxingly fell into a welcomingly pleasure.

"Was I a pleasant surprise," I teased?

"Always," he whispered.

"Tell me why I am here again," I directed to Keisha, who had me surrounded by drunken spirits? Joddy, Diane, and Keisha had persuaded me into having a few drinks with them, later that afternoon to celebrate 'no particular reason'. With my desk nearly clear of paperwork and files and the silence of the phone ventilated the air, I had no particular reason to say no.

However, the allurement of drinking was more of their idea, than mine. I was just gonna to sit and laugh at their mindless behavior. That was my idea until Joddy ordered me a single drink. And then another glass of rum and coke quickly replaced the first one. Keisha summons the waitress for another round before I'd barely finished the last. But I didn't even touch that one. I just allowed the ice to water it down, while I watched Joddy, Diane and Keisha carry on like fools trying to out drink one another.

"You are here because, you work too hard," Joddy slurring words came together. "You never have any fun," she continued loudly, in this senseless high pitch tone.

"I do have fun," I whined. At least, I thought I did. I mean, I don't go out to late night bars and go clubbing of that sort. But, I was convinced that my life did contain some area of fun.

"Yeah, yeah," Joddy brushed me off. "You spend more hours at work than anyone that I know. I know it's your business, but you're still entitled to loosening up sometimes," she insisted. Keisha raised her glass next to Joddy's near empty glass and toast on behalf of my pathetic life according to Joddy.

A new song blared through the sound system that had Joddy up and grooving. "Ooh, that's my song," she nearly scream. On the other hand, every since we had arrived at the bar, she proclaimed every song to be just that.

Joddy is such an interesting person. She leaves little to anyone's imagination about who she is personally and professionally. She has huge breasts that overshadow her small body. Most of her blouses are cut low to accentuate her deeply stack chest line. And she uses the 'goods' as she refers to them, as her secret weapon to make a sale. When I questioned her on how does her chest impact a sale when the client is a woman, she arrogantly relayed, "she is probably looking at the goods too because she wants a pair just like them."

In the midst of all this laughter and drinking, I now felt sad and depressed rethinking my life and my accomplishments as dull and boring. "Hey, what's the matter," Joddy returned her free-spirited intoxicating vibe to me?

"I'm okay," I said aloud, even though I was telling myself.

"Rocqui, I understand that you work so hard every day all day. But, you need to take some time to unwind a little", she returned in much more sensitive tone. "That's what tonight is about, unwinding." And then she began to shake her body loosely to the rhythm of the music, as if to demonstrate to me what unwinding looks like and feels like.

Her playful, free-spirited view shook off my despair. I laughed soothingly.

"There are some decent looking men in here tonight," she implied darting her attention towards the bar where a few men causally straddled on the bar stools.

"They are okay," Diane answered filled with skepticism in her voice.

Diane who had been maintaining a silent voice through all the yelling and laughing going on at our table had finally invited herself into a conversation. "I don't think the man whom I'm suppose to marry is sitting up in here, though."

"Who is interested in getting marry," Joddy retorted, appallingly?

"I am," I quickly reminded them. Then I held my engagement ring up before their astonished faces.

"Well, if I had a man like Zoric, I would be too," Joddy quite frankly, answered.

"I hope I don't offend you in anyway," Diane led off her dialogue to me. "But, would a man like Zoric be in a place like this? Because he is very good-looking and well to do. I want a man, not just like him, but someone of his caliber. You know what I mean?"

I didn't know how to even attempt to answer her question even though I tried. We were seated at an unknown corner bar under a sky-rise building. The outside reeked of urine and sewage. The open room looked dark and gawky under poorly dimmed lights. Burning cigarettes still filtered the air when you first walk through the door. Some tables still resonated spills and mess from previous customers. This place was not of Zoric's forte, but it did appeal to a wide number of people according to the crowd we staggered onto, when we arrived.

"Zoric is a very casual, but refined. He likes a cozier more catered exclusive setting. I guess if you are looking for someone like him, you probably wouldn't find him in here." I couldn't believe what I'd just heard myself say, after I said it. It sounded so superficial and ridiculous, even to me. I mean, who am I to pretend that Zoric is so inaccessible that he wouldn't be caught dead at a downtown bar. Yet, Diane seemed impressed by my answer as she listened intently with dreamy eyes.

The waitress returned to our table and placed a new apple martini before me. Feeling like I had quite enough consumption of alcohol, already, I declined to accept the drink. "I told you Keisha, I have had my last drink for tonight. So quick ordering me drinks," I asserted.

"I didn't order you another drink," she quickly denied. The others girls simultaneously replied they didn't either.

"If you didn't and neither did Joddy and Diane, then who did," I investigated?

The waitress that brought me the drink remained at our table to clear away the empty glasses answered, "the gentleman at bar with the brownish shirt did."

We all quickly shifted our eyes towards the bar and immediately connected with the gentleman, who raised his glass at us, as a way of saying hello.

"Who is he," Joddy questioned gawking curiously at me?

"I don't know," I defended.

"I know who he is," Diane stated. "That's my Zoric or Keith or John…or whatever his name may be."

"Well, after you find out, tell him 'thank you' for the drink, but no thank you." I began to search for my keys in my purse and through my bag over my shoulder.

"Where are you going," Keisha asked?

"I'm going home to be with the REAL Zoric," I answered veering playfully into Diane's face.

When I finally arrived home, the house appeared dark from the street. I parked in front of our brownstone, along the curb and entered through the front door. I wanted Zoric to be home, but I assumed by the total darkness that enveloped me as I entered inside, that he wasn't. It was going to be another night I resided alone, I conceived.

I walked into the kitchen and poured a drink of water. As I was getting ready to march up to my room, the glare of the television shadowing through the darkness leading down the stairs caught my attention. The TV was obviously left on, but I was even more startled by what I found. It was Zoric, tiredly draped over the sofa, with his mouth gaping open. When I reached for the remote to turn the TV off, a snore erupted from his throat. I stood over him and silently shook my head, with a smile. Why bother to wake him when he looked so humble and sweet, I decided. I searched inside the storage closet for a blanket and some extra pillows. Then, I found a cozy spot right under his arm and laid next to him. The rest of the night, his snore growled in my ear. But, I didn't mind. He was home. That's all I really wanted.

10

*Hope to hear your voice one day soon...*just a few irrelevant words that appeared across my cell phone screen got me feeling confused and discombobulated.

It was a text from Avery. He obviously was not affected by the last and final text I had sent him about a week ago that was supposed to have brought closure to our relationship. Maybe he didn't get that message. Maybe I should be angry and upset and resend another firm text. But instead, I was flattered and smiled deeply as my heart fluttered.

I waited patiently outside of Bridal Elegance in my car for the arrival of Ciantra. Originally, the plan was that she and I were going to try on 'however many dresses necessary' until I found the right one. Yet, now I suddenly felt overwhelmed with emotions that I thought I had buried a long time ago...emotions that instantly came alive throbbing vibrantly, inside of me, as soon as those words spelled out on my screen. I couldn't do it. I couldn't walk into a showroom full of bridal gowns to choose a perfect dress to marry one man when I obviously still had feelings for another. Not this day.

As I waited for Ciantra anxiously tapping my fingernail against my steering wheel, I contemplated what I was going to say to her. What lie was I going to give her this time on our third attempt to try on wedding gowns? She had taken time out of her schedule and created an all day agenda just for her and me. Next, she wanted to go by this printing company and help me choose the right invitations. Following that, she wanted me to tour her reception cite in hopes that I would be impressed enough to reserve my date there. And then, she wanted to spend the rest of the day at the spa getting mani-pedis, as we gloat about our wedding day. That was all too much even if I wasn't distracted by the immediate attention of Avery.

Telling her that I didn't want to marry Zoric would have certainly been a lie. Of course, I want to marry him, I convinced myself. I'll just postpone today. I'm sure she is use to it by now. When I return from Fayetteville, I quickly thought, my decision will be final. The next time, I will be one hundred percent be ready to buy my wedding dress.

Fayetteville was just a day away. Whenever I thought about going back home, I thought about Avery and the obvious affects he still had over me. I didn't know if I could withstand from not texting him or wanting to 'just call' him.

The last time I talked to him over the phone, he talked about going to go kill a pig.

"That sounds so disgusting and nasty," I protested.

"What you mean? Wouldn't you rather I kill it before I cook it?"

"I'd rather not hear the details of a pig being sacrificed to feed thousands of greedy mouths?"

"It's Barbeque season. Don't act like you've never been to Fayetteville's Annual Pig Roasting Contest and seen a sea of grills everywhere, while people come as far as South Carolina and Georgia to taste the best cooked pig in the south."

"I'm quite aware of the annual pig roasting contest, but I've never been there before. That's just not my scene."

"What if I told you that besides earning the title of the best Barbeque in the south but also five thousand dollars is given to the winner of the best tasting pig? Would that still deter you away?"

I thought for a quick minute about what I would do with the five thousands. A couple pair of shoes, a nice bag and dress to match. Now I could see some favorable incentives in it for me. "I might be a little more understanding," I said.

He laughed. "Well if my dad and my brothers and I win, I will figure out some impressive way to convince you that pig roasting is not all bad."

"You don't have to impress me with anything. I get that there are certain things between us that are different."

"I get that too. But, I'm in love with you. What's a brother to do, besides try hard as hell to get the one thing he wants the most out of life?"

My heart had fallen to my stomach. I was so touched that I didn't know what to say. "I'm sorry to cut this short, but I have to get to the farm early enough to pick out the perfect...you know," he quickly interjected.

"I know. Have fun, I guess. Poor pig. He just doesn't know that today is his last day."

We laughed.

I continued to wait for Ciantra, looking impatiently over at my digital clock on my dashboard, contemplating calling her to reschedule. Yet, it wasn't about a minute later as I held my cell phone in my hand that she arrived pulling up beside me.

"Hey Rocqui. Sorry I'm late. I got caught up in traffic," she relayed innocently.

"That's okay. I was just about to call you..." I quickly conjured up an excuse. "One of my realtors needs me to urgently sign off on the sale of a house. I need to return immediately to my office to meet her. I'm so sorry."

"That's okay. I figured while I'm here I should browse around for some bridesmaid gowns," she replied, never swaying from her congenial gesture.

"Okay. Maybe, we will reschedule for another day," I suggested, maintaining a friendly mannerism.

"Let's do that."

"Bye." I started my ignition and exited the parking lot. Looking through my rear view mirror, I observed Ciantra happily strolling through the front doors of the store, slightly envying those same feelings I held just moments ago.

Four hours of driving have returned me to the doorsteps of my mother's house. Instead of my mother appearing before the widening door, following my persistent knocks, the door slowly unveiled the presence of Monty standing in the entryway. He looked like he had bathe and was dress in cleaned clothes. But a bar of soap couldn't wash away the disappointment I now held against him. My feet slowly moved inside the house within arms reach of him. I looked at him like he as a total stranger... like a man I've never known before.

"Hey sis," he spoke mildly.

"Hi, Monty", I replied uncertain of the words that may follow.

"Well," he initiated, like he was waiting for me to say something else?

"Well what," I retorted?

"Aren't you gonna give me a hug, or something?" He waited until my tense shoulders had fallen flat before he paced forward with his arms held out for me.

I received his embraced tightly not wanting, for a brief moment, to let him go. My arms fell to my waist side and I studied his humbled face. "How are you doing?"

"I'm living. I'm breathing… I'm home," he added with a quirky smile.

"You know, you really scared me when I ran into you at the gas station that night."

"I don't know what to say. That scene at the gas station seems to be the story of my life, right now."

"It doesn't have to be, Monty. You have a family and people that are willing to do whatever they can for you," I pleaded.

"I hear you Rocqui. But you can't put a band aid on this one. This is my battle." His words echoed the voice of hopelessness.

"This is your life you are talking about."

Becoming disconcerted over my pessimism, he finally pleaded, "Could we not do this right now? I love you and I understand what you are saying. But, not right now, ok?"

"I'm glad you decided to come home." I unreservingly implied.

"I know." He disappeared up the stairs caring my luggage in tow.

I walked into the kitchen and observed my mother from a distance joyfully prancing around, circling the counters with a dish rag in the palm of her hand.

"Hi Mom", I interrupted.

"Hey baby", she sung. Her face mirrored the look of a woman, who had just been reunited with her long lost love.

I stepped down into the sunken den, where Tamra was fully extended on the sofa glaring attentively at a cartoon on television.

"What are you watching," I questioned frowningly?

"The Princess and the Frog," she answered never removing her fixed eyes from the screen.

"Don't tell me...the frog kisses the princesses and they live happily ever after, right," I guessed?

"Shush" she returned obviously agitated by my persistent interruption.

It's seems to me quite strange how all of these grown and able people leisurely filled this house, like the term *working* was never apart of their vocabulary. My sister lazily stretched herself along my mother's sofa watching cartoon, while my brother roam the night, like the next day is promised. On another day, this scene would have been enough for me to bring the house down. But, I was too tired and too anxious about my mother's appointment to let that bother me.

Somehow I found myself flopped on the sofa opposite of Tamra watching a world of animation as if I was watching a Lifetime movie. I couldn't peel my eyes away from the screen until it was time for my mother's doctor's appointment.

The drive to Cape Fear Valley Cancer Center, felt like a journey separating life from death. Music echoed from the sound system in my car, but I don't think anyone was intone to its lyrics. My mother's eyes set outside the window pane. Tamra's attention was lost into her own world of music. And my thoughts had revisited 5 years ago when we first visited this very same hospital and it was announced that my mother had cancer. That time, even though, I was scared, I was confident that she was gonna be okay. Why would I think anything less about the strongest woman I've ever known?

Nevertheless this time, I'm absolutely terrified that the vengeful return of the cancer would constitute the last days of my mother's life.

But I gotta be strong, I kept reminding myself. I needed Tamra to be just as strong, too. Her relaxed mannerism towards this doctor visit showed me that she wasn't prepared for the worse to come, as I've began to imagine.

Before we left the house, I pulled her into the main bathroom, to prepare her for anything that may come out of this visit.

"Listen. We don't know what may come out of this doctor's visit. But, there is a strong possibility that the news we hear today may not be good, at all." I straightforwardly admitted. "But, no matter what, we have to be strong for her and promise not to cry. Okay," I concluded?

She nervously nodded at every word I spoke and vowed not to shed a tear, nor show any sign of worry. But it was I that was weary. And apart of me, did not want to go on this appointment. If I could, I would have been the first to say 'I don't like the way hospitals smell' before Monty made it well known to all of us. Somehow, however, during my lifetime I was chosen as a leader. People have always expected me to lead, even at times when all I really want to do was follow.

The glass doors pulled apart as we made our entrance and I checked my mother in, at the front desk. We worriedly sat amongst other cancer surviving patients and their families. Each showing no obvious evident of which stage the tumor had invaded their bodies. Each seemingly, hoping for another chance at life and maybe, wishing God, had made a mistake.

Dr Aditri, an Indian woman with long silky black hair, made her presence and announced my mother's name. She led us down through a narrow corridor and into the examining room and remained there until she changed into the hospital gown. Then a nurse escorted Tamra and I into Dr. Aditri's private office, while my mother remained in the room, alone.

This office had become unwelcomingly familiar to me. Tamra and I sat along side each other on the very same black leather sofa flanked against the dark forest green wall, once again. There have been some added images of laughter and happiness framed along her mahogany antique desk of friends and family that I merely glanced at the last time I was here. All in all, being here once again made me realize that life has no guarantee. One moment you are smiling and full of joy and in the next, you are drowning in tears and sorrow.

"Mom's gonna be alright, right Rocqui," Tamra whispered? She searched my face desperately looking for an answer of hope.

I looked into her timid eyes and tried to hide any doubt that I may have felt. "Of course she will be. She is still young and beautiful. Plus, I don't think heaven is ready for her sassiness, just yet." I added to draw a bit of humor into these frightening minutes of my life.

I didn't believe completely the words that I spoke. I felt just as lost and uncertain, as she appeared. Sadness began to stir at the pit of my stomach and I urgently wanted to cry. I tightly held my eyes closed to hold back the flow of tears and called on God. My mother had always reminded us that 'God answers all prayers.'

God, it's me, Rocquelle. It's been a few Easters and occasional Sundays since I've called your name. And now, I seek you once again, when my world starts to crumble and fall. I need a big favor God. And I know that no favors are too big or too small for you to handle. But, I'm begging you God to share a few more birthdays, a couple more Christmas', and throw in some holidays, with my mother and I promise her that I would try to be a better faithful servant and go to church every Sunday. I promise God.

Before I began to repent for all my sins, the door knob turned and Dr Aditri and my mother entered inside. My chest felt tight and I had to remind myself to breathe.

Tamra's fingertips pressed firmly against my hand, as we waited for the truth to be unveiled.

Dr Aditri sat comfortably behind her desk and opened my mother's medical file containing X-rays of her distorted organs. She spoke in her Indian accent, eyeing my mother with great concern. "Your right breast is showing some evident of cancer cells."

"You mean the same breast that we've treated once before," my mother asked surprisingly?

"Yes. It seems that those cells are returning and have spread to your brain, as well. We could operate and remove your right breast and possibly remove the tumor from your brain. There are a lot risks involved. But, it is quite evident that the cancer is spreading rapidly."

"What other treatments do you offer for my mother in this stage because it's evident that what you all did last time was not effective enough because it came back," I upsettingly interjected.

"It's very unfortunate. But this happens sometimes. The cancer returns more aggressive than what it started out and spreads to other organs," She eyed me with gentleness on her face.... I do recommend continual radiation treatment and chemo therapy and immediate scheduling for a mastectomy. I would like 1 to perform a biopsy on the tumor to first to see if it operable." she added.

"And if it's not operable," I yelled?

"Then, there is really nothing more that we can do," she firmly stated.

The news that she delivered was too much to swallow in one setting. Nothing she said affirmed that my mother would have many more years added to her life. I looked at my mother to read her expression, but her face was sterile. There was no frown, nor smile, not even a slight hint of emotion that was captured on her face. Silence began to increase until finally she asked, "You mean you want me to continue to add toxins to my body?"

Dr Aditri calmly explained, "Chemo will reduce the size of the tumor and allow you a fighting chance for survival."

"What's the point," my mother starkly stated. The air in the room was thick. Yet she continued, in a very composed matter. "I know that removing my breast will stop the cancer from returning there, but now you are saying that I have a tumor in my brain. And you want me to continue to submit myself to that poison, just so that I *might* live. There are days I can't even carry my own laundry from the laundry room to the family room. And I've just given up on going up stairs every night to sleep in my own bed... I'm tired of my body being constantly weaken explored and injected. That's not living. That's dying."

She paused for a moment before continuing and then took a deep sigh. Her eyes met Tamra and I, like her words were deliberate yet freeing. "I want to enjoy the rest of the time I have here on this earth without my life being interrupted by meaningless trips to the doctor to fight something that is evidently gonna kill me, anyhow", she pleaded, as if she had long made this decision before this day.

I was in total disbelief. There were a series of emotions that drowned my thoughts. Was I hearing her correct, I asked myself? The woman that I come to love and respect was giving up on life, without a fight to the end. The vow that Tamra and I made before our arrival had shattered like glass, when the tears began to spill from my eyes. Trembling, I interjected, "Mom, but what about us? It's not just your life. It's my life and Tamra's and Monty's life too... We need you," I begged knee-deep in sorrow.

"The one thing I want you all to understand is that God has always been on my side. I'm not gonna let this cancer and now this tumor dictate how I live my life. I'm gonna live blessed and abundantly throughout the days of my life, as God would allow me too."

She carefully studied our lost and pain-stricken faces, hoping her words had consoled us. But they didn't. "You kids are grown now. You'll are just starting your own lives. I don't want your last memories of me to be of me being too weak to get up out bed because of the chemo or the constant rotation of me being in and out of the hospital." I felt her soft fingertips stroke the top of my hand as she continued to objectify her decision. "I've done well by you girls. I'm proud of you and Tamra." She looked over at Tamra whose eyes had reddened from her fallen tears. Her words were peaceful rather than of pity. She never cried, not even a single tear; but displayed a poised smile.

"All I ever wanted was to live to see my kids to become grown and make a life of there own. And I've done that. And I'm thankful that God had allowed me that. It's okay. It's gonna be okay. I promise you. Trust your mother on this. You may not understand right now, but someday you will."

By this time, my mother's arms had tightly extended to encircle Tamra and I into her bosom. "I think I've done well as a mother. You girls are certainly evidence of that.

"What about Monty," Tamra unexpectantly blurted out?

Well, at least two out of my three children aint bad," my mother jokingly conceded.

A bit of laughter escaped over our tears.

The drive home was silenced with deep thought. I wasn't ready to conceive the idea of this world existing without my mother. But, as I looked over at her and saw how beautiful she was, I understood that she had lived well... a life full of happiness, ambition and determination for herself, as well as for her family. Her eyes seemed to sparkle with light, as she caught my stare. No words were needed when she reached over to tightly hold my hand that I laid in her lap... like everything was going to just fine.

The house was evidently empty. Monty had unsurprisingly disappeared again. I was kinda relieved. I wasn't so sure if I would have backed off the strong words I felt I needed to say, with my emotions weighed on my shoulders.

Tamra and I intimately cuddled around my mom, smothering every bit of her, like we were trying to hold on to as much of her as possible before she was gone. On any normal day, she would have easily fussed and became irritated by this overwhelming display of affection towards her. But tonight, she embraced it. Maybe at this time, she needed us just as much as we needed her.

Tamra rose from the sofa to answer the phone while my mother continued to fill our lives about the stories of her life. She smiled through her poetic tales of her first kiss by Johnny Holt. She was 13 years old, she recalled and he discreetly passed her a note at school to meet her at Rock Stream Park, a couple blocks from school. My mother admitted she didn't know what made her trail skeptically along this narrow path to meet him under the monkey bars. She didn't even necessarily like him. However, the proposal was intriguing, I guessed. Johnny wasn't even there when she arrived and she began to rethink her impetuous decision. A moment later, Johnny arrived toting a knapsack over his shoulders strutting forward full of cockiness. When he stood to her directly he outwardly stated, "Well, you ready to do it?" My mother displayed such innocence in her mannerism when she recalled how she answered him, with a simple, 'I guess.'

Her lips nervously trembled as she eyed the puckering lips landing on hers. There were no fireworks in the sky, she'd admitted. No thank you. No I'll call you later. Not even a 'will you be my girlfriend' was offered in exchanged for a kiss, from our mother's lips. Tamra and

I dangled in disbelief. We couldn't believe that our mother was ever so easy.

Her stories continued with an exciting tale of her and her girlfriends trailing off to Chicago right after I was born on a church convention, leaving daddy behind and me and Monty with Aunt Jennifer to tend us. She was impressively amazed at life in a big city. But she was totally clueless over the existence of one-way crowded streets until she and her girlfriends got lost and attempted to enter the wrong way down one, during her visit. Even though her reminiscent of her getaway brought about laughter and joy, she sternly admitted that that trip was her only trip ever away from her husband and kids. If she had to go somewhere that did not include her family than she wasn't including herself.

Some stories caught me a bit by surprised. Like for instance, who would have ever guess the greatest cook on earth, actually almost burn the house down because she went upstairs to finish ironing daddy work clothes and forgot about the bacon fat frying on the stove. I was, she told, playing in my room with my dolls and came frantically crying into her room when the smoke alarms screeched throughout the entire house. She rushed to call 911 and removed the pan from the stove, while she and I escaped outside until the firemen had arrived. Monty was at school at this time and daddy was at work. She continued to relay that the fireman urged us to go to the hospital to make sure we have adequate oxygen in our bodies.

At the hospital the doctors made us sit and wait patiently with oxygen masks covering our faces until our oxygen level was appropriate for release from the hospital. The firemen placed huge fans into our homes to allow the smoke to quickly escape. But no subtle damage was caused. When daddy finally came home, his first words were, "It smells like bacon in here," as my mother easily recalled. She laughed so hard she nearly cried.

"Monty's on the phone." Tamra reentered from the kitchen to hand me the phone.

"What does he want", I asked before retrieving the phone from her hand?

"He wants to know if you would come pick him up from some crack house," she answered, in an apathetic manner.

"Crack house?" I pulled the phone to my ear. "What up Mont?"

"I need you to come pick me up, sis." His voice sounded more casual than desperate, as I had assumed.

"Pick you up from where," I repeated in a disapproving tone?

"I'm all the way over here in the valley. I need a ride home."

"In the valley," I repeated, like he stated a foreign country."

"Yes. Come and get me. Tamra knows where I am."

"Aight." I hesitantly decided. "I will be over there in a minute or two."

"Where's Monty at," my mother asked in a concerned manner?

"Somewhere were he shouldn't. But, I am going to go pick him up...And Tamra's going with me."

"No I'm not," she quickly snapped.

"I don't know where this neighborhood 'the Valley' is and he said you do.

"It's over off Raeford Rd. If it's the same neighborhood that I'm thinking, it's actually not a crack neighborhood."

I didn't want to get into her ideas of a crack neighborhood. I just brushed off her comment, as we headed out the door to find our lost brother. We entered through a typical middle class neighborhood, where the detailed features of houses exemplified home owners. Most of the homes had vinyl siding with a few brick veneers and two car garages. The streets were clean and lawns were carefully maintained.

My opinion immediately repeated Tamra's thought of it looking nothing like a crack neighborhood I'd imagine. The manicured lawn that I parked next to was not parallel to a boarded up ramshackle house. The street light that brighten up the dark skies did not bring to life street-corner hustling glowing on the fierce faces of our young African American males. And the bare streets did not etched the picture of these 'thugs' swaggering around with their pants sagging low packing 'rocks' in one leg, money in another, with a gun strapped to their backs.

I turned my ignition off and called Monty from my cell phone the number he had given me before I left.

"Why are we here picking Monty up? His ass should have walked home or managed the same way he got over here to get his ass back home." Tamra continued on sparing no sympathy for Monty whatsoever.

"Monty is our brother. And he needs to be home especially now, with mom being sick."

"Whatever. Monty needs to get his shit together. He is older than us, but yet here we are driving around town trying to save him...trying to rescue him. And for what," she irritably conveyed?

"Because he is troubled. And he needs us. We are his family."

"He is not my brother. I don't claim crack heads as kin. If you ask me, Monty needs to grow up and become a man. By us saving him we are enabling him. He will never become responsible and take ownership as a man. And speaking of *your* brother, here he comes now."

He quickly strode from the front steps of the two-story house he'd visited and entered inside the backseat of my car. His appearance still held up to being clean and his breath only reeked of brown liquor. As soon as the car door slammed behind him, Tamra couldn't wait to tear into him with her interrogations. "Is this the house of one your high-priced crackhead friends."

"Who, Jarvis? Jarvis doesn't sell crack. He works for Department of Transportation," he defended.

"I didn't know you had friends with real jobs," she wittingly insulted him.

"I have real friends just like you have real hair growing all over your back like a man."

World War Three had been ignited in my car with words being hurtfully tossed back and forth between them. I stopped the car and threaten to put both of them out if they didn't straighten up.

"Rocqui, Let's go back to that bar I took you to the last time we were together," Monty excitedly suggested.

"She can't. Apparently, she likes the guy that owns the place. But she doesn't want him to know that," Tamra interjected.

"I do not." I heard the whiniest in my voice. "He is just a friend."

"A friend, huh??"

"Is it that same dude that I saw you with at the gas station," Monty questioned?

Reluctantly, I slowly nodded.

"Dang sis! What happened to Zoric?"

"We are all wondering that," Tamra cunningly added.

"I thought you were getting married to Dude," my brother continued to inquire.

"Nothing happened to Zoric," I defended, veering my eyes towards Tamra. "And I am getting married to Zoric. So, mind your business?"

"Hey, do whatever you like. I am not one to judge. I just thought maybe we could shoot some pool for a bit. Maybe we could have a few drinks and have fun like ole times" he continued to try to entice the situation.

I really didn't feel comfortable with the idea, uncertain with whether or not I would run into Avery. But the idea of hanging out with my brother and sister interested me enough to say "Aight", without any further deliberation.

However, before I could carefully outline the specifics of what I would say to Avery, if I, by any chance ran into him, our plan was suddenly folded. Monty's hawk eyes spotted an 'ole partner' of his as we headed in the direction of the club. Instantly he urged me to pull over.

"I thought we were going to play pool," I questioned, as I merged over towards the side of the road?

"We are. Go ahead and I'll meet you there. I promised." He words ended and the door closed behind him.

"Well, there goes that idea?"

"We came all the way over him to pick him up for nothing. Where is he going now," Tamra puzzled, watching Monty hurry across the quiet street to where his friend remained posted.

"Aint no telling. It doesn't matter so much now." I eased my car off the curve and returned to the open road.

"Where are we going, now?" Her eyes maintained on the side of my face.

"Home," I disappointingly answered.

11

The sound of a lawn mower roaring outside my window started my morning. For a moment as I laid in bed, I fantasized that it was my father carrying out his Saturday morning routine. He was the only person I knew in their right mind that got up with the rising sun on a Saturday to work, while everyone else maintained a snore. However, as the swift blades edged closer towards the side of the house, I began to consider that someone else was impersonating my father's labor. I sprung from my bed to eye Monty intensely pushing the very same lawn mower that my father faithfully used, up and down the yard creating a perfect evenly layer of grass behind in his path.

It's been three days ago that I last saw him. Never was there a phone call or any indication that he was alive or even okay, until now that my eyes see him. I wondered what brought him home this particular time. I wondered what interested him in cutting the grass, seemingly that my mother had contracted a lawn service to maintain her yard. I wondered if my father was alive, spying on Monty as I was doing today, what would he think of his son. The son that he'd taught how to throw a football in the backyard and to toss a basketball through a metal hoop. The son that he had awaken early every Saturday morning to pass the tradition of sculpting a perfect lawn and then later, bonded over a few fishing rods soaking in the middle of a lake, somewhere. Once being his son's little league baseball coach and the most admired man from other fatherless sons, I wondered how he would take to find his own son's failures and sufferings bring on such hurt and pain to his family. I hunched my shoulders over these pessimistic thoughts and relaxingly settled on the notion that at least he had found his way home, again.

On my last day visit at home, I wanted to relax, a bit, maybe catch a movie with my mother and sister before I returned to Richmond early in the morning. Maybe, I'll invite Monty to tag along with us. I showered and dressed and crawled back into the bed, with my back upright while my fingertips clambered over my laptop keyboard until someone else rose to their feet.

Before long, I heard a poetic caroling voice that brought me to my feet. I tiptoed silently down the stairs only to stand closely in range to be an invisible audience.

'If any body ask you… Where I'm going. Where I'm going? I'm going up to yonder. I'm going up to yonder,' belted out from my mother's soul with such strength, that I thought God Himself was sitting at the table listening. My mother sings on countless occasions. 'However, the spirit moves me', she says, is what would come from her mouth.

Her beautiful voice had always brought about a soothing calming spirit over me, every time I heard her sing. But this time, it nearly brought me to my knees in tears as my body fell weak on the stairway. I could feel my body swaying in a sobbing rhythm of pain. My sadness suddenly moved to anger as I wanted to shake her and make her understand how much I needed her to fight a good fight over this.

"Good morning Rocqui," she joyfully sang as she walked right passed me overlooking my obvious hysterical state and headed out the front door.

I knew at that moment that she was not interested in a pity party from me. I quickly sucked up my tears and dried my watery eyes with the hem of my pajama shirt.

"Good morning" I replied over my sulking, when she returned inside with the newspaper in her hand.

She continued again, passing me like I was invisible. This time I decided to join her at the table where she was now sitting hidden behind an open newspaper. "How are you feeling today," I asked, trying to sustain as much casualness in my voice without sounding overly concern? Every moment I felt anxious to investigate her health status. Does your head hurt? Have you noticed any sudden changes in your breast recently? Is your heart beating regularly? Does anything feel different than it did yesterday? I could bombard her with questions every waking hour of her day. But then... she would, literally, kill me.

"I'm fine. You're the one that doesn't look so good. Are you sick," she asked as she studied my face carefully?

The irony in that question. "No Mom. I'm just fine. Happy to be here with you," I answered lightly.

"What are you up to this morning?" She relaxingly removed her heavy stare from my eyes.

"I was up trying to organize this program to help people who need financial assistance to buy a new home."

"Humph... I wished they had programs like that when Randy and I were buying our first house."

"Why Mom? You and daddy didn't need any assistance to buy a house. You guys bought the biggest house on the block."

"That's because me and your daddy both worked pretty good jobs and we had to save every dollar we had to make this happen. But there were other families out there that worked just as hard as we did and had to live in subsidized housing or even 'the project' all because they were either too intimidated by the process of buying a home or they just didn't have enough money saved up for a down payment. What you are doing is good...real good"

I smiled. "Thank you mother."

"I don't understand why people have to get up so early on a Saturday morning to cut grass." These were the groggy irritable words from Tamra as she staggered into the kitchen, heading straight towards the refrigerator. Her thick bottom was covered in boxer shorts, with a camisole covering her chest.

"It's Monty. He came home last night." I couldn't resist alerting her with the news, even though I knew she could care less.

"So...," she predictably snapped, as she strode right passed us and returned upstairs. My mother and I immediately exchanged humorous glares.

"Rocqui, where are the keys to your car," Monty eagerly asked after entering through the kitchen side door?

"Why," I frowned?

"Cause..." he continued, with the chest-line of his t-shirt already drenched in sweat. "I want to wash your car. You know, you shouldn't let a nice car like that get as dirty as it had gotten."

I contemplated for a minute. Well, maybe longer than a minute before I found my keys in my purse and handed them over to him. When he returned outside, I turned to my mother and puzzlingly asked, "Mom, do you ever wonder what Monty could have became if he wasn't so hooked on drugs?"

"Of course I do. I use to think about it often enough that it use to make my head hurt. Now, I just live with the fact that my son is lost in a world of darkness. And I don't know if he would ever find his way out."

"Monty could have been fabulous, you know. He is smart and physically equipped to handle anything. I could help him get on his feet, if he would let me. I could pay for him to go to rehab. And then when he finishes the program, maybe he could come and live with me in Virginia. I could get him a job.

"Honey, you are gonna worry yourself sick trying to make everyone's life better...." She paused and took another sip from her cup. "It sounds fantastic. I mean, it really does. But, do you really think Monty would willingly accept treatment again. Remember when we tried that before and it became money gone down the drain. It was only a few weeks later that he returned to the streets, doing the same things he did before."

"But what else can we do. There's gotta be something else... some other choice we could make to help him," I maintained my relentlessly effort to make Monty into a better man.

"There is something you can do. Just pray for him. That's what I've learn to do. You have to at some point just let him go and put him in God's hand."

I have prayed many long awakening nights that the brother that I had once admired and loved so deeply would come home again to stay. I have spent many long awaken nights pondering, how long would he stay this time, before he is gone again. And every time he leaves, apart of my feelings I have for him, goes away too.

"How much," I blatantly asked Monty, as I inspected the perfected shine on my now clean car.

"How much," he repeated, as he knelt beside my tires to finish spraying its glossy finish with Armourall?

"Yes. How much," I returned, noting the fact that a man without a job doesn't work this hard for anyone, for free? Brother or not, he certainly was no different.

He towered next to me wrestling with the towel between his hands. Cunningly he grinned, "Well...since you asked. How about thirty?"

"How about twenty-five," I offered, outwardly implying no less or more?

"You gotta deal," he quickly accepted.

Before I reached into my pocket to pull out his money, I asked, "Mom and Tamra and I are going to the movies tonight. I was wondering if you wanted to tag along with us."

"To the movies," he frowned, like those were words he hadn't heard before?

"Yes. And it's my treat," I added.

"Nah sis. I got a couple of things lined up for tonight. But thanks for the offer."

I place the two bills in his hands and turned to return to the house, until he shouted out, "You know...I really appreciate how you are always there, trying to look out for me. Thanks," he added.

"Yeah...well, I'll let you repay me some day when you get yourself on your feet." I smiled and entered inside.

I anxiously searched for my car in a sea of darkness that seem to have become lost in a the crowded parking lot adjacent to the movie theatre, while my mother and sister argued back and forth over the movie we just saw.

"Just because a movie have black actors in it, doesn't necessarily make it a good movie," my mother noted.

"But mom, aren't you tired of seeing movies with white people in them all the time. It is like they are the only ones making all of the money in Hollywood," Tamra voiced back.

"Going to the movies is already expensive enough. We all had a drink and each a bag of popcorn. And that was almost fifty dollars..."

"Mom", Tamra continued to defend, "if we don't support black actors than there won't be any black movies."

"Tamra, you can do what you want to do with your money. But, I think if black Hollywood want to create movies depicting 'black experiences', than they should be worthy of the time and the money loyal fans pay to come and see them. That's why bootleg is popular now"

"There's my car," I joyfully trumpeted, after circling an area over and over again until I spotted it. I unlocked the doors, just before my cell phone rang. It was Zoric. I waited outside my car to talk to him, while my mother and Tamra got inside.

"Hi Love. How are you doing?"

"Hi Baby. I'm doing fine. What are you up tonight with me?"

"Missing you. Waiting for you to come home to me."

"Aahhh. That sounds so sweet. I miss you too."

"I haven't heard too much from you. I was calling to make sure that you haven't forgotten about me."

"Umm, maybe for a minute. But, never forever," I jokingly implied.

"Good. What were you doing?"

"Tamra, my mom and I are just leaving the movies."

"Tell your mother I said 'hi'. And tell Tamra I've missed her. I'm quite sure she would return the same sentiments," he implied sarcastically.

"Yeah, I'm sure she would too," I laughingly went along with his joke.

"Well, I don't want to hold you from them. I just needed to hear your voice."

"You must really miss me," I convincingly detected from the sensitive nature of his voice.

"Of course I do. You're gonna be my wife. That should tell you right there that I can't live without you."

I was at awe...nearly succumbed by his words of endearment.

"Hold on one second Rocqui, I have a beep."

"Okay." My eyes glanced up at the dark skies as I waited for his return.

"Hey, Honey... It's Calvin. And you know with Calvin. It's always about business."

"Isn't it a little late for business?"

"Yeah. Well, I told him whatever we needed to do, it needed to be done tonight because tomorrow is about you and me."

I smiled. "Don't work too hard. I don't want you too tired for me when you see me in the morning."

"As soon as you walk through the door, I will be ready for you."

"I love you. I will see you tomorrow."

"I can't wait. Love you too.

When the call ended, I glanced up at the stars. There was something quite peculiar about them. Even though talking to Zoric made me slightly warm and fuzzy inside, my mind drifted on thoughts of Avery. I didn't understand why at first, but then I quickly remembered riding on the back of his motorcycle and staring up at the stars. I was easily mesmerized by its perfected glow. The sky was beautiful ...just as it was tonight.

"Are you gonna daydream all night while leaving us in the car or take us home," my mother anxiously blurted out, interrupting my moment of fantasy.

With her cue, I got inside the car and drove home.

When we arrived home, the lights from the living room beamed from the window. Monty was still, surprisingly, home with his long legs totally extended across the ottoman in the den, while the remote was held in his hands. We all leisurely gathered around in the den, eyes fixed on the TV screen and our mouths closed. My thoughts were far removed from the Grey's Anatomy episode viewing from the TV screen that when Monty dropped an unopened deck of cards in the center of the coffee table it nearly startled me.

"Anybody wants to play a game of Tunk," he propositioned?

"It depends on how much money you got to play with," Tamra quickly responded.

"I got a little change in my pocket," he modestly disclosed.

"I'm not rising up from my spot for some change," she sharply replied.

He shut her up when he reached into his pocket and pulled out what looked to be a thick roll of dead presidents held in place by a thick rubber band. My eyes widen with curiosity of how he'd obtained such substantial loot. However, I easily rested on the notion of not asking him. It wasn't any of my business to inquire. On the contrary, Tamra didn't share the same sentiment. "Where did you get that money," she investigated?

"Don't worry about my money. It's mine", he arrogantly upheld.

"Have you upgraded from being a crackhead to a crack dealer?" She couldn't resist the opportunity to insult him.

"Look! Are you gonna put up or shut up," he bated her?

"I got money too. And I can't wait to pocket all of yours, big brother," she agreed.

Monty caught my intriguing eyes and asked, "What about you? Do you think you are too good for an old fashion spanking?"

"If you've ever beaten me in anything, it's because I let you," I reminded him. Monty and I have always been quite competitive. I was book smart and he was athletic. He could always outrun me and even out swim me even though, I damned well tried. However, he could never outthink me. My trophies and honor recognitions were framed or displayed solemnly for my family to admire, around our home. Yet, Monty's Friday Night catch or 50 yard touchdown was publicized on the front page of the Saturday newspaper for the world to see.

He was like a small town celebrity. Everyone that loved the game of football loved my brother. From the front page news to college scouts, he had thousands of people holding their breath and waiting to hail him as the next great sensation. His best friend and teammate, McKenzie, which everyone called, 'Mac' were like peanut butter and jelly. They went everywhere together. People clearly noted their inseparable bond and nicknamed them 'Mac and Cheese'. Mac didn't have a father. My dad was always around to fill whatever void that he sometimes needed. From the playing field to our house and countless family vacations, Mac was there, just like he was a part of our family.

I used to overhear them fantasize about how their lives would be when they made it to the NFL. They promised if they didn't make the same team, that they were going to buy their houses, side by side in Miami where they would spend their off-season fishing, swimming and chasing women. I even bought into their dream by imagining me being at every game and going down to Miami to chill with them during the summer.

Their dream was quickly becoming a reality when Monty and Mac were offered full athletic scholarships to the University of North Carolina at Chapel Hill. They celebrated non-stop from the time they sign-off on their acceptance letter, until the time they both proudly walked across the stage to receive their High School Diploma.

I don't think no one was more proud of them, then the way they were of each other. They acted like we were walking on air, as if they could do anything, because they had already proven that could. No one could understand why everything had to end so fast. Why was Mac, just two days after graduation shot and killed just four feet away from Monty after a party?

Monty came home late that night, staggering through the door with Mac's blood on his shirt and his eyes feel with pain. We all walked around like Zombies for a while, until we finally settled on the truth that Mac wasn't coming back. He wasn't going to join us for Sunday dinner and he wasn't going to Chapel Hill that fall, with Monty.

Monty disconnected himself from everyone around him, including me. I watched him painfully exist, wishing that all he needed was a little love and attention to make it all go away. But, there was nothing that I could do. My dad encouragingly helped Monty through. He told him to go on to Carolina, because that's what Mac would have wanted it. However, somehow, I knew that was not what Monty wanted anymore.

But, in the fall, Monty did arrive at UNC-Chapel Hill. His high school stardom and notoriety had quickly diminished to a mere number. His limited time on the field made him nearly invisible amongst a swarm of NFL hopefuls. By the end of his first season, he probably played in a handful games. There were no front page cover, no loose girls running up to his side to offer him pleasure and no Mac.

By the second season, too much hadn't changed for him. He played in a few games, but his athletic ability was crumbled up by guys that were bigger them him and better. Besides all that, he couldn't shake the pain he still harbored from Mac's death. Soon, he began to seek refuge and comfort in smoking a little weed, during the summer. Soon, the evidence of his habit overlapped into football and he was kicked off the football team and lost his scholarship.

After my father died, weed was no longer sufficient enough for him to cope with death. And he was soon introduced to crack. His life, eventually, lost its meaning to him.

A few hands of easy winnings from Tamra resulted in her withdrawal from the game. She was out of insults and out of money. I, on the other hand, pulled twenties after twenties from Monty's tight folded bills. Finally, he relentlessly caved.

"I got your money. I got your money," I sung into his desperate eyes. I rose from my chair and realized that Monty's head was lowered in silence. I felt sorry for him, at that moment. I didn't really need to win. But, a small part of me believed that the money that I've now folded away into my pocket was money that could have been exchanged for drugs.

Trying to make light to his obvious unsettling lose, I walked around the table and stood over his head, while my fingers stroked through his tangled hair. A half smile flanked across my face as I attempted to pacify him. "Next time, I'll let you win."

He held his head up so that I could see the forced smile implanted across his face. "I'm okay. You rightfully earned every dollar."

"I know I did," I jokingly conceited. "How about I give you a twenty for your hard effort?"

"I'm good." He shunned. "I'll be alright."

"Okay." I patted his shoulder. I left him alone at the kitchen table, glancing back at the hopelessness that now surrounded him, not giving too much thought to his disappointment.

Hours later, I found myself asleep in my mother's room. The humming sound from my cell phone had startling awaken me. I got up disturbingly trying to find it in total darkness that enveloped me.

The blinking light signaled from across the dark room on my mother's dresser where I had placed it earlier. It was a text from Zoric. It read 'Our last night together was amazingly delicious, desiring me to want more.'

"What," I baffled. My brows pulled tightly together while my mind boggled with confusion. This doesn't sound right. What last night was he referring to?

As I stood motionless in total darkness, I tried to remember the last time, Zoric and I had sex. It's been a while, I concluded. Maybe he is anticipating my arrival tomorrow. But, why would he text me. Zoric doesn't text me.

I was confused. I needed to figure out what was going on behind this message. My first instinct was to call him. But as I was about to maneuver towards the bed, I heard laughter and voices outside my mother's window. I looked across the yard and onto our longtime neighbors, Mr. and Mrs. Carmichael. They appeared as if they'd just returned from a night of partying.

Mrs. Carmichael or Vivian, as my mother called her, was wearing a swanky shimmer short dress and Mr. Carmichael or Ronald as my dad refer to him was dressed semi-formal, with his shirttail pulled halfway out of his slacks. Mrs. Carmichael was teasingly hanging on to his loosen tie dangling from around his neck, whispering words of intension, that I could barely hear. I was surprisingly entertained by their flirtatious antics. After all of these years, they still seemly kept the fire burning between them.

I was enjoying their youthful act and display of affection, until my eyes veered towards my mother's driveway and noticed my Lexus was gone. My heart fell to the pit of my stomach. Instinctively, I thought Tamra had taken flight with my car without my permission. But swiftly, I raced to her room and observed her body tightly wrapped under her covers.

My chest began to heave in and out, as I nervously began to conceive the unthinkable....that my car was stolen. I followed the darkness of the deserted hall and down the stairs, till I reached the front door. I met the warm temperatures of the summer air, as I stepped outside. My feet hastily patted along the cemented walkway and into the vacant space to where my car should have been parked.

'OMG! OMG! It's gone. It's really not here. My body had stiffened with fear. Mindlessly, I dashed inside the house and desperately fled to Tamra's room.

Tamra," I frantically yelled in between each desperate gasp for air!

"What" she mumbled tossing the pillow over her head to block off the sound of my voice?

"I think my car has been stolen!"

She quickly jumped from under her covers and opened the blinds for an intense look. And then she turned to me and in an urgent stake and implored excitedly, "Your car is really stolen!"

"Exactly!" Reality hit me hard, like a ton of bricks and I felt a rush of anxiety.

"Oh my god! Oh my god!" Tamra was increasingly becoming more anxious than I was. "Where did you leave your keys?"

"I thought I brought them upstairs with me. But, I must have left them on the sofa." While I was still stuck in disbelief, Tamra's thoughts were moving a million miles ahead.

"Wait a minute." She grabbed my arm and led me down the stairs and into my mother's other room. "Mom, where's Monty?"

Blinded by the blaring light that Tamra switched on above her head she answered, "I don't know."

Tamra turned to me and straightforwardly declared, "Monty stole you car."

With those uttered words, my mother's attention became fully alert. "Monty was just here, a few hours ago," she attempted to defend.

"Yeah, now he is gone and so is Rocqui's car," Tamra summed up. Then she turned to me and asked, "Who are you calling?"

"I'm calling the police!" My mother rose from the bed instantly and raced behind me into the kitchen.

"Calling the police," she excitedly repeated! "Why?"

"Mom, Monty stole my car," I angrily stated, trying to remember that she is still my mother and not a stranger.

"Rocqui. But that's your brother. . Do you understand that he is still on probation? He probably just went to the store or something," she nervously uttered any excuse she could creatively come up with. "Just wait a few more minutes before you do something you'll regret."

We all knew that Monty did not just go to the store at one o'clock in the morning. "Mom, I don't care where he went. He has my car. Aint no telling what he is using it for!"

"Rocqui, I know. I don't want you to make a mistake that you might regret later."

"Mom, do you realize that he is probably out there, somewhere, driving around trying to buy some drugs. Or maybe trading my car with some drug dealer, just to get a hit. I worked hard for my things. And I'm not going to let anyone, even my brother just stripped me of the things I've earned because of the stupid choices he had made with his life!"

In a calmed and manipulative matter she justly added, "Rocqui, you know I'm sick. And they are gonna arrest your brother and put him away and..."

"That's really low, mom." I looked painfully at her and could no longer stand anymore of her sympathy she had towards him.

Once I had spoken with the police, I waited outside in the middle of the lawn, wearing some shorts and a t-shirt I had thrown on. Tamra came outside and met me at my side, only to say, "You are doing what's right, Rocqui. He is better off in jail then on the streets. Maybe, this time he'll come out and be a better man." Then she returned inside.

I looked at my phone and strolled down my contacts, until I highlighted Avery's name and pushed send, without any hesitation.

"Hello," he answered in an uncertain matter.

"Hi," I paused. I stumbled over a few words trying to find the right thing to say, before saying, "I need you, right now. I know I haven't talked to you in a while. But, there's a lot going on with me right now... And I just need you."

"Where are you," he anxiously asked?

"I'm here. I mean, I'm at my mom's."

"I'll be there in a few minutes."

The invasive blue light, from the patrol car, circled in front of my mother's house while I stood outside of her door reporting to the policemen that my brother had stolen my car. Avery arrived moments later and I know longer felt so alone and scared. He got out of the truck and walked up beside me and worriedly asked, "Are you okay?"

His presence gave me a sense of security that stabilized my pulsating heart rate. "I'm okay," I assured him.

Long after the police had left, we sat inside his truck talking about the incident. I looked at him intensely trying to compose the words that I wanted to say. I knew what my heart felt. I openly confessed, "I miss you."

"You do," he returned full of uncertainty in his voice?

"I know. I'm..." I stumbled over my words. I didn't know what to say besides, "I'm sorry." I uttered in a mere whisper, yet I felt it whole-heartedly. My eyes fell shamefully down into my lap.

"No need for apologies." When he spoke, his husky soft voice warmed me all over. "You asked me to come. Now I'm here."

I was beginning to realize that he seemed to always be there for me. "I was trying to make things in my life as simple as possible, before I ever met you. I figured if you were out of the picture, it would be. But, the harder I tried, the more I feel like I need you... And I've never really needed anyone before."

My words did not provoke any sudden expression from his face. "Where do we go from here?"

"I don't know. Things in my life are complicated. To make things worse, I have the police on a relentless search for my brother because of me, on top of everything else." I shook my head in disbelief, as I looked through the total darkness that had now filled my mother's house.... "I don't know. I just know that I need to be away from this house right now. And that I want to be with you."

"Okay," he softly voiced. Moments later, we drove off. My eyes distressingly held the view of my mother's darken house, until it was fully out of sight.

12

The last vision that I held was of the gas station on the corner, before my eyes closed. I wasn't even aware that we had arrived at his house, until he gently shook my hand and asked 'do you want me carry you in.'

I followed behind him through the front door. The first thing I noticed when we entered inside was a huge bronze trophy standing next to the fireplace inside his bare living room.

"I see you and your dad won the pig roasting contest," I smiled.

"Oh yeah. We did," he conceited. "And if it adds any comfort to you, we prayed over the pig before everything went down," he added.

I returned a smile at his sentiments while he led me directly up the stairs into his bedroom. But, as he waltz inside his room and sat on the edge of his bed to unlace his shoes, I halted at the doorway.

"Do you have a t-shirt, I could sleep in," I asked, looking into his room, contemplating a night of sexual seduction?

He looked at me curiously as to wonder what exactly I was doing. I wasn't quite sure myself, but I followed my instincts anyhow. He walked over towards his dresser and reached inside for a t-shirt, before handing it to me. I turned and walked into the hall bathroom and stripped my body of everything, except for my underwear and draped the t-shirt over it.

Before returning to his room, I glanced into one of his extra bedrooms. It was empty of everything, except for brown boxes aligned against the back wall filled with stuff. The other room right next to it, however, was neatly decorated baring only a full size bed, with a burgundy duvet and oversized shams centered in the middle of the blank room.

I returned to the entrance of his room and became instantly aroused by sight of him unveiling his broad tight shoulders and his defined washboard stomach, from under his polo shirt. I felt my heart beating. Oh gosh! He looked delicious. I'd almost forgotten what I was about to say until he gazed at me with a smile and asked, "What?"

I restrained myself from all temptation and bellowed out, "I think, I'm gonna sleep in the other room tonight."

He strode closely towards me, as to minimize my space between him and the door. I inhaled the scent of Creed from around his bare chest and desired to caress the enlarging bulge I noticed inside his unfastened jeans.

"You're gonna pass on a nice looking, lonely man, like myself, to sleep in the other room" he amusingly entertained?

I thought for a quick second and then answered, "Yeah. I think so," I stated, full of lustful hesitance. "It has been a long night and I don't want you to think I just want you for your body," I continued with humor.

"That's okay. I want you to want my body."

We shared laughter.

Then my eyes became lost behind a sudden screen of passion and sensuality. Suddenly I needed to touch him, like I needed water to drink. My hand found its way to his face and slowly traced his perfectly line lips with my fingertip. His mouth slightly parted to welcome the taste of my finger inside. But it was my lips that he wanted more. It wasn't long afterwards that our tongues intertwined. My body shivered at the touch of his hand sliding under my t-shirt and vigorously clenching my bare waist. I remained intensely still, lacking any desire to move. His lips then moved smoothly along my neck covering it with gentle wet kisses. I purred with pleasure, as I moisten from each passionate kiss. Abruptly, he interrupted this moment of lustful intensions and pulled his body away from me. I was left feeling weaken and in a bit disarray. The framed doorway held up my weightless body as I steadily tried to retain each breath that I breathe. We stood in companionable silence, absorb by the intensity of the moment that we'd just shared.

"Can I at least tuck you in," he finally spoke in an intimate low voice?

I couldn't think of any words to say. My thoughts had fallen into a submissive state...willing and wanting for any part of him to have full control over me. The word 'yes' just kinda fell from my mouth. I pulled myself together well enough to follow him into the other room, where a full size bed awaited me. He folded the comforter back for me and my body, still tingling from excitement, crawled into its awaiting place. He leaned over and tucked the comforter neatly around my body. We exchanged a few short kisses, before the moment ended. "Get some rest,

Baby," he whispered before leaving me in full solidarity yearning for more of him.

The bottom half of me wanted to spring up from this remote isolated room and joined him in his bed. But, the upper half, rested on the fact that my brother was out there, somewhere, lost in his own state of being succumbed by his craving of drugs. And my heart had weighed heavy on the fact that I actually defended myself, by standing against my mother, something I would have never imagined doing in my life. I dwelled through a restless night on whether my actions were finally necessary or just simply selfish.

The next morning, I'd awaken to a deserted house. I walked downstairs, nervously, thinking that Sasha was going to spring out around a corner and attack me. But, she was absent, as well. I sat at the breakfast bar, dwelling in deep thought over the comfort that surrounded me. Even though his house held little decorative space, it gave me an overwhelming feeling of warmth and security. I strangely felt like this house held some meaning for me.

I waltz around the kitchen and cleared my plate of the remaining bite of croissant and butter before placing it into the sink, as if it was my own kitchen. I strolled through the family room to perfectly align the pillows to the sofa, like that was part of norm. My hands rummaged through a few sports and Black Enterprise magazines that laid scattered across an Asian inspired hand-carved coffee table. I looked into the refrigerator for orange juice like I was certain that there would be some. The cream colored wooden blinds added privacy to the picturesque patio view, that I stood before. But they still lacked the softness that drapes added to any room. I studied a few photos of laughter and gatherings he had hung opposite of the wall where the flat screen television was mounted and immediately noticed the same beautiful align teeth and sparkling eyes gleaming from every unknown face in the photos. For a moment, I romanticized what it felt like to be apart of that happiness that they all shared.

I revisited the open sparse living and dining room areas and wondered what decorative touches I could bring to make the empty, yet well extended areas rich in texture and comfort. My eyes shifted upwards and embraced a beautiful abstract painting hanging above his fireplace. I could pull the colors of red and black, from its framing as my focal point to make this area perfect. In a complete three-hundred and sixty degree turn, I decided that this felt all too easy for me.

It wasn't so much of my decorative ideas that carried me away into wondrous thoughts of what this house would be like if it was my home. The feeling that I breathe in as I strolled over the carpeted floor in the living room and onto the hardwood floors leading throughout the kitchen and into family room was that I was home. The only things that were missing were my clothes and my car. I held no hesitance to answer the house phone when it rang.

"Hello," I casually answered.

"Ah… I think I have the wrong number," a female voice stammered.

The call abruptly ended. The dial tone that hung in my ear rang the truth-of-matter in my head. Even though the innocent cordial voice from the other end of the phone could have been the tone of his mother, his sister or even his cousin, it could have just as likely been the voice of a fling. Who am I kidding? I am just a fling, too. I couldn't explain this sudden audacity that reign over me. I had quickly gotten beside myself, I admitted. None of this would ever be mine, I quickly swallowed. My world exists many miles away. And it was with this subtle reminder that needed I returned to where I belonged.

No sooner as I was dripping wet from the shower I'd just taken, my cell phone rang. With a towel barely gripped around my chest, I hurried towards the bed to search for the persistent ring. "Hello"

"Good morning, Sleeping Beauty." It was Avery. A smile creased easily across my face at the sound of his voice.

"You had an early morning today, I see. I didn't know you were even gone," I implied. I settled at the foot of his bed.

"I had a meeting this morning and a couple of errands to run. I started to wake you, but figured you really needed to rest."

"Thank you. I was more tired than I had imagined, I guess. But now I have a few things I need to do before I head back to Richmond."

"Oh." He was obviously taken aback by my plan. "You're thinking about going to Richmond tonight," he questioned surprisingly?

"Well, if the police have located my car, I was thinking that I should", I said cautiously. "Unless you were planning on keeping me hostage," I playfully added.

"Even though that thought may have crossed my mind I'd rather not keep you under false pretenses." He laughed.

"While you are laughing, I'm sitting here naked at the foot of your bed, with water dripping off my body."

I can be there in *at least* thirty minutes and cover you up?"

That time, I was the one laughing silly, like a schoolgirl. "The idea sounds intriguing, but today may be just as frantic for me as yesterday. I've called my sister to deliver my luggage over here so that I could actually put on some clothes, rather than being draped in a towel all day. And I need to rent a car... I don't even know if my brother is okay at this moment. And my mother..." The mere mentioning of my mother caused my stomach to twist into a knot.

"Rocqui." His voice sounded like it came from the heavens above. It quickly layered a humbling essence over me. "Everything is gonna be okay. This would all pass in time. And you don't have to worry about renting a car. I have another car in the garage that you are more than welcome to drive. The keys are hanging next to the kitchen door entrance."

"Are you sure?"

"Of course, I'm sure. I hope your day goes well. But, I would be heartbroken if you left town without even a subtle goodbye."

"You've been more than wonderful to me. I would give you more than a simple goodbye."

"Okay. Take care of your business and I will see you later on then.

"Okay."

When I hung up the phone, I snug his robe around my body and paced down the stairs towards the garage door. I flipped the light switched on and stepped barefooted along the cool cemented garage floor. The halogen light from the ceiling glowed over his motorcycle, which got my attention immediately. My fingers smoothed over the black leather seat as I recaptured the spine-tingling sensation I felt riding on its back. However the presence of a glossy pearl-white Escalade, sitting on twenty-inched shiny chrome wheels, parked beside it, nearly floored me. I was suddenly breathless. Not by the actual presence of the car. But by the fact that I had no idea that he had the financial means to acquire such luxury. At that moment, I was guilty with premature superficial ideas, yet reprieved with joy that he was a man of exceeding finance.

Tamra finally arrived with my bags.

"Good grief, girl! You opened this door like you live here," Tamra implied holding one of my bags over her shoulder.

"Thank you sis, for my bags" I gladly replied, releasing my bag from off her shoulder. We strolled into the dining room and sat at the long cherry oak table flanked by high-back parson chairs. "Did you bring all of my bags?"

"Yes. Have you permanently moved in? Should I forward your mail and all of your calls to here as well?"

"You're funny."

"Seriously, you are living with one dude, but engaged to another. Isn't there something wrong with this picture?"

"Will you stop saying I'm living here. I don't live here. As a matter of fact...I'm going home today?"

"Why are you going home so soon?"

"Because I have many things I need to do. I can't just sit around here all day. I have money to make."

"And what about your mother? Are you just gonna leave town without even talking to her first?"

"I don't really know what to do. I still can't believe last night happened. Can you believe that I actually stood up to mom? I have never taken a position against her like that before?"

"I can't believe it, but she can."

"What do you mean? Did she say anything about me?"

"She sure did. She said tell that hussy, 'you can't buy another mother or brother, like you can buy a car," she spoke in her comical impression of mom.

Startled, I asked, "She said that?"

"No. But it sounded good, didn't it?"

She laughed hysterically.

"I don't need this from you. I don't think you or anyone else understands what I did was not just about my car being stolen. But, it was about our brother who had taken from all of us. Our time, money and patience waiting to see if he could get his life on the right path. I've given Monty a lot of things and a lot of money. But you know what? There would never be enough anyone can give him unless he helps himself. I can't help him anymore. AND YES, that was my freaking car he stole. That was the first car I ever bought with my own money earned from my own business unlike the Honda Accord that mom bought me."

"Well at least she bought you a car. She didn't buy me one."

"Then you should have gotten a job and bought one yourself."

"It's always about money with you, isn't it?"

"Look, I don't have time for this. I need to get back to Richmond today. I am suppose to be meeting this girl again to help me pick out my wedding dress and it doesn't seem like I'm gonna make it back on time."

"You haven't picked out your wedding dress yet? What are you waiting for? How long have you've been engaged?"

"For seven months. But, I've been busy," I felt compelled to say.

"Yeah...you've been busy," she repeated questionably.

I couldn't stand to eye her directly with her piercing glare, at that moment. She looked at me like she knew more than what I wanted to say. After allowing my fingers to tap nervously on the table, I raised my head to her hard glare and openly stated, "A large part of me feels anxious to marry him and to create this life that we've plan together. And then there is another part of me that is scared too death."

"What do you mean? I was a little scared of getting married too?"

My voice had soften to a near whisper. "I'm sure that what I feel is normal. But something happened that I can't tear away from my mind?"

"What? Did he hit you?"

"No. It's nothing like that. It's really not a big deal. However, one day, Zoric told me he was leaving to go play golf, which is typical. He plays golf every Saturday. But, when I cruising through Highland Springs I swear I thought I saw Zoric kissing another woman in front of this restaurant."

"You didn't go over there and say something to him? And confront him?"

"No, only because I was at a red light and there was a car in front of me. By the time the light turned green, they were gone."

"Did you call him?"

"Yes, but Zoric never answers his phone anyway when he is golfing. He didn't answer that time, either. Anyway, by the time he got home, he had on his golf clothes unlike the slacks and shirt that I thought I saw him in."

"When did all this happen?"

"Right after we got engaged."

"Did you ever ask him about the incident?"

I shook my head. "I just blew it off, as if I was being paranoid or something. I'm probably just having cold feet"

"Having cold feet and being paranoid are not the same thing. You can only be paranoid if you have reasons to be that way."

"I know. I just need to get past it."

"How are you gonna get past it? I mean, we all know that I don't like Zoric. To me, he is just not the right guy for you."

"Why do you say that?"

"Because, he is too vain. And despite your expensive taste, you are a lot more down home than what you pretend to be."

"I don't pretend to be anyone. I like nice things. And Zoric just so happen to be something nice."

"I don't think *something nice* is apart of the traditional wedding vows."

"Well maybe I will have to write them in, then."

Tamra looked overly displeased with my reply. However, she held back her words and just shook her head.

There was silence before she continued. "You should at least go by and see mom before you go back to Richmond?"

"I don't think I can do that just yet. She is not ready to stop acting like the world owes her son something."

"Well, while you are waiting for that to happen, you may want to hire an interior decorator. It's a beautiful house, but it needs some color and furniture," she commented, looking around the sparsely furnished white walls.

"The longer you sit here talking to me about nothing, the more of my time that you are wasting. I need to get on the phone and try to locate my car."

"Your car has been found."

"How do you know?"

"Because the police called and stated that they had found your car."

"Is Monty okay?"

"Sure he is. He has returned safely to his steel-block cell downtown."

"How do you know?"

"Because, Monty called this morning from jail."

"Is mom gonna bail him out?"

"Honestly, I don't know. I didn't ask her and she didn't offer to tell me."

"Well, the least I can do is go and see him. Do you want to go with me downtown?"

"Sure. I'm quite sure I will run into one of my ole boyfriends probably locked up too. I can visit them, as well. It would be like a reunion."

"I swear you have to have been adopted."

Tamra behaved like a child inside a candy store, as she ridiculously explored every compartment of the Escalade.

"What are you gonna do with Avery, when you are done with him," she inquired, along our drive to the jailhouse?

"What kind of question is that?"

"I mean if you don't want him after you are done, can I have him? I could use a man, who had a lot of extra spare change. And it is obvious by the size of his big empty house and this limited addition Escalade, that he had plenty of change."

"And what about Diesel, your love muffin?"

"Diesel will always be my love muffin... Thank you very much?"

"Tamra, don't get all worked-up over your husband. I understand that you love him. What, I don't understand is why you rushed off so fast to get married. You were only nineteen years old."

Her hands relaxingly fell into her lap. I could sense her glare on me as I tried to maintain my focus on the road ahead. "I rushed off and married Diesel because I loved him. And I never had moments of paranoia or cold feet, because I knew undoubtedly that he loved me too, especially after I lost our baby."

"What", I screamed! I nearly rear ended a car the in front of me. "You were pregnant," I uncontrollably yelled?

"Yes," she openly admitted.

"Why didn't you tell me," I asked slowly calming down? My eyes now witnessed her humble glare. I totally ignored the moving traffic in front of me until the car behind me blew its horn.

"Because, that is not why we got married. Before I even got pregnant, Diesel and I were in love. But, then when it happened, he automatically felt like he had to marry me so that he would be there completely for me and the baby. I didn't feel any rush, but I loved how he quickly stepped up to the plate to take responsibility. You know what I mean? At first I told him 'no'. But then, when we went through the miscarriage, he still wanted to marry me. Plus, he was going into the Army... I didn't want to lose him. I really wasn't sure what love was. But, I knew that I wanted him in my life forever."

"I can't believe after all these years you never told me."

"You are the one who didn't want to believe that I really love Diesel. You wanted me to be like you. You wanted me to wait around on love and become some successful business person like you."

"That is not what I wanted. I wanted you to be able to take care of yourself and have your own without depending upon the happiness of some man."

"I love Diesel. But, I don't depend on him fully for my happiness. Do your beautiful home and your expensive car fulfill you with happiness?"

"No it does not. But, I know that I'm happy with myself and who I've become. Love is great when you find it. But love isn't everything."

"Love is enough for me, right now."

"Oh really! Then how come you beckon me when you need some extra money to get by, because you and Diesel have overdraft on your account once again. Or you've found these fabulous pair of two hundred dollar shoes and you are calling me, begging me to buy for you."

"I enjoy those things too."

"Then you need to get a job to be able to afford those things and not count on me for those things."

"I have a job. Being a wife of a soldier is a full time job. When he is here, in the states with me, I get up with him at 4am every morning. I iron and clean his army fatigues. I make sure that whenever he wants it, I give it."

"But, you want to walk around in Manolo Blanik shoes, like Sex in the City, yet live in Boys in the Hood."

"Ha, ha. I really don't need all of those things, like you. Of course, certain luxuries are nice, sometimes. But, eventually, all of those things end up being, just THINGS. What's real is finding that someone that makes your life whole. And you look forward every morning, to waking up beside him. And that's Diesel and I."

"Well, the next time you want me to buy you the latest Coach bag, I'm gonna remind you that, it is only a *thing*. And it will not make you whole, okay?"

We laughed.

As I cruised into the visitor's parking lot of the county jailhouse, my thoughts retraced the last time I had visited the chamber walls of criminals. My father had been buried no more than two years before Monty's troubled mind led him to seek more than just the fifty dollars he occasionally stolen from my mother's purse.

He and some of his thuggish acquaintances quickly became menaces to society breaking and entering into houses. They pocketed over ten thousand dollars in loot in exchange for the extravagance and sentimental values innocent victims had acquired through their hard earnings. Even, I had become a victim of Monty's illegal activities, once before.

I was at Howard University when my mother, disturbingly called to warn me not to be alarmed by the absence of my monthly allowance. She cautiously continued that she needed a large share of it to be used as bond's money to get Monty out of jail. I was livid. How could she have unthinkingly taken money reserved for my education and used it towards bailing him out on a crime, he obviously committed.

I didn't know who to be angrier with....my mother or Monty. By the time Spring Break had arrived, I thought I would be over my hurt and anger. Seemingly, the money that was inconsiderately borrowed from my account was replaced. Monty was temporarily released back into society. All was well, but not forgotten.

Yet, I didn't understand why the first sight as I arrived home of Monty hanging out in the front lawn with some of his boys damn near sent me in near rage. I wanted to ram my engine over his ass with my car. But, instead I turned the ignition off, got out of the car and aimed my keys with all force, to his head. It barely missed his eye.

"What the hell is the matter with you," he yelled, as his fierce eyes met my anger?

"If mom ever calls me again to tell me she is taking my money for school to bail your dumbass out of jail, she is gonna have to post bond money for me too. Because I'm gonna kill your ass," I promised!

That summer, I returned home before his sentencing. His words were few. However, he apologetically handed me half of the money my mother had taken out of my account. I was at a lost of words. I knew that the money was never truly his, to offer to me. Yet, I understood that that money held more meaning than the words 'I'm sorry.'

I relayed the cash to my mother to hold, for any sudden emergencies, like bail money she could use in future for him. The anger and hurt surpassed between us. And our bond held on. It had never been easy for me to see him caged up like criminal. He was more than someone that had been strayed down the wrong path. He was and will always be my 'big brother'.

After the sheriff, searched my bag, my body and everything else in between, Tamra and I were free to enter inside the visitors room. I sat on the visitor's side of the Plexiglas window and waited for his arrival.

A swollen chest, fair-skinned sheriff escorted Monty, tightly gripping his arm, like he was weightless. He was wearing the usual orange county jumpsuit. I was a bit nervous, wondering if I would have anything to say to him.

I reached for the phone. His eyes reflected through the clear window. He extended his hand for the receiver and placed it up to his ear. "Hi Rocqui," he mildly spoke.

My eyes burned to look at him.

"I'm surprised that you came to see me."

"Why? Because you obviously don't give a shit about anyone, but yourself," I angrily tossed back. "Why did you do it? I would have given you anything. And you know this, but yet you still chose to take from me."

"Believe me when I say, I'm sorry. And I really didn't mean to hurt you."

"You never do Monty. But, that is all that you've been doing to me lately…is hurting me. You are hurting me, mom, and yourself. And you are the only one that seems to not to care."

"How can you say that? You know I care. And you know that I love you?"

"Deep down inside, maybe I do. That's all the more reason why when I look at you Monty, it makes me sick. It tears my soul to realize that the brother that I use to know, admire, and love would be nothing more than what a quick high would ever allow him to become. And no one, no matter how hard we try, can do anything about it."

"You're right. You can't. Every time I try, I lose. That's why I'm here, right?"

"What were you going to do with my car?"

"My intension was to just borrow it for a couple of hours and return it before you ever knew it was gone."

"Where were you going? Was this a drug deal or something?"

"Or something… I owe people, Rocqui. I owe people 'Big Time'! I was hoping to easily win money off of you and Tamra 'cause I knew that you wouldn't just give it to me… And when I lost the money that I had, everything began to crumble around me."

"Why didn't you just ask mom? She would have given it to you, you know."

"Whose money did you think I was playing with? But, I needed more. And she wouldn't have been able to help me until in the morning. And I needed it right then. I bated you and Tamra into playing cards with me."

"Damn Monty," I pleaded. "How could you?"

"I don't know. I just need what I need when I need it. That's how pathetic my life had become. I'm off the streets right now. I'll be alright."

"But I don't like to see you locked up?"

"I'm sure you didn't prefer me stealing your car either. I talked to mom, already. I asked her not bail me out. It's not even worth it. I might do something else stupid. I swear Rocqui, I didn't mean to. I just didn't know what else to do. Did you get your car back?"

"Yes, I got my car back. But it's damaged slightly. My insurance will cover that. I just wish there was something I could do to help you."

"Believe it or not, you probably helped me, just by calling the police. I know growing up, you've always looked up to me. But, now I look up to you. I'm amazed by the woman you have become... Dad would have been proud of you."

At the mere mentioning of dad, my emotions began to stir. "I will always look up to you, Monty. No matter who or what you'll become. You'll always be my big brother."

"What is 3ft doing back there," he asked looking over my shoulder at Tamra standing behind me? He invited Tamra to sit at the desk and I handed her the receiver.

"Hey 3ft," he grinned.

"What's up crackhead?"

"Can't argue with you there... I expect by the time I get out, you will have grown a little."

"I expect by the time you get out, I will be fifty!"

"I want you to help your sister out. She can't do everything by herself, even though she tries."

"I will."

"I love you, Tamra."

"I love you too, Monty."

"Let me talk back to Rocqui." Tamra got up from the chair and handed me the receiver. "Hey my time is about up. I want you to know that I am sorry and that I love you," he continued.

A forced smile emerged on my face. "I love you too."

13

The front panel on the passenger side of my car was recklessly damaged beyond recognition. The sleek black polish now embedded senseless scratches alongside the passenger door. I was so sickened by its disfigurement that I couldn't stand to see my car being chained to the tale-in of a tow truck and dragged off to the Lexus dealership. A week they said is all they needed to reinstate its beauty. Where was I gonna stay at a whole another week in Fayetteville? What was I going to do while I was here? It wouldn't be too much for me to rent a car and return back, in a week to pick up my car... But, then I didn't really want to. Not after I saw him again. That rush or sense of urgency that I felt earlier to get back to Richmond quickly vanished at the site of observing Avery from across the emptied room as he maintained his attentiveness on a white gentleman and papers spread out across the edge of the bar, where they both stood.

I don't know how long it took him to realize that I was watching him and admiring him, from across the open floor, with his shirt-tale drape over of his neatly fitted jeans and wearing a fitted baseball hat over his head. Yet, his warm smile that immersed his face hinted a sense of gladness that I was there. He waved me over and I joyfully flounced myself over near him until I was next at his side. Just a simple kiss. That's all it was on my forehead, as his arms tightly wrapped me into his body that made me surrender all that I felt and knew unto him. There was no other place and no other body that I could think of where I would have rather been, at that moment.

"Are you okay," he softly spoke, sensing the tenseness in my weary mine?

I became entrance by the sight of his glittering brown eyes. With an all knowing smile, I confirmed, "yes."

His hands fell to his side and his smile had faded. Seriousness now mounted his face. "I know that you are under a lot of stress right now. But, I would like to sincerely open my doors of my home to you."

I was content over his warm gratitude, but felt slightly uncomfortable about accepting his invitation. "I don't Avery…"

Before I could finish my sentence, he rushed right in with, "You don't have to sleep in my bed with me. You are free, with no obligations to continue to sleep in the other room, if you would like."

"With no obligations," I repeated.

"With no obligations," he confirmed.

I had already quickly decided but wanted to toy with the idea a little. "That would make us something like roommates."

"Okay, if you prefer the term roommates."

"In that case, I'm all yours."

As my eyes darted around the open space, in view of a few hard-hat workers sawing and cutting, I asked, "What is this place?"

"This place is my new project. I am in the process of opening a jazz club. This place has a lot of potential to bring a different scene to town. Hopefully it will work out."

I noted the extensive bar and the raised platform for a stage. "I think it has the right atmosphere to make it happen."

"I sure hope so. I'm supposed to check out this other potential spot tonight. But, not before I take care of some other important things."

"Take care of some other things. Like what?"

"Like sitting down and chatting with my new roommate over a glass of wine. And offering her this." He reached behind him and handed me a small gift bag.

My fingers rushed over the gift paper and found a small red crushed velvet box on the inside. "What is it," I asked nervously holding the box in my hand.

"Open it."

And I did. It was a platinum bangle bracelet. "Wow," was all I could gasp from my mouth. He took it out and slid it over my wrist and I stared at it deeply.

He'd broken the silence with, "It's just a simple 'Thank you' from the pig."

"Well, I thank the pig and the beautiful person behind this," I approvingly stated.

While we were dreamingly starring off into each other eyes, I quickly remembered the call this morning that I boldly answered. "Oh I meant to tell you. This morning, I answered your phone," I crooned apologetically. "And there was a female voice on the other end."

"Humph. It probably was no one but my sister Angela." He unaffectedly stated.

"You're not mad at me for answering your phone."

188 -C L Alexander

"No, not at all. I don't have anything to hide from you, Rocqui. As a matter of fact, my family is having this cookout on Saturday. And I want you to come with me."

I took a few steps back to view if he was seriously asking me to meet his family.

"What," he chuckled? "It's just a cookout. Anyhow, I think I should introduce my family to my new 'roommate', unless you don't feel comfortable with that."

"I am okay with it," I answered slowly. "But, I don't want you to feel like you have to do it because I'm with you."

"There is nothing I feel like I have to do, but be with you." I was locked into the intensity of his eyes. He waited on no earth shattering event to occur to say to me "I love you." Yet, I felt like my world did.

I wanted to say something. But, I just wasn't quite sure if *I love you too* were the right words for me to say.

"Avery," I mumbled, feeling breathless. "I don't know what to say."

"You don't have to say anything. As a matter of fact, I didn't plan on saying it myself. But I sure couldn't lie that I wasn't feeling it. I don't think I ever told anyone that I love them and meant it as much as it means to me right now."

My eyes narrowed as I puzzled over his last comment. "What do you mean by that?"

"What I mean is that I remember using 'I love you' growing up, like it was a catch phrase when I dated women. It was like the next thing to saying *I like you a lot*. But, never did I ever think that it would actually feel the way I feel at this very moment when I look at you."

My head was overloaded with thoughts and emotions. I could no longer, hold his eyes that pierced through me. Instantly, I shunned away. "Hey Rocqui, I'm not trying to scare you or back you in a corner with all of this. I just thought you should know how I truly feel. And if this isn't something that you honestly want to deal with, you could walk away and I promise that it would be okay," he convincingly stated.

I returned a peculiar glare at him and studied his secured disposition for a brief moment. "I'm not scared of you," I declared. "I'm probably more scared of myself," I unguardedly admitted. "Just that I've never met anyone like you before."

"I've never met anyone like you before either," he replied.

"It's not that I am not in love with you. I just need to take things slowly. That's all.

He held up his hands in as a gesture of surrender. "Okay," he defenselessly voiced. "But, you will."

I undeniably felt something at that moment. It was that unmistakable feeling that made you glow from the inside out. He obviously saw it too, I sensed, as I watched his swaggering walk move closely on me. Without any hesitation, he coated my unremitting smile, with his lushes' lips. In returned, my watering mouth received his wet tongue. Time was of no importance to us as our souls connected through our exchanged of a long passionate kiss.

Last night seemed to go on forever with his thickness filling my weakness, his mouth sucking my tenderness and his hands gripping my firmness. Sweat beading off of his temples dripped on me endlessly, as he stirred, tasted and further deepen inside of me. The next morning gave birth to a new me. A renewed 'me' that felt empowered to do anything... even cook.

As I searched relentlessly for pots and pans, the startling sound of the phone ringing reminded me that I was in foreign territory. What was I doing, I questioned myself as I blankly stared inside his pantry like I knew what I was looking for.

I dug through the cabinets, and looked through the refrigerator to find all the ingredients of love. Yeah...

love is what I was feeling. Barefooted, with my body adorned in his terry robe, I whipped together a few eggs, laid several links of sausages side by side and slid the pan into the oven. Then, it was time to for my grits to be stirred and butter added to make it just right.

I sampled every thing, before I found a wicker tray neatly stacked in his panty and carefully carried his food upstairs to his room. I was very proud of my great achievement.

"Good morning," I happily sung as, I placed the tray carefully in his lap, where he was positioned in the center of his bed.

"Wow. I'm not the only one full of surprises," he welcomingly replied. A simple kiss almost took us back to a night of knee-bending, penetration. But, I remembered that he did have a plate of hot grits on his lap.

"Now, I'm no chef, like you. As a matter of fact, I can't remember the last time, I cooked. But, I did the best I could do," I justified before he opened his mouth to a big disappointment.

"Because, it's from you, I know it will be the best thing I've ever tasted," he gladly assured me.

I was at a stare as he took his first bite. I waited anxiously for his critique. He swallowed it. That was a good sign. Then he implied, "it tastes good.

"Are you sure its okay," I asked, not fully convinced?

"Yes, baby. I mean, I may have would have added a few more seasonings, but I still love it."

He saw the disappointment that had fallen from my face. I was hoping he would be in love with my cooking, as I had obviously fallen in love with him. His eyes soften and his voice lowered to add, "I am enjoying your breakfast. I promise. You did a really good job. But, I don't want you in my life to cook for me. I can do that. I want you in my life because you complete me… And I love you."

At that particular moment, the words had fallen from my mouth before I could stop myself from acknowledging it, too. "I love you too," I faintly whispered. It could have been the way his eyes intensely gazed at my vulnerable face. Or it could have been the warmth of his hand that gently stroked my arm that rested next to his relaxed body. On the other hand, it could have been every thing I've thought and felt about him had finally added up at this very moment. Regardless of what defined this profound moment, I knew at that very instance that I whole heartedly did. Yet, it intimidated me slightly to feel this way.

His eyes held mine, with a relaxing smile unfolding across his face, like he was deliberating my sudden admission. Yet, his immediate expression switch. His lips pulled tight and his forehead creased.

"What," I questioned, a bit thrown off by this sudden change.

"Nothing... I just didn't know that a few pots and pans, on the stove, would bring out your true feelings." His face relaxingly fell into a grin.

"That's not funny," I smirked, even though we were both laughing.

"Seriously, you've made me the happiest person on this earth."

"Why?"

"Because, I honestly see that you love me too."

"Because I cooked a few sausage and eggs?"

"No, because you went to great lengths trying to make me happy. And I am happy...whether you had cooked for me or not."

The tray I'd originally carefully placed on his lap was now on the floor. My hips comfortably straddled his lap now. He had evidently lost his appetite for food, but not for me.

Later that day, Avery had to go into Georgia's to demonstrate a new dish he wanted to add to the menu. He invited me to stroll along and I happily obliged.

The restaurant was empty of customers. Yet, the tables were adorned with crisp white linen and the mahogany wood floors were polished to reflect a glossed finished. Each booth and leather back chairs were dust free and perfectly aligned under the cherry oak tables.

Even though the dining area was quaint and docile, the kitchen was thundering with the rattling of pots and pans and the anxious shouting from everyone strapped in white chef's jackets. I excluded myself behind the boundaries of quietness within his office door, while he orchestrated the preparations for the dinner rush. After a long patiently wait, Avery walked inside, wiping his hands dry in a white towel, covered in his white chef jacket.

"Are you bored yet", he asked, easily detecting the signs written across my face?

"I've been more entertained before," I responded modesty.

"Are you hungry? I can fix you up something quick."

"No, I'm okay. I was thinking of leaving for a little while and coming back." I regretted that my laptop was left at my mom's house. There are a million and one things I could have been doing at that moment, rather than pretending to be watching TV from his flat screen.

"I don't want you to leave just yet."

Off guarded, I asked "Why?"

"Because there is something I think you should do first."

Peculiarly I asked, "What do you mean?"

"I mean, I spoke with your sister and she and I decided that whatever this distance that has become between you and your mother is not worth it."

"You talked to my sister?" My brows tightly frown to display the dumbfoundness that was now embedded across my face.

He nodded.

"When did you do this?

"When she called this morning for you and you were downstairs cooking... She was quite entertained by the mere mentioning of you cooking, by the way. Then, she started asking me a million questions about you and me. Your sister is one straightforward person. She doesn't hold anything back, I tell you. "

"How did you and her start discussing my mother and I", I asked sharply?

"When she said your mother really misses you. And she said that these days that are passing with your mother and you apart, you can never get them back once she is gone. I decided that I didn't want that to be something you will regret for the rest of your life, knowing you love her so much."

I couldn't believe any of what he was saying. Mixed feelings were surfacing from this announcement. I felt misunderstood about my abrupt intentions towards my mother, so I was compelled to say, "I wasn't going to disconnect from my mother forever. I love my mother. I was just giving her some time."

"How much time does she have to give?"

"I don't know."

"Exactly," he affirmed. I was taken aback by his interest in my relationship with my mother.

I'm a smart girl. I knew what I was doing... at least, I thought I did. "When is she supposed to arrive?"

"She and your sister are here now.

Just like his efforts had been made, he exited the office and returned back into the kitchen. I was left alone, feeling uncomfortable of decisions being made on my behalf. I make my own decisions. He has yet to discover that about me, I arrogantly conceived.

However, it was a little too late for contemplations. The stage was already set. All I had to do at this point was await the opening of the curtains.

My walk felt mechanical as I pushed through the swing doors and entered into the dining area. I scanned the area until my eyes met Tamra and my mom sitting casually at a table, as if they were waiting for their orders to be taken. Mellow jazz now soften the area, harmonizing the atmosphere. Guests had begun to arrive, being ushered in by waitresses in white blouses and black pants carrying oversized menus in their hands. I walked over with caution of every step I made and presented myself before their table.

Tamra naturally spoke first. "Looks like Georgia's has a new waitress," she wisely conveyed.

Observing her relaxed face me informed me that she was fully aware of this reunification, even though I wasn't. "Hi Rocqui," my mother casually spoke.

I uncertainly responded, "Hi Mom... You look good."

"Are you gonna just stand there and talk to me like I'm a total stranger, or do you prefer to join me and your sister?"

"No ma'am." I moved in and sat next to Tamra.

"By the way, Avery is fine as hell," Tamra lustfully praised.

"I know. He is cute, isn't he?"

"And obviously in love with you."

An uninhibited smile spread across my face, as my eyes locked on the concerned face of my mother's. "I can't believe you ran off that night, like I had disowned you or something, Rocqui," she noted.

"That's not why I left." I slowly spoke, being mindful of the fact that I was talking to my mother. "I left because I didn't think I could lie there peacefully the rest of that night after all that had happened.

"All that happen is that your brother had stolen your car and you felt that it was time that he paid for all the hurt and disappointments that you've endured through his struggle with drugs, right?"

"Yes. But you certainly felt like his action only merited a slap on the wrist and a promise that he wouldn't do that any more."

"Maybe so, Rocqui. Or maybe, you just don't understand no matter how wrong he was to have stolen your car, he is still my child. To see Monty out there hurting and lost, hurts me just like it hurts me to see any of you going through pain and there is absolutely nothing I can do about it. Even though I don't necessarily agree with your actions, I understand it. And at this point, I have no other choice but to deal with it."

My heart had weakened. "I'm sorry mother."

"No need for pity now. He is safe and you seem to have found a pair of warm comforting hands to sooth you over."

"It's not like that," I bashfully replied.

"That big grin you are carrying around with you is fake?"

"No... I mean." I began to stumble over my words. I relaxingly took a deep breath and added, "He is great. He is also so thoughtful and sweet and..."

"That's a lot more you've said about him this time, then you did the first time I asked you about him," she blurted in? "Looks like to me that he is revealing himself to be more than just a friend."

"Can we not talk about him, anymore? I got this under control." I knew she would not understand. It did not make any sense to me to further this conversation about him.

"I don't think you really know what you are doing," she acknowledged. "If you did then you would be in Richmond planning a wedding with Zoric and not here pretending to be babysitting me."

"I'm not gonna throw away four years of what Zoric and I have together over some minor interruption." I added like I was reminding myself.

"Now, he has moved from a *friend* to a *minor interruption*", she continued.

"Mom, who ever he is to me will be my decision. And I'm not ready to make that decision, just yet. So, will you please let it be?"

"Yes, ma'am," she finally surrendered. She turned her attention towards the menu. "I guess since we are here, we should order something."

"I'm not really hungry."

"Well, we are," Tamra loudly announced, as she began skimming through her menu.

"When are you going back to Richmond," my mother asked?

"I'm not quite sure. It needs to be real soon though."

"How does Zoric feel that you are spending so much time here and not there with him?"

"Zoric is a big boy. He understands that I'm here for you."

"You can use me as your excuse all day as long as you are honest with yourself the real reason why you are here."

"You are my real reason. And speaking of Zoric, he is calling me at this instance." I recognized his obvious ring tone before looking down into my purse. I excused myself from the table and walked outside. A smile plastered across my face as I tried to create this cheerful voice to say, "Hey baby!"

"Hey there. I was beginning to think you had moved away from me. You still know where your home is, right?"

"Of course. I've been going through a lot of things since I've been here." I went on and explained about Monty stealing my car and lying about staying in a hotel and exaggerating about my issue with my mom. I could tell by the quietness and humbleness in his voice that this was no ordinary *I miss you* call.

Sunday was the golf tournament, he reminded me. He expressed sincerely how he wanted me to be home as his good luck charm for the tournament. All of the years that I've attended the Bofa Tennis Tournament with him, he has never lost. And he wasn't expecting this year to be the first. I simply agreed and told him that I would be home by Sunday, regardless if my car was ready or not.

Returning back to my mother's table, my mother sighted my discontentment in my face. "Did something happen?"

"No. Nothing happened. Zoric just wanted to make sure that I would be home by Sunday for this golf tournament."

"That means that your little rendezvous will be coming to an end soon?"

"I'm gonna leave early Sunday morning. Hopefully, I will have my car back by then."

"And what if you don't?"

"Then, I'm loading my things up in a rental and driving home. I've been away too long. It's time that I get back to my life."

"You don't seem too happy about that?'

"A week ago or maybe two weeks ago, I would have been. But not now. I just don't know what to think or how to feel anymore."

"I see my daughter who has always been one hundred percent sure of every thing she has ever done now, got herself in an interesting situation."

"Is it possible to love more than one man?"

"I'm sure it is. Of course, I've only loved one man. But which one are you gonna be with? You are gonna have to chose."

"That question is getting harder and harder for me to answer."

"My vote goes to Avery," Tamra jumped in to say.

"That's not a shocker," I added.

"You'll figure it out for yourself," my mother replied

"I'm glad someone understands that."

"Hey, I understand. I'm the one that's married. It's you that is confused," Tamra interjected.

My mother, sister and I continued our dinner and entertaining conversation, until they left to go home. Avery had longed finished up prepping for dinner. He patiently waited behind his desk watching a football game, when I reentered.

I sat across from his desk, a bit disturbed and uncertain of what to say. But, I knew I had to frankly point out that, "You know... I am a boss too. I have a business just like you."

"Okay." He listened on.

"And... I don't like people to make decisions which I am capable of making for myself."

"I can live with that."

"And..." My words softened. "I really appreciate what you did. That means a lot to me."

"Sure. Anytime." He smiled.

I smiled back. However, remembrance of Zoric's phone call faded my smile away into a tight lip stare.

"What's wrong," he asked with concern in his voice?

"I have to be in Richmond by Sunday." I slowly revealed.

His head fell comfortably back against his chair. "I guess that means that I will no longer have a roommate.

"I guess so."

"Are you coming back?"

"Yes, as soon as I can."

"Then, I will be here waiting for you when you do."

14

All week long, the auto repairman would promise me another day that my car would be finished, but it wasn't. I tried to pretend that it mattered to me when my car would be ready, but it didn't. I was loving every minute, day and night spent with Avery. My mother actually invited him out of his truck, when he was dropping me off one night and welcomed him inside. I knew to expect several rounds of interrogations from her as he settled across from her at the dining room table. Her mouth immediately spun off a list of questions, investigating his life before and after he had met me. However, I didn't foresee her smiling and giggling in a girlish manner and then offering him a slice of her infamous Sour Cream Cake. Quickly, my appearance next to him seemed to vanish as they sparked a conversation around food and started exchanging cooking secrets. I was as displace from their dialogue as I would have been if two doctors were standing in front of me diagnosing a cure for an illness.

She said to me one night, after I had returned to her house from a late date with Avery, "After loving this man all this time since you've been here, how are you gonna love Zoric when you go back to him?"

I didn't know that answer. I tried not to give it too much thought. I was spellbound by this moment in my life when I never felt so happy before. I could live with returning to Richmond and robotically falling back into the patterns of my everyday life. But, I don't think that I could be in Fayetteville without the comfort and security of Avery being near me. I craved him that bad.

Saturday came and I was as nervous as a puppy that was about to be given a bath. The entire drive to his parent's house, I could feel my chest tightening as I tried to force myself to breathe. His hand gently caressed mine to ease my anxiety. Yet, it only escalated when he turned into a secluded gated community with luxury custom-style homes lining the wide curving street. I knew from my distant view, that the approaching two-story grandeur home with stone finished nestled high on a gently rolling hill was his parent's home. The street lined with expensive foreign cars beside it also gave hint to my conclusion, as well. I felt like we were entering on the set of MTV Cribs. We pulled up the curving driveway in front of the side-angled three car garage and I took in a deep breath of air.

Always being more than a gentleman, he walked over to my door and opened it, even though I sat momentarily and deliberated what I was about to embark on.

"You ready," he asked, maintaining self-confidence and poise?

"Yeah," I whispered. I step out nervously feeling my knees wobbling and locked my fingers around his hand as he led me to the laughter and music in the back.

"It's Avery," I heard someone scream! There were so many faces that I saw, I didn't know who and what to look at first. Then a pair of small hands and long legs raced up in front of him and near trampled him with a tight playful hug. Once her face captured my timid stare, I saw how absolutely stunning she was. She was obviously teenager with a slight curve in her slender hips that fitted effortlessly into a two-pieced bathing suite. Avery mumbled her name, but I was too tense to comprehend it.

"Hi Rocqui," she spoke than scatted off for a quick dive into the pool.

One down, many more to go. Avery's name was shouted and sung and yelled from every voice that comfortably relaxed along the stone covered patio. He walked up to some, hugged and talked to others, but not before introducing me first, as I hung at his waist-side. Bearing the introductions of the aunts, uncles, nieces and cousins was nerving but effortless. However, I knew the matriarch of the family awaited somewhere behind the tall patio doors leading into the impressive family room. My fingers tighten around Avery's grip when we entered through the doorway.

"Wait," I spoke, halting in the center of the two-story family room floor. I put my trembling ring finger into my mouth and moisten the skin around my engagement ring until it slid off. Then, I dropped the ring inside my bag.

"You didn't have to do that," Avery firmly stated.

Oh yes I did, I was certain. And then we moved forward through the palatial living space with high arch beams and into the impressively spacious custom built kitchen that complemented top of line stainless steel appliances. She stood with her back facing our entrance while leaning over the farmhouse style sink cleaning fresh vegetables.

"Mom," his voice echoed, without any forewarning to me that I was about to enter into the lion's den.

She turned nonchalantly and was smitten with eyes of surprise that we were stood just a few feet away from her. "Avery," she crooned. She displayed the ageless beauty and elegance of Nancy Wilson, with her gray streaks pulled back into a neat bun and an apron tied over a casual dress. Her feet paced quickly towards us. Immediately, her extended arms sealed tightly around her son's body. "Don't you look handsome as always," she marveled like it's been long since she had seen him.

"This is...." He began his introduction of me.

"This is Rocqui," she sweetly finished. Her arms filled me with the same embrace she had just given him. Something about her arms holding me tight let me know that everything was going to be okay. And I was. "I'm Georgetta. I've heard everything about you. I'm finally happy to meet you."

I was bit taken aback by her familiarity with my name. "Come join me for a glass of wine," she directed. Avery and I pulled up a seat at the large center island while she gathered two wine glasses out of the cabinets and poured an already opened-bottle of wine into them.

"I'll have a beer, mom," Avery requested.

"You know where the beer is, don't you," she reminded him?

It was only seconds after she placed the glass before me that an older coffee-tanned man with smooth gray hair and a diamond stud in his left ear entered into the kitchen. His maturity only made him more handsome. His poise and casualness was identical to Avery's wearing a loosely fitted short-sleeved button shirt, shorts, and flip-flops with an empty metal pan in his hand. But, I knew immediately that he was Avery's dad.

"I want to know why when my son finally brings a woman home, I'm the last one to meet her," he demanded slyly.

"What's up dad?" Avery greeted his dad with a beer in one hand and a brotherly handshake with the other.

"Dad, I would like for you to meet Rocqui?"

"And she is beautiful too." He also welcomed me with an affectionate hug. "Thank God because we don't let too many ugly people into our family," he laughingly entertained. "I'm Virgil, by the way."

I couldn't help myself from smiling. He was impressively charming and scented in a rich trendy cologne, just like his son. "Nice meeting you."

"Son, I thought you were gonna help us out with a little grilling today."

Avery nodded his head. "Not this time. I am strictly a guest today."

"You see that Georgetta. The boy thinks he is too grown for us, today. Any other time we would have to make him get out of our way in the kitchen."

"Umm, hmm," she agreed.

"Well, don't keep your beautiful girlfriend all hidden in the house. Bring her outside where the rest of the family is."

"Okay," Avery agreed.

"And Rocqui, my home is your home, okay," he finished, before returning outside to his grill?

Avery's brother Chris made his entrance into the kitchen. He made no immediate interest by my presence whatsoever, as he buried his face between the refrigerator doors searching for a snack. Avery, of course, made his formal introduction of me. A familiar smile that I've seen a million times before on Avery unfolded on Chris' face. Their conversation quickly sparked instant competitiveness involving a latest PSP game that Avery felt compelled to oblige his brother in a quick game.

"I'll be right back. I need to teach my baby brother that he is never too big to get a spanking from his brother." He leaned towards my lips for short kiss and then he followed his brother up the winding wrought iron staircase. That left me and his mother alone in the kitchen.

"Avery tells me that you live in Richmond?" She turned and face me with finely chopped vegetables placed in the pan, her husband had brought in for her.

"I do." I couldn't have answered that anymore simpler.

"Do you like living Richmond?"

"It's nice. It's definitely a different place than Fayetteville."

"Honey, I don't know too many places like Fayetteville." She settled in the barstool across from where I sat, with her wine glass within reach. "Fayetteville is very unique in its own southern way. It's not big. Yet, it's not small either. I'm from Raeford."

She easily read the look of surprise on my face. "Yes, small hick-town Raeford. Could you imagine how naïve I was to once think that moving from Raeford to here was like we were doing something grand? Fayetteville was quite big to me growing up in a small town like Raeford. I remember when, I was a young girl and my family use to get up early Saturday morning and plan an all day shopping trip in Fayetteville."

"Are you kidding me?" I almost laughed at how funny that sounded.

"Not one bit. When we spoke of Fayetteville growing up in Raeford, it was like we were talking about New York City or something. Now, mind you, my husband and I have traveled all over the world... just about. We've been to some magnificent places and seen many things. But, nothing had impressed me enough to want to move there. What made you want to live in Richmond?"

"I don't think I ever wanted to live in Richmond. It has been more so, circumstances that have led me there like school and work."

"I understand. I really had no intensions on leaving Raeford. But, my husband was driving every night back and forth from Raeford to Fayetteville to go to work. Finally, we realized that it was costing us more to live in Raeford rather than to just move and settle in Fayetteville. And we've been here every since."

"Do you like living in Fayetteville?"

"It's not so much that I like or even love Fayetteville that has kept me here. It's more of the fact that my husband is here. We raised our family here. We have ties to the communities, with the restaurant being here. Those things have become more meaningful in my life rather than a city address. Did Avery tell you about how we open the doors of the restaurant every Thanksgiving and Christmas and feed the homeless?"

"No. He had never mentioned it." I was moved.

"That was his idea even though he would say that it was me that started it. Before we had money to afford the restaurant, I use to cook and sale plates from my home. And sometimes we would have so much food left over Avery and I would load up the car and donate it to the homeless shelter."

I was in awe.

"Do you think you would ever move back to Fayetteville?"

"I don't know," I sadly stated. "My business is very important to me. I would hate to just let that go after I'd work so hard for it."

She smiled knowingly. "You sound like my daughter, Angela. She would rather be as far away from Fayetteville as she could be. The city life is certainly for some and not for everybody. If all of my children decided to move as far away as they possibly could, my husband and I will be right here. And if he decides one day that he is ready to move, then I will be ready to move with him. Unless it's some place like Alaska or somewhere cold like that. Then, he'll have to go by himself."

We chuckled. "When are you leaving to go back to Richmond?"

"In the morning."

"So soon." She sounded sincerely disappointed. "Well, I hope this is not the last time I will be seeing."

"No ma'am," I quickly answered.

"Listen, I have three grandkids that answer to me 'ma'am.' Call me Georgetta. Everyone at the restaurant surely does."

"I'm sorry." Then I corrected my answer. "No Georgetta. I hope this will not be my last visit with you, either."

"Well good." Then she grabbed her wine glass and the pan of fresh vegetables and headed out the back kitchen door onto the patio where her husband was orchestrating as the chef within their outdoor kitchen.

When Avery and I gathered outside surrounded by the likes of his extensive relatives, I fully understood what his daddy meant, when he said 'they don't allow too many ugly people in their family because everyone was literally beautiful. They could have been easily related to the Jackson's. From the darkest berry to the lightest hue, all of their faces shared the same marbled eyes and stunning smiles that made up their flawless faces.

Avery's oldest brother, Ezekiel or Zeek as everyone referred to him looked identical to Avery and his father behind his full facial beard. His wife Marie and their daughter and son all paraded around with pleasant smiles displayed on their honeyed faces. Shatoya, his sister, seemed to be a bit edgier and spunky, like my sister even though her expression carried the look of innocence. She had returned to live with her parents after having a daughter and enduring a failing relationship with her boyfriend. Chris was the youngest of all the siblings. I could only imagine the player he is as a high school senior. He was understatedly handsome…tall, broad shoulders with dreamy eyes and an entrusting perfect smile. He kept his cell phone clipped to the waist of his designer logo jeans as it hummed every other minute of the hour. "It must be another one of his groupies," his mother insinuated, as we watched him repeatedly excuse himself away from the laughter and talking, for privacy. "They act like the child is some kind of celebrity or something," she added with slight narrowing eyes.

They all greeted and talked to me like I was some great surprise. Like they were all so amazed to see their brother so happy. Always with humor, their joyous tones didn't have any reservations sharing how entertaining their lives have been with all that gathered in the family area. I joyfully laughed and settled comfortably amongst the Smith's, like the newness that I had felt hours ago had never existed.

After a barely-eaten plate of grilled chicken and other delicious fixings, I wandered alone up towards the gazebo that sat on a slight slope above the pool. I was just simply relaxing, taking in the air and the atmosphere of pure genuine love. I didn't necessarily need Avery's company, but when I saw him gravitating up towards me, I welcomed it.

"I guess you found my family to be a bit too crazy for you, huh," he began, leaning up against the post?

"No...not at all," I rushed my words. "I think your family is wonderful...the picture of an American dream, to be honest."

"That is because today is Saturday. We just missed all the crazy, deranged, obscene family members yesterday. They always come over on Fridays."

We laughed. He settled comfortably next to me and stretched his arm around my shoulder. My head leaned on his side as we spied on the continuous joyous gathering of his family.

"Your parent's house is beautiful. Did you grow up in this house?"

"Hell no. When I was growing up, we lived in a three-bedroom ranch style house. You know there are five us. My two sisters shared a room and had their own separate beds. My brothers and I shared a room. But there were only two beds, because the room was so small. Who ever didn't get to bed early enough to claim a bed had to sleep on the floor or on the sofa. Most of the time it was my oldest brother, Zeek. That's probably why he was the first to leave the house and get married before anyone else. I was the next to leave and join the army. When I came home, my dad had taken money he had earned as a worker from a distributing company and became part owner of that very company."

"Wow. That's impressive."

"The only ones that have basted in the lap of luxury are my youngest sister Shatoya and my brother Chris. They, unlike the rest of us had their choice of bedrooms and hired a decorator to come in and design their room for them."

"Where is your sister Angela? I thought I would meet her today."

"Angela is Atlanta attending graduate school at Clark. She said that she was going to try to make it. But knowing Angela, she probably stayed up all night partying and couldn't get up this morning."

"Your family is cool. I really like them. Being around them actually makes me think about my family and how much I miss the days when we were a family," I admitted.

"What do you mean?" His arms maintained its security around me.

"I mean...my daddy is gone. My sister is always too far away for me to reach. My brother is locked up. And now my mother is dieing." Suddenly, I was burden with sadness. A tear had fallen slowly down my cheek and onto his shirt.

"Family is hard sometimes. Even in my own family, things haven't always been right. When it's good, it's really good. But, when things are rough, it's hard. There is not much that we could do about our own family, but to accept them and love them for who they are. And you know, sometimes, that aint easy. I don't know how much of it may matter to you, but I'm here for you."

"Thank you. That means a lot to me."

"I have heard people say, 'you choose your friends but not your family. I don't necessarily agree with that. From the moment a man and wife say 'I do', they have made that choice to be a family. Sometimes, it's a good choice and sometimes it's bad. But it's always a choice. Everything else, the drama and the imperfections are all apart of the package deal. And that's really what makes every family what it is. No family is perfect."

"Yeah, well. Your family seemed to exemplify the word 'family.'

"That's because today is a good day. No matter what you may have witnessed between us down there, there have been some bad days. But that's with anyone. Over the years and through the hard times we figured out how to make it work. And who ever or whenever I decide to marry, we will just have to make it work, too. I think that's important."

His eyes met mine. I nodded.

"I look forward to the day when I get to choose my wife. And she and I could start our own family." I closed my eyes gently and felt his lips touching mine. I envisioned that those words he spoke were intended for no one other than me.

I had Avery drop me off at my mom's house for a brief visit to say my 'goodbyes' while he went on to the restaurant to take care of a few things. "Tamra will drop me off later on," I assured him, seeming all of my clothes and luggage were still at his house and I was leaving in the morning.

"Guess what Rocqui," Tamra yelled when I made my entrance through the front door? "Diesel is coming home from Iraq in a few weeks."

"How do you know," I asked unmoved by her excitement?

"Cause he just told me," she exclaimed, still grasping tightly her cell phone after moments earlier from ending her call.

"Aren't you excited for me?" She observed my indifferent mannerism.

"Sure," I answered short.

"And guess what else?" She followed me anxiously into the family room, maintaining her enthusiasm. I flopped onto one of the sofas and listen on as interested as I could pretend to be. "We've been granted temporary orders to move back to Fayetteville!"

"Is that supposed to be great news?

"Of course."

"Why would you want to live back here?"

"Because, this is our home. And we miss living close to our families."

I deeply inhaled tiresomely. "If that's what makes you happy."

"Oh yeah, I forgot. Big city girl thinks she is too good to live like country folks. I wish you could be happy for me sometimes," she pitched at me in a sassy tone.

"I'm sorry. I just had a long day."

"What's wrong? Did you and Avery have an argument?"

"Not at all. I met his amazing family and they were all extra nice to me. And I thought about our family and how amazing our family was back in the day."

"Yeah, we were. It was a lot of fun growing up here."

"I miss that a lot."

"Just think, we had two amazing parents, mom and dad. No one could compare to them. And they raised us to be amazing too."

She made a lot of sense. And I needed that. "Thanks Tamra," I said subtly.

"Sure. When you come back from Richmond, do you mind helping me find an apartment or maybe even a house?"

"I think I can help you out there."

"Cool. Well, if I don't see you in the morning before you leave, drive safely."

"I will."

15

I was digging relentlessly inside my bag to reach for my phone before the ringing ended. Why am I so compelled to buy these over-priced, over-sized handbags only to find nothing inside of it when I need it, I frustratingly questioned? Oh, I remembered why. I remembered how big and glossy the leather bag sat on the nickel stand on the display counter at Neiman Marcus. And I was instantly taken by the way the halogen light shone on the shiny brass plate and thick links that chained the strap to its glossy leather grey sack. And no matter how many times I deliberately distracted my attention away from it by turning to study a pair of Italian heels, Louis Vuitton kept whispering my name, arousing my senses and compelling me to believe how beautiful and expensive I would look when it hung from my shoulder. Finally, I decided as I reached in my purse for my credit card, I deserved it.

What I didn't deserve was to find my hand swimming at the bottom of that very bag trying to fish out a simple phone the size of deck of cards out of its bottomless pit. Just as I shuffled enough things around to grab hold of the pressing ring, someone forcefully bumped into my shoulder and made me drop my phone to the floor. My mouth dropped with it, while I watched compartments of the phone scatter across the tile floor. I could not believe what had just happened.

"Sorry," the passing voice tossed at me, like she was throwing away a used up paper tower. She didn't even have the decency to ask me if I was okay. Of course I was okay. The obvious eye would have seen that I was just fine. But, no one knew how badly at that very moment that I wanted to snatch her by her neck and eye me in my face so that she would recognize me and show me some human courtesy. Yet, something bigger than me held back my intent and helped me to remain my composure while my eyes pierced into her back as I watched her joyfully prance on about her business right through double glass doors and out onto the patio.

When I quickly knelt down to pick up the pieces of my phone and tried to meticulously assemble it back together, I couldn't remove my eyes from her, while she easily and gracefully distanced herself further and further away from me. Her long and narrow unshapely figure was an image that I had captured in the back of my mind from somewhere before. I know I've come across that overextended weave swaying from side to side along her back as she smiled so innocently like she had just done God's good deed before those that welcomed her bitter charm. "Bitch" I mumbled.

Quickly I became absorb in my thoughts trying to remember where I may have seen her before, that I didn't even realize that I had successfully put the phone together ...until my phone hummed in on my thoughts.

"Where are you?" It was Keisha sounding anxiously impatient.

"Where are you," I returned? "I'm standing in the lobby of the country club."

"Come out back. Me and Joddy are down near the crowd." The phone called ended. Effortlessly, I found myself easing down the very same path that 'Bitch' had just walked on. She was no longer in my sight and no longer apart of my thoughts especially after spotting Keisha and Joddy holding their hips and poking out their chests like two silly school girls at the bottom of the perfectly aligned green lawn, waving in my direction.

I couldn't understand why Joddy and Keisha marked their calendar every year to attend this event. It didn't really matter so much to me if they felt their luck on meeting a successful businessman would likely improve in this surrounding. Yet, to stand here and pretend to be excited like cheerleaders over eighteen holes, just to get a man was utterly ridiculous.

"That's because you already have a man," Joddy blatantly stated one time before.

And I answered, "Yes I do. Which furthers makes this situation worse for me to stand here in the company of two desperate house women."

"Wait a minute now," Joddy cut in sharply. "Who are you calling a house woman? Desperate yes...but I will never be labeled a house woman or even housewife, for that matter."

"Yes of course. And that sounds so much better, right?"

After finally pacing my steps down the walkway, I met up next to Joddy and Keisha. "Why is it so damn hot today," I irritably acknowledged, feeling the sun beaming down on my back.

"It's only in the eighties today," Keisha reminded me.

"Yeah but, it is October. Don't we usually start pulling out a sweater or something around this time of year?"

"I see a sweater was the furthest thing on your mind when you scooted your butt into that tiny skirt," Keisha answered looking down at my newly purchased khaki pleated golf skirt."

"Girl, I had to stop somewhere in Raleigh just to buy this golf outfit because I had nothing suitable for this engagement in my luggage. Do you like it?" I did a quick celebrated twirl.

"Yeah, but did you have to buy a pink sun visor to match your shirt too? You are looking too much like one of them." Keisha and my eyes followed Joddy's pointed finger at a few white women that apparently had the same style in mind, as I did.

"Yes. Why not dress the part since I unwillingly had to be here, anyway."

"Well, at least you don't look like a golf hootchie, like that woman standing over there," Keisha pointed out.

All of our eyes immediately veered in the direction of the flirtatious giggling and laughter, as the woman who had just minutes ago nearly mowed me over was now hanging loosely from the shoulders of Calvin trying to capture his every attention. Her white polo shirt was identical to Calvin's, Zoric's and other executives signaturing the name of Merrill Lynch on the left side of their shirts.

"That Bitch just bumped into me, inside the Country Club."

Jokingly, yet with a serious undertone Joddy eagerly suggested, "Let's go over there and jump her silly ass. She aint even nothing for the wind to take." Her feet started pacing into that direction until, Keisha and I snatched her back.

"No," we chorused!

Then suddenly, it was like someone turned a switch in my head. "I knew I remembered her from someone. She was in Zoric's office one day when I came to visit him a few weeks back."

"Well now she is in Calvin's arm trying to seduce him", Joddy stated.

"I should tell Ciantra how her man is enjoying himself too much with some hoe dangling from his side. She should kick *his* and *her* ass," I stated.

"A woman like that is never to be trusted. She hangs from one man's side today and another one, tomorrow."

"You better keep your eyes on that one, girlfriend. If not for you than especially for your girl, Ciantra," Joddy earnestly advised.

Aren't they getting married in June," Keisha remembered?

"I suppose," I answered.

"Humph. I'm sure they will live happily as soon as he finishes banging her." Joddy has never been one to hold back her quick tongue.

"Shhh!" I embarrassingly looked around to make sure no one was in ear range of our conversation.

"I'm just glad you made it back in time. It's a close one between Zoric and that dude Matt," Keisha stated politely detouring the conversation.

"I really hope Zoric wins. Matt would never let it end, if he takes home the trophy from winning this tournament. What hole are they at?" I tried to extend my vision beyond the greenery and spy Zoric into full swing a few yards away.

"I don't know. I've been standing here wondering which one of these gentlemen will be paying for my dinner tonight," Joddy candidly replied.

We couldn't help ourselves by laughing out loud over that joke, even though we were surrounded by the company of a more conservative and docile members of society.

"Come on. I think we are moving further towards the pond," I motioned for us the follow the trailing group of golf enthusiasts. We reached the lawn of the green grass bordering the white sand, where Zoric stood in the midst of an imperative swing. His arms extended tightly around the metal club, focusing carefully on his aim and the white flag that stretched out of a subtle hole, yards ahead of him.

As the crowd grew into to a silent enthusiasm, I prayed and crossed my fingers tightly that he would make it. This hole would place Zoric in the lead, if he hits it. In full swing above his head, his club rushed down over the powder sand and forced the ball into its destination. The crowd cheered and applauded his triumph. I would have nearly leaped into the air, if it wasn't for this sudden tightness and uncomfortable feeling that pinched the side of my stomach.

"What's the matter with you," Keisha asked, noticing my intensely frowning face, when I should have been exuberating with joy?

"I don't know," I softly spoke. "My stomach just started acting up."

"Are you gonna be okay," she continued, with a slight worry line across her face?

The piercing pain did not show any immediate sign of easing up. As a matter of fact, it became even more intense. "I don't know, Keisha. I don't think I'm gonna be able to make it through the rest of the tournament.

"You look awful," Joddy noticed. "Maybe you should go home and lie down. You are probably just tired.

"Yeah, Rocqui. Go home and get some rest. We got this. Your man is winning anyway," Keisha prompted me.

"I think I will." I quickly had to submit to the intensifying ache and pain and staggered up the lawn and into my car.

Before I knew it, I was home in my bedroom, with a glass of water and the opened Tylenol bottle placed beside my bed. After swallowing the two capsules and chasing it behind a sip of water, I was comfortably asleep within minutes.

Hours had passed before the arrival of Zoric. I heard the garage door chime to alert me of his return inside the house as he made his way up the stairs and into the bedroom. By this time, I had awaken, but comfortably lounged still in the bed, while I flipped the page of an Essence magazine.

"Whose car is that in the garage," he questioned, as he entered the room without relaying any warm and friendly welcomed?

"It's my rental. And a nice to see you too," I sarcastically implied.

"Oh baby. I'm sorry. I'm glad you are home." He made a better attempt to sound welcoming. "How come the Lexus dealership did not give you another Lexus to drive, rather than a Nissan Altima?"

"Because they didn't have another one available. Besides, it's just a car."

"All that damn money you spent on that car, you should be given what you deserve." His tone became increasingly assertive.

"What's the matter with you? It's just a car. If I would have known that driving a loaner home would have been more important to you than just me getting home, then I would have stayed in Fayetteville for a few more days and waited on one," I voiced angrily.

He inhaled calmly and sat on the edge of the bed near my legs. "I'm sorry Rocqui. I lost the golf tournament and I guess I'm taking some of my frustrations out on you."

I whimpered disappointedly. "I'm so sorry. I know how that must make you feel."

"I thought you were going to be there for me. You know I would have won, if you were there?"

"I was there, but I started feeling really bad, so I had to leave. I don't know if it was something I ate too much of or not enough of, but it became excruciating for me to just to stand there...Does that mean that Matt won?"

"Yeah," he reluctantly admitted. He slowly raised himself off the bed. I knew it would be moments before he would find a reason to leave again. "I need a drink. Calvin and I are gonna meet up at the bar for a minute or two." He looked at me like he suddenly remembered to ask if I was okay. "Are you okay? Do you need anything before I go?"

"Yes. As a matter of fact, I do need something."

He was surprised by my response. It had been a few occasions that I have needed anything from Zoric, even though his trailing list of 'needs' from me is constant. "What?"

"I'm hungry...I would like some McDonald's."

"McDonald's," he exclaimed, like he was caught off guard by that request!

"YES, McDonald's. I would like a Big Mac, with large fries and a Coke," I answered full of certainty.

"When was the last time you've eaten at McDonald's?"

"I don't know. But, it sounds really good right now."

"Okay. Whatever..." He grabbed his keys he had placed on the dresser and exited the room. Thirty minutes later, I was devouring two all-beef patties with special sauce, like I was eating a filet mignon.

"Tomorrow, I want you to call the Lexus dealership here, where you bought your car and see about them getting you a Lexus to drive while your car is being repaired rather than that other car," he insisted before finally departing to meet up with Calvin.

Wow!" My lips widely parted. I was totally taken by surprised as I stepped over the threshold of what once was an abandon colonial-style house that Ray had lured my interest and my money into. Dust floated in the unfinished areas. New plaster and drywall now replaced rotted rat-infested walls. My eyes couldn't blink away from the carefully crafted winding oak stairway that welcomed your entrance through the front door. The unfinished walls frames out a formal living and dining room, both were retaining its original crown molding features, encasing ten feet ceilings.

I curiously trekked up the stairs, carefully stepping over nails and around tools that were left carelessly on the newly refurbished hardwood floors. The sound of my four-inch heels echoed throughout the blank hollow walls, as I carefully inspected the tile layout in each of the bathrooms making sure the constructors thoroughly followed the blueprint that Ray and I approved.

"What do you think," Ray asked. His unexpectant attire of faded dingy jeans, overly worn t-shirt and paint splashed workmen boots, made him almost unrecognizable by me from my view at the top the stairs.

"Ray, is that you?" I teased.

"Of course it is. Don't let the hand-me-downs fool you. So, tell me what you think?"

"You know what... I really don't know what to say. I'm really impressed." I amazingly continued to circle around the open interior, still in disbelief that this was same condemned house that Ray showed me from the picture. "I mean, we've taken this neglected colonial and modernized it while maintaining some of its historical character. I think this is going to be a beautiful home once it's done," I concluded as I made my way down the stairs, to where he stood.

"Have you seen the kitchen yet?" He eagerly inquired, anxious to lead me through the framed entrance into the kitchen.

"No, not yet. I can't tear my eyes away from the entrance."

"While you were away out of town, I was here expending blood, sweat, and tears. There were days when I was the only one on site, doing little jobs here and there and trying to keep the cost down. Man, I'm just glad the end is the near. I don't know what being pregnant feels like, but I'm ready to give birth to this." As I returned down the stairs and stood next to Ray, I continued to observe his out of character attire, noticing his unshaven beard and white ashy knuckles.

"How much more time do you think you'll need to finish this house?"

"It depends on how long you are gonna be here in town. You are like the roadrunner on TV. I can't keep up with you long enough to help me order the finishing touches."

"What do you need me to do Ray? I promise I will stay put long enough to see this through the end. What time span are we looking at?

"Possibly, by the first of November. Could you stay still long enough to select light fixtures and appliances for the kitchen?"

"Yes sir. When I leave from here, I will go immediately to Home Depot."

"Thank goodness. We got a lot more work to do. But we could get it done faster, as long as I don't have to wait around for *you* to add all of your fancy touches."

"I got this, because I am ready to make some money. We need to get this house on the market as soon as possible. We are moving into the slower months. The quicker we get it sold, the quicker the digits in my bank account could move into its rightful place."

"You are telling me! I had to cut back on my little extra spending myself to see this through. But, we are almost there."

"Did you give up on bathing too, because you're starting to blend in with the drywall?"

"Laugh if you may, but the profit off of this house would allow me to bathe anywhere I please."

"If we could get this houses listed by November, it would then allow us a couple months to market it effectively and get it sold by the end of the year. By December thirty-first, I want this house to be in escrow."

"By December the thirty-first, I want to be on a two week vacation on some island reaping the fruits of this labor. And you my dear business partner, could pay for that big elaborate wedding that you and Zoric have been bragging about."

My mood was almost altered by the mere mentioning of the 'wedding'. "I hear you Ray. I'm sure this wedding would happen for us whenever the time is right."

"What's up with the lack of enthusiasm in your voice? I remember not too long ago, you were twirling around singing the 'I'm getting married song," he dramatically reminded me, impersonating my excited behavior, that I carelessly displayed after Zoric had given me my engagement ring.

I chuckled, at his mimicking performance. "Well, sometimes life throws you a curve ball. Maybe, even two at a time. But, I can only hit one ball."

"Amen to that. But, I'm ready to hit this ball straight out the park." He imitated a MLB hitter, lowering his extended arms together and stretching them high above his head, like he was swinging with a bat.

"I certainly feel you there. I am at your service to get whatever you need to get done."

"I haven't thanked you enough for helping me on this project. I knew I could count on you to help me make things happen. When do you want to start our next flip?"

"I don't know yet. Lets see how profitable we do with this one."

"I'm telling you, Rocqui. This is my new business. I'm jumping in with both feet on this business venture. There is a lot of money that could be made off of this. And you and I as a team, just spells out dollars."

"Well, lets make sure that both feet are dry before you start jumping, Ray. I would like to see this do well, also.

But, money and time are not favorable for me right now. I'm just taking things one day at a time."

I left Ray at the construction site and headed out towards Broad Street to shop at Home Depot. Darkness was starting to fall early on the autumn skies. A gently cool breeze began to sweep the colorful leaves from the whispering trees. When I arrived home, Chee Chee curled up next to me on the sofa, while I searched through the MLS, on my laptop for comparable home prices in the area of Ray and I flip. The main level door chimed and Chee Chee raced upstairs with his dog tag jingling in strive to her every move.

"Hey Rocqui," Zoric yelled from the top of the stairs. "I brought dinner."

I didn't have a big appetite for food, but I yelled, "I'll be up in a minute."

Slowly I marched up the stairs and entered into the kitchen where Zoric was hidden between the cabinet doors reaching up for plates to prepare our food. I opened the refrigerator and grabbed a bottle of chardonnay. As I moved in closer towards Zoric, searching in the cabinets for two wine glasses, my senses became aroused by the smell of his cologne. I knew that scent anywhere. My bodies had lain naked and absorb the aroma of that very same fragrance. But it wasn't with Zoric that I shared these memories. My movements paused, holding the wine glasses steadily in my hand, while my mind recaptured the images of Avery's strong bare body. I could see his face and how intense it felt when he looked at me. I could feel his hands smoothing over my body whenever he would touch me. Lost in the moment, I imagine Avery was here. As I walked up behind Zoric, I pressed my hands against his chest and inhaled sweet memories.

He turned around and kissed me. "I didn't know you love Japanese food that much," he implied, receiving my hug and my love, as if it was intended for him. My arms fell disappointingly to my waist side. Forging a smile, I replied, "I sure do. Thank you for picking up dinner." I tried to sound as sincere as ever, but I couldn't hide the disappointment I now felt. I knew then at that point, that this is no ordinary love I was feeling towards Avery. It was that type of love that made you strong when you were weak and filled your soul when you were hungry.

Over my pretentious use of the wooden chops sticks that I held my shrimp, my thoughts were at a distant from Zoric's handsomely presence. Before I met Avery, I would easily get excited and all tingly inside, in the company of those same hazel brown eyes that I now sat across from. And I would savor the moments he would lay his head in my lap so that I could run my fingers through his soft curly hair. Whenever we were out, I caught the jealous glares, wishing it was their hand he held. I would smile right back into their desperate stares knowing that they could not have him. None of those shallow ideas seem to matter too much anymore, particularly when someone had opened up something much deeper inside you that you never knew existed.

"I know I didn't tell you this when you first came back from Fayetteville, but I really missed you when you were gone," Zoric sincerely stated.

"I miss you too," I said lying to myself and him.

"So how's your family doing?"

"They are doing okay. Things could be better."

"What are you doing down there to spend so much time away from home?"

His question made me nervous, but I proceeded with caution to answer anyway. "The same thing I do while I am here... working and trying to be as helpful as I could be for my mother." I obviously couldn't state that I have been spending my days and night loving someone else. That would have been the truth of it all.

"When are you going back to Fayetteville?",

"I'm not quite sure. There are so many things I need to do here. I can't really pinpoint an exact date." I thought about the Halloween Party that Avery had planned at Georgia's Club and knew I was hard-pressed to be present for that occasion. But, then three weeks felt too long to be absent without seeing him.

I had to throw out a plan to let him know about my upcoming intensions to attend the party, without my actions becoming too suspicious. "There is supposed to be this grand Halloween Party, in Fayetteville that I would like to attend. I don't know if I'm gonna make it or not." That was a partial lie, because I was gonna do whatever I needed to do to be present at Avery's side for this occasion.

"That sounds interesting. Maybe I would come with you," he casually implied. I could have choked on the rice I had just place inside of my mouth. I would have never predicted those words to depart from his lips or I would not have ever mentioned my plan.

But then I thought rationally and conceived the notion that Zoric wasn't coming to Fayetteville. He hasn't been to Fayetteville since we first started dating. There was no reason I decided that I should feel worried over his sudden interest in coming to my hometown, when there have never been one before.

I faked a smile and added, "That would be nice."

"Speaking of partying, you know the company is holding our annual Investor's Ball the week before Halloween."

I was quiet, still a bit distraught over that whole Fayetteville thing. "You didn't forget, did you," he pressed?

"No baby. I haven't forgotten, I just had a few things on my mind," or person, I thought. Before he asked me to empty my secrets, I swayed the conversation in a different direction. "The house that Ray and I are flipping is beautiful. I'm glad that I wasn't around for the intense labor part, because that house was a mess. I am really impressed with Ray and what he had done. But I think we are gonna do well. It's a seller's market right now, so we should get multiple offers."

He smiled. "That's great baby. Do you think that this is something you may want to keep doing?"

"I don't know. The money is good, but it seems like a lot of work if you don't know what you are doing."

"You could be the investor. And leave the construction part to Ray. You already have the real estate business. You could manage the business side, easily."

"It sounds exciting. But, I have to give it a little more thought. Maybe, after the sell of this project. Then I could have a better perception of what exactly I'm getting myself into.

"Have you chosen your dress for the Ball yet?"

"I haven't had the time to shop for anything."

"Well, whatever you decide, you know blue is my favorite color. I would love to see you in something blue."

I'd swallowed hard and lowered my stiff shoulders against the back of the chair. My face became heated as I stared at Zoric's egotistical demeanor that continued to fork down his food without any awareness of my sudden irritation I now felt towards him. It was a feeling of resentfulness that often plagued my disposition towards him every time he slyly suggests what he wants over what I want. Just like the issue of the Nissan Altima. Every morning he pestered me about calling the Lexus dealership to replace the rental I had driven from Fayetteville. After the third day, of his constant reminding I finally ordered him to leave me alone about that damn car. "IT'S JUST A FUCKING CAR," I finally released!

He backed off cautiously fearing of what I may say next. At first, he didn't even want to me to buy a Lexus. He wanted 'his fiancée to own a classier car', like a Mercedes Benz, because one of his friend's girlfriend had just bought one. Mercedes, Lexus, Audi, they were all overpriced foreign cars to me. But, my heart easily swayed towards the Lexus IS convertible because they had just made their feature debut on the market. The dealer swore by every word that they only had two in stock and that I would be the first person in Richmond to obtain one. And if that didn't win me over, the breathtaking test drive seduced me in believing the world was orbiting around me, surely did.

Finally, I woke up early one Saturday and drove to the Lexus dealership in my old Honda Accord that I had since my undergrad studies. I returned home later that day, in the car that I wanted and not the one that Zoric was trying to convince me to have. When he finally spotted my new car parked in the garage he simply uttered, "Nice car."

"Well, I may not find anything I like, that's blue," I sourly retorted.

Sensing the obvious irritation in my voice, he calmly replied, "That's okay Rocqui. It could be any color, you like. I just thought maybe you wanted a suggestion on what I think looks beautiful on you."

There was more that I wanted to say, but I chewed on my last words citing that it wasn't worth any more energy spent squabbling over. My attention easily had fallen back on thoughts of Avery and I wondered what colored dress would he prefer me to wear for him. Hmm... something simple, but not too fussy...definitely sexy. And then, a tainted smiled creased on my face when I determined that Avery is into loving me full body and soul...not under the stipulations of what color dress I'm wearing or rather or not I'm driving a Nissan Altima as oppose to a Lexus.

I kinda starred across from him, at the table like I was examining who this man really is. When I first met him, he came from a place of nothing. He didn't have a set of towels to add to my collection when he moved into my apartment. Now, he is dictating to me what color dress

I should wear. That was pretty damn funny to me. And then I noticed...

"Where is your watch?" I was surprised by its absence. I bought him an exclusive leather watch for his birthday two years ago. And never have I seen him without it.

His hand immediately felt his wrist, as if he had forgotten that he wasn't wearing it. "Oh. I had accidentally cracked the glass and so I took it to the repair shop to have it fix."

"Why didn't you tell me? It's under warranty. I could have returned it to the jeweler and had it replaced without any cost."

"You haven't been here, remember. It's no big deal. It should be ready next week."

I let the matter rest at hand.

After spending a few hours in the office, on a Saturday morning, I headed off to Regency Square Mall in search of a formal gown for Zoric's annual Investor's ball. Ideally, I have somewhat enjoyed attending these affairs with Zoric, to showcase to the world how perfect we are together. He as my prince and I'm, his princesses, as we made our grand appearance through the doubled-doors of the ballroom, hand and hand. All eyes would appear to be on us and smiles would greet us, as we were repeatedly reminded 'what a handsome couple we make.' And I would gracefully stand by his side while he would exchange business jargon with his colleagues, as his trophy.

However, on this particular occasion, I was lost in another world... a world full of lust, and love and romance over another man, that had overshadowed my real world.

"Hello," I answered, receiving a call through my Bluetooth.

"Hi Rocqui. I need your help." It was Avery. And his voice sounded urgent.

"What's the matter," I anxiously responded?

"I just couldn't figure out what color to pain the guest bedroom. I mean I want it to look perfect, just in case you ever have to use it again." His husky voice calmly softened. I could tell he was even smiling on his end of the phone. I certainly was.

I decided to play along with his game. "Well, I think an eggshell color would go perfect along the walls."

"Eggshell!" From the excitement in his voice, I knew he wasn't expecting a comeback from me like that.

"I tell you what, if you would wait until I return, I will go with you to the store and help you pick it out," I flirtatiously suggested.

"I like that idea," he easily replied. "I just couldn't bear to keep walking past that room and seeing it without any color or even without you."

Even though, I only slept one lonely night in that room, I totally understood his sentiments. "I miss you a lot Avery."

"I'm missing you a lot too Rocqui. I feel like I'm just holding on to each day, until the next time I'm with you."

"So am I. My weeks ahead appear to be very tight… more than I anticipated. I really don't know how soon I would be able to see you again."

"Maybe we could work out something where we could spend a few hours together, rather than a whole day, if that's easier for you."

"That sounds like an excellent idea."

"I'm glad you like that."

"I have a workshop next Saturday at my office. I know I will have the rest of the day to myself, afterwards. If your afternoon is open then let's make it a date."

"If that day wasn't free for me, it is now."

"Then, it is a date."

16

As I entered through Macy's grand doors, I strolled through the crowded make-up and perfume counters and headed towards the upper level of the department store. I was one step away from gliding upwards on the escalator, when my name was summons by an unrecognizable voice, from a distance.

"Rocquelle!" I looked to my right, far and beyond the sea of customers crowding the aisles and counters. "Rocquelle!"

Then a familiar face appeared from around the Fashion Fair counter and rushed up to my side full of energy and excitement. It was Yolanda McKenzie. She and I were at VCU together. We shared similar course loads and often were the only two African American women, in the same class, surrounded by our white counterparts. Ironically, our relationship only amounted to nothing more than casual acquaintances, in which we spoke or exchanged words when necessary. She stood before me wearing Juicy couture jeans with a vibrant wrapped silk bloused tied around her waist. Her neck and her arms were accented with a bit of sparkle and bling, while her walnut complexion was perfectly made-up in posh punch eye shadow and matching lipstick. She is naturally a few inches shorter than me, but her stacked heels gave her some height. She had an oversize Coach bag thrown over her shoulder, while her hands handled several large shopping bags.

"Hey girlfriend," she glowed as she braced me with her arm thrown around my shoulder.

"Hi Yolanda! It's been a long time since I've seen you."

"I know, girl. You look good. How have you been?" She sounded overly excited.

"I'm good. My real estate business is doing quite well. And, I'm looking into the possibility of investing and renovating old homes. Other than that, everything else is great."

"Are you still seeing that guy you were dating at VCU? What was his name? He was so handsome....," she cooed.

My brows tighten from her surprisingly bluntness. "Yes, Zoric and I are engaged." I even held my hand up so that she could marvel over my engagement ring.

"It's beautiful," she complimented touching my finger tips for a better view of its sparkle. "I just got married two years ago. My husband works for the Department of Defense at the Pentagon and I am working out of our home as a Computer Analyst for IBM. We are doing quite well. We are living in DC now, but I came home to visit my family for a few days."

"That sounds really nice," I responded, even though I could really care less. "How do you like living in DC?"

"Oh girl. I don't really like it at all. The traffic is ridiculous. The crime rate is senseless. And the schools are horrible. But my husband, Kenneth makes all the money to afford me a little time and luxury to go shopping whenever I want to. Just last week, I was in New York at fashion week. Have you ever been?"

"No, I've never been." Even though it would be nice to go one time in my life, I was not interested in having this conversation with her about it. "Sounds like everything has really worked out for you. I'm really happy for you," I tried to hurry up and say and be on my way.

"Yes, it has," she gloated. "Your life is gonna be just as fabulous when you and Zoric get marry."

"I suppose it would be." I smiled mildly trying to conceal the lack of interest I held in this dialog between us.

"Maybe you and I could get together to have lunch or something," I kindly suggested, anxious for this reacquaintance to end.

"That sounds like a fantastic idea. Here, take my number." We exchanged numbers and stored them in our cell phones, pretending like we were really going to keep in touch, like longtime friends. Well, it was good seeing you again, Rocquelle. I wish you well."

"Same to you, of course." She and I turned in opposite directions and I proceeded up the escalator.

I arrived into the section of taffeta, silk and tulle adorned with illustrious and glittering gowns hanging from the clothing racks. My initial plan was to buy a gown for Zoric's ball. Yet, now I was distracted over the lasting words of Yolanda. 'Your life is gonna be just as perfect when you and Zoric get marry.' That was my exact thought three months ago. But, now my heart and mind come from a different place. I didn't know what to believe. I could not dispel the fact that I there was a tinge of jealously of Yolanda and her life she boasted in front of me. She seemed to have everything I was looking forward to having, one time ago.

I thought about what my mother had told me. She said I was going to eventually reach the point when I would have to choose. But, I wasn't at that point yet. I was not ready to decide between Zoric and Avery when I couldn't even decide on a simple dress to wear to a ball.

I tried to refocus my attention less on my love triangle and more on this beautiful sapphire taffeta strapless gown that had caught my eyes. I resented the fact that it was blue, but I couldn't resist its bold strapless silhouette with a sweetheart neckline. I wanted something far from the images of Zoric's mind. Yet, I grabbed it anyways and draped it over my arm. Then I turned in view of another overstocked rack. Easily I spotted an off-white strapless tulle gown with an unforgiving hemline that sweeps the floor with pure grace. Its impressive details could have been misunderstood as a wedding gown...something in which I was far from being ready to buy. However, I was still intrigued.

With both dresses hanging over my arm, I walked into the fitting room and closed myself off from the world. I slipped off my shirt and jeans and starred up at the two gowns. I knew that one of these dresses I was certain to buy yet I felt less inclined to try them on. Just pick one, I pushed myself. Both were quite beautiful in its own way. However, I can only wear one dress, for this occasion, just like I can only truly love one man. But who do I really truly love? Wasteful minutes were counting away as I continued to dwell over the matter. Until finally I redressed and grabbed the blue taffeta, without trying it on and bought it.

The house phone rang just as I'd stepped through the basement level garage door. Chee Chee loyally met me at the entrance, as I raced to answer the phone.

"Hello," I answered, nearly bracing myself.

"Hey baby. How was your day today?" It was Zoric.

"It was okay. I just spent most of the afternoon at the mall," I answered, as I waltz upstairs and fumble through the kitchen cabinets, in search of a light snack.

"Oh, OK. Did you buy anything I would like," he slyly asked?

"I guess you could say that," I passively responded, trying not to disclose the frustration I felt from the whole shopping experience.

"That's my girl."

"Listen, I was thinking tonight we watch 'The Notebook'. I borrowed it from Keisha and she absolutely swears by this movie. But, I gotta warn you. It is a chick flick. I believe Keisha said she has watched it four times and cried every single time."

"Uh, baby," he interrupted. "Calvin had already set up this dinner with a few clients that I wasn't aware of until about an hour ago. You may want to start the movie without me."

I should not have been surprised or even allowed a hint of disappointment to tamper my mood. But I was surprised and genuinely disappointed. We once made a commitment, a long while ago, to honor Saturday nights as our date night...no matter what. And whoever was the last one home had to pay for dinner. We playfully enjoyed the challenge and had a lot of fun with the idea. But, that was before money began to steadily flow in and settled between us.

"Now baby, don't be upset with me," he tried to ease over. "I promise I will be home as soon as possible. Two hours top," he guaranteed.

"I'm not upset," I tried to convince him, but I was. "Go ahead and take care of your business and I will see you whenever you get home."

"Alright love. I love you."

"Yeah. You too," I uttered.

I crammed the bag of Tostitos chips back inside the opened cabinet...and slammed the door. In place of hunger I had felt moments ago, I was pissed and needed a drink. The search to quench my thirst was not long when I opened the refrigerator and grabbed an already half open bottle of a Seventy-Eight Merlot. With the bottle in one hand and a wine glass in the other, I trekked upstairs to my room.

I looked at my cellphone and contemplated calling Avery. I needed to hear his voice to comfort me from my soreness. But, I couldn't. He was much more than just a pacifier to me. I resorted instead to a hot bubble bath in my claw-foot cast iron tub and tapped off my empty glass with some wine, while I soaked. Each time the glass bared emptiness, I made it full. My skin began to wrinkle under the cooling hot water. But, I was determined not to move from this position, until my bottle was empty and I was drunk.

"Ladies and Gentlemen, thank you for coming out today on this early Saturday morning. I am Rocquelle Johnson, realtor and broker of Dream House Realty and I am here to get you into a home of your own. I have several financial advisors that are here on behalf of Bank of America and they will walk you through several plans and grants to make the home buying process easier and more comfortable for you."

I was standing before an intimate crowd of sixteen to twenty people hosted at the Marriot. I wore a penciled skirt and high heels. Guests sat at round tables with light linen, with brochures place in front of them while, the three financial advisors that Matt allowed me stood in strategic corners of the room with a few chairs and flow charts beside them.

"Please feel free to ask any questions. We are here to be at your service. If you haven't already grabbed some food in the back of the room, help yourself. We have plenty of muffins, fruit, coffee and juice for you all. And please, please tell us what we could do to help you buy your dream home." People began to steadily rise from their tables and line themselves aside the table where the food was. I organized my space and made sure my business cards and available homes brochures were lined up along my display table, so that people could easily see some choices they may have.

Slowly, people began to circle around myself and the other financial advisors. An African-American woman appearing to be in her early forties walked up to me. Her puzzled face read of a million questions she was eager to be answered.

"Hi Rocquelle. I'm Leah."

"Nice meeting you Leah. How can I help you?"

"I got married when I was very young. And just recently I've gotten a divorce. My ex-husband or even myself for that matter, never really kept a steady job. Basically, we have lived from paycheck to paycheck and never really could maintain our debt. The thought of actually purchasing a house was the furthest thing from our minds." She deeply sighed, like a burden just had been lifted from her shoulders. A smile appeared and she continued. "However, now I have been a Dental Assistant, for at least four years. I make a decent salary. But still not enough to save for a down payment on a house... You said earlier that there are several grants available to help people make a down payment?"

"That's exactly right. The purpose of this informative session today is because there a lot of people just like you, who are hardworking individuals that still may need some financial assistance in buying a home. And I want to help you in any way that I can to make that happen."

"Thank you so much."

"You're welcome. One of these advisors standing in the back has a plan for you to help you to make this possible. I guarantee it. And if they can't help you, just let me know." She maintained a hopeful smile. I wanted her to know that my words are sincere. "You are standing here now in front of me. But, just imagine, within a year at the most, you could be standing in your own living room."

"That's all I ever wanted."

"Here. Take my card and take one or several of these brochures of these houses that you may be interested and you and I could go and take a look."

"Thank you, again. I really appreciate it."

"You are very welcome."

A few other patrons walked up to me and openly discussed their financial situations. Some were young. Some were older. Some were white and some were black. However, they all were desiring and thankful for the opportunity to possibly own a home one day.

I knew it wouldn't be long before Matt made his appearance. He swaggered into the conference room and led his steps right before me.

"Well, hello Rocqui." He smiled slyly like a cat that just swallowed the canary.

"Hello Matt," I indifferently spoke.

"I see you have a fairly nice turn out today," he observed, eyeing the participants attentiveness in the information his advisors were relaying to them.

"I did okay. I was hoping for more."

"I was expecting less."

I didn't want to get into this with him, so I rushed my words, with what I expected he had come to hear me say. "Thank you Matt for all you've done. I really appreciate it," I added superficially.

"What's up with the cold shoulder? I thought you would be more welcoming to see me?"

Maybe he did have honest intentions for coming here today. I eased up a bit and changed my tone. "I didn't expect to see you today. I thought you were busy."

"I am. But, I wanted to make sure that my people were doing their job...And I wanted to also show you something?"

"What?"

He pulled out his Blackberry from his pocket. "Look." He held his phone up in my direct view and displayed a picture of the trophy he won from the golf tournament against Zoric. "Doesn't it look so much better in my office", he arrogantly added?

"I should have known." I rolled my eyes away.

"I'm sorry Rocqui. It's just that it has been a long time coming, that's all."

"I'm happy for you. Now, if you would excuse me, I have other things to do." I turned towards my display table and began to store the remaining brochures and business cards into my briefcase.

"Where are you off too?"

"This is over in thirty minutes. And I have additional plans for the afternoon." A cunning smile erased the sourness that I felt towards Matt from my face.

"You and Zoric must have something special plan," he tried to interpret.

I have plans, but they didn't include Zoric. But, I wasn't telling him that. Yet in still, I nodded happily. "Thank you again Matt," I reinstated sincerely. "I couldn't have done this without you."

"I'm just moved by this opportunity to make money."

With all I sincerity, I added, "Good for you." And then I continued to put my things away and loaded up my car.

The skeptical faces that earlier entered the room departed with hopeful faces. I was overwhelmingly pleased at the turnout. Before I departed from the Marriot, I changed into a more casual attire…a matching velour jogging suit. I released the clip from my hair and brushed my hair to flow down my shoulders. I added a little lip gloss and touched up my face with a little powder. Then, I was ready to head south to spend the rest of my afternoon with Avery.

The plan that he came up with was we are to meet in Raleigh and have an afternoon picnic. Nothing else could have sounded so perfect and more romantic. I could not have gotten on the interstate any faster, than what I did.

"I'm on my way to you," I voiced when Avery picked up his call.

"The words that I've been waiting to hear all day," he replied.

"I have a head start since you're closer. I guess I will be seeing you in two hours."

"Yes indeed. Drive safely. I love you."

"I love you too."

I think I had smiled for an entire hour, when I had gotten off the phone with him. It was the start of a perfect day. Along my drive, I kept remembering how he felt, the way he kissed, and the amazing feeling I felt when I was around him. How could I deny myself this type of happiness?

Finally, I zoomed passed the highway sign that read Raleigh...45 miles away. And just minutes afterwards, my phone rang.

I presumed that it was Avery telling me that he was there. But when I looked at the incoming call it read Zoric.

"Hello," I stammered to answer.

"Rocqui, I need you," he desperately voiced.

"What do you mean? Are you okay?" I felt my heart beating faster.

"Yes, I'm okay. I'm at Rodolfo's Taylor shop in Georgetown. I've seen to have ran out of money. Could you come by here and help me pay for my tux?"

"What? You got to be kidding me." I was livid.

"I know baby, I'm asking for a lot. But, I need you, right now."

"Couldn't you just wait until tomorrow and we could return to the store together?"

"Believe me, I thought about doing it. But, I need you also to help me to decide on a few choices. Baby, I don't know which one to get."

I was mowed over with anger, that I couldn't even utter a word.

"You weren't busy were you," he decidedly now to ask? "Could you come? I'm standing here in the dressing room, undressed waiting on you. Please."

I took a deep breath. Less than forty-five miles I was away from Avery...and suddenly Zoric had called out for me to rescue him. I didn't want to believe that I was turning around, but I was.

I called Avery. "I have everything ready, under the perfect shaded tree. I got the wine, the delicious deli sandwiches and my mother's potatoes salad. She insisted that you tasted hers over mine. Now all I need is you. Where are you?" His voice was so cheerful and warming that I didn't even know how to tell him.

"I'm...I'm returning to Richmond," I cried.

"What's wrong?"

"I can't say right now... I'm sorry Avery. I'm just really sorry."

He was expectantly quiet. I continued, "I will call you later...okay?"

"Okay," he answered. Then it became official. My day was ruin.

17

I was so mad at myself for returning to Richmond and missing my date with Avery. The next couple of days I couldn't stand to even look at myself or let alone Zoric. Avery stated that he understood. But I wondered how could he understand when I didn't understand the choice that I had made?

I lost myself in my work. With the phone constantly ringing, it seemed near impossible to get anything done. Paperwork piled high and unopened mail covered the corner of my desk. There was a list of important phone calls I needed to make and not enough hours in the day to get them all done. I finally decided to give my hand a rest from pushing the pen and return a pertinent call to Andrew Spencer. "Mr. Spencer, how are you? This is Roquelle Johnson of Dream House Realty," I asked in my professional voice.

"Heaven speaks! It is my realtor," he exclaimed with genuine excitement. I would have never guessed when I stood in the center of one of Richmond's five dollars a day gravel parking lot, placing my business cards on hopeful client's windshields, that the voice that followed behind me with, "What are you selling," would actually become my most lucrative client. He conveyed a sincere interest in listening to my business ideas and was eager for me to show him a few houses. - Well not so readily. But in a few months ahead, a short stature white man waltz through my office doors with enthusiasm he still shares today, ready to buy a new home.

I sat anxiously at Keisha's front desk and greeted him with "Welcome to Dream House Reality" without a clue that this was the same man that I met briefly a few months ago, now wearing a light blue collard shirt and khakis.

"I remembered the name of your business, even after I passed your card off to another colleague," he begun to say. My mind dauntingly chased the memory to make the connection between where I may have met him before. It wasn't until he added, "how did that exchange of business cards in the parking lot make out for you," did my memory ring a bell.

I never led on to the fact that I was oblivious to who he was. That would be tacky, even after I sold him a one and a half million dollar home in Alexandria. However, I've always been the most grateful that he waltz through my doors, just three years ago.

"I was beginning to think you've moved on to a wealthier client and wasn't interested in a poor man like myself anymore," he jokingly implied.

I chuckled. "No sir. Not at all Mr. Spencer. My hands have been tied up for a minute. But, I am here at your service, at any time."

"Great! So, how's Virginia Beach looking? You know, I am really anxious to make a small investment on some property there. Nothing grand. Just a weekend getaway, for some easy living. With that being said, it would be FANTASTIC if we could get it on a golf course. However, if there is nothing reasonably available on the course, certainly, in close proximity of one. You know what I mean?" He spoke at a fast momentum, but full of sureness of what he wanted.

"So how much money are you looking to spend?"

"I'll say in the neighborhood of three hundred to five hundred thousand dollars. And I would like for it to be already furnished. I don't want the added stress of furniture shopping. I want to be able to throw a suitcase and my golf bag in the car and feel like I'm on weekend vacation."

"I will check the listings and give a few associates a call in that area. And I'll enlist the help of my assistant as well so that she could do a little shopping around for us to see what's currently available. How soon are you available to go there to see what's available?"

"I tell you Rocquelle, it would be wonderful if we could sign on something this weekend."

So soon, I thought. I had no intentions on traveling to Virginia Beach this Saturday, when I was anxious to return to Fayetteville to make up for skipping out on our date last Saturday. However, I needed to make this deal. Not just for the financial gain, but because Andrew Spencer took a chance and became my first major client when my business doors first opened. If it wasn't for him exchanging my business card to some of his loyal patrons, my business would not have flourished so quickly and successfully. Therefore, I postponed my romantic weekend and confirmed, "I'll get right on it," before hanging up the phone.

My vision was strained by my flat screen monitor, carefully scoping and dotting the details of some perspective homes in Virginia Beach. I didn't even turn to acknowledge Keisha's presence when she knocked and slowly entered inside, whistling like a canary. "My, my, someone wanted to remind you how much they love you," she sung.

"What," I uttered, without ever blinking away from the computer screen?

"These flowers were chosen with a lot of thought and attention given," she continued as I scarcely tuned into the words she was saying.

Then the picturesque bouquet of long stemmed pink orchids and red tulip escaping a tall crystal vase, were placed in the center of desk, crowded next to my monitor on my right and my office phone on the far left.

Immediately, the vision of the freshly blossomed flowers took me far away from the boundaries of these four walls. I anxiously dismissed my endless task momentarily and reached for the pink envelope tucked neatly on a stick inside the bouquet.

It read, *'To the one that has filled my life with joy and my heart with love. Love, Avery'*.

I couldn't let go of the smile, I held. I palmed my cell phone in my hand and touched send after highlighting Avery's name.

His phone rang several times, before I listened to the recording of his voice. I contemplated for a moment to leave him a message, but ended the call abruptly before the sound of the beep. What I wanted to say to him, like how beautiful the flowers are he sent, how much I miss him and how I was counting down each day when his lips are just a touch away, could only be delivered directly from my mouth to his ears.

With my eyes at a daze and my hands mounted to my cheeks, I dreamingly fantasized about spending the rest of my life with Avery. The memorable pleasures that he gives me left my body yearning and feeling sultry, with a tinge of excitement flowing through my blood. The cool air that once circulated through my blouse and between my thighs had now become oppressed by the gentleness of warmth I get each time my eyes gazed on the beauty that has now overwhelmed my desk. Maybe if I take a break away from my office and grab a Coke out of the staff lounge, I would regain my composure and return my focus on work.

The tall glass door mini-fridge was just a few steps away tucked in the staff lounge directly behind my office. There are just two chocolate leather chairs circling a cream fabric sofa and a dark stained coffee table, with magazines fanned over it. I recently added a toweling water fall flanking the entrance wall, to create a relaxing ambience to a sometimes, overwhelming day. On the opposite wall was a tapered counter positioning a coffee maker and coffee mugs, which was always my first stop of every morning before beginning any task. Yet, it was now one o'clock. And I still wasn't half way completing the extensive list of things to get done by five.

The Coke felt refreshing showering down my parch throat. A few more sips were all I had taken before carrying the bottle in my hand, as my feet led me in the directions towards the corners of my office. But the exchange of laughter and a few words that traveled from Keisha's desk gave way of my immediate intentions and stopped me in my path. Suddenly, I realized, as I moved around the fica tree that sprouted eight feet tall, along the narrow hallway, that the familiar tenor belonged to Zoric.

My knees instantly buckled as my eyes met the startling unannounced arrival of Zoric, in full view, leaning against Keisha's desk. His hand extending high up into the air to acknowledge his awareness of me, made me even more nervous, when I remembered my flowers gracing my desk just a few feet away from his eyesight.

I couldn't think fast enough. I dropped the remaining can of soda into the small wastebasket outside my office and nervously trotted to intercept Zoric's path at the sight of his Prada shoes prowling towards me. Hoping to screen a glimpse of my flowers reflecting through the glass partitions that framed out my office, my arms enveloped his body, when we came into contact.

"Hey Baby," I muttered trying to contain my nervousness and mumbling silent prayers to God that my bouquet of flowers were not in his view.

His face was charming and welcomingly pleasant as he leaned in towards me and pressed his soft lips against mine. "Hey Love. Thought I come by and take my baby out for lunch."

Trying to keep nervously still, I apprehensively played along with his plan. "Where were you thinking about going?"

"Where ever you like… I have the rest of the afternoon off. So, it doesn't matter."

My chest punctuated each rapid heartbeat. A sense of urgency overflowed through my veins. I quickly agreed, hurrying for us to leave right now, without me ever stepping foot inside my office.

Zoric's arm had widened the office door to free me like a bird in a cage. I deeply inhaled a sigh of relief as the afternoon breeze combed through my bare arms. Then Zoric suddenly gripped my right arm tightly and halted my strive, just a few feet away, outside of the building.

His startlingly stare pierced through me. "Aren't you forgetting something," he detected?

I barely was able to formed my lips together to reply, "What"?

"Your purse," he answered, eyeing my bare shoulders.

I tapped my empty shoulder and recollected the displacement of my grey Louis Vutton Mahina hand bag that probably still sat on the tall file cabinet, where I placed it this morning when I arrived to work. "Oh yeah," I sighed.

I hurried back to my office, thanking God every step of the way, that Zoric did not spot my flowers. When I walked inside and grabbed my purse off the cabinets, the red light was flashing on my cell phone. I reached across my desk and saw that I had a voicemail message left by Avery.

I stood there for a quick moment, holding on to my phone like I was standing at a crossroad. Should I return his call and relay my sentiment of love and excitement that I was experiencing earlier or should I just walk away and ignore the message like I never saw it. Zoric was here... and now... and standing outside my office building waiting for me to return. I had to go... I had to ignore it.

We arrived at Acacia on W. Cary St. It's been since the days of newness in our relationship that we've eaten here. I had to ask him, "What's the special occasion," as he parked in front of the tall steep steps leading into the converted mansion?

He reached over and locked his fingers around my hand that rested intensely tight in my lap. I watched his answer empty from his mouth when he stated, "Because I love you... that's all."

My eyes were at a blank stare even after he had risen out of the car. I felt numb and unaware that he had opened my car door. "Baby, do you want the waiter to take our order from the car... or do you want to go inside with me," Zoric motioned, as he waited for me outside my door.

I snapped out of my daze and stepped out of the car. Once we were seated, I knew I needed a quick hard drink. "Rum and Coke, please," I answered to the white waitress with a Jennifer Aniston resemblance.

"Rocqui... don't you think it's a bit early for Rum and Coke," Zoric puzzling asked?

"I know. It is early. But I figured a few drinks could help me unwind from stress that I've been feeling lately. It seems like I have a lot to do and little time to do it all."

"Well, yeah you do... I mean, you are driving back and forth from here to Fayetteville and taking care of your mother. You are trying to run a business and keep me happy at the same time. I say that's plenty."

With the last words he spoke, I felt like I needed two drinks. Fear of incriminating myself, I kept my lips pursed while forming a half smile. But, he proceeded, "You are an incredible woman, Rocquelle. And I'm glad you are in my life."

With the arrival of my drink, my confidence started to build and I relaxingly ask, "Tell me... how do you know I am the one?"

He took a short swig of his apple martini and answered very surely, "I knew you were the one the day I bumped into you at the bookstore."

I shook my head in disbelief. "Come on now... It's been four years between us. I'm even wearing your engagement ring... See?" I twinkled my fingers before his face that encircled his diamond engagement ring.

He chuckled. "I'm serious. When you and I had that moment on the floor trying to gather all of those heavy ass books, I looked into your eyes and knew that you belong to me. Why do you think I kept bumping into you around campus?"

This time after he relayed his feelings of endearment, I knew I had to get drunk. So, I ordered another drink.

Zoric, frowning at my awkward behavior, pointed out that, "If you keep drinking like that, you won't be able to go back to work."

"Maybe, I shouldn't." A sip from the second glass felt like something was literally punching me in the chest.

"I know that we've been busy lately... and kinda distant. But, I don't want us to forget about us. I'm excited about the day when you meet me at the end of the aisle and promise 'I do'."

Now, I was easily drunk. My emotions set hauntingly at the tip of my tongue. I opened my mouth and "Zoric, I've made some bad decisions" spilled out.

Before the hole that I had begun to dig for myself, could get any much bigger, he interjected. "We've all made mistakes. People make mistakes. But, there is no mistake about how I love you."

His words were killing me softly. At that point, I felt like throwing a rope around my neck and hanging myself. But, instead, I kept drinking more and eating less of my grilled salmon.

"Did you ever pick out a dress to wear tomorrow night to the ball," he asked as his fork picked over his grilled zucchini?

"Yeah…And it's blue." I reluctantly shared.

"See what I mean. We are perfect together. You knew exactly what I wanted. Just like I know exactly what you want," he implied, as I watched his hand reached into his pocket. He raised in front of me a small black velvety box.

My fork dropped to my plate as my heart hit the floor. I couldn't extend my arms to reach for it, even though he held it over my plate. The box was so small, yet larger than life. I couldn't take my eyes away from it. "I don't know what to say."

"You don't have to say anything. This is just a simple thank you for helping me get my tux. I know you didn't have to. But I appreciate that you did. Here, take it," he insisted.

Finally, I did. My fingers trembled as I lifted the top of the black velvet box. Inside, there were two glistening princess cut diamond studs. Everything around me suddenly vanished. Zoric, the couple sitting next to us and the restaurant were gone. It was just me and the studded earrings. Ironically, the image of Avery suddenly emerged right before my eyes. He was standing, patiently waiting to see what I was going to do. But, I couldn't touch him, even though I felt desperate to do so. Within a quick blink of an eye, I looked up and he was gone. But Zoric wasn't. My eyes filled with hurtful tears when I looked into his congenial face. "Do you like them," he asked?

"They are beautiful."

He placed his napkin into his plate and moved in closer towards me to pierce my ears with the 2-carat ice. His hands brushed my face so gently. When he caught my eyes, his kisses covered my lips.

He wanted to love me immediately once we were home. But I felt lost in remembering what it felt like to love him. His shirt came unbutton. My blouse drifted to the floor. His pants dropped to the floor and my skirt slid down my legs. Nothing but emptiness now filled me even though he lied naked on top of me. I was hopeless and buzzed, but understood that I couldn't continue to go on this way.

The moonlight dimmed through our sheer drapes. . And Zoric still rested tenderly on the other side of the bed. I laid awake, my eyes piercing through the darkness, pondering thoughts that would not let me rest soundly. I love Zoric. But I'm undeniably in love with Avery too. Avery excites me and caresses. He is the air I breathe. While Zoric adores me, compliments me and had asked to marry me. Zoric and I share dreams of the children we would one day have together...long slender legs, soft wavy hair, attending the best private schools, fluent in three different languages and graduating at the top of their class...maybe one of them would even become President some day. I wanted to believe in our dreams again. I wanted that feeling back when I thought of Zoric as my everything. I needed it back.

Morning had arrived fast. I got up, showered and headed out of the door to the office. The presence of the flowers captured my thoughts, periodically of the times I spent loving Avery. Then there were stolen moments when I smiled and felt him near. Bothered by constant reminders of what Avery and I could have been, I hesitantly finally decided to move the vase out into lobby on the glass coffee table.

"I think the flowers looked better on your desk," Keisha acknowledged in passing from her desk to another agent's office.

I wasn't compelled to respond to her hint but I wanted to. As she crossed my path, again returning to her desk, I sat across from her. "Keisha, I think I am on the verge of making the biggest mistake of my life."

She dropped the pen she held, on top of her paperwork and gave me her undivided attention. "What are you saying," she whispered, like I was going to disclose some secretive mission?

"I'm saying that I don't think that I should marry Zoric?"

Her mouth fell open. She braced herself before she replied, "You have to marry Zoric. Zoric is the epitome of a man. He is handsome, successful and very intelligent. Who else are you gonna marry?"

"I love Zoric, but... what if I'm not in love with him?"

"Rocqui do you hear yourself? I don't think you do. I mean, I've seen in movies about these women who meet the perfect man and do something stupid and ruin everything that they have going for themselves. But Rocqui, your life is not a movie. This is real. And I know the love you have for Zoric is real too."

"Maybe it's just cold feet, right?"

"It's gotta be. Do you know how many black women that will never get the chance to be asked by someone to marry them, during their lifetime? Too many. And the saddest part of it is I may be one of those women. So you hold on to what you got because what you got is damn near better than what most women will ever have."

I listened intently to her meaningful lecture and drifted back to my office. She was right, I decided. I have everything I have ever dreamed of. So there should be no one other then Zoric in my life.

18

Tonight was the night of the Investor's Ball. I had a one o'clock closing and a four o'clock hair appointment. I really didn't feel like meeting the phony expectations of people, hiding their true selves behind their silk lined tux, BBS cufflinks and diamond clad necklaces. All of that was exciting the first year Zoric and I attended this affair. Back then, we were just ink blocks surrounded by the likes of pointy noses and stiff collards. Our money was new and limited. And theirs were old and plenty. It wasn't an occasion in which I immediately fell into comfort. Yet, I left no questionable doubt that I was just as, sophisticated and intelligent as the company that surrounded me.

Now, I was at a status in my career in which I didn't feel compel to prove anything to anyone. I just wanted to attend this event and honor Zoric for the man he was and for his distinguished title in his career.

I was always impressively pleased with Maya's finished style of my hair. I quickly viewed my hair from different angles in the wall length mirror at my perfected sculpted bun and I was ready to begin this night.

When I arrived home, I rushed up the stairs to my room to only find Zoric already showering. His tuxedo hung neatly on the bathroom door. His sleek shine shoes waited at the side of the bed, along with his white tuxedo shirt and black bow tie.

While Zoric filled the bathroom with steam from the shower, I walked into the closet and grabbed my gown off the rack and laid it across the chaise in the dressing area. I rummaged through my dresser drawers searching for a strapless bra and matching lacy thongs, to wear. Or maybe I should grab a girdle, I considered. I did grab that dress off the rack without trying it on, I remembered. Like my mother always tease, "It aint like you're gonna be a size six forever". She insists that after my first child was born, my body would transform into a more womanly figure, with curvier hips and thighs, rather than the youthful fit I now embodied.

Lately though, I haven't been feeling like a size six. In certain clothing, I noticed a more snug fit around my waist than before. I'm sure it's only bloating or slight water retention that I carry. But, I began to question as I stood before the ceiling to floor mirror, how would that extra weight fill out my dress. I stepped out of my skirt and pulled my top over my head, being careful not to mess up my hairdo.

I stood before the mirror and posed with my hands grasping my hips. Slim waistline…check! I turned around with my back towards the mirror and tilted my butt upwards. Nice firm booty…check! I released by bra strap and cupped my size Cs with the palm of my hands. Full plump breasts… check! I was rather pleased with what I saw.

I still got it, I concluded from my self-evaluation. I reached down to grab my gown that I laid across the chaise and made a few steps forward to get dress in the other room. I had almost stepped out into the bedroom, when Zoric's blackberry that was once hidden under my gown, now lit up like a beacon. First thing I noticed was that his phone was on silent. Now why would his cell phone be on silent? That in itself sparked a curious mine to discover more. Or was I feeling a tinge of insecurity. Should I have room to be suspicious? I probably wouldn't be if it wasn't for the fact that I have been busy with my own secrecies.

However, at this point, my manner of dishonesty was irrelevant to his cell phone glowing distinctly, as if it was summoning me to see what had really been going on in his world without me. I didn't ever want to live with someone whom I had to check their pockets, questioned their in and outs and whereabouts. I believed that I was more worthy of sneaking and stealing their cell phone when they were not looking or even taking a shower to try to find out the things they wouldn't tell me. I had those thoughts while my dress hung within my folded arms, without any subtle movement from my body.

And I then I conceived that I will never become that woman, at least, not after I take this one look. Then I vowed to myself that I will never look again.

I quickly retraced my steps back towards the chaise and settle my behind on the edge of the chair. Nervous...why should I be nervous, I pondered, as my fingertips moved swiftly across the palm-size screen towards discovery? And there it was smaller than an eye glass lens, yet bigger than the world that I'd imagine. Everything that I didn't want to know.

It read *Hey baby. I know she is going to be with you. But, I'm gonna try to hand over your watch you left at my house whenever you appear to be free. Can't wait to see how handsome you are gonna look.* From Julia. Who is this Bitch 'Julia' with all of her boldness and disgracefulness that had interfered on my dreams and my promises that he had given me.

And there were more. I skimmed through every text that noted the name 'Julia' underneath it. My fingers impelled through their secrets to read all of their 'I love you', 'I miss you' and 'I want you'. And even 'she will never love you the way I love you' that she and him have exchanged. I couldn't stomach anymore. I read too much. But, I hadn't seen everything.

There were pictures, just a simple touch away that identified the name to the face. Immediately, I knew who she was. She was the legs in front of Zoric's desk. She was the woman outside the restaurant that I thought I mistakenly saw Zoric with. She was the arm that bumped into me at the golf tournament. The text that Zoric wrote, that I strangely received in Fayetteville was intended for her. She was every bit the skank hoe that I perceived her to be, with a pair black lace panties all twirled up in between her ass. There was even a picture of her, knee deep in the bath tub with lathered soap glossing over her naked body. However, nothing shocked me more than the picture of her red fingernails gripping her satin panties to the side unveiling her tapered bush for his eyes to see. Her legs were parted so wide I could have seen her heart beating from her insides.

The rage that fired inside of me could have launched an automatic warfare. While, Zoric showered totally oblivious to my detection, I could have ripped him to shreds with my claws. But, I thought rationally and calmly. My mother had always said before, there is always more than one way to skin a cat. And I couldn't wait to fry up this p.....

Quickly, I dropped the phone on the chaise and began remembering the lie he told me. This Mother' led me to believe that the watch that I had bought him for his birthday was in the shop. But, instead he left it accidentally over that Bitches' house. She had deserved an ass-whooping from me for a long time and I think tonight might be the night she gets it.

The shower abruptly ended and I could hear Zoric motioning out of the shower and drying off. Alarmingly, I rushed out of the room and ran off into the other bathroom, before he was ever aware that I was there.

I pressed my hands firmly against my tight chest to steadily hold on to each rigid breath of air that escaped me. My body was fused with fiery and range. My life stood still, as I tried to conceive what was really happening to me.

I couldn't erase the reflection of hurt that now painted my face. The random late night meetings and the all day of absence from home came to be about another woman. And to add, she had in her possession, a three thousand dollar watch I bought for him.

This type of discovery makes a woman want to do things beyond reason to another human soul. The nerve of her to go about her business thinking that she doesn't have to answer to anyone for her reckless behavior. She just doesn't know that tonight isn't gonna be the night she had hoped for.

I cried a little as I stood under the shower. Hurtful feelings that I had long buried from Curtis Jackson began to stir in the pain I now held.

Curtis and I grew up together. He lived just a few streets over. For the most part, he was just like the other little aggravating boys growing up that use to tease me and pulled my hair. By high school however, he had convinced me that I needed a boyfriend. And that he was the one for the job. By then, he had filled out nicely and was impressively cute. So, I believed that there was some truth in his disposition. I loved him deeply and honestly for two years, like most young love. Until one day I drove up on the sight of him leaning up against his car, with his arms straddled around another girl's shoulder. Their bodies were sandwiched together as if the idea of me loving him was obsolete.

With every pucker, she swallowed up his kisses and held onto his body like he belonged to her. No matter how much it pained me to sit there and watched her rob me from every thing I had hoped for, I couldn't motion myself to move. A part of me wanted to recklessly run up on her and scratch her eyeballs out. And then there was the other part of me that hated me for loving him. It was like I was standing in front of my yard watching my house burn down. You want to do something. You should do something. But, in actuality, there is nothing you really could do. What's gone is gone.

Those happily ever after pages turned and ended like a childhood love story... never to be read again. Curtis arrived at my front door, all cool and casual on our graduation party from high school. Since, my family adored him like a welcoming son they had planned a big party for the two of us. I didn't know what to say to him the weeks that led up to our graduation. When I had asked him about that *girl*, he lied easily, as if he had prepared perfectly for that very moment. "Nah Baby. That was my cousin." Being young and dumb made me want to believe him, so I did.

Yet on the day of our graduation, when the gift bag and balloons arrived in his hands, I was a fool no more. Never did he anticipate me to be emotionally strapped and ready to do battle when I met him on my doorsteps.

"We did it Baby! We are graduates! Can you believe it?" His mouth stretched from ear to ear full of excitement. "You looked beautiful...Now we can start our future together the way we always talked about it."

When he stood before me at his very best I had ever seen him, I did not know who he really was. That very moment felt as real and honest to me as the day I sat there in my car watching him love all over that girl.

Suddenly I realized that I did not want to go another day feeling uncertain and scared about loving him, when he obviously did not know how to love me back.

A troubling frown appeared across his face, when he began to take noticed of my nonchalant response. "Rocqui, are you okay? What's the matter? You were happy earlier. What's wrong?" This time, he reached out to touch my hands, but I snatched my hand away from his gentle pull.

"What's the matter with you, Rocqui," he demanded?

My royal blue graduation gown still hung over shoulders, while I stood stiffen by his shameful presence. I finally felt compelled to say what I need to say three weeks ago. "There is nothing wrong with me Curtis, besides the fact of me loving you."

"What are you talking about now?" The octave in his voice heightened. "I told you weeks ago, that what you saw is bullshit. She is just my cousin."

"Looking at you right now, on my daddy's steps holding up those lame ass balloons and pretending to love me is bullshit. And I don't have room in my life anymore for any type of your bullshit."

"You gonna throw all of this away between us over some shit you thought you saw?" His words implied stupidity on my part.

So I tossed back, "Yeah. Just like you should throw that fake ass present away that you're holding in your hands."

"Aight then. But you're gonna be calling me tomorrow wanting me back." Curtis voice was heightened with enough anger to cause my daddy to appear behind me and asked 'Curtis, is everything alright', in an assertive matter that implied that this business between us was over?

"Yeah Dad. Everything is alright. Curtis was just leaving." My words were final, even though my heart was hurting.

Curtis turned around with the white balloons floating above his head and got into his car and left.

After Curtis, I promised myself that the next time I love, it will be for real and forever. When I met Zoric, the timing felt right. My heart was opened and ready. Yet, once again I have found myself again standing on the steps at my daddy's house feeling this same kinda way, I did then.

"Honey, are you almost ready," Zoric yelled outside the bathroom door?

Trying to compose myself, as much as I could, I answered, "I'll be out in a few."

I anticipated seeing her walk up to him, while I'm at the bar or something and secretly hand over the watch without my watchful eyes. Then what was I gonna do next? Inside of me there was so much fight in me, I was ready to take on the world and win. But, that's not really who I am. That's not who my mother raised me to be. How was I gonna handle myself tonight now, after all that had been unveiled to me? I really didn't know. However, no matter how the situation presents itself, I was going to try to keep myself as well composed as I possibly could. I am a well respected professional in Richmond. I was quite sure I was going to be in the midst of some of my colleagues and clients. So, I had to remind myself to be professional.

I stalled in my completion of getting dressed, often having interruptions of sorrow and disbelief. I forcefully made up my face and masked the confusion and stinginess I know felt, before meeting Zoric at the bottom of the stairs.

Even though I nearly hated him then, I couldn't deny how handsome he looked awaiting near the front door. His tall stance was all decked out in the black tux that I had purchased. When his eyes focused on my appearance swaying down the stairs, he looked at me like he was seeing me for the first time, with glazing eyes and white sparkling teeth. His thoughts were at a distance from the disturbances that had now plagued my thoughts and the pain I felt. "You look so beautiful," he serenade, just before his lips softly graced my blushed cheek.

"Thank you," my voice steady replied, trying not to disclose the hate and anger that had now taken possession over me.

He stopped and intensely stared at me, before opening the front door. With his brows pulled tightly together, he inquired, "What's the matter? Are you okay," he questioned, noticing the stillness along my face?

"I'm fine. At least I will be," I conveyed, biting back the distaste of hurt and anger that lingered in my mouth.

The drive to the Doubletree Hotel was quiet. When the maitre'd opened the door for me, I found something of a smile and plastered it across my scorn face. Fictionally, I became the happiest person that anyone had ever seen. I drew my shoulders up and sucked in my breath, as we entered arm and arm through the grand doors of the main ball room...passing through the pretentious admirers decked out in their tuxes and gowns. Their faces were all aglow with luxuries and richness tapering their bodies. Yet none of them carried the face of Julia. My eyes scanned the entire area of the ballroom in search of her, with my right hand tightly clinched into a fist. But there were no sighting of her just yet, even though Calvin and Ciantra quickly noticed us.

"What's up Zoric," Calvin cheery voice spoke trying maintained a steady tone?

"Hi Girl. I love your dress." I praised Ciantra's peach flowy gown.

"You look beautiful also. If your dress was white, it would be the perfect wedding dress," she romantically beamed at her conspicuous gesture.

The fake smile, I exchanged, hid what I was really thinking what she could do with a wedding dress right now.

"I tell you what, my man... we have the best looking women in this place," Calvin conceited.

"I second that my brother," Zoric agreed. They exchanged a brotherly fist pound. Zoric excused us from their presence and gently tugged my fingers towards the dance floor.

Thoughts of mistrust and deceitfulness were concealed as I swept the floor, dancing and twirling, in my newly purchased Jimmy Choos. I anxiously awaited the meeting of her. I wondered, as Zoric pulled me close into his chest, where was she? Was she at that very moment, watching us from a distance with envious eyes? And what would I say or do if she comes in arms reach of me? I didn't want to come off derange and out of control. So, I coached myself to keep cool, Rocqui. You are the bigger woman, I reminded myself.

Before I could go beyond any more thoughts in my head, I had to first to get beyond the throbbing pain my ankles now feel from dancing around in these heels. I couldn't stand it any longer. My feet felt like they were crumbling right from under me.

"Zoric, I have to sit down for a minute," I admitted.

"Are you okay," he spoke with concern.

"Yeah, I'll be fine. I just need to sit down for a minute." With all the coolness I had left, I tried to disguise my impetuous limp I made towards our table. Zoric, I left idolizing and falsifying, surrounded by a pool of black suites. Once I settled in my chair, I looked down at my pulsating perfectly manicured red painted toenails to release the strap that was restraining pressure from around my ankle. Carefully, I removed the left sandal from my throbbing foot. A cool 'aah' seeped from my lips.

I needed a waiter for a drink. But, they were out of my proximity of my table, circling around only those that were closer to the bar or chattering within a circle of acquaintances. My ailing feet weren't going anywhere. I tried waving one waiter down, but he dismissed my signal like I was of no relative importance. Feeling frustrated, I settled back into my chair and tapped my fingers along the silk linen table until a waiter approach me along side and stated, "I'm sorry I couldn't get here sooner, but I was busy trying to serve a few other customers. Is there anything I could get for you?"

My heart fluttered. In that quick instance when I scanned over his smooth chocolaty body, complimenting his tall manly physique, he mirrored the exactness of Avery. His spellbinding eyes glared over me, holding a silver tray with empty drink glasses and asked, "Would you like a drink ma'am. I braced my heart, with pressure from my hand and stuttered, "I've changed your mind."

"You're sure. I can get whatever drink you like, if you want one," he confidently conveyed.

Boy, I thought, he even sounded like Avery. With settling nerves, I gave a quirky smile and assured him, "I'm okay."

Accepting my reply, he wandered off to other tables cleaning up empty martini and wine glasses. My solitude now resumed with clouded memories of Avery. I miss him. But those thoughts of him and I had to wait. Not tonight, especially with all that had happen.

I exhaled like I had just unzipped a tight dress from around my sucked-in waist and try insistently to relax... that was until my cell phone began vibrating inside my clutch purse. I took it out and saw that it was Tamra calling me.

"Is everything okay, Tamra? How's mom," I anxiously asked?

"Mom's fine. How are you," she asked, straight to the point?

Feeling relieved, I answered, "I could be better. What exactly do you want this time, Tamra?"

"Gosh, you don't have to sound all snappy. I just wanted to know if you have talked to Avery lately."

"No, I have not. Not that it's any of your business. Look, if you called me to give me your speech on life and love, I'm not interested in hearing it right now."

"What's the matter with you? You sound like something's wrong."

"Everything's wrong right now," I belted out, with tears streaming down my face.

"What happened? Did Zoric do something to you?" Her voice had peaked with intensity.

"No! I mean, yes!" My boohoos were starting to grasp the attention of other's round me.

"You know, it aint nothing for me to be up there in a hot minute. Especially for Zoric's ass. I've been wanting to smash him in his face for a long time."

"Will you just shut up and leave me alone right now. I'm busy"

"I'm not gonna do that until you tell me what's wrong. And you better tell me fast before I start looking for mom's car keys."

Realizing that I my voice was starting to sound louder than the live band, I rose up from my chair and grabbed the hem of my dress, while holding one shoe in my hand and hopped on my aching foot to the bathroom swiftly. "Okay Tamra. I just found that Zoric has been cheating on me all this time."

"And..."

"What do you mean *and*?"

"I mean what I said. You are acting like you have just been run over by a bus. What do you think was gonna happen when you decided to get involved with the campus hoe?"

"Really Tamra. This is exactly what I need to hear from you right now."

"I'm just telling you how I feel. If I was you, I would wait until he falls asleep tonight and cut his thing off."

"You're sick and crazy. I can't talk to you anymore about this."

"I'm just saying. Tell Zoric don't try nothing stupid. I know where he lives."

I pressed end on my cell phone. Her words were so hurtful, yet so true. I couldn't stand to hear any more of it. My eyes began to fill with tears again. I grabbed some tissue out of the bathroom stall and forced my eyes tight to retained them from flowing freely down my cheek.

Breathe, Rocqui, I told myself. Breathe. It's too late to be crying now, child. Listening to other women merrily gather at the sink, on the other side of the bathroom door took my attention off of me and allowed me the chance to gather my composure. I slid my shoe back on my foot and I tossed my damp tissue into the toilet. I waited for a minute for the room to clear before I made my exit. I didn't want anyone to see me crying.

Yet, just as the few women who were talking just outside the stall exited, two new voices entered inside. Damnit! I placed a toilet sheet cover on over the toilet and sat back on it and waited for the voices to disappear. I was listening to their conversation until I heard one of the women say Zoric's name. Immediately, I jumped up and stood at attention to hear more.

"I can't stand it any longer to see Zoric standing there pretending to be all happy with her. He was happier with me," the first voice spoke.

The second voice agreed. "I know, right. And you look so much better than she does...But don't worry about it. He already told you that she is gonna be here for another week. And then she is rolling out again to North Carolina. And what the hell was she over there crying about?"

"I know right. She already looked stupid thinking her man is all hers."

"Where you able to give him his watch back?"

" No. Too many people have been standing around him. I got it though right here in my purse. I'm gonna save it for later when he drops her off." As soon as I heard those words, I widened the bathroom door and looked at this Bitch with disturbing eyes. Everything ugly I'd ever thought of about her stood before me at that very instance. Finally she was just a breath away from me, lining her lips with lipstick and wearing a blue dress... just like mine.

My warm blood ran cold. My widen eyes became hard. "Excuse me," I said tapping my nail into her shoulder "but that watch you have in your purse belongs to me, not Zoric. And I want it now." Her face froze with fear.

"What watch," she nervously quivered?

"The watch in your purse." Before she said anything further, I snatched her purse from off the sink. When she reached to grab it, I suddenly became someone else. I held it tightly in my hand long enough to slap her in her face a few times with it. When she tried to fight back, my hand released her purse and folded tightly into a fist. I swung with all the force I had within me upside her head. She fell lifeless into her friend's side, forcing them both to tumble to the floor. My fist intensely pulsated from the impact from her face. Everything from that moment on happened too fast before my own eyes.

When it looked like she was scrambling her way up from off the floor with the help of her friend pulling her up to strike at me, I reached down and clawed her face with my hand again and tangled my fingers into her weave, yanking with each strength I exhaled. I don't know how we ended inside one of the bathroom stalls. I had her and her friend pressed tightly against the stall, as if I was attempting to flush them both down the toilet. However,

I wasn't that strong. My fingers on the other hand, intertwined with her bracelet had somehow snapped the clip apart. The miniature diamonds instantly scattered to the floor, as I watched her face drench with despair.

The women who entered the bathroom stumbled upon the vicious fight and ran right back out only to scream for help. I heard a crowd of voices forming behind me, but I didn't see any faces.

Before I knew it, I was overpowered by the arms of a man yanking and pulling us apart. My body was lifted up in the air and tossed over the shoulders of Zoric. He rushed me out of the crowded bathroom and into the lobby. Not without a few, 'I'm gonna kick that Bitches ass' belting from my lungs and forceful kicks and heavy blows against Zoric's back.

I recklessly fell from his shoulder when he dropped me down. "What's the fucking matter with you? Do you realize what you've done?" His chest was heaving heavily in and out. His shirt was entirely distorted and hanging out of his pants.

"Do you realize what you've done," I returned, not allowing him the chance to place this blame for this situation on me?

"I can't believe that my fiancée was in the fucking bathroom fighting at this occasion around my friends and my business colleagues," he angrily expelled with emphasis on each word he spoke.

"Oh really. Well, I can't believe that all this time I've been seeing my sick mother, you have been here focused on swinging your dick with that Hoe." Heavy stares maintained on us.

"I don't know what you are talking about!"

"Is that it? That's all you got to say is 'I don't know what you're talking about' to me. Well let me tell you something. I hate you Zoric. I will never in any day of my life marry you."

He was stuck somewhere between deliberating over what all had just taken place and the last words I sternly tossed at him. His mouth seemed to have run dry. He suddenly looked confused and displaced, while I shuffled around the lobby, wondering where my clutch was. I seemed to have left it in the ballroom, I concluded.

"What are you looking for," he asked, noticing me retracing my steps.

"The fucking watch I bought you on your birthday. The one that was at the repair shop, remember? Apparently, one of the workers decided to personally deliver it to you. Wasn't that sweet of her? You can tell her I said 'thank you' when she finishes picking her face up off the floor."

I made strides toward the ballroom door, before he halted my reentrance. "Where do you think you are going," he nervously questioned, with his hand firmly gripped around my arm.

"Get your fucking hands off of me. I'm not the one you need to be worried about right now. You need to be checking on that beat down low class hoe I left in the bathroom."

He had the nerve to shush me. "Lower your voice," he insisted.

Spitefully, my voice became even louder. "You lower your damn voice," I exclaimed from the top of my voice. My hand jerked away from his hold and forced the double doors to open with all might.

Embarrassment captured my face, as I returned to the presence of many pale and perplexed faces, targeting my next intention. This irate behavior is not becoming of what my mother had raised me to be. On the other hand, she did not raise no fool either.

I casually went about my business, retracing my steps, trying to locate my silver sequin clutch. I strutted towards the bar when my eyes caught a glimpse of Calvin and Ciantra's, ghastly faces. Their startling eyes followed me like they were watching a scene from a horror movie, then I walked over by the table where I had sat earlier.

Zoric was just a foot away, trailing my every move to make sure I wouldn't resort to killing that Bitch next time. I found my purse where I left it. It was on the chair next to where I had sat earlier before Tamra called. I grabbed it and gracefully exited through the ballroom doors, with all the dignity I had left and Zoric still stumbling behind me into the lobby.

"We will talk about this tomorrow," he tried to downplay the catastrophe that had just occurred.

"You can talk it over with her because I don't have anything else to say to you."

I tucked my clutch tightly under my bare arm and staggered outside the building to wave down a taxi.

The first thing I did when I entered through my front door was kicked off those tormenting shoes and massaged my throbbing feet, on the steps of my stairway... Then, I raced upstairs to my room, locked the bedroom door and bellyached in tears the rest of the night.

19

My right arm felt like it was embedded in cement, as I tried to extend my hand over to reach for the ringing phone. I was sore and nearly paralyzed to move. Each subtle movement in my arms and legs made me groan with pain. I still couldn't believe after all the years of my life of never even having to raise my hand at another person I have found myself in a shameful demeaning brawl with another woman...over a man.

My eyes were too sore to open from the unrelenting flow of tears all night long to open. My face was buried tightly under the blanket and pillows that covered my bed as my hand gripped around the phone. "Hello," I moaned.

"Whoa! You must have had a long night last night, the way you sound," Keisha echoed and sounded overly energetic.

"You wouldn't believe what kinda night I had last night, because I still can't," I reluctantly admitted.

"Well, it's Saturday. And we have an hour and a half drive ahead of us. So, wake up!"

"I can't get up. I'm in too much pain," I whined.

"For fifteen to twenty thousands dollars, you do," she replied.

I finally revealed my eyes to the hint of sunlight that pierced through my open blinds. I looked over at the clock that read eight o'clock. Then my eyes glanced towards my nightstand and I wondered why my cell phone wasn't in its normal place. Damn. I must have left it in the bathroom at the hotel, I concluded.

"I've almost forgotten. We are driving to Virginia Beach today, to help Andrew Spencer find a vacation home." I was numb. I didn't want to see the light of day. I didn't have any desire to get dress and be apart of society, especially after my embarrassing disorderly conduct last night. All I wanted to do was lie here in bed and wait. Wait for happiness to arrive again in my life and the actions of my behavior to become a distant memory. And it didn't matter how many days it took, just as long as it got here. Because today was not the day.

However, the thought of loosing an opportunity to make money was not quite sensible either, especially since it's been almost two months since I have sold a house. Using work as a distraction would probably benefit me more so than wallowing in my sorrow.

"I have to go by the hotel on my way to your house. I think I lost my cell phone. Give me about an hour or so."

"Cool. I will be ready." We ended the call.

I slowly stepped into the shower. Before long, I was throwing together what looked to be decent outfits and zipped them inside my luggage.

Reluctantly, I unlocked my bedroom door and opened it slowly, hoping not to deal with the issues of Zoric today. I really hoped that he didn't think that I was playing when I told him not to bring his black ass home last night. But he didn't. As soon as I trekked down the stairs, with my suitcase next to me, I came in view of his leisure along the mahogany leather sofa, still dressed in the tux he wore last night.

I spotted my cell phone on the dining room table as I entered into the kitchen. He must have found it after all the commotion had died down and brought it home. How considerate, I hatefully thought. I sensed him motioning in my direction where I was standing, fixing a cup of coffee. Looking down at my luggage, parked next to the breakfast bar, he asked, "Where are you going?"

I continued to mind my business, hoping that he would do the same.

"You're not talking to me?"

"I don't really have shit to say to you. Everything I have to say has been said, already," I reminded him, waiting on the coffee to finish brewing.

"We need to talk, Rocqui. A lot of things were said and done last night that we need to talk about."

"What?" I harshly replied.

"What do you mean 'what'?"

"What do you have to say to me, Zoric?" My voice became aggressively louder, as I turned and eyed him spitefully.

"I would like to start by saying that you've accused me wrongfully. I have not been sleeping with that woman." His words stammered slowly from his lying parting teeth.

"That sounds really nice and well rehearsed. Now if you don't mind, I have other things to do rather than listen to this bullshit that you are trying to feed me."

"Why didn't you just come and talk to me about what was on your mind, rather than meeting her in the bathroom and causing a senseless display of ignorance and jealousy?"

"If you think my beating her ass was over jealously, than you're the dumbest man I ever known...You disgust me Zoric. I would have never imagined in a million years that you would stoop so low. You probably brought her here to our house."

"I swear to you Rocqui, on everything, she has never step a foot inside this house." He convincingly pleaded.

"Oh yeah. Well, can you also swear that you've never slept with her too?"

I studied his shameful face as it drop towards the floor. "That's what I thought." As I stared at him tensely, I realized that he was still dressed in the tux that I had to abruptly end my perfect plans with Avery to go rescue his 'no good lying ass'. I despised the sight of him wearing it. "You know what I want you to do for me?"

"What?"

"Take off **My** damn tux!"

"What," he sharply repeated?

"**Take Off My Damn Tux**." I repeated myself this time enunciating each word specifically.

"You can't be serious."

"I'm dead ass serious," I finished, with my hand on my hip and the tight shift in my neck.

"I'm not taking off a damn thing!"

"Oh, okay. Then give me my twelve hundred dollars that I paid for it in order for you to wear it."

"You have lost your damn mind, you know that," he replied hotly. Yet, he slowly stepped out of his pants. He pulled his jacket off and laid his shirt over the rest of his things in my hand.

He was standing wearing only his silk boxers and black socks. "What you gonna do with it," he asked?

"Burn it," I retorted after grabbing a garbage bag, from the bottom cabinet and tossing it inside.

"I can't believe this. You are actually for real, aren't you? You want me to take all the blame for this whole situation and play along in your little world like you've been so innocent and honest. And all this time, your trifling ass have been creeping with someone else too."

He had me stumped. His eyes bored into me, as I timidly gazed towards him. "What are you talking about," I asked, skeptical of what he might add?

"Come on, Rocqui. You thought I was *stupid*. Who in the *hell* sent you the flowers the day I arrived at your office, huh? Keisha obviously thought they were from me." He condescendingly laughed. "And I just stood there, surprised as hell. Damn near floored, playing along with your little silly love game." His face was burning hot, as his husky voice continued to escalate. "Do you know how stupid I felt? And let's not omit the mysterious cell phone calls that you all of a sudden could not answer and the texting you thought you were being all secretive about. You didn't know that I already had your shit all figured out, did you?"

"Thank you for reminding me about that whole cell phone issue," I retorted with just as much anger in my voice, as he held. "I really appreciated when I was away in Fayetteville, receiving a text from you that you were trying to send to that Bitch! How do you think that made me feel... just as stupid as you!"

Our voices were high, filled with emotions and intensity, as we both tried to out talk and out yell one another. There was a moment of silence when the exchange of fire between us had temporarily ceased. I couldn't bear to look at him. His eyes looked away from me, as they found a resting place against the burnt orange painted wall.

"Where do we go from all of us this?" His voice softly posed.

"I don't know. I don't want to do this right now." Looking at the time, I realized that I was on the verge of being late.

Calmly he announced, "I just want you to know that I really do love you Rocqui. And I don't want us to end. We could squash all of this, if you could just tell me who he is Rocqui. I think that's important enough so that we can move on from this situation," he insisted on knowing?

My mannerism quickly returned to anger. "You know what, it doesn't really matter who he is. What matters is that you are not who I thought you were." I grabbed my keys off the dining table, along with my cell phone. I maintained the garbage bag in my hand and tightly gripped the handle of my luggage, with my other hand. With it in tow, I stormed out the front door leaving behind the echo of a slammed door. I was so anxious to escape from Zoric's presence, that I unintentionally left my coffee mug on the kitchen counter. Damn.

I waited outside Keisha's apartment complex, in my car, for her to bring her things down the stairs and load up the car. My head continued to throb. A range of motions flowed in and out my mind. For a minute, I wanted to be mad at Keisha for running her mouth about those damn flowers to Zoric. But, deep down I knew it wasn't her fault. It was Zoric's fault for being trifling and thinking I was a fool. It was my fault for believing in such fairytale bullshit! No. It was all that Bitches fault for not knowing who she was messing with. The nerve of her calling me stupid.

Zoric sounded almost convincing about not ever having her in our house. But, once a cheater is also a liar. And he probably lied about that too.

"Good morning" Keisha spoke after she loaded the trunk with her bags and sat in the driver's seat.

"What's up with that trash bag in the trunk of your car?"

"Good morning," I answered barely eyeing her directly in her face. "Oh gosh, I almost forgot I had that in there." I sat up quickly skimming the parking lot for a place to dump the tux. "Is that your apartment complex dumpster over there?"

"Yeah, why? Are you okay?" Keisha stared at me strangely as I got myself together and got out of the car.

When I returned to the car from heaving the trash bag into the oversized dumpster, I noticed Keisha's eyes studying me like I was alien from another planet. "Oh my Gosh! You look horrible. What was in that bag you threw away," she asked like she had reasons to be worry?

"Just trash," I answered, hopefully to relieve her from her concern. "Do I really look that bad," I asked as I pulled the sun visor down and noticed the redness and puffiness in my eyes?

"Yeah. But it's nothing that a tall Latte can not cure," she concluded, before driving off.

Along our trip to Virginia Beach, Keisha disappeared from my current state of mine. I occasionally tune into the lyrics and rhythm of Mary J., but was often lost in my destitute of pain and sorrow. Some where along the way, Keisha spotted a Starbucks and pulled over to buy us both some coffee, I placed mine in the cupholder next to hers, untouched. The last thing I desired was a stimulant to keep the imagines of Zoric and that Bitch from reappearing in my mind. I leaned my head to the side and closed my eyes, until we arrived at our destination.

We arrived at the Courtyard by Marriot, in Virginia Beach, about ten. I estimated that we had at least two hours to settle down and relax before Mr. Spencer arrived. Once we checked in, I went up to my room and applied make-up to my pathetic face. Keisha called me and suggested that we eat something before he arrived. I met her downstairs, momentarily, in the hotel restaurant at the Ocean Grille.

Lacking much of an appetite, I just ordered coffee.

"You still are not hungry," Keisha wearily asked, after she ordered a full size breakfast?

"Not really. I just have a lot on my mind, right now," I replied.

"I'm not use to seeing you this way. You always seem to have everything in its perfect place."

"I guess. Looks can often be deceiving."

"Well, that may be true. But, I really admire you. You have everything I want... the successful business, a beautiful home and a handsome fiancé. What more could a person want?"

I was beginning to feel like Keisha was forcing me to have a conversation that I did not want to openly share. I told myself to keep my answers simple and short, but when I opened my mouth, my words flow like a roaring stream. "I use to share that same foolish thought. I wanted to believe, for so long, that I'd found my prince and that he would always be the man that I'd wanted him to be. But, maybe the glass slipper that I tried to squeeze into is really someone else's shoe that I'm trying to wear."

"I know you are not going to tell me that fairytales do not come true. I am not gonna give up my prince charming showing up one day on a white horse and lifting me up on his saddle to carry me off into the sunset."

"Girl, there is nothing in those fairytale books that prepare you for real situations. I mean..." I felt a little embarrassed to say, yet relieving... "I had to beat a Bitch down last night."

"What," she worriedly gulped?

I nodded.

"I can't believe it. What happened," she captivatingly pressed for more information?

"Let's just say that Prince Charming aka Zoric was not sitting up at night, alone waiting for me to fill my glass slippers. He had some other skank ho' from the town village to keep him occupied."

"Nooooo," she crooned.

"Yes. That damn Cinderella has all of our minds fucked up... (Laughter) believing in glass slippers, horse and carriages and forever after. I'm at the point in which I'll buy my own glass slippers and ride off in my own horse drawn carriage, alone."

"I still can't believe it," she continued to utter in total disbelief.

"You know what bothered me the most? It wasn't so much that Zoric cheated on me. It was more of the fact that *SHE* had no respect for herself and certainly none for me. I had to give her a quick class on it in the bathroom at the hotel.. She deserved to be punished. And if I ever catch her ass on the street, I will punish her again."

"Wow...You really are a Rocky."

I chuckled.

"What are you gonna do now," she inquired?

"I don't know. I'm kinda glad that I am here and he is there. Because right now, I can't stand the sight of him."

"I don't blame you, at all. I wouldn't put up with any shit like that either."

I couldn't help myself from laughing at her now over dramatized composure. "What ever happens would be for the best for both of us."

"I get the fact that life is not perfect. But, I know its gotta be better than living paycheck to paycheck each month and going out to those lame ass clubs every Friday night and listening to the same ole tired ass lines."

I laughed. "It might be a little better than that. However, I really don't know. I'm still trying to figure my life out, just like everybody else. I guess we are all trying to be happy. And sometimes we try to find it, in all the wrong places... In the club, in our clothes, in our man. And when we find it there, we still, sometimes, feel incomplete."

"Well, I rather be incomplete and have money, than to be incomplete and be broke as hell, like I am now. "

We both laughed.

My cell phone rang.

"Hello, Mr. Spencer," I answered.

"Hello Rocquelle. I'm standing here inside the Quality Suites Hotel, getting checked in. Have you arrived here, yet?"

"Yes. I am staying at the Courtyard Marriot. My assistant and I are having breakfast before we meet up and start house hunting. "

"Okay, great. It's gonna take me an hour to get situated. How about you two enjoy your breakfast and I will meet you all there in about an hour."

"Sounds goods."

"Well, I will see you then."

After an exchange of a few moments in laughter and words, my depression subsided and I actually regained a bit of an appetite. I'd taken a couple bites a croissant with butter and eaten a bowl of fresh fruit, when Andrew Spencer entered into the restaurant.

"Here comes the little white man," Keisha pointed out.

My head turned and I saw him exactly as Keisha described him as. Short, with a narrow frame along with gentle blue eyes and cropped blonde hair. But, I added, "Little white man, with A Lot of money."

"Hey ladies," he spoke, looking like he just step out of a jcrew magazine.

"Hello," we harmonized in sinc.

"Did you ladies have a great breakfast," he asked after sitting down at the table between Keisha and me?

"I am nicely full," Keisha answered.

"I've had enough as well. Would you like to order something," I asked?

"No thanks. I grabbed something from Starbucks before I got here."

"Okay. Well... lets go find you a weekend getaway," I suggested, grabbing my purse and then reaching for the ticket.

Spencer took the ticket out of my hand and implied, "I got this. Breakfast is on me, since you all had to sit and wait until I arrived."

"I can't let you do this, Mr. Allen. It's just twelve dollars," I added.

"Exactly, it's just twelve dollars. I will be right back," he concluded before walking up the cashier to pay for our breakfast.

"You know what? Lil white man is kinda cute," Keisha pointed out with a glow reflecting in her eyes.

"Girl, money would make anyone look good. But he is sort of cute, I guess," I replied, observing him from a side view, while he stood at the counter and paid for our ticket.

He returned back to us, laid a $5.00 bill on the table and asked, "Are we ready to go?

We visited several different sites. The homes were either too big or too small or way of out his asking price. There were moments when I had fallen back into my state of solitude and Keisha immediately stepped in and went over the details of some of the homes, keeping Spencer entertained with her flirtatious sales pitch.

The last home we visited was a newly built all brick condo. He was impressed by the outside interior from the driveway. We stepped into the living room that had a wide open living space. Standing in the center of the floor allows your view to continue straight through the kitchen. Keisha took the lead and led him through the main level master suite with Jacuzzi and lower level media/entertainment room. I was pleased to see the golfing course right outside his French patio door. I stood parallel to the patio door, quietly looking beyond the greenery and the tall aged trees.

I reached into my purse to check for any missed calls on my phone. There were none. There wasn't a call from Tamra, my mom or even Avery. Deep down inside I'd hope that Avery would have called me by now. A simple *hey* would have suffice. It's been too many days that haven't heard from him. I wondered where he might be at this very moment. I wondered if he still smiled when he thought of me, as I now displayed. I was missing him. I needed him. But, my sentiments are probably a little too late. Trying to have it all has left me with nothing.

"I think I have a new condo," Spencer joyfully implied, returning from downstairs.

"You like it, even though it's not furnished," I asked seeing his enthusiasm sparked across his face,?

"Well, Keisha made me realize that it could actually be more fun than I imagined. Especially if I could enlist some of her decorative ideas."

I looked over at Keisha, who was blushing like a schoolgirl and wondered if they were more to this interest she has developed all of sudden to Andrew. "Well, then lets make an offer," I concluded.

After two counteroffers, Andrew finally signed on the purchase of his new condo, by nightfall. I was exhausted and relieved that the sale went through a lot faster than I'd imagined. To celebrate, Spencer offered to take Keisha and me out to dinner at a seafood restaurant. I was not enthused by the invitation, but Keisha insisted that I had to be there, since he was my client.

"Keisha, I don't know what's going on between you and Andrew, but nothing better not happen till I make commission off the sale of this house," I firmly stated while she was waiting for me to get dressed in my hotel room.

"Nothing is gonna happen. I don't even think I really like him. I mean he is kinda cute and very intelligent, but he is not really my type."

With those last words she spoke, I was reconnected with memories of Avery. I paused for a second and looked in the mirror at myself. Loneliness reflected through the metallic sable eye shadow and the 'onyx' mascara that curved my lashes. My 'bronze lights' lips outlined in a light brown pencil were folded into sadness.

"Are you okay," Keisha asked noticing a sudden change in my demeanor through the mirror?

"Yeah, I'm fine."

"Are you sure you want to go? You could stay here. I promise I will be well behaved," she assured me.

"That Kool-Aid smile, you are showing, tells me differently. Now, I know I have to go and keep my eyes on you." I finished up my make up and we exited the hotel to meet Spencer at Lynnhaven Fish House.

I was feeling a bit hungry and the impressive atmosphere of oceanic blue walls and dark wood paneling stirred up my appetite, even more so. But, instead of my tastebuds becoming aroused at the arrival of my lobster tail, with melted butter on the side, my stomach all of a sudden began to feel quizzy and ill. I tried to act as if I was fine, surrounded by Keisha and Spencer. However, the deeper the aroma filtered inside my stomach the weaker and tighter it tried to fight off the scent. Until finally my stomach won. I went dashing off to the bathroom helplessly begging over the toilet for mercy. .

"Are you okay, Keisha," frightfully asked as she appeared behind me in the bathroom mirror?

"I thought I was… I don't know where that came from. I was feeling fine earlier," I answered as I tried to reconfigure my appearance.

"Do you feel well enough to stay, or do you want to go back to the hotel room," she concerningly asked?

"I don't know. I'm gonna see how the rest of the night goes, first… You're just trying to get rid of me early, so that you could have Andrew all to yourself."

"Not really", she blushingly replied. "Okay… Maybe a little bit. He is really cute. I think I like him", she happily admitted.

"I think he likes you too. He hasn't taken his eyes off of you, all night."

"I mean he is white, but he is funny and his conversation is different from any other guy I've met before."

And I went on to add, "That's because he is WHITE. And he has money. And you like the way he pulls out his American Express Card."

We laughed. "Yeah, that's appealing too. But, it's not like we are getting married, or something. We are just having a good time."

"Yeah, ok. As innocent as it may be, you still need to maintain a certain level of professionalism. Look, I don't want you to get caught up in your little schoolgirl crush until we have officially closed the deal."

"Then I can go out with him?"

Sounding like her mother, I answered, "Then you can go out with him, sleep with him and do whatever you want with him."

"That sounds exciting"

Laughter

After I recomposed myself and my mind, Keisha and I returned to our table and rejoined Andrew.

"Is everything okay," he wondered?

"Yes. I just had an unexpectant moment. I think I'm gonna nibble on these crackers to get me through the night and have them to box the rest for later," I answered.

"I certainly wish you could enjoy this lobster. It is really delicious," Andrew boasted as he savored his meal.

"It really is," Keisha concurred. I looked over at her once again and she was all smiles. The obvious attraction between them was making me feel even more nauseas. I was about to excuse myself and tell them I would meet them in the morning before checkout, when my cellphone rang.

A bit of excitement rushed through me as I searched relentlessly throughout the bottom of my handbag. Finally, my fingers encased it and I saw that it was no one other than Tamra. My emotions had easily subsided and calmingly I answered, "What's up now, Tamra? Are you calling me again to give me more advice on love?"

"Ah... Rocqui. I'm calling you to tell you that your mom is in the hospital," an unexpectant male voice relayed from the other end of the phone.

"Who is this? Is this some kinda joke. Where's Tamra," I quickly asked, as my heart began to race?

"This is Diesel, Tamra's husband. Tamra and I are at the hospital, with your mother, right now. Earlier today, your mother started throwing up. And we weren't quite sure what it was. And, then, she wouldn't get out of bed. She kept complaining of being in a lot of pain. So, Tamra and I brought to the emergency room. And that's when the doctor decided to admit her....She seems to be doing much better, now. But your sister wanted me to call you to ask you to come home."

"Why didn't Tamra call me the minute she noticed mom wasn't doing well?"

"Because, I don't think she felt that it was serious, at first... Not until her doctor decided to keep her overnight."

"Rocqui, are you still there?"

"Yes, I'm here... I'm on my way." I was stumped. I ended the call and looked over at Keisha and Andrew, who were engaged in a jovial conversation amongst themselves and announced, "I'm leaving."

"Why? You still don't feel well," Keisha worriedly asked.

"No. Not at all. I'm leaving right now to go to Fayetteville. My mother's in the hospital." Even after the words parted from my lips, I still couldn't believe I was saying it.

Andrew stepped in and directed. "You go ahead and see about your mother. Everything is a clear deal with the house and it will be my pleasure to see that Miss Keisha returns back to Richmond, safely."

I eyed Keisha sincerely, "Are you sure you will be okay?"

"Oh yeah! I will be fine," she answered more merrily than I had expected.

"Okay. I will call you and keep you posted, once I find out about my mother's condition. I took a deep breath, grabbed my keys and left in my car down Highway 165.

20

There were a few occasions, throughout my young adult's life that I thought I was grown. Thought I knew all that there was for me to know at the early age of fourteen. My chest had become bouncy and my hips had curved to define my apple bottom behind. Hello world, meet the new me. I thought I was ready.

It seemed like I was a minute or two behind everyone else, in middle school to blossom. But when I did, everyone took noticed. Even those 'nappy headed boys' as my mother would often refer to them as, starting dropping a few lines on paper and discreetly passing it on to me

School was no longer an avenue for an education. It was a place to hang out, socialize and find out who you really are. Homework wasn't the only thing that I made sure I had everyday before I went to school. The hair had to be right... my pants had to be tight. And my lips had to shine.

Boys trying so desperately to find out what girls are made of. And girls were trying eagerly to find their way. For a moment, I was flattered by the silly schoolboy games of having my booty grappled by their young curious mind. But a classmate, by the name of Monique Hargrove schooled me on the rules that separated the men from the boys. Her stories convinced me that I had arrived at the peak of maturity and no longer needed to be toyed by childish games.

Monique wasn't necessarily the type of person I normally hung out with, on any occasion. She wasn't necessarily cute or even smart. However, she embodied the mind and the shape of a grown woman. She had wide hips and big tits that gave evidence of her promiscuous mannerism. People tagged her as 'fast'. Yet, she was rather clever and smart in the way she used what she got, to get what she wanted. Her voice and her laughter automatically invoked an audience. Boys, as well as girls rallied around her like she had lived twice. And I was just as engrossed by her popularity and the immediate attention given to her by her peers.

"Those are some cute jeans," Monique floated up beside me, one day eyeing my latest trendy style. "What name brand are those," she investigated, veering her sights on my behind that tagged the popular logo.

Modesty, I answered, "Jordache." I confidently knew that they looked good on me. I anxiously tried them on ten times, with ten different tops, before the morning arise, hoping their dark rinse snug fit would attract the attention of Kadeem.

Kadeem was as cute, as the eyes I held from him. Yet, he reserved any forward attraction he may have had for me. That was until this one particular day, when he finally slipped me a note in my hand, in between class. It was the day I had been waiting for. All of the 'he say she say' had finally paid off. The note indicated that he liked me and if I liked him the same write my phone number down on that piece of paper. I thought this was it for me. He was all that life had to offer me. I was smiling as hard as my mouth could stretch, when Monique settled in a desk right beside me. Her eyes accompanied the letter that I'd openly held in my hand.

"Girl, you like Kadeem," she questioned with obvious objection in her voice?

"Yeah. I think he is cute," I answered passively.

"Well, my boyfriend has this friend that looks way better than Kadeem. And I told him about you," she frankly stated.

"You told him about me," I shyly repeated?

"Yeah. And he said he wants to me you. He is not a pee wee like Kadeem. He is real dude...and fine."

I carefully noted her last words, 'fine.' Who could possibly be finer than Kadeem, I pondered? Kadeem was tall, slightly lanky, but had the prettiest, thickest eye lashes, I had ever seen on a boy. I liked him every since the moment he sat next to me in Algebra. Yet, he wouldn't even acknowledge my presence, if the matters didn't pertain to anything other than Math. Even after I wrote my number down and returned it to Kadeem, he still resigned to his obvious shyness. Maybe, I deliberated, what Monique was saying was true. There was no other way to find out, but to see for myself.

On a spring day, she invited me into her 'fast' world, even though I was quite uncertain why. It could have been that she envied my style or my clothes or the latest kicks laced around my feet. She was always the first to express admiration for the way I dressed. Or it may have been that day, when the principal stumbled on her repeated attempts to skip school and I just so happened was there and lied to save her from getting into trouble. She acted like I had saved her life or something. Afterwards, we hung around each other like best friends.

Eyebrows raised and whispers sprayed when people observed me and my new friend. Something about the instant attention was entertaining to me. I would look for her to walk down the hallways with and waited to see all eyes on me.

I deceivingly persuaded my mother that morning that I would be riding the school bus home with Kim, my best friend. "You better be home before the streetlights come on," she ordered, as her last words before I bounced out the front door and headed off to school. However, at the sound of the of the three o'clock bell, instead of exiting to the bus lot, along with the herd of students at dismissal, I trotted along side Monique, with my book bag thrown over my shoulder, to the Corner Mart, which was the hangout spot for high schoolers, in hopes of being flattered by the mature minds of some older guys-.

It wasn't long once we had arrived standing on the corner, along side of the store, that a couple of older and appealing guys stumbled upon our young interested minds and initiated conversation with us. Monique spoke as if she had known them for years, casually and full of confidence, smiling and displaying a sense of cockiness. Often I felt lost and displaced from the dialogue that made me question my foolish presence. I was like a fish at a cattle ranch. What was I doing, I began to anxiously ponder, as my eyes darted around the busy intersection of cars, feeling lonesome and unnoticeable. I should have been home by now doing my homework. I remembered that I had an Algebra exam coming up soon. What if my daddy drives by and sees me standing here? How would I explain to him that his innocent little girl is hanging out on the street corner gloating in the faces of total strangers?

My knees buckled and my hand nervously gripped my other arm, in a childlike manner, as I recklessly tried to build up enough courage to oppose this situation. However, before, I'd announce my apprehensiveness to continue our plan, a long dark green car with tinted windows pulled up along side the curve, blurring music and a rattling bass from the speakers. Monique, without any hesitation, carrying a gentle flirtatious smile, swayed towards the car with her hands on her hips and got inside the front seat. Her lips twisted and slurped with the driver, before she had remembered that I was still standing parallel to the curve, as cemented as a statue.

Her hand waved to summons me to get in the car along with her but I stared awkwardly at her, like she was talking to someone else. 'Its okay. Nothing is going to happen to you' she promised before my feet began to slowly trek towards the car. I took one quick glimpse at the corner mart and all of its surrounding, like I may never ever see it again and got into the backseat behind her, which was shared with a guy whose colorless face was dotted with freckles.

I didn't know where we were going. I was too scared to ask any questions. My head just simply pressed against the window, looking wondrously, watching my familiar surroundings become a distant memory. The apartment complex where we'd finally arrived looked like it was built in the middle of nowhere.

Once we were all inside the compact apartment, Monique and her fellow quickly disappeared off to a back bedroom, leaving me all alone with the freckled face guy from the backseat, who appeared to be just as uncomfortable as I felt. Nervously, I sat on one end of the dingy worn-out sofa, while he sat on at the opposite end. The TV was on and I pretended to be interested in a show until freckled face guy finally stumbled on a few words to say. "I've seen you somewhere before."

"Where?" My eyes examined him, looking beyond the red dots that sprinkled his face. He wasn't bad looking. He had a reddish-brown low cut hair. His smile was soft. The appearance of stubbles over his top lip led me to believe that he was old enough to shave.

"Have you ever been to an Dunwoody High School football game before," he asked?

"I've been at every game. My brother is number forty-four," I proudly admitted.

"Your brother is Monty Johnson," he asked surprisingly?

"Yes." I chuckled, astounded by his reaction. "Do you know him?"

"No. I don't really know him. But, I've seen him around school a few times." He began to look at me observantly, like he saw something in me that wasn't there before. "Now that you mention it, you look just like him."

"That's what a lot of people say."

"Your brother has probably made the Fayetteville Times more than any other high school player I've ever know. You think he'll play in the NFL one day," he inquired?

Thoughts of my brother forced a smile along my face. "Umm, I hope so," I modestly replied.

"I've never seen you around campus. What year are you," he asked?

I hesitated for a moment, citing the fact that he was older than me. But then, I figured that he probably already knew that, being in the company of Monique and her boyfriend. I muttered to him, "I'm in Middle School."

"You are in Middle School," he loudly voiced!

His temperament caused my heart to beat fast. But I nodded, anyhow.

"I thought you were in high school. You're just a little girl", he stressed.

I felt embarrassed by his proclamation, hoping that he saw through my grade, as a minor factor.

"You have some long nice legs for a young girl," he politely asked.

"Thank you," I answered not really sure if that made sense for me to say.

"You must play basketball?" he continued calmingly. "

"Only with my brother. At school, I'm on the tennis team."

"The tennis team!" The way he answered, you would have thought I had answered him in French. I betcha you are the only black girl on team...out there trying to be like Serena or Venus Williams." He was actually humoring himself, laughing ridiculously over his own comment. The sound of his laugh made him suddenly look ugly to me.

Immediately I tossed back, "I bet I can beat you."

"No doubt. I bet you can. Give me a basketball any day and court. That's my name to fame," he felt proud to say.

"I'm just as good at basketball too," I relaxingly bragged.

"Why don't you play basketball then?"

"Because winter and spring sports overlapped, I had to choose one. I chose tennis. "

"Tennis looks hard, as hell to play. Maybe one day you could school me on a few tricks on how to play."

"Sure. But, I don't think that I would be a good teacher."

"Why not?"

My eyes cross-examined his long slender physique slouching comfortably on the opposite side of the sofa, leaning towards me. "Because you don't seem like the athletic type," I reckoned.

"I play a little basketball now and then... I'm no Monty Johnson or anything, but I can take it to the hoops and throw a pass now and then."

"If you say so." A quaint smile unfolded along my face. We both chuckled.

For a moment, when our eyes met, I felt awkwardness between us that compelled me to quickly look away.

"You have some pretty eyes." I heard him say.

"Thank You," I shyly answered, keeping my sights focused on the television in front of me.

"Do you want something to drink," he asked as he rose from the sofa and entered the kitchen?

"No. I'm okay."

He returned to the sofa with a tall glass of red Kool-Aid in an iced glass that he placed on the coffee table before us. Then he relentlessly began rattling an unopened bag of family-sized chips, until his mouth filled disturbingly with each crunch.

I wasn't thirsty, necessarily, but the sound of those chips echoing between his teeth, stirred up a hunger inside of me.

I wanted to ask him for some chips, but I didn't feel comfortable enough to eat, in a presence of a stranger. After a couple of handfuls, in which he gobbled down his throat, his manners finally made an appearance and he asked, "Would you like some chips?" Slowly, my head turned in view of the opened bag that he held out towards me.

I, gracefully, reached into the bag and grabbed as many chips that my hand could handled. "Thank you."

"You're welcome."

Words were empty between us, while our mouths were filled with the sounds of munching and crunching from the Sour Cream Chips.

"You were starting to look a little hungry," he jokingly noted.

I'd nearly choked, on the last chip I crunched, from embarrassment. "I don't look hungry."

"Yes you do," he teased. "Look." He pointed towards my face. "There's a crumb on the side of your face."

"Where?"

"Right there." He inched closer into my comfort zone, to brush his hand against my cheek. I never saw a crumb fall from my face. However, I did start to feel a little tingly feeling on the inside, when I felt his eyes resting on me this time. He, obviously, felt something too, because his lips moved in closer towards mind before they touched.

Slowly, I opened my mouth and accepted his tongue. It didn't feel as passionate, as I'd imagine it would be at first. But the longer he kissed me, the more spellbound I became. His hands slowly began to creep up my buttoned blouse. I felt like I had been hypnotized, as I allowed his fingers to gently explore unguarded territory... my breast, my nipples and even my thighs that were still concealed in the jeans that I wore.

I'd never experienced this before. *Please don't stop, my thoughts echoed.* I took full pleasure in the foreplay, allowing his lips to tickle the center of my neck and then travel down to my breast, circling slowly with his tongue, until.... He reached for the snap on my pants and pulled it apart.

A bright red light flashed in front of my eyes. That red light that intercepted his sensual persuasion, I later discovered was called 'common sense'. His interest in me did not even stretch beyond asking me for my name, let alone to assume that he could have my body. The warmth and tingly sensation were suddenly interrupted and I began to pull my body away from him.

"What's wrong," he moaned?

"I can't," I softly objected.

My words held no validity, as his fingers moved swiftly inside my pants and stroked the top of my panties.

I gripped his hand tightly and pulled his intrusive fingers away from my anatomy. This time, my words held still, when I stared deep into the intensity of his face. "I can't."

"Why not?" He frustratingly pierced into my eyes.

I could have honestly said that, I'm too young, I'm scared, I might get pregnant, and even, I don't even know your name to hand you my virginity, so easily. All were the exact reasons why. Yet, I told him, with all certainty, "cause I don't want to," even though, a few minutes ago, I did.

His shoulders fell back, disappointingly, on the sofa and I, anxiously, readjust my clothing.... Zipping up my pants and readjusting my bra. "Why are you here," he sternly asked?

"I don't know," was all I could muster up to say, regretting the fact that I was there and not at home where I should have been.

"She doesn't seem like your type of people." His words were more of a big brother, rather than of a molester.

"Who, Monique? She really isn't. She is cool, though."

"Maybe. But you seem to be on different level than she"

Deep down, I understood his words to be true. Freckle face guy, didn't pursue any further sexual contact with me the rest of the time I was in his company. Our words were short and few, as we both pretended to hide our thoughts behind a show on TV. Time steadily passed by. At a glance out the window, the tall trees began to hide the sun.

I asked him, "Do you know what time we are suppose to be leaving?"

"Nah. You want me to go ask Chris and Monique?"

"Please."

I heard him knock on the backroom door. Monique appeared before me, wearing a long t-shirt barely covering her exposed behind.

"What's up girl," she forwardly asked. "You ready to go home?"

"It's getting late. And I have to be home by eight," I pleaded.

"Well... Chris' brother took the car and said he would be back in a minute," she responded in an as-matter-of-fact manner... "Just chill out and relax. We got some beer and some cold chicken if you are hungry," she added flatly.

I searched her face in total annoyance, as she profoundly stood before me, signifying disinterest in my well being. My eyes sneered, in anguish when she turned and disappeared off to the back room. What have I gotten myself into, I tried to rationalize? Why did I ever conceive of venturing off with her, on this reckless journey? I needed a way home. But I didn't even know where to begin. There was no phone and I was totally clueless of where I was. As the sun gradually disappeared, darkness arrived and I was scared to death of never seeing my mother and my home ever again.

I grabbed my book bag, off the floor, next to the sofa and started to head towards the door. Freckled face guy asked, "Where are you going?"

I paused in my strived and looked over my shoulder. "Home," I assured him before exiting through front door. The darkness that I'd stepped into only heighten the anxiety that was now stirring inside of me. My feet drummed down the wooden steps until I landed on the base concrete floor, arriving to the openness of the parking lot and apartment doors to my left and to my right. I noticed a rubber welcome doormat at the base of one the doors, to my right. I, assumingly, took that as cue, that it included desperate lost frighten young girl, trying to find their way home.

Nervously I asked, when a white man responded to my persistent knock at his door, "Please, can I use your phone?" With my words trembling in desperation, he led me to his phone and I called home. He was quite helpful in giving me directions to where I was and I relayed it to my mother.

I waited outside, in the dark, alone sitting patiently on the harden concrete until the arrival of her headlights greeted me. There were a million things she could have said, and a million and one things she could have done to me. However, she didn't do or say anything, for weeks. She had me nervously on edge awaiting the wrath of her anger to appear. Even if I had to go outside to check the mailbox, I made the cautious decision to ask for her permission first.

I found out, once my life resumed to normalcy from Kadeem that he truly did liked me. Yet, my newfound friendship with Monique deterred him away from pursuing me any further for a potential relationship. We did eventually go out, after my friendship with Monique ended. However, just like most young impressionable minds, we were on one week and off the other. The respect that I have for my mother matured as well. Even when I began to 'test the waters' again, I knew that no matter where I was in the world, she would always find me and bring me back home again.

This time it wasn't I that needed to come home again. It was she. This time it wasn't she that came running to my side, at a time of weariness and despair, it was me... gently holding on to her hand as she rested soundly in her hospital bed. The sterile white walls breathed only cool air, as the tone of her heart echoed from a monitor, alongside her bed. Bearing the thought that my mother facing death erupted a continual state of panic along my expeditious drive from Virginia Beach.

But now, my mind easily rested seeing that life was still breathing through her. My lips pressed gently against her warm forehead. I folded my body into the recliner positioned next to her bed and eyed her presence, until she fell deep into my dreams.

I don't know what it was, but early the next morning, I'd awaken to a weak stomach. I raced to the bathroom to bring up whatever that disrupted the sense of flow within me. Am I coming down with something, I began to wonder? It was late October, but it felt like August. It must have been the constant change in climate that's causing me to feel uneasy, I presumed.

After I'd washed my face and brushed my teeth, I opened the bathroom door to see that the nurse had just arrived placing a bouquet of flowers next to my mother's bedside. They were beautiful, long, pink orchids. Something about them felt quite familiar when I walked closer to touch the petal of an orchid.

"Aren't they beautiful", the nurse implied, with a wide irrepressible smile, as she continued to check my mother's blood pressure?

"They sure are. Where did they come from," I wondered, filling entranced by its beauty?

"Oh… There was a guy just up here…A handsome fellow, who brought them. It wasn't visiting hours but, he wanted to make sure your mother got them, before she woke up."

A handsome guy. Who could that be, I oddly thought? "How long ago was he here?"

"He just left, probably seconds ago.

Before another question arose from my thoughts, I acted on impulse and raced out the door and down the stairs. I knew I didn't have time to wait for an elevator, if I'd hope to see, who I was wishing it would be.

Four flights of stairs and nearly out of breath, I arrived in the lobby to see no one. I did a complete three hundred sixty degree turn, nearly breathless, only to be bypassed by a couple of nurses and a doctor, draped in scrubs and white coats.

I felt ridiculous, standing there in the center of the lobby waiting, hoping that the handsome guy the nurse was describing was Avery. I wanted to believe that he still remembered me…that what he once felt for me was enough to make him come to the hospital, on this particular day and by chance, see me again… And maybe love me again.

The fantasy that I conjured up in my mind wasn't gonna happen, I concluded. With my hands on my hip, I exhaled and I shook my head at my foolish behavior, as I walked over towards the elevator. Just as I looked down to press the up-arrow next to the elevator doors, the door in front of me slid open and revealed Avery standing before me.

I couldn't believe it, at first, but he was real. He had on an aqua-blue crewneck sweater. It felt like I was seeing him for the first time. "Hi," I fretfully uttered.

"Hi Rocqui," he spoke, seemingly unmoved by my unexpectant presence.

"How have you been," he asked?

"I'm okay. Just taking everything, in stride," I responded, still feeling tense by his overwhelming presence.

"I was just up delivering your mother some flowers. I heard that she is doing better."

"Yeah. I think she is going to be okay... How did you know she was here?"

"Your sister called and told me."

"I just found out last night, myself. I think I'd arrived here about two this morning. I've only had about four hours of sleep."

"You still look beautiful."

"Thank you."

Then, there was that awkward silence, like I was waiting for him to say something or maybe he was waiting for me to say something. Then finally, he did. "Well, it was nice seeing you again." Then he turned and began to walk away.

"Avery," I cried out, as I watched him distance himself away from me. "Is that it? You're gonna just walk away... just like that?

He stopped and hesitated for a moment, before he returned to my presence. His eyes pierced through me, as he conveyed his confession. "I've called you, text you, and sent you flowers. And not once did you ever called me back, to say anything. I've stayed up nights, wishing you were here next to me. I've even wanted to get into my car, a couple of times to drive to Virginia... But I didn't... I couldn't....Because no matter how bad, right now, I wish that the ring you are wearing on your finger was from me… It's not. And there is nothing I can do about that, but walk away."

I looked down and was caught off guard by the engagement ring that was still locked around my finger. Throughout all the bullshit I had just gone through with Zoric, I had forgotten that I still wore this ring.

"It's not like that, Avery. I swear." My voice sounded child-like.

"Oh really. You mean you are ready to be in my life forever. Because, right now…right here, Rocqui, it's ALL or NOTHING. I can't do that part-time love, bullshit anymore. I love you more than that."

He stood patiently watching me intensely and waiting for an answer. But I didn't have one. I needed a little more time to make things right; one more day or even one more week. But not right now.

"Avery, please believe me when I say, I love you." The sound of desperation in my voice was loud and clear.

"I wish that was enough," he softly concluded… And then he was gone. I stood there lost and pathetic, as he disappeared on the other side of the glass sliding doors.

By the time I had returned to the fourth floor, my face had succumbed with tears. I carefully tried to erase my sadness before reentering into my mother's room. To my surprise, she was wide awake. Her back was erected upwards, supported by pillows. I sucked up my pity and blanketed it with my excitement over seeing her awake and talking. "Mommy," I exclaimed! I sat on the side of her bed and leaned in for a tight hug and kiss.

"Hey darling! I wondered what happened to you so quickly," she implied.

"Oh yeah… I had to step out for a minute." Quickly trying to change the subject and not allowing my true emotions to show, I added, "But, I'm so happy to find my favorite person on earth doing so much better.

"I woke up a few times, in the middle of the night and saw that you were here. You don't look so well. How are you doing?"

"I'm feeling fine. I'm just dealing with some issues, that's all."

"What kind of issues? When you left here a week ago, you were happy. What's going on now, with you?" She continued to probe, patting her hand alongside her white blanket, welcoming me to confess my manners of the heart.

I didn't want this moment to be about me whining over my complications of love. "I'm more concern with how you are doing." I quickly interjected.

"I'm doing better. You see that I'm alive and kicking again." She gave me her vibrant smile as means of downplaying her abrupt admission into the hospital, just yesterday. "So, tell me what's really going on with you. I'm still your mother." Her direct words made me understand that she was not gonna rest until I shared my heartache and pain. I moved off the side of her bed and fell comfortably into the recliner, like I was in therapy and began.

"Well, apparently I'm not the only one caught up in triangle love affair. Zoric has been the center of his own love affair, as well. (Paused) I guess I wanted to believe, all this time, that the guy that I fell in love with was a different guy from the one I first met, at the bookstore. But, he's not." I regrettably wanted to admit that much information to her.

"Why did you think he was gonna be any different just because you fell in love with him?" She had to add.

"Because, he loved me. At least I thought he did. And that should be enough to change any man."

"Oh really? Love is not enough to change a man. As Tina told Ike, 'What's love got to do with it?'

"Mom, you are not listening to me."

"I am listening to you. You thought you had changed Zoric. He became the idea of another man through your eyes. Now you realized that he is just a man and obviously not the man that you fantasized him to be. You should be happy that you are now seeing your relationship for what it truly is. Some people waste years and years in a relationship, walking around blinded, trying to pretend that they are living in a fantasy. You should thank to Avery for this.

The mere reference of Avery made me uneasy, especially after his renowned disinterest in me. "What does Avery have to do with this?"

"You are obviously in love with the man, just as he is in love with you. And you didn't dream him up, did you?... Like I've told you and your sister many times before, the only true love story that is written in a book is the Bible. Everything else is just a fantasy or make-believe."

I glanced over at the bouquet of flowers on her table. "He brought these flowers by for you."

"I know. They are beautiful aren't they?" Her eyes veered towards the bouquet that left her with an impressionable.

"What you are going to do," she resumed?

"I don't really know. What would you do?"

"Child, please... I've lived my life. I've made my choices. And I don't carry one regret whatsoever." She drew her shoulders up and sucked in her breath and exhaled the pure pleasures of life.

I exhaled deeply, gazing down at my engagement ring that huddled my tensed finger. Even through the instability of my relationship with Zoric, it still sparkled.

The monotony that held the room, momentarily, was broken when the nurse's assistant wheeled in lunch, covered with a plastic lid. When my mother pulled her bed table closer towards her and released the cover, the pungent taste of her food, floated in the air and settled within the pit of my stomach. Without a moment wasted, I was sent rushing off to the bathroom, forcefully straining and clearing my stomach of its ailment.

Returning to my mother's fixed eyes looking through me was like looking head on at a deer standing in the middle of the road. "What", I sharply question?"

"What's the matter with you? Are you sick or something"

"Nothing," I quickly defended! I'm think I may be coming down with something." My words were calmer.

"Is there something you would like to tell me?" Her gazed followed me as I returned to her bedside.

"No."

"Are you pregnant?"

"No," I quickly objected.

"Have you been having sex?"

Shyly, I answered, "Mom, what you mean have I been having sex?"

"I mean, have you been committing sexual acts that could result in you becoming pregnant."

"I feel like I'm on trial or something." I returned to my position in the recliner and pressed my hands tightly against my stomach to ease the soreness.

"Cut the Virgin Mary act, Rocquelle. All I want to know is if you are pregnant or not?"

"Mom, please don't. I am not pregnant. I've been on the pill for ever. I may have missed a pack here or there, but I know I am not pregnant."

Her direct attentiveness drifted away from me, as she began to look beyond the white wall of her room. "It would have been nice to have been called 'nana' before I had left this earth. I don't know what your sister and her husband are waiting on. Maybe now that Diesel is home, Tamra would be the one to honor me with a grandchild."

"Mom, why are you so concern about someone getting pregnant, now?"

"You think because I may be dying that the idea of me wanting a grandchild is dying with me. I may not live to meet who this person may be, but I still desire for our family lineage to carry on."

Not quite sure how to feel about her message, but I listened to her like an obedient child yet, nodded like she may be losing her mind. She continued, "And I would like for my first grand baby is a boy. We need more boys in our family."

"Why, because you particularly, like boys," I was quick to slyly ask?

"I know that you and Tamra think that I was harder on you two than, I was on Monty."

"Sure was," I readily answered.

"Maybe I was. But, there is something that you don't understand. Monty was the first boy in a family of women. I was grateful to have a son. Your grandmother and your aunts worshipped the ground Monty walked on. They thought that every bad behavior by Monty should be simply excused by saying 'oh, he is just being a boy.' And maybe that was the case for some of his mannerism. But for the most part we were all guilty of trying to ease him over through life by spoiling him to death.

And I believed at the time of Mac's death, Monty was so use to us giving and protecting him that we enabled to handle real life situations. And things only became worse for him when your dad died.

"But mom. It wasn't like Monty didn't get whooping. Monty got more than me and he still ended up jail," I interjected. "Daddy didn't play with Monty like that."

"No he didn't. And sometimes it doesn't matter how many times you beat a child. The number of whoopings they get will not determine whether or not they would turn out to be good or bad. Do you understand what I'm saying? There is no secret formula to raising a child. You just have to keep trying and trying your best until there is nothing left you could do but pray. I miss my son every waking moment of the life. Yet there is still apart of me that is relieved to know that he is jail rather than out in the street somewhere. When you have your son, learn from some of my lessons. Don't enable him. Do everything you could to prepare him for the world, by teaching him to be responsible for his actions. And don't let anyone excused his behavior as 'just being a boy.' I often wished that I did."

`I was nearly floored by her admittance of guilt for safe guarding Monty, all his life. All of my feelings in the past were finally validated and I just wanted to tell her 'Thank You'. And then subtly reinstate that, "I'm not pregnant, so you may want to repeat this same speech to Tamra and Diesel when they get here, seeing that they surely have been doing more practicing at it than I have been lately."

"Don't play games with me, Rocqui. I'm not crazy. Just watch and see what I'm saying is to be true."

"Could we talk about something else, please. Like, when are you getting out of here?"

"Dr. Aditri said that she will be by this afternoon to check on me. If all is well, she promised to sign me out today."

"I hope so, because I couldn't take the smell of this place much longer."

"Isn't that interesting," she stated with a peculiar smile? "When I was pregnant with you, certain scents made me sick too."

"That's very funny, mother. But, I'm not pregnant."

21

The Lexus dealership called days before I had arrived in Fayetteville to tell me my car was ready. I was more than ready to leave from the hospital, after my mother had been discharged and pick up my car. When I opened the door and settled in the driver's seat, it was like I had been reacquainted with a longtime friend. My mother frowned at my senseless behavior eyeing me strangely at me hugging my steering wheel and sliding my hand down its tan leather seat, like I was Vanna White or someone. But I couldn't help it. I was unarguable elated to have my car back. We even rode from the hospital with the top down, allowing the hint of fall to breeze through our hair.

"What was daddy thinking wearing those polyester plaid pants and an afro, with a big black afro-pick in the back of his hair," I heard Tamra humorously asked?

"That was way back in the day. Your dad was fly. He had to be the coolest cat back then," Diesel complimented.

"What are you guys talking about," I asked, as I entered into the family room, where they were seated side by side. Their eyes were buried deep between the pages on a wide leather black book.

"We are looking through the photo album," Tamra replied, catching a quick glimpse of my presence before refocusing her attention back to the album.

"Is that you holding on to the hem of your mother's dress, when you were little," Diesel asked Tamra, never stirring his eyes away from the aged photos?

I immediately knew exactly which picture that he was referring to before Tamra interjected with, "That's Rocqui. Can't you tell by that gonzo nose she has?" I smiled at her comical gesture and recanted the picture in my mind of me adorned in my white Sunday dress, with pink flowers darting along the pattern. Pink ribbons tied two long curly ponytails dangling to my shoulders. My mother was just a beautiful as sweet lemonade on a summer's day. Her legs looked longer in her stacked heels and her waist appeared slimmer in her A-line floral dress. I couldn't recall the actual day, because I was five. However, she once told me that we had stopped over my Aunt Jennifer's house after church to pick up a chocolate cake my mother's sister had baked the night before. Daddy and Monty preferably waited in the car because dad did not want to permit my mother to an all day visit by settling along my Aunt Jennifer's sofa. And Tamra, at that time, wasn't even a 'thought' as my mother would laughingly imply.

Aunt Jennifer, being childless, declared Monty and I her favorite niece and nephew and swears by every word to give us the world if she had it to give. Taking pictures and buying us gifts on any given day had always been apart of her nurture towards us. This particular day was no different from any other. Even though my mother had already used up nine of the ten minutes my dad had allotted her visit, she couldn't deny her baby sister the opportunity to capture this moment on film.

"Now this is a beautiful picture", Diesel announced.

"Let me see." I rushed to his side to see what captivated his attention.

"Oh yeah," I agreed. My face warmed with delight as I envisioned this still moment like it was taken just seconds ago. My little head and puny arm rested along my mother's pregnant belly, while Monty's scrawny body stretched from her opposite side to affectionately kiss her cheek.

"Was that you inside your mother's tummy," Diesel asked, looking at Tamra?

"Of course," Tamra conceited. "Last, but not least", she affirmed.

"It was taken by daddy," I recalled.

I easily thought about the memories of the man I once knew. The man that was my first and greatest love. At times like these, I miss my daddy. He was and will always be the greatest man I've ever known. I was so delusional and dreamy of a life of ahead of me that I could not have even imagined when my family drove me six hours up to Howard University that it would be the last time that I would ever see him alive.

I remembered looking at my daddy and Monty carefully carrying all of my luggage and a heavy trunk up to my dorm room, hoping that I had packed everything because I had no intentions on moving back to North Carolina. I was all smiles and full of excitement. My dad stood before me full of emotions in his eyes, but with unspoken words, like I had broken his heart for leaving him.

"Oh daddy," I moaned, as his arms unreleasingly held onto my waist. "I'm gonna be okay. Thank you for letting me come to Howard. I love you."

He affirmed, "You just let me know if you need anything. Okay Rock." as his watering eyes held mine? He initially gave me the nickname 'Rock', during my playful childhood years. My mother, however, arguably said it sounded too mannish. Instead, she added the 'Qui' part to its ending and I became 'Rocqui' to everyone else in the world. However, to my father, he proudly maintained my name as *Rock*, reminding me of the bond that he and I shared. It all seemed not so long ago, that he was here.

As I was still taken aback from the photo, Diesel spotted another interestingly funny picture. "Here is your mom and dad looking like they were lost band members of Parliament, with their platform shoes on and wide rim dark shades."

"They were so young," I concluded. "I think this was taken before any of us were born."

"They were so happy," Tamra noted. Her detail implied that she had zoomed into their parted mouths of joy and laughter, dancing together, with clear plastic cups filled with drinks in their hands.

"Oh my word! Look at Monty," Diesel pointed out on the following page.

We all began to laugh at the photo of a young boyish Monty wearing superman pajamas, in a ridiculous pair of brown leather cowboy boots. His tiny lengthy arms were tightly bent to force his undeveloped muscles to show, while a towel draped around his neck like he was Superman. He had to have been at least five years old at that time and stubbornly would not go anywhere or do anything unless he had on those silly cowboy boots, as my mother would playfully relay to us, time after time again.

Just standing over Diesel's shoulders, my mind had traveled back down memory lane to a time when everything from a child's eye, looked perfect... when love was undeniably forever. And the mere idea of my parent's demise were unconceivable. The thoughts stirred a moment of emotions.

I felt my heart weaken and then suddenly a rush of sadness overflowed my mind. My starry eyes turned watery. I needed to distance myself from the pages of memories before the tears began to spill down from my face. Instantly, I settled on the opposite sofa across from Tamra and Diesel with my eyes glazed at their casual intimacy.

The unspoken realization was tantalizing, as I studied their enduring love. Her full bodied-shoulder length hair curtain the view of her face from him, as she leaned over still marveling over the pages from the past. Yet, his hand mindlessly and gently, swept her hair behind her ear to expose the beauty of her face he so admired. She gazed up at him, spellbound with a full smile embarked across the face, desiring his affection. And he instinctively adhered to her wish. He leaned in closer towards her face as his lips pressed sweetly against her cheeks.

A tinge of jealous pervaded me as I watched them like I was viewing a scene from a romantic movie. She had found love and happiness whereas I was left, in my current state, swallowed up in solidarity. But, that was my choice. I made that deliberate decision to be a successful business woman over succumbing to the matters of the heart. Love was an afterthought. Being financially independent was my comfort and my destiny.

It took everything that I had inside of me to purse my lips when the justice of the peace asked, 'If anyone sees any reason why these two should not be married, please speak now or forever hold your peace.' She was only nineteen years old and just a little over five feet tall in heels. Her dreamy eyes held only Diesel, who wore his dress green Army uniform. He was a head taller than she, with an awkward narrow build. He looked wimpy and languid like he was easily breakable with brownish skin, sporting a freshly new military buzz cut, just five days after completing basic training.

Up until that day when mom and I joined Diesel and Tamra at the county courthouse, I believed wholeheartedly that she would not go through with this impetuous decision. I yelled, debated, and pleaded with her the night before, that she should rethink this brash decision. However, my words only filled her youthful girlish bedroom with air. When I looked to my mom to back me on my viewpoint, she unmovingly justified that, "She is nineteen. That's her life, not mine." Finally, Tamra quieted my frustration and deliberation of reason by sternly concluding, "Whether you like or not, I'm gonna marry Diesel.

Disappointingly, I forced myself to stand by her side, while the desperate words of 'don't do this' warned repeatedly throughout my mind. The judge offered me a last attempt to reinstate my opposition on this marriage. But as I stood stiffly behind Tamra and studied the way Diesel gazed at her, intensely and unconditionally, I knew that what they shared was far comprehendible for me to understand. Decidedly, I willed my mouth shut and I congratulated them afterward.

To this very day, at this exact moment in time, he still embraced that same look of everlasting love for her he held in his eyes five years ago. I felt my cheeks pulling back into a smile. Without any hesitation in my voice, I spoke "Diesel."

Yet, there were no response. His head remained downcast into his lap while Tamra and he continued to browse through the photo album.

Next time, "Diesel" sounded more stern and direct when I repeated his name.

His head jolted upwards to display questionable eyes towards me. His glare reflected a certain surprise as to be caught off guard by his name being uttered from my mouth.

The realization that I hadn't found too many words to say to him in the past, suddenly drew my mind a blank.

I quickly scrambled my thoughts to speak, this time in a much softer and sincere tone. "You've seem to have gotten taller since the last time I've seen you." When Tamra and Diesel arrived at the hospital earlier today, he was almost unrecognizable. His youthful slender had broaden to a more manly physique.

"How long has it been, about two years, since we've last seen each other," he stated? I've probably put on a few pounds, as well."

"You look more mature." I was ineffectively trying to break down the wall that I'd built many years ago between us.

"Ah...Thank you, Rocqui," He scrambled to say. "I'm gonna assumed that you are given me a compliment."

"Baby, we need not to worry about going to church anymore, because Hell has frozen over", Tamra quickly interjected with sarcasm.

"Funny," I hissed at Tamra before returning my attention towards Diesel. "But, what I really want to say is 'Thank You', I added.

"For what," he puzzled?

"For protecting our life and our freedom, as a soldier, in that God-forsaken war."

The tensed lines in his face began to relaxed. "You're welcome."

"This is the first that you've had more than two words to say to Diesel. I wonder what this unexpectant niceness is all about," Tamra seriously asked.

"Maybe, after all of these years, I get it. I get you and Diesel. I get the whole idea of love and what it should be. And not necessarily what I thought it to be."

"And..."Tamra asked probing for more information?

"AND, I see that he truly loves you and you truly love him. And it doesn't matter what anyone else thinks or believes."

"And... what about you," she continued making me feel more and more like I was on trial?

"What about me?"

"Are you still in love with Avery?"

"I can't deny that I love Avery. But, I don't think he is still in love with me.

"What are you talking about? You are all he talks about. You and Avery belong together.

"Yeah, well, for a quick moment, I may have believed that to be so, too. But, I don't think that's gonna happen."

"You know his Halloween Party is Saturday? Are you going to go?"

"I don't know. I don't think I should."

"You need to go. He would be very disappointed if you were not there. Diesel and I are going."

"Good for you. But I don't feel comfortable going. I don't feel like I can see him again."

"What do you mean? If you have a chance at happiness and true love than you should take it."

"I know you mean well, Tamra. But right now, I am emotionally drained. I think it's time that I just focus on my business and my life in Richmond. I just need to be by myself for a while. "

"Does that mean that you are gonna stay with Zoric?"

I cringed at the sound of his name being said. I impatiently answered, trying not to rethink the cheating incident once again "I haven't figured out yet what to do about my relationship Zoric. I just don't need to talk about him right now."

"What did he have to say about him cheating on you," she continued to probe?

Her continuous questioning started to irritate me. "Don't ask me anything else about him," I demanded.

"I hope you are not seriously considering staying with him," she immediately objected.

"And if I were, what would be so wrong with that? He is not the only person in this relationship that had cheated. Have you forgotten that part?"

"Have you forgotten about the reason why you probably cheated on him in the first place? You're the one that said that you caught him outside a restaurant with another woman long before you even met Avery. You knew the truth then. You just were too afraid to face it. And now you don't have no other choice. Unless you're planning on keeping your head buried into the sand until the rain goes away. But, I always assumed that you were a lot smarter than that."

"When you wanted to get married, I totally objected. If I could have kidnapped you and hid you away from Diesel until you had gotten over your love craze, I would have. And through the years, I've learned to accept your choice. And your life seems to have turned out perfectly fine, with the choice you've made." I argued, easily dismissing the obvious captive audience of my mother and Diesel, who startling watched our warfare

"You sound crazy. You are making this way too hard for yourself, when it really isn't. But, I'm gonna let you figure this one out by yourself, since you've always seem to have the answer for everyone else," Tamra declared holding a steady voice.

"Would anyone like to something to drink," my mother asked trying to break the awkward silence that now fell throughout the entire room. Since her arrival home from the hospital, she had yet to concede to the word of 'sickness.' She was wearing her usual floral house robe, with slippers and looked as if she had never spent two days in the hospital, nearly at the mercy of God's will.

Upon her arrival home, she immediately carried on with her life as if Dr Aditri's profound assertion that it would be a blessing if she lives beyond Thanksgiving was ludicrous. And even though we insisted that she relax and take it easy, her strong objection only epitomized her anger and forced us out the way to leave her to do what she loved to do... cook. And deep down inside, I was happy that she did.

"No mom, I'm good. Do you need any help with setting the table," I asked?

"No, I don't need any help, because you all are gonna get your own plates and serve yourselves. I may be sick, but I'm not crazy."

"Hey Mom, do you remember right after daddy died and we spent that first Christmas away up in the mountains?"

"Yes."

"Do you remember the name of that resort?"

"It has been so long." She rested her wide heavy hand along her hips and pondered. "I think it was near Boone NC? Why do you ask?"

"Because I was thinking that maybe we should go there, right after Thanksgiving. I think it would be nice to get away for a minute. What do you think?"

"That sounds like an idea. I think we all deserve a vacation from here. The air is becoming too thick between us, with us all being confined to this house," she smoothed.

"I'll look up some resorts on the computer and make reservations to rent a cabin when I get back?"

"Get back from where?"

"When I return from home. I have to go to Richmond in a couple of days to put this house on the market that Ray and I have been renovating."

"When will you be back?"

"I will be back in a few days. I just need a few days to tie up a few loose strings."

"There you go, up the road again, trying to stir a wagon into two different directions."

Tamra jumped in with her quick tongue and asked, "Mom, why do you always use some ole country-fide cliché, just to deliver one simple point?"

"Because, that's how I was raised. My mother had a saying for everything. And to be honest, it wasn't until I had you'll that, I actually remembered them."

"What wagon am I trying to stir mom," I hesitantly asked?

"Your home...your life, child."

"What do you mean? I live in Richmond, Virginia. The only reason why I keep driving here to Fayetteville is because of you." I replied becoming more and more annoyed by listening to everyone's opinion on how I should live my life.

"I am very appreciative of that my darkling. But there are other factors that have kept you here a lot longer, besides me. You can't deny that to anyone, but yourself."

"No disrespect to you mother, but I would like it if everyone would stay out of my business. I'm quite capable of making my own decisions without everyone trying to tell me what to do," I settled before, upsettingly, exiting the room.

22

"**R**ocquelle, I think we should talk." Zoric has never called me Rocquelle before.

"Talk about what," I vaguely replied? I had avoided answering his calls for days deciding to deal with our issue when I returned to Richmond. But, twenty missed calls later, I decided to hear what it was he urgently had on his mind.

"You can't hide down in Fayetteville and pretend that you and I don't exist."

"You did," I nastily reminded him.

"I know. I really fucked up. But, so did you. And I'm not ready to end this because we both got a little sidetrack in our relationship."

"Is that what we are calling it, sidetrack?"

"Whatever you want to call it? I don't really give a shit. I just want you back," he adamantly pointed out.

"Zoric, I don't think the direction of our relationship should be discussed over the phone. I just need this time while I'm here to clear my mind of some things. Because right now I'm not quite sure what I want."

"I hope you are not trying to decide between me and that Negro down there. I'm your fiancé remember. We bought a house together."

"Well, did you think about all that when you were with her?"

"Fuck it. You can do what you want to do. I am trying my best here to make things right between us and you're steady holding on to that bullshit."

"Damn it Zoric! I don't know if you have realized it or not, but the problems in our relationship are much deeper than him or her. All they have done is to allow the real issue between us to surface."

"What's the real issue between us besides the fact that while I may have been seeing someone, you were also screwing someone down there?"

"I don't want to do this now, Zoric," I warned. "Just wait until I come back to Richmond."

"No, we are going to talk about this now. I want to hear it all right now," he demanded.

I didn't have any answers or energy left for his demanding questioning. Without a second thought, I smoothed my thumb over the end button on my cell phone and pressed it. The tension between us was starting to make my head spin. I dropped the phone from my hand and let it fall from my mother's kitchen counter.

"Are you okay?" I was awaken to the sound of Tamra's voice. She stood over me with a garment bag in her hand, as I had obviously fallen asleep in the family room.

"I'm okay." I sat up on the sofa and took in a deep yarn. "I'm just a little tired."

"Good." She sat next to me and continued. "I just wanted to say that I know you are having a rough time right now. And I just wanted you to know that I love you."

I was a bit taken back by her moment of sentiments. "Where is this coming from? You and I normally argue all day long and you never exchange one hint of an apology. Why now?"

"Maybe it had something to do with Diesel being back and I'm realizing how much I really missed him when he was gone. Loving someone has never been easy. But seeing and being with him again made me thankful that I have him to love. And I guess I just want the same thing for you."

I nodded replaying imagines of their playfully exchanges of hugs and kisses. "Don't worry about me sis. Everything is gonna work out fine."

"I know it will." She smiled promisingly.

"What do you have in the bag?"

"Oh. This is my costume for the Halloween Party tonight."

"What is it?"

"It is Little Miss Muffet outfit, with short ruffle panties and dress. And it comes with a matching bonnet." She unzipped the bag and held the pink tiny outfit out in front of her.

I began laughing. "You can't be serious. You are really not gonna wear that are you?"

"Oh yes I am. And… I brought you one too."

I was surprised. "No you didn't. I am not wearing some outfit like that out in public."

"It's Halloween. Plus, I didn't buy you a costume like mine. We are not twins. I got you a Tina Turner short glittery dress, like the one she wore when she was still with Ike. Plus, a wig." She pulled the wig from out of the bag and swung it playfully around in her hands. "Isn't it perfect?"

"You have really lost your mind. I am not going to this Halloween Party. And I'm certainly am not dressing like a rundown version of Tina Turner"

"You have too. Diesel has to be on post all night for a weapons inspection and I don't have anyone to go with. Please, Rocqui. It will be fun, I promise."

"I really don't want to, Tamra. The last thing I feel like doing is partying."

"But, I need you. This outfit is too cute to go to waste." She pouted for a minute, turning her bottom lip down pathetically.

Finally, I gave in. "Alright. I will go. But, I don't want you running around playing Cupid, with me. I do not want to see Avery. I'm just gonna go and have a few laughs, because I know it's gonna be hilarious. And come home."

"Fantastic. Come on and let's start getting dress. The party starts in two hours."

I got up and followed a few steps behind her and added, "It's gonna take about an hour to squeeze you into that outfit."

I had transformed into the saddest impersonation of Tina Turner, with the tight booty hugging thigh length dress, I've ever worn. After repeated efforts of standing in front of the mirror trying figure out a way to make this work, I actually felt like belting out 'Proud Mary' and throwing my legs around like I was on stage or something.

Before Tamra and I skipped out of the house to depart on this entertaining night, we were confronted by our mother. "You two looked like two cheap hookers," she smirked.

"Well, mom if we make two hundred dollars tonight, we would owe you at least one hundred dollars of it because you made us," Tamra playfully tossed back.

We entered inside the club that mimicked the set of horror film. With all the ghastly and haunted faces we encountered, it almost left me little frighten. There were vampires, big tall furry rabbits, hookers and pussycats dancing, laughing, and drinking animatedly. I stood with my back against the wall, keeping my guard up over the wild company that I was surrounded by. Tamra skated away from me, leaving me alone and prancing around like she was queen of the party.

Moments later of uneasiness, I spotted Avery in the center of a group of people dressed as Dracula. His black cape hung over the black suite he wore. It was too painful to see him cheerfully standing in a midst of a crowd talking and moving on with is life, like I was nothing more than a memory. I peeled my eyes off the site of him and anxiously walked over to the bar to order a soda. Drinking alcohol was not a perfect suit with this hootchie dress I had on. Any alcohol consumption would have made me start acting like a hooker rather than just looking like one. After a few sips, Tamra finally remembered that I came here with her and found her way back to my side.

"I don't know why you even asked me to come with you, if all you're gonna do is leave me standing here by myself," I fussed.

"Since when have you needed me to help you stand on your own two feet?"

"Every since I told you that I didn't want to come in the first place."

"Why are you standing here looking lost anyway? You should be partying and having a good time," she advised.

"You know why. I'm trying not to run into Avery," I reminded her.

"He already knows you're here. You matters well get over it, really quick."

"You couldn't wait to run up to him and blast your big mouth."

"I didn't have to. When I saw him, the first thing he asked me was if you were here. Then, he said something about he wanted to talk to you."

"I'll be gone by then...with or without you."

"Don't be so hostile. It's still a party. Come and dance with me." She began pulling my hand toward the dance floor. Michael Jackson's *Thriller* filtered from the speakers and everyone, no matter how insane and spooky some looked, rushed to the floor and began dancing. I was really beginning to feel the vibe of the party and threw my hips from side to side like Tina, with my sister dancing with me like my backup singer.

I was in my groove, thinking less about Avery and just enjoying the moment when Tamra suddenly stopped dancing and announced "What the hell is he doing he?"

"Who," I asked, suddenly scurrying my eyes across the dance floor to see who she was talking about? Yet, it only took a second or two for him to come into my full view. It was Zoric. His appearance was hardly disguisable dressed in regular casual clothes… khakis and with a blazer over a light sweater.

I moved off the dance floor and into this path. "What are you doing here Zoric," showing no sign of happiness that he was here?

"I'm here to get you," he answered confidently.

"How did you find me?"

"I went to your mother's house, first. And then she told me where you were."

My face steamed with anger. Why would she tell him where I was? "Zoric, whatever you expected to accomplish by driving all the way down here is not going to happen tonight."

"I just want to talk to you. Could you at least give me that? I did drive for three and half hours just to see you and I'm not leaving without you," he convincingly reminded me.

I threw my hands up in the air. Trying to avoid causing a scene especially with Avery possibly nearby, I escorted Zoric outside. We got inside his Land Rover and I waited for his insisted first words to be said. "Rocqui…" his tone was soft. "I know that our relationship had not been as idea as we both imagined. I work all the time. You work all the time. There have been nights that I've waited up for you to come home. And you've done the same for me, as well. I understand how frustrating you must have felt at times, when I wasn't there for you. You were so right when you said that we have allowed other people replace what had been missing between us. But, I have never, in all my life loved anyone the way I love you."

My harden face had relaxed. Slowly I began to speak, unsure of what it was I was about to say. "I love you too Zoric. I have always loved you. Even though it's easy for me to walk around here all day and pretend that this is all your fault. It really isn't. You and I have allowed things to happen outside of our relationship that should not have happened. But, it did. And I accept responsibility for it."

"But what scares me the most is," I continued. "...I don't think I can get beyond it and move on with our relationship."

I couldn't look at his face, but I know that he wasn't expecting me to announce that. There was silence between us. And then he spoke, "Is it because of that guy? Are you in love with him?"

I couldn't answer him honestly, even though it was true. But, it wasn't the only reason that I no longer wanted to marry him. "For a while, Zoric you had my head so far up in the clouds, I couldn't see anything in my day, but you. But, before any of this happened between us, I was increasingly becoming suspicious of you...Did you know that one day I was at the stop light, just a week after we got in engaged and I saw you outside of that restaurant kissing and hugging on her? I saw you Zoric with her, in plain view of my eyes! And I tried for so long to ignore what I saw. I've tried to ignore the random phone calls, the texts, and the constant late night meetings. I tried so hard to ignore what was really happening between us, that I went into denial. I didn't think you would ever do that to me. I tried to make myself believe for a long time that it wasn't you that I saw...that you wouldn't cheat on me. Because I wanted to believe that what we had together was made for no one other but you and I. Yet in reality, it wasn't. I would have done anything for you, because that's how much I loved you. But, I don't think I could ever trust myself to love you that way again."

"Wow. I wasn't expecting all this. If I knew that you had intentions on breaking up our relationship, I would have stayed in Richmond rather than driving all the way here for nothing," he stated point blank.

"This wasn't easy for me either. But, I think it's for the best, that you and I stop pretending, to live happily. And live our lives honestly...I'm sorry Zoric," I concluded.

"Me too." He cranked up his truck. I took that as I cue that enough was said between us. I opened the door and step out of the truck. Before I closed the door, I slid my engagement ring off my finger and placed it in the seat. "Bye," I uttered.

He exited the parking lot. I walked in a daze towards the club doors, until Tamra reached out for my arm and stopped me in my tracks.

"Are you okay," she asked?

"No. But I will be."

"We don't have to go back inside. I had enough partying for one night. Let's go home," she suggested.

I could not have agreed with her more.

23

I stood over the welcome mat at my very own door hesitating to enter inside. On the other side of the door, I wondered if I would still have that feeling of home that I once had when I opened the door. I took in a deep breath of the cool autumn air as I slid the key into the lock.

When the door opened, everything looked as I had left it. The air inside was slightly much cooler and crisp than I expected. I suspected that Zoric had not been home since he left me last night in Fayetteville. I wondered where Chee Chee' had been kept all this time. Apparently not at home. His canisters, next to the stainless steel refrigerator were empty and clean. I suspected that he had not eaten from it in days. As I glared at the stairway, I puzzled over what I would find upstairs. I imagined the bed would be unmade bed and socks and shoes would be left carelessly across the floor. And I just knew that the unwelcome view of Zoric's underwear would lay scattered across the room, as I would usually find them. Those were the thoughts I carried, along with my luggage, as I made my way up the stairs.

As I entered inside my room, I was surprised to see a flawlessly made bed. Esmeralda, my housekeeper, had obviously been here. Zoric would have never taken the time to clean up behind himself. The pillows were fluffed and propped perfectly up against the wrought iron head board. The room was immaculate and organized projecting an image of a showroom. Even the anticipated display of Zoric's worn clothes were missing from the normal view I'd witnessed many times before. I speculated that he may have being staying in a hotel room or, even more likely nesting over at Julia's trying to create cozy quarters for them to live. He had better not have my dog over there, or I'm gonna have to whoop somebody's ass again. And next time, I plan to start with him.

A thunderous roar echoing outside my window cut off any further deliberation I had about Zoric's whereabouts. The rain quickly followed, cascading against my window pane.

I don't know how long I had slept before I felt Chee Chee's paws trampling across my comforter and over my legs. My eyes opened to his fury body settling across from me and his charcoal eyes gazing upon my restful face. I softly stroked his coat and remembered the day that Zoric presented him to me.

It was Valentine's Day, when everyone else were racing home to be greeted by flowers, balloons, a romantic intimate dinner or even a little lingerie, I was fifteen miles west of the James River showing a beautiful traditional brick home to a disconcerting client. This was our fourth house we had toured that day. She was determined to find a five hundred thousand dollar home, with all its upgrade and luxuries, on a two hundred thousand dollar budget. I anxiously watched her navigate slowly, surveying and deliberating over the two bedroom house, while Zoric repeatedly rang from my cell phone to lure me home.

"Baby, what time are you gonna be home," he frustratingly asked again, during his second phone call within an hour?

"This will be my last showing. I promise," I tirelessly decided. "If she buys this house, I'm gonna have to make a stop by my office so I could finish up the paperwork, in order to finalize the sale. Maybe in about another hour, I should be done," I projected. I had already noted that it was three minutes past seven o'clock, when my readily voice trumpeted through the vacant house, "What do you think?" I carefully maintained a level of professionalism in my tone, even though I was obviously cueing to end this unremitting search.

Finally, after her meticulous assessment and her extensive leisured tour of the house, she finally decided to purchase it. The sellers were much more easily receptive to her offer than the time she took to decide to buy it. We rushed quickly to return to my office, before the sale became legalized.

Feeling rushed and a bit anxious to see what Zoric had romantically planned for me, I made sure all the computers were shut down. I hastily turned off all the lights and grabbed my purse before securing and locking up the building. The night air was brisk. A slight wintry breeze made me quiver under my white double-breasted wool coat, as I quickly strutted in my leather black boots down the dark deserted sidewalk.

I was just a few steps away from my car, when I noticed the shadow of a man posted under the corner streetlight. The closer I gravitated towards my car, the more nervous and unsteadily I became before I came in full view of the identifiable figure that stood, just a few feet before me. It was Zoric. He was unquestionably strikingly handsome, as the streetlight radiated over his black Burberry coat, with a fedora tilted on the side of his head.

An ease of relief escape my alarming state, as I stepped closer under the hazed light and gazed merrily into his affectionate eyes. My lips instinctively parted when he stepped forward to welcome me with a passionate kiss. However, our embrace was quickly interrupted when a puppy with a beautiful red bow tied around its neck, popped out of the top opening of Zoric's coat.

"This is for you... for being everything I could have ever imagined in a woman," Zoric declared to me, before placing Chee Chee in my arms.

"He is beautiful," I adored. I took one quick look into his timid, yet round eyes, and fell in love. He whimpered and moved frenziedly in my arms when I nestled him close to my coat. I was so lost in the attentiveness and cuddliness of the puppy, that I almost missed Zoric kneeling to the cold cemented ground, before asking "Will you marry me, Rocquelle Johnson?"

My heart answered 'yes' before the word escaped through my breath. A kiss had sealed our promise of love, forever, on that cold winter's night. Everything about that moment couldn't have been better scripted for two people that were in love. Our immediate plan was to be married on June 17th, exactly a year and four months, because I always wanted to be a June bride. Happily ever after, I dwelled. I would have bet everything I've ever own that on that day, we would have been just that.

"He misses you." Zoric's voice broke me out of my trance as I looked up and saw him standing well poised in the entrance of the doorway.

I mumbled, "Hi" seemingly I was at a lost for words.

"I'm just here to get some clothes," He was wearing grey windbreaker pants and a matching jacket, which was apart of his usual weekend attire when he had nothing particular to do.

"Oh, okay." My answer didn't feel fitting for his statement, but that was all I could think of to say.

"I didn't know you were coming back today or maybe I would have waited another time to come by," he implied waiting for some type of signal that I was okay with him being here.

"Zoric, you don't have to do that. We bought this house together, remember?" I sat up in the bed, still stroking Chee Chee coat in my lap.

He moved into the room and settled beside me. "If I haven't said it yet, I just want you to know that I'm really sorry how things turned out."

"I know. So am I."

"You know what I was thinking about the other day?"

"What?"

"Do you remember when we didn't have money? Well, you did. But, I was still struggling. And we were in bed one Saturday morning and you said, 'let's drive to New York City.' We got dressed, packed an overnight bag and just hopped in the car like nothing else mattered and spent the rest of the day in New York."

I was smiling. "Yes, I remember. That was the good ole days." My mind quickly recaptured the time when we didn't have a lot of furniture, after we first bought this house and we use to camp on the living room floor with lots of pillows and blankets and have romantic candle lit dinners and partake in dessert afterwards. I couldn't bring myself to share this memory, feeling that it would only make this awkward situation feel worse.

"Yeah, it was. I'm gonna miss that."

"Me too." He leaned over and placed his arm around me and kissed my forehead. I watched him rise from the bed and enter inside the closet. I couldn't understand why I all of a sudden I felt sad. I began to question whether or not I believed that ending our relationship was the right thing to do. We shared some incredible times.

He came out of the closet, a little later with luggage filled with clothes. "I'll get the rest of my stuff later on in the week."

"You don't have to be in a hurry. I probably won't list the house for sale until the end of the month."

"What are your plans now? Are you gonna stay in Richmond? Or are you thinking about moving to Fayetteville?"

"No, of course not," I stated adamantly. "I don't have any intentions on returning home to live whatsoever. I just think it's for the best that I sale the house, since both of our names are on the mortgage and find someplace smaller around here somewhere. You deserve your half."

"Alright then." Then he began to walk out of the room. "Oh, I'm forgetting something." He pulled his keys out of his pocket and twisted the single house key off the ring into it was apart from the rest. Then he laid it upon the dresser. "Guess, I won't be needing this," he concluded. Zoric's glared at me with deep eyes. His head drop low and shook in dismay. "I will see you around," he stated before exiting the room.

I've never seen him look so sadden and hurt before. Even though he had evenly hurt me, I would have never thought that I would be the one to bring upon such pain to him. With my head held low, I waited until the slamming of the front door confirmed that he had left, before I was able to hold my head up again. My eyes drifted slowly around the room. Memories of Zoric and I, past and present, trophied every angle in which I turned. Chee Chee hopped off my lap and exited the room. Suddenly, I was alone.

Somehow, sleep was not a factor for me through my disparity. I woke up feeling the urgency to use the bathroom. The luminescent of the bathroom lights shined upon Zoric's assortment of cologne and shaving kit he'd left behind, cornering the bathroom sink. The ending of Zoric and I certainly merits a few flow of tears from my eyes. But, I was empty of emotions. I sat long on the seat of the toilet, in deep thought.

I couldn't help but to think about Avery. I needed him now. There was this one memory we shared when I had arrived at an unfamiliar night club spot, alone. I waited patiently and anxiously for his immediate arrival, but there was no sign of him being present. I sat in my car, gazing at a few people freely and excitedly entering under the green and white awning that umbrella the entrance of the club. The narrow building was camouflaged by the black skies. The asphalt parking lot began to increasingly thicken with a balanced mixture of people. I began to feel anxious over my awkward displacement, until, Avery sent me a text. *'Enter through the side door. I'm inside waiting for you'.* My eyes shifted to the narrow two-story building and I tried to make out a side door from the obvious darkness that surrounded the building. Yet, there was none. Maybe, he meant the same entrance as everyone else, I interpreted.

I stepped out of my car, feeling a bit skeptical and leery in my setting and paced quickly across the black lot, heading towards the extending line out front of the main door. I had decided to enter through the main entrance, until a slight head turn, put me in view of a white gentleman who had just exited from the side building.

I, carefully, stepped out of the line and gracefully strutted towards the hidden side entrance. There was a black door that blended in with the rest of the shadowy building, with a distinctive shiny brass doorknob. I lightly knocked on the door, timidly. There was no response.

Next time, my knock was more forceful and filled with anxiety. An oversized bald-head white man jerked the door opened and nearly scared the life out of me. "Yes," he yelled over the loud blaring music drowning out the sounds of voices coming from within. His voice was quite brute and very unfriendly.

"I-I'm here for Avery Smith," I stuttered.

"Come in." His tone lighten. "He is waiting for you," I barely understood him to say.

I felt immediate relief. Yet, there was no sight of Avery swarming amongst the sea of strangers in such an intimate setting.

I was lost and confused. Just then, I received another text from Avery. 'Come closer towards the dance floor. I'm near the bar."

I stumbled around and through the crowded groups of people until finally I found myself under a disco ball, rotating at the center of the dance floor. People were tending to their own vibes, dancing and sweating and lost in the groove of the music. Yet, I profoundly thought to myself, what the hell am I doing here? I pivoted my feet in the direction in which I came. I was about to leave until I received another text. 'Don't leave. I'm right here.'

"Right where?" I voiced out loud, with the sound of my words being drown out by the overbearing music.

"Right behind you," he words softly answer in my ear. Slowly I turned around. And there he was. As beautiful as the first day I met him.

Minutes passed, as we stood just a foot apart, with his intimate eyes romanticizing me with each passing second. Closer and closer, he moved in towards me until he was just a breath away. My heart drummed with excitement and passion, as he held my head between the palms of his hands and slowly seduced my lips with his passionate kiss.

I had recanted it all in my mind like it was a pleasurable dream. Yet, it was so very real. Now, it had fallen to nothing more than just a memory...a memory of a love that I still held for him.

My behind had become increasingly numb and tender due to my extended position on the toilet seat. It was time for me to get up. That's when I realized that there was no toilet paper on the holder. I leaned over to extend my arm under the bathroom sink and fumbled through all the hair care products and body scented collections to find a roll of toilet paper hidden in the far, next to an unopened box of tampons.

Instead of reaching for the toilet paper, I grabbed the pink unopened box of Playtex and starred at it intensely. Subtly, my fingers began to tremble as I tightly gripped its sealed contents, between the palms of my hands. Thoughts anxiously raced through my mind to recall when I bought this box. There was no answer. When was the last time I actually used a tampon? Every answer that I sought felt trivial. Am I pregnant? I gasped with horror over the thought of that being so. A sharp jolt pierced through my stomach. I couldn't be, I was sure. I'm quite sure I had a period last month. Or did I? This unopened box says 'no'. But haven't I bought a box in Fayetteville? I squinted my tiresome eyes trying to recall the actual day and time that I went to the store to buy a box while I was in Fayetteville. However, there was no particular memory that I could recall. It's just stress. That's what it is. I heard some people say that stress can cause irregularity in periods.... But, to go months without a period is a bit unusual... or is it?

"Keisha, are you awake?" It was after 1:00am. I obviously knew that answer before I called her, but I desperately needed her.

"Barely. What's wrong," she mumbled?

"Everything. Could you come over here?"

"Right now?" The sound of surprise echoed in her high pitch response.

"Please. I really need you, right now," I whined.

She took a deep exhaled and replied, "okay".

"And Keisha... stop at Walgreen's on your way to pick a pregnancy test, for me." I didn't give her a chance to reply before I pressed end on my cell phone.

About an hour later, I heard my front door open and closed... Followed by Keisha's voice. "Where are you, Rocqui?'

Her voice traveled in and out of all the bedrooms, as she searched upstairs to find me.

"I'm in here," I yelled.

"In where?"

"I'm in my bedroom."

"I just looked in there."

"Look harder next time."

I could sense her entrance into my room, leading up to the bathroom door. "What the hell are you doing in the bathroom, on the floor," she curiously asked, looking down at my senseless position. I had been sitting with my nightshirt tucked underneath my folded legs, every since I'd gotten off the phone with her.

"Losing my mind... Did you bring it", I asked looking up at her dressed in a trench coat over her striped pajamas and oversized t-shirt?

"Yeah, I got it." She placed the bag down in my lap. I then got up and sat on the top of the toilet. "Do you mind telling me what's going on? And where is Zoric?"

I read the instructions off the blue narrow box. Then my eyes rested upon her, who was still standing, looking down at me wearily. "Zoric is not here... Indefinitely. And...." I did not know how to form my lips to say it. "And.... I may be pregnant." My lips slightly trembled as I voiced those exact words. I looked up at her desperately as to hope that she had some answer to my encroaching problem.

"Wow," was all that she could stutter. She looked just as lost and displaced as I now felt. "But, we don't know for sure yet until you pee on that stick that you are holding", she continued offering a ray of hope.

"Okay. I'm gonna pee. You will sit on my bed and we will both hold our breaths together."

Two long nervous minutes of my life later, I held the same white stick in my hand, only for it to reveal two definite straight blue lines. "This couldn't be happening", I mumbled over and over again.

"What are you gonna do?" Keisha only echoed the exact thought that I had in my head.

Too much was happening to me in one day. Zoric is gone. And now I am left, burden by his unborn child. I felt trapped. Trapped between a fantasy of what I once shared with Zoric and a reality that I so desired with Avery. Keisha and I both laid side by side parallel to the ceiling waiting and searching for some mysterious answer to fall from the sky.

I resorted in a deep sigh and answered, "I don't know."

"It's the unexpectancies that brings about life's greatest joy," She poetically song.

My head turned in view of her elongated body still gazing marvelously up at the ceilings. She was still young and believed that real life and fairy tale were all the same. She had no notions of my onward realities....like my mother is willfully dieing. My brother is incarcerated, on my behalf. And my sister is too far away to add any comfort to my life. And now this.

"Are you gonna tell Zoric?"

My eyes rolled back towards the ceiling, full of uncertainty about everything else, except that. "That's the last thing I'm gonna do right now. Plus, I just peed on a stick. This couldn't be the defining moment of my life, in which I discover that I'm pregnant. Nothings going to be said until I see my doctor," I concluded.

After a couple more hours of worrisome babble from me, Keisha went home. And I failed at every attempt to sleep the rest of that night.

24

A new day had brought about a new life. I sat alone motionless in my room listening to silence. I tried at best, to understand the interruptions that have happen to me. My life after all of these years of me carefully crossing my 't' and dotting my 'I' and methodically creating a perfect plan had now become a mystery.

I hopped up out of my bed and stood before my full length mirror. I saw a total stranger in the eyes that I held. I had become someone else. Someone other than the person I had known, just yesterday. I had it all planned. I would have settled contently in a happy marriage and financial comfort before I was given the joy of a new life settling into my reality. But, today was a different day…a brand new day. And I was pregnant. Single, unhappy, financially well-off and pregnant.

I pulled my oversized t-shirt up above my waist. My waist was too narrow and too tight to believe that a life was living and growing inside of me. I wanted to think that my hourglass figure that I now held would maintain throughout my nine months of conception. But, I laughed at myself, for having that thought. I modeled, in the mirror, viewing my body from different angles, poking out my belly and standing at different views trying to imagine the look of my stomach stretching out to the size of a watermelon in the months to come...until the phone rang.

"Hello," I answered.

"Hi Rocqui. It's me, Ciantra."

Immediately, I hoped that she wasn't calling me to try to get me to go shopping for a wedding dress. Hesitantly, I answered, "What's up?"

"Oh nothing. I was just calling to see how you were doing?" Her voice sounded bubbly and cheery, as usual.

"I'm doing well. Why do you ask?" I seated on the side of my bed, because I instinctively knew that this was no casual call.

"Well, Zoric has been staying with Calvin and me for the past few days. And I know that this is really none of my business, but he said that the wedding is off. Is that true?" Her tone mirrored more a disappointed mother, than of a casual acquaintance.

I had to deliberate over my words carefully, trying not to respond too quickly and overly sensitive. "Zoric and I have decided that it is for the best that we move on separately, with our lives."

"I'm sorry to hear that. You and Zoric were so good together. I really hate to see you two apart," she empathetically relayed.

"I know. But, I guess that's how life is sometimes. It doesn't always work out the way you've planned," I implied, becoming increasingly restless with this conversation.

"You know, Rocqui... I know that you are hurt and all. But sometimes, men mess up. I mean...they are just men. And they need us to help them get themselves back on the right path. When Calvin cheated on me, I thought I was gonna lose my mind. Yet, I knew that I loved him. I knew that we could get beyond this and move on with our lives together."

Was I hearing her correctly? Was she justifying the affair that Zoric had with Julia and implying that I should simply dismiss his behavior and stay with him? "What are you gonna do Ciantra, when Calvin cheats on you again", I tactlessly retorted?

"Excuse me." Her words stumbled.

"Next, time," I deliberately repeated, "when Calvin cheats on you again, are you gonna excuse his behavior as, 'he is just being a man' or what? Because I'm just curious on how I should have appropriately handled this situation," I spitefully added.

"You don't know that he would cheat on me again," she pathetically replied.

"The only person who doesn't know that is You."

"Maybe I shouldn't have called you. I'm sorry that I did." Her trembling words abruptly ended with a dial tone.

I sat stiffly holding onto the phone in my hand, pondering over what I've just done. I shouldn't have been so heartless and callous towards her, I regretted. The phone slipped through my hand and onto the floor, as I began to relinquish a few tears of my own. I cried. I cried for Zoric. I cried for our unborn child. I even cried for Ciantra.

"I don't know if it's that I haven't seen you in a minute, but you look different," Ray suspiciously stare at me.

"I'm just becoming more and more fabulous, with each graceful day," I jokingly replied.

"I know what it is," he continued to analyze. "It's that bride-to-be glow," he speculated.

I unnervingly chuckled. "I really wouldn't say that that's what it is?"

"Oh really," he uttered, examining my face questionably.

We were at the renovated house that Ray and I flipped anxiously awaiting the arrival of guests for Open House. I was not about to relinquish the turmoil of events that had my life spinning out of control, at this very moment. Yet, his eyes waited patiently for some sort of fascinating revelation. "I tell you what... if an offer is placed on the table tonight, I will tell you what this glow is really all about?"

His fixed eyes relaxingly fell into a smile. "I will be all ears."

Trying to distract Ray's interest away from my unveiling glow, I admitted, "Ray, you are a genius. The house turned out amazingly beautiful," I marveled!

"I know Rocqui. It's been a tough labor of love. But it is finally done. Time for the money", Ray sung, rubbing his palms together like they were itching to scratch the face of a few dead presidents.

We were standing professionally dressed, me in my formal navy suite and he, in cocoa tailored slacks and an argyle sweater, in the formal living room area of the house. The walls were coated with a classic taupe, while the ten feet ceiling were cased in a startling white crown molding. A modern-style sofa and wing-back chairs along with a few traditionally pieces were placed strategically along the refurbished mahogany hardwood floors.

"Where did you find time to create this fruit and desert tray," Ray jokingly implied looking over the display of food I brought in and placed on the round coffee table.

"That's pretty funny. You've never known a day in my life that consisted of my time being spent in the kitchen. I preordered it from Sam's Club. I figured if we sprinkle a little more sugar in the cake, it would sweeten the deal even more so for potential buyers."

"I like that Rocqui. That's pretty clever. I know I keep saying it over and over again, but we make an incredible team… How does Johnson and Goodman Investment Team sound" Ray excitedly stated, as he held his hands up high to demonstrate our names being hung in lights?

"It sounds like we have potential buyers," I cued at the entrance of potential buyers entering through the front door.

I eagerly sought to approach a tall white man dressed in the likes of Kenneth Cole, because he embodied the look of money, as I am often persuaded to believe by society conflicting ideas of race and money. Yet, a more mature African American woman with slightly grey streaks sweeping the edges of her hairline, wearing a pair of wool slacks and sweater and gorgeous pearls adorned around her neck appeared just as equally qualified and financially suited as the white gentleman that I almost darted towards.

She strolled casually and proudly gazing at the architectural details of the home. "How are you?" I extended my hand towards her and introduced myself. "I am Roquelle Johnson, broker and owner of Dream House Realty."

"Hi," she pleasingly welcomed. "I am Beverly Howard. I've just moved here from Charlotte NC. And I am looking into a more traditional-style home, but with all the modern upgrades."

"You've come to the right place," I cheerfully acknowledged. "This is a Twentieth Century Victorian with all of its historical character still intact. What my partner and I have done is renovated from the inside and out and completely updated the most important rooms, like the kitchen and the bathrooms. This house has four bedrooms, three baths and three exposed brick fireplaces. One here in the parlor as you can see. There is another in the family room, right off from the kitchen and upstairs in the master suite. And you are gonna be totally amazed at what we've accomplished in the master suite."

"Thank you so much. This house is absolutely beautiful," she complimented.

"Here's my card. Please enjoy and ask any questions. I hope to make this house your home," I finalized my sales pitch, as she escaped off towards the back rooms.

I was readily prepared to approach the white man, who appeared to be quite attentive to the restored fireplace, before I eyed someone who looked identical to Julia passing through the living room and up the stairs into the other rooms. It couldn't be her. I couldn't imagine at of all the places and homes for sale in Richmond, she would have found her way in this house, in my presence once again.

I waited and watched anxiously, until I behold her coming down the stairs. My eyes quickly darted around the room to count the number of people standing closely by. Too many for my taste to cause a scene. I spied her trailed off in the opposite direction of me like she maybe was heading towards the kitchen. I veered left to meet her in her path. The back rooms weren't so busy with onlookers. I, of course, had no intentions of fighting. I certainly was in no physical condition for that type of behavior again. However, I kept my guard up to ready for any and everything.

Slowly, she slithered into the kitchen, eyeing the decorative details of the room, totally blinded by my presence. "Now, that you have my fiancé, I guess you want my house too," I casually released, to catch her attention.

She was obviously shocked to have stumble upon me. It took her a minute to or two to search for words. But then she nervously spoke. "What are you doing here?"

Energetically and confidently, I answered, "You're standing in my investment at my Open House."

"Well, I guess I'm here trying to buy a house, then," she returned. I detected a slight cockiness in her tone. I began to edge in closer towards her. She stood on the opposite side of the island. I used that as I a barrier to keep me from tearing into her ass again. "Look, I'm not looking to get into this with you here," she quickly defended, taking a few steps back away from my confrontation.

"And I have no intentions on repeating what happened at the Doubletree with you. This is my place of business."

"Business," she laughed, like what I said was jokingly funny? "Did you think it was very business-like to corner me in the bathroom the way that you did, at my place of business?"

"I thought about business just as much as you did when you started fucking around with Zoric at work," I sharply retorted.

"He came after me," she insisted, shifting her neck from side to side.

"And you just so happened had your legs opened and ready when he did?"

The air between us was becoming increasingly hot and thick. I kept feeling myself wanting to pick up something and knocking her with it. But, instead I kept my right fist held tight, pinned beside my leg. She arrogantly announced, "I could have had you arrested. You should thank Zoric for that."

"Really? Well, you should have thank Zoric for stopping me from whooping on your ass," I threw back maliciously.

"Let's just call this conflict between us even. I don't want to keep running into you and feeling like I have to defend myself."

"I'm done with it," I finalized. As she started to strut away from me and exit the kitchen I had the urge to say one last thing. "But Julia, if you ever bump into me again the way you did at the country club it won't be just my cell phone dropping to the floor."

Her lips sneered at my promise. And then she left at a hurried paced out the front door.

Every potential buyer had deserted the house and a few offers lay waiting in a wicker basket along the dinning room table. Ray and I relaxed our tiresome bodies across the living room sofa, side by side. I filled his ears with joy and a few tears, of my life's current events. I even told him about the expectant arrival of my 'glow'. He comically filled me with laughter. "You mean to tell me, a brother still can't get no break. First, there was Zoric and now...Avery" he said questionably. "And to top it all off, you are pregnant!"

I listened on, entertained by his overly exaggerated emotions.

"I'm really sorry to hear about your mom. But, I think you are going to be an incredible mother, just as she had been to you," he touchingly relayed. He leaned over and gently kissed my cheek.

The very next day, I found my legs yielded apart and my feet propped up in metal stirrups. I anxiously laid on my back, with a white sheet draped over my nakedness, awaiting the official results of my pregnancy. I studied intently at a poster that pictured the nine months stages of pregnancy and denied myself the reality that it could be, until Dr Carmichael, my OBGYN entered into the room and finally sat next to me on her little round stool.

"It's official, Rocqui. You are pregnant", she announced so definitely. I found Dr. Kandice Michaels, in Richmond's Black pages, a magazine that contains a listing of all African American entrepreneurs within Richmond's district. After our first initial meeting, we hit it off instantly. I've been to several of her social parties. And she had been to quite a few of mine. We even hang out with the same circle of friends. She had become my doctor, just as we had became good friends.

"I should have known... I was really hoping that a few drops of pee on a stick would not redefine my whole life."

"Well Rocqui, you know like I know that it wasn't the few drops of pee that got you into this situation," she reminded me, sounding witty and entertained on my behalf? "Besides, I think it's wonderful."

"If it's so wonderful, than how come you don't have one, yet?

"Because I haven't found a wonderful man yet, like you have."

"Why does everybody keep saying that? How come everyone knows how wonderful and perfect he is, except for me?"

"Because we, as women, want to believe that a perfect man exists. We have to believe that despite knowing that deep down inside, he really doesn't.

"Yeah, but the reality is they are only perfect when you first meet them. They smile perfect, feel perfect, and even make love to you perfect...until the relationship gets real. And then you discover that his black ass wasn't so perfect after all."

We chuckled.

"You are so right. A perfect man does not exist. But a man can be perfect for you. Hell, any man can be perfect for me right about now."

"Well, I've ended my search for perfection. I just want happiness. If I could just obtain that long enough, I will be good."

"This baby may open up new doors of happiness for you. If you haven't found happiness by now, you'll have about another seven more months until you'll rediscover it."

"Seven months," I exclaimed! I just got pregnant! Doesn't pregnancy suppose to last for nine months", I asked?

"From all of my years of practice, it does. That's why you have seven months left, because you are"... she opened up my charts to make sure she was giving me accurate information.... "You are ten weeks pregnant. You are a couple weeks moving into your third trimester."

"Are you serious?" I gasped with disbelief.

"Deeply."

"Do you know what that means," my voice languidly trailed?

"That you need to get started on a nursery, ASAP?"

"That I got pregnant in August. Is that right?"

"Pretty much. According to your last period, your baby was conceived between the 26th and the 29th of August, to be exact."

"Wait a minute! Did you just say August the 26th through the 29th?"

"Yes, I did."

I suddenly reached for my Blackberry that was tucked next to me, because I had just text Keisha a message. Anxiously, my trembling fingers searched through the stored data on my calendar. August 26th, 27th and 28th were clear of any pertinent memos. However, August 29th noted my sister's flight arrival to Fayetteville. This memo instantly connected my memories with the sexual interlude with Avery, the night before.

"Oh...My...God! I was in Fayetteville!"

"I guess you and Zoric did more than just visit family while you were there."

"Zoric!" I exclaimed, like I was living through a nightmare. I was with Avery. Oh my God! I'm carrying Avery's baby. I can't be. This can't be. "I gotta go," I nervously mumbled, as I rose from the examining table and began to fumble through my clothes trying to put them on.

"You know you need to see me next month. And here is your prescription for your prenatal vitamins."

"Yeah, yeah."

I drove, mindlessly, having no idea how I had arrived in the parking lot at Regency Square mall. My mind rushed back and forth to the night Avery and I first made love. It had to have been the night that we conceived this baby.

I was dumbfounded in thoughts. Why, in the millions of times that Zoric and I had had sex, I never got pregnant. But the very first time that I'm with Avery, it happened.

I tried various types of birth control methods before. The pill, I kept skipping a day or two. I was advised against using the patch, because Kandice said it could lead to blood clots. Consequently, I'd allowed Zoric convinced me not to be too concerned about birth control, at all. "We're getting married anyway. Do you know how beautiful you'll be as a bride to be pregnant when you walked down the aisle," were his convincing words. And I naively believed him.

Granted, my mother had always reminded me throughout my young adult life that 'it only takes that one time'. But, there were many opportunities between Zoric and I that neither one of us used protection and I didn't get pregnant. It just couldn't be true. Or could it really be? I continued with my pessimistic thoughts until Keisha's heavy fist pounded against my windshield and scared the hell out of me.

"Excuse me ma'am. Do you mine getting out of the car, sometime soon?" Her voice sounded muted through my raised window.

I rode down my window. "What are you talking about," I responded, feeling displaced and weary? "You just got here," I added.

"Did you not see me standing in front of your car, waving at you hoping that you would get out some time soon?"

"All I see right now is a pile of mess that I've gotten myself into."

"Well, get out of the car and let's do a little browsing so that you could clear your head of some of this mess."

"As much as I love to shop, I'm really not in the mood right now Keisha."

"What are you saying? How could you not be in a mood for a new pair of shoes?

"Do you understand that buying shoes would eventually become secondary in my life to buying diapers and milk, now?"

My words meant nothing to her. She waited outside of my car door until I forced myself out of the car and moseyed through the grand mall doors.

Walking along side of Keisha, through the Macy's entrance, I relayed, "shopping right now is like putting a band aid over a swollen stomach."

"That's exactly what we are looking for. A lot of cute maternity band aids to keep you comfortable and looking good. Let's go into *A Pea in a Pod*. That's more of your style." I followed along Keisha's attempt to make me feel content through the pleasure of shopping. But all it really did was add more stress to my anxiety. Everywhere my head turned my eyes captured all of these women with their swollen tummies. And if it wasn't a pregnant woman I was noticing, it was a stroller or bratty kids running up and down the walkways. Finally, we settled down at the food court for dinner.

"I have something for you," Keisha hummed as she reached down next to her and pulled up a small white gift bag with yellow wrapping paper propped out.

"What is this," I asked, as I reached across the table to grab the bag? I opened it and pulled out the most adorable cutest white knitted baby booties, I've ever seen. I gasped with joy and held it in my hand like I was holding on to all of life's joy.

"Isn't it cute? I could not resist. I just had to because, I think that out of all of your accomplishments, this will be by far your greatest."

I reached for a napkin to wipe away my tear. "Thank you, Keisha. This is probably the best gift I've ever been given."

"Tell me how did the Open House go?" She must have sensed my emotions beginning to unravel to redirect the conversation.

"It went well. We have multiple offers. Now the three potential buyers are in a bidding war."

"Darn. I was hoping that it would have stayed on the market a little longer, so that I could sell it."

"I know," I agreed. "This would have been an excellent opportunity for you to get your feet wet. But, your scores are not back yet.".... Right as I said that, her facial expression changed oddly. I could sense a tinge of secrecy in her mannerism. And then I added, "Unless you have already received your scores and you just haven't told me yet?

"I did", she excitedly admitted!

"I'm so proud of you! I got up from the table and grabbed her around her shoulders for a tight hug. "When were you going to tell me?"

"Well I figured with all of your unexpectant news, I would wait until it was appropriate."

"Girl! This is a great fulfillment for you. I am just as happy about you passing your real estate exam, as I am about being pregnant."

"Wait a minute. I'm not quite sure, if that's a good thing or not."

"No. It's good. It's real good. Even if I have to raise my baby alone, it will be a beautiful blessing and I am thrilled about it."

"What about Zoric? Have you told him yet?"

I thought rationally and calmly, before I declared, "Zoric will never know about this baby."

"What? You have to be kidding me, right," she said in a startled voice?

"Zoric is not the father," I felt comfortable to admit. "The father is someone who I met very briefly and intensely while I was in Fayetteville and fell in love with."

"Are you gonna tell him?"

"I don't think it matters, anymore. He has moved on with his life. I think its time that I do the same with our baby."

25

Tamra and I were on our way back from getting our hair done when I spotted an expansive shopping area to my right. As I sat at the traffic light waiting for it to turn green, I had the sudden urge to turn right and enter into the widen entrance of retail shopping.

"We should go over there"

"Over where?" Tamra didn't see anything particular to determine where *there* was, as her eyes scrambled out the window's view to see what I was talking about.

"Here, at the grocery store." I turned right and eased down the driveway towards the main entrance of the building.

"Why are we going to the grocery store? Does mom need something to cook for dinner?" She asked as if the thought of going into the grocery store repulsed her.

"No. We are going to the grocery store because, I'm hungry." I maneuvered cautiously through the parking lot searching for an empty space to park.

"Rocqui, there's a Bojangles over there and a McDonald's right there. And I think we passed a Chick-Fillet about a mile back." Her pointed finger veered right before me as if I was blind to the obvious towering signs and arch of fast-food heaven within my view.

"I don't want any fast food. I want some real food." I finally found an empty space and eased between two cars.

"What's the matter with mom's kitchen? I'm sure she would have some real food ready for us when we get home."

I turned the engine off and pulled my keys from the ignition. Finalizing my intentions, I turned to her and said, "We are going inside the grocery store. It will be fun."

"You are really serious, aren't you," I heard her say even after closing the car door behind her trailing words?

I walked to her side of the car and awaited her emergence from her side. "My gosh. This is really doing too much. I have other things I could be doing with my time rather than pushing a buggy up and down a grocery aisle," she continued to growl.

I ignored her and continued through the opened glass doors. "Could you just be quiet for a minute and go get a buggy? This would be an enlightening experience for the both of us."

We walked over towards the fresh produce area. I began to pick over the apples as if I knew what to look for in a perfect apple. "How come you've never really learned how to cook? You are the one with the husband and jobless."

"What do you think I do all day, sit around and watch soap operas?"

"Pretty much." As funny as my words may have sounded, I was being quite serious.

"I do more in a day than most people do in a week."

I bagged some grapes and oranges and placed them in the shopping cart.

"That's a commercial, not necessarily your life." I was too busy examining potatoes like they were foreign objects to see if the sincerity in her voice matched her expression.

"I'm serious. I'm enrolled in a community college taking classes to become a Licensed Practiced Nurse. And I'm teaching an aerobics' class part time on base."

I eyed her intently. "Even though I'm rather proud of your effort. That however, hardly sounds like more than what normal working people do in a day."

"See, this is why I didn't want to tell you. You are always doubting me."

I held back my immediate desire to smile. "That's because you're always worrying me about something. I always feel like I need to keep two eyes open for you, because you often walk around with both eyes closed."

I silenced her. But only temporarily. She pushed the cart along side of me into the bakery and deli section. We walked towards a sample table of what appeared to be rotisserie chicken, thinly sliced and laid out on small paper plates for anyone's tasting.

"This looks good." I took a plate and savored its taste.

"What is that?" Her nose tightly crinkled and her brows raise when I tried to hand her a sample.

"Food. Try it."

"This doesn't look right." She continued to resist tasting, while I waited patiently with the thin slice held before her face.

"That's because it's not closed inside a white Styrofoam box labeled Take-Out."

She finally took the plate from my hand and bit into the chicken. Finally, she agreed, "This is pretty good."

"You know what I have a taste for right now?"

"What?"

"A banana and peanut butter sandwich with honey."

"IIIILLLL. That sounds so nasty."

"Mom use to make it all the time. You never had any?"

"I think our mother has better sense to know that I would not eat any mess like that."

"Wait right here. I'm gonna go back and get some bananas. Maybe mom will make me one when we get back."

"Suit yourself."

We paraded up and down the aisles looking for nothing in particular. After convincing Tamra to join me at the grocery store, I wasn't quite sure of why I was here. Maybe I thought that now that I'm pregnant, I should at least become acquainted with one. It's not like I've never been inside a grocery store before. I do occasionally run in with my list of twelve items or less and speedily head towards the check out counter.

However, now that this new role had been given to me, it's my responsibility to make the most of it, even if it meant trying my hand at something new. Tamra and I walked over to the meat department and I studied the various types of red meat. I looked at a package of ham and was puzzled by where to begin to turn this into something edible. The departmentalizing of these packaged uncooked foods was starting to bore me.

"Can I help you ma'am," said the man, whose face looked as reddish as the meat he butchered?

Even though I heard him quite clearly, I couldn't bring any words to say anything. Instantly, my mind traveled six years from that very moment when my child would come home from school and ask "what's for dinner." In my current existence, dinner would be whatever I ordered on my way home from work. I recalled the top left drawer right next to the refrigerator where every take-out menu, in Richmond was kept. Everything from *PF Chang to Maggiano's Italian Restaurant* were stuffed inside that drawer of my house, more so than what I could offer inside my refrigerator. Then suddenly, it hit me. I was overwhelmed with shame and fear when I realized that I would not be able to offer my child a home cook meal, something that I'd taken advantage of in my mother's house growing up. At best, I would be able to serve up a turkey bacon avocado sandwich on rye bread and call it dinner.

I didn't even notice at first that water had spilled from my eye until I felt it running down my cheek.

"Ma'am, we have some rib-eyed steak on special today. Would you like to order a pound," he proceeded to engage my thoughts on what I should be interested in and less on where I emotionally stood.

Finally, I muffled up something to say, shielding my pity behind a smile after wiping my cheek. "Rib-eyed steak sounds really good. But, I think I'll have to pass on that today."

Tamra instantly appeared out of nowhere beside me. Without catching a glance of my disparity, her eyes pierced through the presentation of meat behind the glass counter. "I think mom has some leftover of this same boneless prime rib roast, I'm looking at. If we hurry home, I'm sure she wouldn't mind slicing up a few potatoes to go along with to it," she hinted.

I smiled at her suggestion and began walking away. She kept up the pace next to me, occasionally, shooting a few ideas that she may have observed from mom or a television show on how to best prepare a meal here or there. However I felt like she was just as clueless as I was.

I decided to end my search for nothing and conclude this visit with the purchase of some milk and juice, that I presumed my mother needed for the house. As we headed towards the dairy products, I caught a quick glimpse of the aisle sign that read Baby Needs and Dry Cereal. I detoured off my path towards the refrigerated aisle that was in my visual distance and strolled up the aisle.

The shelves were stacked with all sizes and shapes of diapers. Baby formula stocked two levels of shelves. And pacifiers and baby toys twirled off the hanging racks, enticing the minds of motherhood.   It was all so overwhelming to see. I inspected the various diaper sizes and then noted the prices. Wow. Having a baby isn't cheap.

"Why are you looking at diapers?" Tamra interrupted my trance.

I tried to find a few quick words to say. "Oh... I don't know," was all I could muster up, still holding on to the view of pacifiers and the different bottle styles.

"Wait a minute... Are you... You are not" She swiftly shook her head, in disbelief, with her mouth hanging opened. However, she quickly figured it out. "YOU'RE PREGNANT!"

She anxiously waited for me to acknowledge or deny it. However, my smile had to have answered it best. I felt my cheeks holding tightly at my uncontrollable urge to scream "yes".

"That's why we are here at the grocery store. And that's why you are craving that nasty sandwich, right?" She waited for me to confirm her affirmations, looking all wide eyed.

"Yes," I finally confessed with my mouth holding on to my smile.

"Oh my Gosh!! I can't believe it. You are having a baby!" She was more excited than I'd imagine that she would be.

"I'm gonna be an Aunt. That is so cool, Rocqui." She grabbed me tightly and locked her arms around me.

I tried to keep her as settle as possible on our way home. She kept making big plans about the baby. She went on and on in the car about the baby as if she was talking to herself...what was she's gonna buy her. She had already declared the baby to be a girl. What would be the perfect name to give her? She kept throwing out different names and questioning if it sounded right while I listened on just as entertained by her dwelling excitement.

Before I could pull my car steadily into my mother's driveway, Tamra was nearly out the car anxious to deliver the news to our mother.

Mom," Tamra shouted, before her swift disappearance inside the front door. I heard her voice as I slowly guided up to the front steps. "Rocqui's pregnant!"

It was then that I had to remind myself that my mother was knowledgeable of all things when it came to her children. She was the first to announce that I was pregnant, before I knew. I quickly recalled my response, *'Who Me'? Not me'*. I wanted to believe. Slowly, I made stride inside the house and into the kitchen, where they both had gathered at the kitchen table. I moved towards a chair across from them to sit before my mother's awaiting eyes and admit, "Yes Me." The words flowed softly. I officially declared, "I'm pregnant."

My mother, with the look of *I told you so* on her face stated, "I knew that. I'm just glad you finally realized it. How do you feel?"

"Surprisingly well," I confessed. "I mean, it may not be the idea situation. But I am finally coming to terms about having a baby. And I'm quite happy with it."

"And how does the father feel," she probed deeper?

"The father," I answered like that was news. "What father," I continued? "There is no father."

"Sure there is. Now, I know like you know who he is. I'm just curious to know how he feels."

I wanted so quickly to reply, if you know who he is then you should know, already, how he feels. But, that would have been something Tamra would have said, full of sass. I just quietly mumbled, "He doesn't know."

"Well, shouldn't he know," she continued to interrogate?

"Yes mother, he should." At this point, I was becoming increasingly irritated by her badgering. "But, right now, I don't want him to know," I finalized.

I stood up from my chair and was about to turn and walk away from the table until my mother interjected with, "Rocqui, don't get up and walk away. You always do that when you can't solve life's problems."

"What do you mean? I don't always walk away from my problems."

"Yes you do, dear. If you can't fix your problems, you run from them. And that's exactly what you are doing right now. You are too afraid of admitting to Avery how you truly feel about him and telling him that you are having his baby. So, you've chosen to run and hide and carry on with your life, like everything is going to work itself out, on its own."

My sermon did not call for me to stand on my feet and preach. I eased my body back into the chair, with a slight fear that a may be knocked down and professed, "Mom, Avery does not want me in his life, anymore. I had that opportunity and I gave it up. And quite frankly, I don't blame him. If he couldn't give me what I wanted, when I asked for it, I would have walked away too."

"That's exactly my point. You walk and sometimes run away, instead of facing your fears and dealing with the truth."

"I have been honest with him. He knows how I feel about him."

"Does he know that you are carrying his baby?"

"No, he does not. And I don't want this baby to be a reason for him to think that I want him."

"Then give him the *Real* reason. Tell him you love him and then tell him that you are having his baby."

"Of course mother. You are absolutely right. I should do just that. Maybe, when I get up from the table, I'll run and call him and share the great news. Then we could run off and live happily ever after", I sarcastically stated, just to get her to stop hassling me about my dilemma?

"Why do you young people make everything so hard?" Here we go again and again, I thought. Instead of our conversation coming to an end, a another window had been opened as she eagerly shared with us another one of her life's lesson. "Honey, when Randall Michael Johnson came into my life, I toyed with his courting until I was almost at the point of losing him," she proclaimed.

Tamra exchanged silly facial gestures of annoyance, at me from across the table, like I'm the one to be blamed for prompting our mother to relay the same story we've heard over a million times before about how she and our dad met. "Randall Theodore"... she called my daddy by his first and middle name as to add emphasis on whatever she needed to say.... "Didn't have a penny to his name when he met me...just lent in his pocket and love in his heart. But, I thought I was being cute and all...taking my time, flirting with the idea that I had this man. And I did. He would give me any and everything he had to make sure I had what I needed, before he got what he wanted. I knew I had this man, because he loved me unlike any other man I had ever known." Quickly she inserted, "Not that there had been many before him. But, one day, I waited for him to come by, as he always did every Sunday after church. And he never showed up. I waited and waited, until weeks had gone by and there was no Randall Theodore Johnson. Then finally, I went looking for him, at his house and there he was sitting there so calm, cool and collective, like he had been waiting for me. And you know what he said," she asked us, knowingly we all knew what he said, because we've heard this story too many times before. "He said," as she continued, "I got tired of chasing after you. Figured you'd come around eventually to me."

Tamra and I both released an impatient sigh, as if we were both holding our breath until the story ended. Tamra, however, quickly interjected before our mother could get another word out of her mouth with, "And you two lived happily ever after and raised three beautiful kids. Right mother?"

"Yeah, we did. Even to this day, I love your father more and more," she proudly remembers.

"Well, mom, sorry to cut your story short, but, Rocqui and I need to go visit Monty before visiting hours are over," Tamra prompted. She and I anxiously rose from the table, before Chatty Kathy started up again.

"Oh, okay. Tell my son I love him. And Rocqui," she got up from the table and faced me sincerely, and declared, "Everybody does not have a real shot at finding true love. Those that do are few and far in between. If you are given another opportunity to love this man, grab him and don't let him go."

"Okay mom," I nonchalantly replied. Thoughts of Avery and I ever being together again did not exist in my reality at this moment in my life.

"How did mom know you were pregnant by Avery," Tamra curiously inquired along our drive to the Jail?

"I don't know. It's a mother thing, I suppose. Just like she knew you were having sex at the age of fourteen. She just knows, I guess."

"How did she know when I started having sex? Did you tell her, Rocqui?"

"Tamra, seriously, who didn't know? You were hotter than fish grease, in junior high. Boys acted like they were lining up to get their turn to be with you."

"So, what? Shoot! We were all screwing around that time."

Maybe so. But at fourteen, you shouldn't have been. And certainly not with every Tom, Dick and Harry that smiled at you. She thought she was going to have to sew your ass shut until I suggested that I would take you down to the Health Department and get you on birth control pills."

"I remember. The pills have to be the best invention ever."

"Are you still on them?"

"Yes."

"Do you ever want any kids, Tamra?"

"Yeah, I do. This whole war thing messed up Diesel's and I plan to start last year. They keep shipping him off every six months. And it's not for certain if he's home for good or where we are going live next."

"I'm sure that's a bit challenging living under the thumb of the military. But, I don't think there is ever a perfect time to have kids. Look at me, now. I'm not a good representation for the American tradition, that's for sure. But, I'm gonna make it work, regardless."

"I'm still proud of you, sis. And my new nephew or niece is going to be the most rotten thing on this earth."

"I heard the news," Monty announced all cheery eyed from the other side of the Plexiglas window. His muscles in his arms had tightened from all the weightlifting he had returned to. His hair was cut low and his face was well groomed. I thought for a minute, that he looked better in jail than he did when he was out.

"I shouldn't be surprise. News travel fast with you people, I answered, after an exchange of laughter.

"That's because your mother can't hold water. I had just called mom right after you and Tamra left, wondering if she was bringing me a box of cigarettes and some money. She said she gave it to you."

"Yes, she did. I checked it in already. You should have it once they inspect it or whatever they do with it. How are you doing?"

"I'm trying real hard to stay sane up in this joint. I've seen niggas here that were in jail the last time I got locked up. Some did worse shit than the first time they got time. I tell you, jails are set up to train you to become a life long criminal. I promise Rocqui when I get out, I'm never coming back to this place again.

I listened on like I had never heard him vow those exact words before. Looking across at him, into the eyes of what was once athletic stardom and seeing him now caged up like an animal, troubles my mind. I didn't know if I'm happier that he is locked up and safe, rather than being out on the streets trying make a hussle. "Whenever you do get out, I'm gonna set you up nicely so that you'll have a place to live and a job."

"What about mom's house? I can always live there. She is doing fine, right? Someone has to be there for her."

"True. But, mom isn't doing fine, Monty. She is dying. And I don't think she will be around to see the new year. I just want you to know that I will be here for you, no matter what."

"Mom is dying," he uttered in total disbelief? "I thought she was doing better. Whenever I talked to her she sounded fine. Why didn't she tell me?" He turned away from me, holding back the tears from falling from his eyes. I observed his vulnerable moment, wishing I could touch him. But, he didn't cry. I don't think I even remembered him crying at daddy's funeral. Maybe, because it was me that howled irrepressibly enough for everyone.

"It's coming Monty. I believe she understands that it is happening far better than we do. Last week, when I was here, she made me follow her upstairs to her bedroom and then she pulled out her navy silk dress that was hanging up in her closet. And then, she made me promise her that I would bury her in that dress. Isn't that crazy? Man, I thought I was going to lose it, right then and there. But, she was okay. She acted like she was showing me a dress that she wanted to wear on the First Sunday, to church. I'm scared, Monty. Each day that I wake up, I wonder if this would be the last day I would have with her."

My last words cut me like a knife. It was me, this time drowning in tears. I needed to feel Monty's hand that he pressed against the glass window, like he was reaching out for me. I needed someone else to be me just for a simple moment, so I could catch my breath, because I felt like I was suffocating inside.

"Rocqui, do you remember when we played against Waddell High. And that night I was knocked unconscious and the coaches and trainers, mom and dad and everyone else were nervously waiting for me at the hospital to make sure that I was going to be okay?"

I nodded my head.

"Well, when I woke up, I remember you. You were the first person I saw at my bedside, holding my hand, telling me that I was going to be okay. And I believed you. I believed you because even though mom loved me and spoiled me, as you would say, she respected and admired you. She always knew that she could depend on you to take charge over any situation and do what's right for the family. Seeing you there by my side brought comfort to me. Probably the same type of comfort mom feels about dying. She knows that she is leaving behind an incredible person that would try her best to keep Tamra and me from messing up too much."

My sniffles had minimized and my tears had ceased. And I chuckled, "What a job that is."

"Well, I'm locked up right now. You don't have to worry about me too much," he joked.

"You are my brother. I worry about you more than anyone else."

"For right now, you shouldn't worry about any of us… just my niece or nephew growing inside of you."

I reached down and rubbed my small stomach, as a small reminder that there was a new life growing inside of me. "Oh yeah. My greatest achievement, yet."

"I didn't think you would ever have any kids, Rocqui."

"Why? You didn't think I had any motherly instinct? Hell, I've been taking care of you and Tamra, like you'll were my own children."

"I know. But, you were always so career-oriented. You wanted the nice car and the big fancy house and the big dollars."

"Well, if I can remember correctly, so did you? Why did you stop dreaming to have those things too?"

"So many things kept happening to me that I couldn't find the time to dream again. It seemed like every time something good was happening for me, something bad was waiting right around the corner. And I guess I couldn't take it anymore. The whole football career wasn't just my dream, it was Mac's dream, too. And when he died, I didn't want to have that dream anymore."

Monty and I never had this conversation about Mac before, until now. I was heartbroken. At that very moment, I understood my brother's life not to be as easy as I had imagined it to be.

His intense eyes moved from my stare and darted behind me like he was looking for someone. "I thought Tamra came with you?"

"She was with me until Diesel called her on her cell phone from Fort Bragg telling her that he needed her to fill out some paperwork for housing on Post."

"Tamra and Diesel are moving back to Fort Bragg?"

"It looks that way. Diesel apparently received orders to return to Fort Bragg."

"That's kinda cool. Now, we just need you to move back to Fayetteville so that we would all be close once again."

"Don't count on that ever happening."

26

Two days before Thanksgiving and already my mother's kitchen counter is lined up with an array of mouthwatering pies and cakes on display for the weaken tongue. Huge pots and pans covered the stove fill with all the ingredients of a down-home southern cooked meal with seasons and spices searing from under the tight lids. All of my aunts and their families are expected to fill our house with laughter and embarrassing memories as they arrive on Thanksgiving Day.

"Alright, Rocqui. I'm going to show you how to make this Sour Cream Cake, for the last time," my mother decided, as she stood to my side, in the sweltering kitchen. She had already spent part of yesterday and most of last night cleaning and cutting in preparations for the big day. I left her standing in this very same spot late last night when I grew tired, just from watching her dance around this kitchen to the sound of rattling pots and pans.

"Mom, we really don't need any more cakes. Look at this counter," I pointed out to her. We have Coconut Cake, Rum Cake and...What kind of cake is this," I inquired, as I investigated the creamy three layered white icing, monumentally displayed on a tall crystal cake stand?

"That is a Red Velvet Cake," she verified, without ever looking away from her mixing of the dry ingredients into the tin bowl.

"Did Aunt Jennifer bake it?"

"No."

"I know you didn't bake it. Where did you get it from?" My mother cooks or bakes, just about anything without even a glimpse at a recipe. I've never seen her, in my life, use a measuring spoon or cup for anything she had prepared, except for when she had tried to bake a Red Velvet Cake. The icing had always looked perfect and tasted buttery and creamy. Each crimson red layer gave off an impression of moisture and mouth watering flavor. Yet after one bite, it fell to a complete dry and crumbly disappointment.

"If you must know, I got it from Avery. He baked it," she subtly admitted, like she was telling me the sky was blue.

"Avery was here?" I shouted in total disbelief!

"Yes, he was here."

"When was he here?" My words became increasingly louder over the sound of the hand mixer beating against the tin bowl. I could feel my heart thumping through my chest.

She turned off the mixer and rested the handle down on the counter. Slowly, she turned to me to give me her full attention, as if she understood that one simple answer would not allow my frenzy to settle. "When you left to go fax off some paperwork to your office, yesterday," she answered unreservingly.

"Did you call him and ask him to bake you a Red Velvet Cake?" My mind was rushed with questions that needed to be answered.

"No." Her answer was too casual and too short for me to rest on.

"Then, why did he bring a cake by?"

"Because he called me and he wanted to wish me a Happy Thanksgiving."

"And..."

"And..." slowly she continued to linger with each word as I waited breathlessly for an answer. "He said that he had baked a Red Velvet Cake that he wanted me to have."

"Why didn't you tell me he was coming by?" My tone was becoming more agitated by her passive tone.

"Because you said that 'it was too late for you and him," remember?" And you didn't want me to keep interfering into your business." She made her defense as if this conversation between her and me had come to an end.

I felt frustratingly mad. But what could I say. She was absolutely right. Isn't it ironic that the one time I asked her to mind her own business, she actually does.

"What's the matter?" Her tone was a bit more mellow and sincere. She must have read the annoyed look that now mirrored my face.

"Nothing." I shoved off what I was really feeling. Confused. Frustrated. Angry.

And then I remembered that my mother had a mouth that has no limit for words." Mom, you didn't tell him I was pregnant, did you?"

With her hands on her hips, she answered, quite frankly, "That's not my place to do. That's yours."

I wasn't sure if I'd trusted her answer or not. But, I decided that I had to believe what she was saying was true. If it wasn't, he would have called me by now. I'm sure he'd have a millions questions to ask me about our baby. Surely he would feel some level of joy, even if we weren't going to be together, I guessed.

"Are you gonna help me finish this cake or what, child," my mother asked impatiently?

My thoughts were years away from the kitchen as I fantasized about Avery and my unborn baby. Would the baby have my long pointed nose and Avery's soft mocha skin? The little interest I had in wanting to learn the family recipe of a Sour Cream Cake was flattened. "Mom, I'm no longer in the mood now to bake this cake. Could we do this some other time?"

She gazed at me quite peculiarly and repeated, "Some other time" followed by a slight chuckle. And then, she turned away from me and continued to tend to her cooking in the kitchen. "Rocqui, take this, seeing that you are not ready to learn right now. Maybe one day you will be."

I received the index card that she handed to me and studied it. "What is this?"

"This is the recipe for the Sour Cream Cake. I wrote it down just for you, so that you'll have it."

Nonchalantly, I placed the card in my purse that sat on top of the kitchen table and replied, "Thanks mother."

"If your dog chews up another pair of my shoes, I'm gonna have him stuffed," Tamra angrily declared. She suddenly emerged before us holding a tall leather black boot in her hand.

"Oh... poor baby. He misses his toys," I crooned eyeing Chee Chee prancing towards me wagging his tail.

"Poor Baby," she hissed! These are Coach! Do you see this?" She pointed to the stiletto heel nearly at the bridge of my nose, to validate the Coach imprint inscribed on the outer sole.

"Oh really, Tamra," My eyes burned with anger. The fiery that suddenly erupted in me dispelled my past moment of weariness. "Are these the same Coach boots that I spent five hundred dollars for just for you?"

She paused in her moment of selfishness and ungratefulness to rethink if they were actually those exact boots I bought her for Christmas last year. "Maybe," was all her guilty conscious would allow her to utter.

"Just know this, sista girl, when my baby comes, you can forget living off of me lavishly. I suggest that you go out today or after the holidays and find a job, because you will never see another five hundred dollars pair of boots from me again," I settled.

She sneered a look of disgust at me before and mumbled "whatever" before her feet pivoted and exited the kitchen. And even though I had finalized my words with her, I felt like it was only just the beginning, feeling the intensity of my mother's frowning eyes on my back. I turned and looked at her. "What," I asked?

"Rocqui, you don't have to sound so ugly and mean towards your sister," she firmly stated.

"Mom, did you see the way she held the heel of that boot, pointing right in my face? She never says 'thank you'. It is always 'give me' and 'give me some more', with her," I whiningly justified.

"It is nobody's fault, but yours for that. Before I even began to think about having another child, you kept saying, 'mom, I want a sister.' You thought it would be really cute and fun to have someone to play house with and dress up. And you got her. And every since Tamra's been in this world, you've given to her. Don't start trying now to correct the damages you've already created now."

"Mom, she can be so ungrateful, at times."

"That's true. But soon enough, you are going to be all that she has." With her heartfelt words, my harden face had soften. I realized my emotions were stemming from something other than an act of my sister's self-centeredness.

I left the kitchen and trekked upstairs to the bedroom where Tamra was lounging comfortably across the bed, talking on her cell phone. I wanted to say 'I'm sorry.' I have said it only on a few occasions in the past, in which I was actually wrong. She is my sister. And there was nothing that she could ever do to change that. But the love I have for her goes further than a sisterly bond. She was also my best friend.

I could have cleared my throat and interrupted her phone call to humble myself to an apology. But I opted for a more subtle approach to express my regretfullness. Stalling, I moved stiffly into her room towards her bed, where she sat and leaned over to press my lips on her forehead. She continued on with her conversation, unfazed by my loving gesture. I left her room, like that confrontation between us, never existed.

The day of Thanksgiving arrived... and so did Aunt Clara, Aunt Jennifer and Aunt Myrna and all of their additional hungry mouths to feed. I've seen cousins that I haven't seen since we were kids. For some cousins, I saw them more as strangers because, I never really knew them at all.

Aunt Clara and Aunt Myrna, standing along side my mother, with their petite statures, looked like they were derived from a family of hobbits. I sat at the table and marveled at their sisterly presence, arguing back and forth trying to persuade one to be more right than the other.

Even though my mother was the oldest of the three, her youthfulness glowed over her face. No wrinkled forehead. No crowfeet catching her eyes when she smiled. Just pure beauty. She held herself well throughout the days of her life. One of her longtime girlfriends once complemented her on her ageless beauty. And she returned cleverly full of sass and wit. "It's because I had a good man loving me right and keeping me tight."

Aunt Jennifer came and sat beside me. "What are you staring at," she asked? Aunt Jennifer was slightly taller and lighter than her older sisters. She still carried the signature hips and thighs, but she wore it well. Her breasts, however were a shortcoming to all the thickness her body bared. "Not even a handful" her sisters would tease. She seemed unfazed by their humor. Her presence spoke loudly in how confident and how beautiful she felt about herself.

When I was younger, I spent numerous weekends, giving into her occasional motherly desire. We would bake cookies, because she loves to bake and go shopping. Whatever I so desired, she bought for me. I idealized for a long time to be just like her when I grew up. It was because of my experience working in her bakery *A Little Taste of Heaven* that I strongly desired to enter into the business world.

However, there was one occasion that Aunt Jen had me spending tedious, repetitive hours meticulously creating sugar flowers for a wedding cake that she had baked. I felt like a horse with a broken leg. 'Just shoot me' I silently screamed. When she discovered the agony along my face from working in the kitchen, she compassionately, reassigned me a new position in the front of the quaint store. I had become the cashier and the waitress. I felt so much more comfortable, wearing a white apron to greet the customers and handling the money, as opposed to being elbow deep in dough and sugar all day long.

There had never been that one particular guy in Aunt Jennifer's life, but several. Even though she easily rested on the notion of being single forever and being happy and content in her own space, I desired for her to be married. I didn't understand why.

"I'm just entertained by mom and your sisters, that's all," I answered. We both looked onto them like members of an audience.

"They are an interesting group of people aren't they? Too bad they are not like me. I'm more of the quiet and humble one," she laughingly enjoyed. She is certainly much quieter than her older sisters. Her tone is much softer and comforting. Her words are delivered gentle, yet specific. I always assumed that was because she was the youngest and the least affected by problems caused by marriage and children.

Aunt Myrna, on the other hand, is the loudest and the more deranged of the three. I swear she has shot at her husband, Jerry, three times, with a pistol she hides underneath her bed. Why he insists on staying with her crazy ass baffles all of our minds. And there is Aunt Clara, who seems to have the answer to everyone else's problems, except for her own. Her husband, George's obsessive behavior with women and alcohol had resulted in nothing more than her crying to my mother many long awaking nights and becoming broke from bailing him, repeatedly, out of jail.

"I heard you just flipped and sold a house in Richmond", my Aunt Jennifer interestedly inquired?

"I did," I proudly admitted.

"There are a couple houses around my way that has a lot of potential. They just need someone to come in and fix it up to be sold."

"I don't know about that Aunt Jen. I'm thinking about taking some time off from everything. My house is on the market right now. Once I sale that, I'm just going to prepare for the arrival of my baby."

"I still can't believe it. My little sunshine is having a baby." Her face glowed proudly. "For a minute, I thought you were going to be like me... single for the rest of your life."

"There are moments, I still believe that I might be single, forever," I added. Those words were sad to admit. "Have you ever wanted to be married?"

"Not really. I can live my life without ever marrying someone."

"Do you enjoy being single," I asked hoping if her single status would have any profound affect on me to look forward to enjoying?

She inhaled deeply and then softly replied, "For the most part, I do. There are those moments of loneliness that I occasionally suffer through. But, I have a friend. And we have our dates and travel here and there. And then when we both get tired, I go to my house and he goes to his house. I like it like that."

Her life sounded far from being poetic as I had conceived it to be. There was a short moment of silence. She must have read the emptiness I now felt on my face. And then she added, "Now that you are successful and have a baby along the way, what else do you want?"

"What do you mean," I glanced at her oddly, thinking that there was something she knew, that I didn't?

"I mean, is this it for you? Or is there more that you passionately want to have in your life," she profoundly asked?

Her insightful question caught me a bit off guard. But with Aunt Jennifer she would just listen and not try to interrogate your decision. "I would like to get marry, one day, to the right guy." The revelation was shocking at first to hear myself say. Yet, at the same time, reaffirming of what I once felt. For some reason, the idea of me marrying someone felt so long ago.

"I understand. You just haven't found him yet, right?"

"No. I have, but...." I couldn't find the right words to finish my sentence.

"You know what I'm gonna do when I get tired of my sisters and all of their families, today?"

"What?"

"I'm gonna go back to my house, drink a glass of my wine and sleep alone in my bed. That's my story," she concluded before rising up from the table and joining her loud mouth sisters in the kitchen.

I was suddenly lost in deep thought the remaining of Thanksgiving Day. My younger and older cousins joyfully raced in and out my mom's house, like they were at a park. There was a continuous flow of laughter escaping the kitchen table. And of course, the men, including my Uncle Jerry and Uncle George, sat like mannequins in front of the television watching the football game, stiffen by the voices of women that surrounded them. But, all I did was dwell on what Aunt Jennifer said. Unintended or not, it certainly had a profound affect on me. It left such a profound affect on me, that once the house emptied of all the chatter and ruckus, I found myself in the shower.

"Where are you going," Tamra questioned, very observant of me thumbing through the dresser drawers trying to find the perfect panty and matching bra, with my towel tightly tugged around my wet body?

"I'm going out for a minute." I answered, trying not relay too much information.

"I see," I heard her mumbled. "This dress is cute. It would be more flattering around your waistline. You know, just in case you wanted to hide something." It was a black empire waist dress. She pulled it out of the collection of dresses that I had lying across the bed on hangers. I hadn't gained too much obvious weight, just yet. But, I accepted her suggestion anyhow.

I knew, then, that I didn't have to say a word. She understood. "You should wear this diamond pendant," she advised, as she walked over to our mother's jewelry box and held it up high. The glitter of the diamond dangled from her finger.

"Thanks, Tamra. This is gorgeous." I stooped down low so that she could fasten the necklace around my neck.

The dress was nicely fitting for me and I felt quite pretty when I glared at myself in the mirror.

"You know, on a night like tonight, I would go to this new adult spot called, 'Charisma'."

I paused for a moment and studied her through the dresser mirror, sitting comfortably along my mother's bed, speaking as if her words were not intended for anyone particular. "Charisma," I asked?

"Yeah, Charisma. It's a nice spot over there by the mall. You can't miss it. It has a jazzy ambience, which is why I know you would like it. And the owner just so happens to be a good friend of mind..."

I couldn't help myself from smiling. "I know where it is. I've been there before," I slyly replied?

"Alright then. In that case, give him my love, when you see him," she ended. I couldn't move my eyes off from her, until she had left the room.

Okay Rocqui, let's do this. I needed a bit of self encouragement to get out of my car and walked across the full parking lot that was facing 'Charisma'. I exhaled and walked through the entrance. The last time I was here, it was like a big empty shell. Nothing but opened studded walls and Avery. I couldn't wait to see his ideas become a reality.

There was an African American gentleman that greeted me at the door and led me towards the live jazz melodies harmonizing to a nearly sold out crowd. Every seat on the floor was taken. He led me up towards the bar and I took the last seat available. Perfect I thought. I could keep one eye on the musicians at center stage and another eye on the door's entrance, anticipating his arrival any minute.

The room was dark and filled with floating concert lights. After each set the musicians played, everyone rose to their feet and applauded. But that wasn't why I was here. I was here because I wanted to see Avery because, I didn't want to spend my holidays, with families, only to come home to an empty bed. I knew that I loved him more and more with each passing day and I wanted another chance to finally tell him, even if it meant sitting alone, at a crowded club, looking rather ridiculous, waiting for him to walk through the entrance, at any given time.

I knew that Tamra understood what I was doing, but I had to verify that she knew what she was talking about. I stopped a waitress that scurried before me with a tray of drinks in her hand and asked, "Excuse me, but who is the owner of this club?"

She looked at me like my question was quite trivial and then answered, "I don't know ma'am. All I know is Jack is the manager." And she quickly trailed off to deliver those drinks.

"What could I get for you tonight," the bartender, a black gentleman with dreads pulled into a pony tail, smiled and asked?

"A shot of sanity," I quickly answered, becoming increasingly aware of my foolish behavior.

"I don't have any sanity. But I do have Patron. Would you like some?"

I laughed. "No, that's the last thing I need. You wouldn't happen to have any milk, would you," I comically inquired?

"Milk? Now that's a first."

" I know that may sound strange for a person to ask for a glass of milk at a nightclub. I just need something without alcohol or caffeine in it."

"I might have some milk back here somewhere. How 'bout I whip you up something smooth and alcohol-free?"

"That would be perfect," I answered. Then, he walked off to the other end of the bar. I sat and enjoyed the likes of Norman Brown melodies, escaping my thoughts through the musician's guitar, until the bartender returned with a frothy chocolately-style drink.

I carefully studied the drink before I asked, "This isn't Bailey's Irish Cream, is it?"

"No ma'am. I wouldn't give you something that you didn't ask for. Try it and see."

I slurped the creamy chocolate flavor from the straw. "This is pretty good."

"See there. Another satisfied customer," he gloated.

I figured since he appeared to be friendly enough, I could ask a few questions about this place, without coming off as too nosey. "How long has this place been open," was my first question?

"It's been open about a month or so now?"

"I think this is fantastic. I love jazz."

"Apparently, so does everyone else, in Fayetteville. This place has been booming every since opening night."

"Really?"

"Yes, really. The owner knows a lot about good business. He has this other place over off on Hay Street, called Georgia's and it's a nice place too."

"I've been to that place before. The owner name is Andre, Angelo, or..." I tried to play off my knowledge of him.

"Avery," he concluded my sentence.

"Yeah, Avery. That's right."

"Is he here? I haven't seen him in a while and I just wanted to say 'hi'.

"He'll probably come through some time tonight. He usually does."

"What's your name again," he asked, figuring I may be of some importance.

"Tamra," I lied.

"Well Tamra, if I see him, I would tell him that you were looking for him."

"You'd that."

After another desperate hour of waiting and slurping on milkshakes, I gave up. I got up from my seat and strolled through a cheerful partying crowd before I made my way through the door and out to my car. I was sad and hurting inside. He didn't come. Avery never showed up.

Then something interestingly happened. Right as I was starting my car, I looked out of my windshield and saw a white Escalade steer right passed me. I had known, instinctually, that it was Avery. I watched the trucks every turn, until it parked, across the driveway, directly behind me in plain sight of my rear view window. I nervously waited for Avery to reveal himself, recanting what I wanted to say and what I wanted do. Should I tell him about our baby? Maybe I should wait until later. I do have a few months ahead before it becomes obvious. First, I would tell him how much I've missed him and how sorry I was for ever dismissing the opportunity to be with him.

And just as I imagined, he appeared. He was tall and looked mouth-dropping stunningly dressed in a collard shirt and slacks. I double checked my makeup. Then I applied a little more lipstick and puckered in the mirror. I was anxiously excited to open the door and greet him, until out of nowhere another woman joined him at his side. She was brown-skinned just like him, a bit more thickly than me, but had the look of happiness on her gleaming face.

I was stunned, paralyzed in my thoughts and actions. I couldn't think or do anything more. I tried to snap out of my state of shock but I couldn't peel my eyes away from the sight of them joining hands and strutting merrily into the club, together. I just remained stiffed inside my car, while I felt the tears burning behind my eyes.

27

Waking up the next morning was the start of my life changing forever. I laid there somewhere lost between loneliness and sadness, while I stared deeply off into my mother's high ceiling. Water filled my eyes and spilled down my face, creating dampness along the pillow beneath my head. Round and round in a circle, I went, chasing a dream of happiness, only to have fallen into a pit of sorrow. I wished that I'd never met Avery. The thought of me ever being held within his comforting arms, lingers me with pain. It was over now. There would never be an *us* and it hurt like hell to admit that to myself. My depressing thoughts were interrupted by a sudden knock at the door. "Rocqui, are you getting dress?" It was Tamra.

I was hoping that she would not forcefully intrude on my moment of pity. I just needed to be alone. The word 'alone' itself was becoming more and more synonymous with my life.

Last night, my heart weighed so heavy with pain that it paralyzed me from going any further than beyond my mother's favorite vintage sofa that furnished her living room. I sat motionless, staring only through the blackness that surrounded me. My face felt swollen and tender as the tears continued to flow down my face. I wasn't alone too much longer before Tamra's shadowy presence made a sudden appearance from the stairs.

I eyed her curious pursuit, as I remained hidden in the background of darkness, watching her tiptoe in and out of the downstairs rooms to find me. I should have allowed her to stroll back upstairs, but it was more than my voice that called out to her.

"I'm right here Tamra," I whispered, just loud enough so that she could hear me.

Her nightgown gently floated, ghostly-like, as her feet anxiously paced towards the desperation in my voice. "So..." she tried to whisper, but the excitement in her voice was hardly contained. "How did it go?"

I couldn't see her actual smile, but I easily detected that she was hopeful that everything went as she expected. I sniffed again and formed my quivering lips to say, "I didn't see Avery." I couldn't force myself to admit to her and myself again that I actually saw Avery with another woman. The admission would have led me down another trip of wasteful tears.

"I'm so sorry." She was more disappointed than I'd expected her to be. She embraced my neck with a tight hug and leaned her head on my shoulder.

I pressed my lips on her forehead. "It's okay. I'm gonna be okay." I reminded myself but expressed it openly so that she could hear.

She unlocked her arm from around my neck and tightly gripped my hands in hers. "It's gonna work out. I promise you, Rocqui. He really loves you." Her words were pleading and promising, but not what I wanted to hear.

"If anyone else guarantees me that again, I'm gonna scream," I retorted through clenched teeth.

"Okay. I won't say it again." She rested her defense for Avery. "How 'bout we get some sleep for now?" She gently tapped my leg in a motherly fashion. "We have an early morning ahead."

"You go ahead. I'll be up soon." She hugged me one last time and disappeared up the dark stairway. I had no idea when 'soon' came, but at some point, I made it up the stairs and into my mother's bed.

I turned over to my side, in the direction of the door and lied, "I'm almost ready." If I knew my sister, as well as I do, that lie would sustain her weary mind only for a mere second. And then she'll be back, once again to see if I am true to my words. I couldn't really blame her. She, Diesel and my mom are anxious about driving up to Boone NC this morning. It was a mini cause for celebration. Our mother had lived a day beyond Thanksgiving. There was hope that underlined our intentions to make this journey up to the mountains. The same hoped we sought when our dad died...the hope for peace.

When my dad died our house became a strange place. It felt empty and displaced from our memories of what it once held. Everything that belonged to him or reminded us of him sort of hung around waiting for his return. We all subconsciously waited. No one sat in his recliner in the den. His ole beaten-up truck remained in the same spot were he left it parked. His wool hat still hung on the coat rack along the entrance into our home. Our movement became robotic as we all tried to find a way to cope with the lost of his death.

Christmas was a couple of days away. No one seemed to care or have any interest in celebrating. I walked in on my mother sitting in the family room experiencing one of her mournful moments of sobbing uncontrollably surrounded by a sea of unfolded laundry. I eased next to her side and gently stroke her back joining her in a few expelled tears of my own.

"Its gonna be okay, Mom," I softly whispered. I didn't really know that. And on some level, I didn't believe it. But, at that moment, it felt like what I needed to say.

Soon as she recovered from her moment of sorrow, with her back fully erected she glared at me oddly. "I was just folding up some clothes and ran across your daddy's favorite fishing shirt." She looked down into her lap where she had nearly drenched it with tears and held it up.

She released a hollow empty laugh. I smiled at the recollection of seeing my daddy wearing this plaid red and green shirt every Saturday when he was planning to go fishing. A deep inhale of air heaved her chest. She looked at me again and decided, "Christmas is just a few days away. You know what we should do," she asked not necessarily waiting for me to answer? "We should go somewhere? I don't think I could stand to spend this Christmas here in this house, this year." Her lips began to quiver again. And tears flooded her eyes again. But this time, she didn't break down into hysteria, like earlier. She wiped her tears away and breathing easily, added "Let's go to the mountains."

I was astounded by her suggestion. We've always chosen our family vacations during the summer, surrounded by sand and water, with the excruciating heat beaming down on our warm faces. Never had anyone suggested or ever thought of going anywhere cold or even with snow. Yet the idea prompted an immediate comfort through me.

We all spent the remaining day packing our clothes, before leaving the very next day to Boone NC. The gradual elevation drew us closer towards the clear blue skies. Instantly, as I read the green sign that said 'Boone City Limit', we entered a territory covered in snow. It felt magical and breathtaking.

Our cabin was wide with tall skyline windows and a floor to ceiling stone wood burning fireplace. I, Monty, and Tamra raced upstairs to make claims on our bedrooms. The rooms were neatly furnished with logged bunk beds and side by side twins beds. There were at least 5 bedrooms, yet every night we all found ourselves camped in front of the fireplace, cocooned in our sleeping bags.

While Tamra, Monty and myself were easily mode over with excitement from testing the laws of nature, skiing recklessly down the white covered slopes and engaging in continual snowball combat, there were still moments in which I was drawn into my mother's sadness.

One day, I noticed from a distance, her eyes were fixated through the tall picturesque window, looking beyond the snow capped mountains that extended as far as the eyes could see.

I walked up next to her and softly spoke, "What do you see?"

"Heaven," she answered. When she said it, I immediately saw it too.

For, a second, I got over my sorrowfulness and set up in the middle of the bed and contemplated how I was going to live my life, without the man I truly loved. Before I became deep within my pessimistic thought, I felt a strange fluttering motion inside my belly. The movement had taken me totally by surprise, which led me to suspect that it could have been gas. But the gas that I've had before, never felt anything like this. I grabbed the hem of my nightshirt and held it up high to take note of its possible action again. And there it was again. This time, I witnessed the fluttering motion of my stomach and I knew, miraculously that it was my baby. Joy masked over my sadness and I was ready to come alive again and began my day.

Diesel and Tamra had already left to pick up the SUV rental, while I steady gotten dressed and rushed downstairs to check on mom.

"Mom, why have you gotten back in bed," I conceringly asked? Her body was cradle to one side of the bed, while the clothes she and I had selected earlier were still stacked and folded next to her empty luggage. I was dressed, in a wool sweater and skinny jeans neatly snug inside a pair of Uggs suede boots.

"Rocqui, I don't feel so good," she said weakly. I sat along side of her ailing body. I hoped that it was, only, too much Sweet Potato Pie, that she'd eaten yesterday that was causing her discomfort.

"What's wrong mommy? Can I get you something," I asked filled with trepidation in my voice. I was hoping that her answer would be of something that could be easily cured by a dose of Pepto-Bismol.

"I need to go to the hospital," she shockingly announced. All the days of my life, I've never known my mother to willfully request to go to the hospital. My shock was quickly displaced with anxiety, as I quickly gathered some of my mother's things and assisted her into the car. Over all the anxiety and nervousness that I was succumb with, I knew, instictively that she would never return home again.

Along the drive there, I alerted Dr. Aditri that we were in route to the hospital and she assured me that a nurse would be waiting outside the Emergency Room, with a wheelchair awaiting our arrival. The nurse immediately hurried to my car and helped me position my mother into a wheelchair before she rushed her off inside the building. I could feel my chest hurting from the rapid beats of my heart, as I nervously filled out my mother's admittance papers. My world around me began to feel cloudy. I couldn't really see anyone or feel anything except for the desperation to hold on to my mother's love, who was now laying inside her hospital room.

The nurse with the wheelchair, stayed with my mother until the I.V. was inserted inside her arm and her heart beat was monitored on the EKG positioned next to her bed. After the nurse was gone, everything fell silenced, except for the rhythm of her heart beating. And I eyed my mother intensely resting comfortably from the chair next to her bed, crossing my fingers that today would not be the day that she says 'Goodbye'.

The silenced came to an end with the panicked arrival of Tamra and Diesel. "What happened," she emotionally demanded?

I couldn't expelled an answer. My mind were at a lost for words. I wanted to make her think that our mother was going to be okay. But, even, I, at that point, understood that to no longer to be so. I found only these words to say. "We will have to wait and see what Dr. Aditri says."

Dr. Aditri finally arrived wearing her white medical jacket and holding in her hand, my mother's medical chart. She seemed, particularly, taller as she stood at the base of my mother's bed, quietly taking notes and flipping through her chart before she was ready to address us on my mother's status. When her lips parted, I held onto my breath, hoping that something good would come out of the words she would say. She looked frankly at me and stated, "Right now, your mother is resting with the medicine I had the nurse to administer to her... But there is nothing more medically that I can do." Her words felt impersonal and detached.

"Will she wake up, again," Tamra belted out, through her sobbing face?

"She should wake up. Give her about another hour or so... okay", Dr. Aditri answered.

I heard Dr. Aditri, responded sympathetically, "I'm sorry" before she disappeared out of our lives forever.

And like the words Dr Aditri had spoken, my mother had awaken to a more contented and joyful spirit. "I'm really sorry about the ski trip, girls. Her eyes looked over the sadness that covered our faces.

"Mommy, we don't care about any ski trip. We just want you to come home," Tamra pleaded, as she buried her weeping face into Diesel's chest.

"Well Dear... I was thinking that it was time that I do go Home." My mother reached out for Tamra's hand and testified. "Life's has been good to me baby. And now it's time that I see my Heavenly Father. While you girls may cry at my funeral, I'm going to be rejoicing." She smiled deeply at us, as if all of those long Sundays that were spent at church worshipping and praying and adhering to the word of God was about to pay off. Being a believer of Christ, did not console me, one bit, that my mother was dieing, right before me.

Tamra continued to cry out, "We're going to miss you, mommy."

"I'm gonna miss you all too. But, don't spend too much time crying over me. Tears are not welcome in Heaven, only joy."

Over the next forty-eight hours, the hospital room became unbearably crowded, filled with aunts, uncles, cousins, friends and other distant relatives that I haven't seen since forever. There were times, when I selfishly wanted them all to disappear so that I could have a minute alone with her. But, that was often short and interrupted. The few times I was allowed, I sat alongside of her bed and she read a few scriptures out of the Bible to me. We even played a short game of Scrabble. And I was elated in those stolen moments of happiness, we shared between us.

On one visit, my mother's sisters cheerfully brought with them a large gift wrapped in brown paper and a large bow. When my mother ripped the paper off it, she revealed a beautiful framed portrait of her and her sisters sharing her last birthday together at the Rose Garden. They all wore these bright spring colored dresses and exquisite hats on their heads. My mother sat centered surrounded by her sister's loving smiles. There wasn't a dry eye in the room after its revelation.

I scrambled through keeping the details and accuracies of my business intact during her sporadic periods of rest. Each time she closed her eyes, a chill went through me. It made me weary if she would awaken. But the harmonizing beep of her heart signaling, kept me at ease. At ease, long enough to return a few emails and phone calls to my office.

"Have I told you lately, how proud I am of you," my mother meekly implied. She'd awaken from a brief nap.

I sat across the room from her hospital bed, with my finger dancing across the keyboard of my laptop. My rhythm paused, while my fingers rested over the keys. I searched through her soft strained eyes for an answer. "Yes." I mumbled, even though my memory couldn't jolt to the actual time and place.

"Well, I am telling you again. I'm very proud of you Rocqui and the woman you've turned out to be." Her body was slightly elevated in her bed, with all the wires and plugs connecting to her life. "I've always knew that whatever situation you'd found yourself in, you would be okay," she continued.

I listened on, intently even though her words were increasingly making me nervous. "You've always been a leader... When all this is over, I'm gonna still need you to lead."

"I will mom. I'm gonna make sure that everything is taken cared of," I promised"

"I know. But, I don't mean by mothering Tamra or stressing yourself out trying to keep Monty off the streets. I mean... lead by example."

She had me slightly baffled. However, I knew that there was a specific point that she was trying to make. "This cancer thing is serious. And because it had taken over my life, there is a strong possibility that it may do the same for you and Tamra."

"I know mom. I get annual checkups and practice self-examinations, monthly." I tried to maintain a steady voice, even though I told a partial lie. When my mother was first diagnosed with cancer, Tamra and I would have monthly scheduled calls to remind each other to check our breasts. However, as soon as she went into remission, so did we.

"I want you girls to understand how important that you check yourself. Every month." Her words were slow but purposeful..." and go annually for your mammogram tests and be supportive of breast cancer research."

Immediately, pink ribbons, pink hotel rooms, pink lids on sponsoring brands of yogurt, pink cars... everything pink flashed through my head. I understood her completely and answered respectfully, "yes ma'am".

"I want you girls to commit to the fight of breast cancer research, even if you're never diagnosed with breast cancer, which I hoped that you are not, if God forbids."

I felt the strength of her life through her hands as I tightly held them, while standing by her bedside. "Okay." Her heart-felt words were painstaking to receive. But, I nodded my head to reaffirm my agreement.

"Breast Cancer is serious, but it doesn't have to mean death," she concluded.

Yet on December 1st, breast cancer brought an end to my mother's joyous life. I could see that day so clearly in my head, as if I was reliving it each and every moment of my own life. It was just she and I and my laptop. To me, it was just another day awakening from another sleepless night. Tamra and Diesel had planned to come by later because I finally decided that I was going to commit to my hair appointment and make it back to the hospital in just a couple of hours. I had stolen a few glances at her as I always do, while she slept contently, as I checked my email and updated my status and checked on the status of others. I knew that in a couple hours she would be awake and probably hungry. I decided to get some work out of the way until then.

However, she had awoken a little earlier. I could hear her vaguely mumbling something, while her eyes remained closed. At first, I didn't think much to draw much attention away from my laptop to attend to her every word, because she had done this on a few occasions before. But then she suddenly called out my daddy's name, like he was standing right next to her. "Randy" My eyes immediately widen with fear and my heart dropped. I jumped from my chair, tossing my laptop down behind me in the chair and alarmingly raced to her side.

"Mom" I cried out grabbing her hand!

Her peaceful eyes slowly appeared. "Yes Dear," she answered humbly.

"Daddy is not here. I'm here."

"Your daddy is here. I'm looking at him right now," she softly spoke. "Doesn't he look as handsome as the last time I saw him." Her eyes remained forward as if she was visualizing everything she had just said. "I know Honey, she is gonna be fine. She is your daughter," she continued on starring at nothing before him.

"Mom, you are just dreaming. I'm here. Everything is gonna be okay."

"Yes Dear. Everything is gonna be okay. I love you," she mumbled. Then suddenly there was silence. And her eyes gently closed. Before I could think about what to do next, the monitor beside her bed hummed a flatline. I alarmingly rushed out into the lobby screaming, hysterically, for someone to save my mother. But those that summon my call walked slowly and remained calmed while my entire world had suddenly stopped. They all just circled my mother's lifeless body in their scrubs and white jackets, only to read her monitors, double check her pulse and to call the time of her death. After that, everything that once felt normal became unreal.

For many days after she was gone, I tried to remember every meaningful conversation we ever had. I dwelled over and over again if I had told her everything I ever wanted to say. It kept me up at night writing down a list of things that I have always wanted to say. It felt like something was beating me up on the inside. Even though, I told her a million times before that I love her, I wasn't even sure anymore if she knew how much she really meant to me.

The day of the funeral, my body felt seemingly numb. There was an overwhelmingly presence of mourners standing outside, as the black limousine, guided us to the front of the church. Yet, my eyes saw no one. The procession down the aisle leading towards my mother's casket resulted in the touch of many sorrowful hands. Still, I felt no one. And the sympathetic hugs that embraced my neck after they bared witness to my mother deserted body, left no strained on my soul to cry out for sadness.

We were all present, including Monty, as he was escorted by a uniformed Sheriff. And we all held, grippingly tight, one another's hand, as the limousine led the parade to the burial sight. The earth was opened and ready to receive my mother's casket. The grey clouds steadily moved in and sprinkled the earth's crust as her casket was lowered into the ground.

It was then, at that moment, that I began to feel again. I could feel my legs barely move, when I stumbled away from the burial ground. And my heart began to feel heavy, when my eyes were rushed with tears. Then, I felt someone's arm encase my body and guide me up the hill. I heard him say, "It's gonna be okay, Rocqui. I'm right here for you."

For a second, I thought I was imagining the words spoken from a familiar voice. Until I stopped and looked directly into Avery's face.

"What are you doing here," I found myself asking over my muffled cry?

"I was here for the funeral. And I'm here for you," he sensitively admitted.

I pulled myself away from his gentle hold. "I don't need you here for me. I'm quite fine, without you," I affirmed bluntly.

I forced my legs to move quickly away from him. "Rocqui, please wait a minute and let's talk."

The force of anger halted my legs. My eyes veered back and saw his vulnerable face. I couldn't do it. I wasn't going to allow myself to get sucked into this moment of weakness only to be hurt later. "I don't want to talk to you now. I don't need your sympathy just because I just buried my mother. Just leave me alone," I belted out.

Rushed tears nearly blinded me from seeing where I was going. Out of nowhere, Tamra intercepted my path, as I was distancing myself further away from Avery's presence. "Rocqui, here is someone I want you to meet." A honey skin-tone lady stepped into my vision. "This is Angela," Tamra proceeded with the introduction. Angela had a warm smile that replaced her doubtful disposition, when she extended her hand before me.

I, mechanically, reached out to shake her hand. There was something peculiar about her. "Hi," she greeted. "I'm Avery's sister. I'm sorry to have met you under these circumstances. But, I've heard so much about you."

"Hi," I muttered, lost in a bit of confusion. Retracing my thoughts, the picture before me was finally becoming clear. "It was you. You were the one with Avery that night at the club?"

"Yes, I was. He thought you were going to be there. He wanted me to meet you," she easily replied.

I glared back at Avery, who was still standing a few feet away from me. "You came to the club night looking for me," I puzzlingly asked?

"Yes, I was looking for you," he echoed, with his steps in stride moving towards me. "I wanted to see you again. But when I found out your mom died, I decided to wait for while. I know right now is a hard time for you. I just wanted to let you know that I am still here for you if you need me to be," he desperately pleaded.

I was at a lost for words, momentarily. Everything in my past had fast-forward way ahead of me. I had to stop and think and gather my thoughts. And then, I remembered that I was pregnant, with his baby. My eyes looked downward at my hand gliding across my belly.

"I don't really need you to be here for me as much as I want you to be", I slowly revealed.

"That's good to know, because, there is nothing else I want more. You are my world, Rocqui. And it had been too hard to just let that go."

I looked back at my mother's dirt covered burial ground. A part of my spirit fell weak once again as I began to welt out more tears. I could feel Avery's arms tightly holding on to me as he proclaimed, "I'm here now. It's gonna be okay."

I looked up at him through my watery eyes and smiled. "I know. She promised me that it would be."

"Is the limo taking you all back to your mother's house?"

"No. We are going back to the church and then everyone is gathering at my mother's house afterwards."

"Would you like for me to call you later, when you have a moment and then we could talk?"

"No. I would rather if you stayed right here with me."

"Okay." His fingers gently intertwined into mine as we strolled up towards the black limo and got inside. I was held snug under the security of his arms, when I quietly affirmed, "I love you Avery."

He tenderly conveyed back, "I've never stopped."

28

I was walking over ice, as cold as the ceramic tile felt underneath my feet. The stark white cabinets added light to the shadowy room. There was something familiar about this kitchen, even though I've never seen it in all the days of my life.

I looked over the two eggs, the butter, and the sour cream that were lined up along the white marbled countertop. I took a deep breath before I was about to submerge my hands into the ingredients. The first step, preheat oven to three hundred fifty degrees.

Next step, crack open the eggs onto the flour inside a white ceramic bowl. Then, I added the room temperature butter, and folded one cup of sour cream into the mixture, before I was ready to mix. I vigorously blended all of the ingredients with the hand mixer, until there was a creamy smoothed yellowish batter. Carefully, I emptied the batter into a tube pan and placed it inside the preheated oven.

An hour an a half later, the timer dinged. The cake rose to its golden fluffy perfection.

I was beside myself at my beautiful creation. It was the first time ever that I had created a Sour Cream Cake just like my mother's. I couldn't wait to share it with her the likes of what she had perfected as she awaited a slice, sitting at the kitchen table.

"It looks delicious," she praised, as I placed a small crystal plate with a slice of my cake before her. Her flowy, long hair graced her luminous angelic face. A long white gown draped around her ankles. I studied her reaction, as she dug her fork into it and tasted her first bite.

However, the looks of her face had suddenly changed. Her pleased, delicate smile had been suddenly erased by a startling glare. Her forehead tightly crinkled, while I noted her eyes strangely widening. "Rocqui... did you add any sugar to this cake," she asked?

"Here, let me taste it." I grabbed a fork and placed a small bite into my mouth. It looked deliciously sweet, but tasted more like a dry sponge. We both quickly emptied our mouths out into a napkin. I rushed to the sink to get a glass of water to rinse away the taste of disappointment. However, by the time I returned back to the table with a glass filled with water for her to drink, she was gone.

My hand that held the glass frantically opened and shattered pieces of glass fell between my toes. Water drenched along the hem of my nightgown. I felt my chest panting with fear as a flow of blood rushed through my body, before I'd fretfully awaken.

I sat up in the bed breathing heavily. My eyes darted swiftly around the darkness, trying to make-out where I was. But I was still in a dazed and a bit confused. Nothing about that room was recognizable, at first. Until I felt a gentle leg grazed against my stiff body. My alerting state fell at ease when I saw Avery's body lying in a deep slumber next to me. Everything suddenly became clearer.

I remembered that I was where I have been every since the day of my mother's funeral. I was at Avery's house.

There was never any formal invitation or even a slight discussion about if I wanted to live with him, during my stay in Fayetteville. I just simply followed him back to his house after family and guests gathered at my mother's house to pay their respects and share their condolences. And I've been here ever since.

Being here has been comforting and easy, but I've felt a certain absence from my life. I've been so bored, at times, that I had resorted to cleaning. My sister said that I was simply nesting, preparing for our baby. Yet I believed that I have been using cleaning as a way to pass time before my next trip to Richmond. The first time I washed the dishes and picked up a broom and the mop, Avery walked in and announced, "Baby you don't have to do all of that."

"Honey, just because I'm pregnant does not mean I'm handicap," I replied.

He laughed. "No, that's not what I mean. I have a housekeeper that comes twice a week to help keep this place in order."

"Are you serious?" I was overly excited with that news.

"Yes. She will be here tomorrow."

"I love you," I crooned.

"Gawd. If I would have known that this is all it took for you to love me I would have told you a long time ago that I had a housekeeper."

But, that still didn't stop me from vacuuming occasionally and scrubbing the bathroom toilet and sinks. Avery even considerately moved some of his clothes into the other room, so that I would have plenty of room for my things. However, I didn't have a lot of things with me, just a luggage set of clothes. The rest of my belongings remained at my home in Richmond, where I planned on returning to in just a couple of days.

Even though, I hated to admit it, I was anxious to get back on my own turf and return to the hustling and bustling of work.

It's been three weeks now since my mother's death. The house that once filled our lives with happiness and blissful memories had now become an empty space. About a week after my mother's funeral, Tamra and I cleared every wall, emptied ever room and storage to erase the memories of a life we once held.

On one particular day, when I was going through my mother's closet packing away her belongings, I ran across my daddy's favorite black leather loafers. It's been many long years since I last saw them. I picked them up and held them in my hands. The heels were unevenly worn. And along the sides, there were visible scuff marks. Other than the normal wear and tear of shoes, his shoes were perfectly fine...fitting to be still worn by him if he was alive today.

All of a sudden, I had the uncontrollable urge to laugh and cry at the same time. I pictured him wearing them with his black dress socks around his scrawny hairy legs and boney knees chilling at a cookout or a family gathering, caring less about what people thought of him. It didn't really matter the occasion or even the season. He would find some kind of way to include those black shoes as apart of his wardrobe.

He attended Monty's high school commencement, wearing those very same shoes and we clowned him every step of the way. We warned him that people were going to be looking at us crazy if he dared to wear them out of the house. But, he paid us no mind, proudly strutting around town like they were the last of its kind ever to be made. In his defense he would always tell us, "If they are good enough for church then they are good enough for anywhere else."

That was one of my hardest days to get through. I have cried fewer times today than I did yesterday. Avery says sometimes he hears me whimpering in my sleep. I miss her. And on that particular day, I was missing them both.

The movers and packers arrived a few days later and cleared the house completely of all that it once was. I maintained my mother's Queen Rice Antique Bedroom Suite at Avery's, now occupying one of his spare bedrooms. Tamra intends to add the formal dining set to her new home that she and Diesel are planning to buy some day.

We both easily agreed that our parent's house was too big and too expensive to maintain. The remaining furniture was either stored for Monty's release from incarceration or donated to Goodwill. Everything that I connected with the meaning of home was now gone. The only thing that remained untouched was the flower bed my mother religiously manicured, every Saturday afternoon. It now embeds a 'For Sale' sign next to it, in the center of the lawn.

"It smells like a pine sol commercial in here," Tamra made no reservations announcing when she visited. "What have you been doing with yourself besides cleaning," she questioned as she walked through the house?

"A little bit of this and a little bit of that," I answered in a joyful spirit.

"It looks like you have been doing a lot of shopping. I like what you've done with the place", Tamra complimented, noting all the intricate details of my décor of Avery's house.

"It turned out better than I'd planned," I responded, standing next to her gazing up at the crimson accent wall flanked by a white oversized sofa, with vibrant pattern of throw pillows.

"Where did you get this," she asked pointing to the Andover cabinet that was positioned against the opposite wall of the white sofa?

"We got it from the Pottery Barn," I answered smiling, proudly showing off my favorite piece.

"I like it," she admired, as her fingertips glided across the top of its rich licorice finished.

"You should see how we decorated the nursery," I politely implied.

"Looks like someone has been busy turning this house into a home."

"I know," I conceited. "A couple of weeks ago, I was just flipping through the pages of a Pottery Barn catalog that Avery had received in the mail. And he liked everything that I showed him so much that we went to the store and bought them, just like that."

"Just like that," Tamra repeated?

"And he paid for everything, just like that," I maintained. "I didn't realize how big this house really was until I started decorating certain rooms."

"You seem to be pretty excited about all this," Tamra realized after carefully studying the glow on my face.

"I am," I admitted. "Now, if that would have been Zoric, he would have been the one examining the pages of Pottery Barn, trying to find the most expensive piece only to coerce me into buying it later," I added.

"That's because Zoric is gay," Tamra comically implied.

"What," I surprisingly reacted?

"Come on, Rocqui. Any man that uses an extensive line of hair care products and moisturizers and gets his nails manicured more often than a woman is on the borderline of being gay."

My memories retraced back to Zoric's colored coded arrangement of clothes hanging neatly on wooden hangers inside our walk-in closet. Then there were times, I was confronted by his neurotic insistence that his t-shirts had to be pressed and the white tees had to be placed separately from his black tees. In addition, he often reminded me that his cotton briefs had no place near his silk boxers. And in return for all of my effort of trying to please him, he would leave those very same worn clothes fully exposed trailing along from the bedroom floor to bathroom. His obsession with perfecting his look could have been misunderstood as being gay. Yet his greed and selfishness only epitomizes his desire for women. I could hardly sustain myself from laughing to reply, "Zoric is a lot of things. But he is certainly not gay."

"Every time I've seen Zoric, he always looks better than me. Now, that is definitely a red flag anytime a man is more prim and proper than the woman he is with."

"Zoric is very indulgent. He comes from a place of nothing and now his tries to overcompensate with things and women."

"Speaking of Zoric, do you miss him?"

A sporadic chuckle left me before I answered, "I miss Zoric like I missed this corn that I had removed from my right toe. Despite his extracurricular activities, Zoric is still a good man."

"Yeah, right. He was good at looking good. Zoric was fine and all. But, eventually he would have left you for another man." She continued her comic stance.

"Well, if Julia is a man, I hope they live happily together."

We moved into the kitchen. Tamra settled at the island, in a barstool, while I poured us some juice. "Does all this shopping and decorating make it official," Tamra insinuated?

An involuntary smile spread across my face, before I replied "I love him more than I've ever imagined loving anyone. We sit up late at night talking about the baby and our future plans together. But..."

"But," she yelled! "What do you mean *But*? Do you know how hard I've worked trying to bring you two together? Like that night you went to his club. I called him and told him you were on your way there to see him. Did you know that? And when that backfired, I was back at work trying to come up with another plan to bring you and him together again, before mom died. So, don't conclude your sentence with me with a *But.*"

"Yes, I know that you were the mastermind behind arranging for us to run into each other that night. And I do thank you for all of your hard work," I added sarcastically. "But... I don't know if I'm ready to give up my business. I enjoy what I do. I've worked hard all of my life to be successful and now that I'm in that place, I don't want to give it up."

"I know you are not still talking about living in Richmond. You have a baby on the way by the greatest man I've ever met, besides my husband and you are still not sure?"

"Living in Richmond is not the issue anymore. It's just that my business is in Richmond. It's my livelihood that I'm talking about."

"What about being a mother? Isn't that important to you?"

"Tamra, you don't understand. There is nothing more important to me, than becoming a mother. But, who says that I couldn't be a mother and still have my business, or even the man that I love. I'm willing to make sacrifices to make this work. I just don't know how. What would be wrong with him moving to Richmond with me?"

"Maybe he doesn't want to move to Richmond. Maybe he is happier living in Fayetteville."

"And maybe I'm happier maintaining my business..."

"Have you talked to Avery about this?"

"No. Not yet. I went to Richmond last week and even though he didn't say it, I could tell he was not happy about me staying away for 3 days. But, I don't know what else to do."

"You have to talk to him, for one thing. Then, eventually you'll have to make a decision; business in Richmond or family in Fayetteville."

"Tuesday, we have a prenatal appointment. And he's going to Richmond with me. I'm kinda excited, but very nervous at the same time. You're right, though. I definitely need to have that talk before then."

The sensor on the door leading into the garage chimed. CheeChee entered into the kitchen first, followed by Sasha. Avery tagged behind the dogs, being carefully not to trampled on a paw.

"What up Tam?" Tam had become Avery's budding nickname for Tamra. And she absolutely gloats when she hears it.

"Hi Brother-in-law," she cooed, holding no reservations back from her expectation of a marriage happening soon between us.

His hand lightly touched my back and we exchanged a short kiss. I blushingly smiled when I returned my face at Tamra's intense stare.

"What," I retorted?

"I don't know about you, but most women I know would find your dilemma, easy."

"Maybe. But, I'm sure there are many more who understands it, as well," I finalized.

Tamra had long gone, when I decided to join Avery on the patio, where he was grilling our dinner. It was a week before Christmas. Even though the southern climate provides extended autumn temperatures in the winter, the air still felt a bit crisp. Avery graced my shoulders with a throw blanket and started a fire in the stone fire pit to keep me warm.

"I had a dream about my mother the other night," I informed him, as I sat tightly wrapped in the blanket, along the armless wicker sofa.

"Really? What was the dream about," he asked sitting before me at the patio table.

"I think it had something to do with me baking a Sour Cream Cake. I don't understand if I was supposed to have learned to bake this cake before she died or she is haunting because she still wants me to learn."

He chuckled. "If you really want to learn how to bake a Sour Cream Cake, I could show you," he offered.

"That's the interesting thing. I don't think I want to learn. I mean I haven't in all my days been interested in standing in a kitchen to bake anything. Why start now?"

"Maybe, you are just missing her, Baby. It's probably that simple."

"Maybe. Do you think it's bad that I can't cook and have really no desire to learn how I mean, I'm about to become a mother real soon. Shouldn't I know more than how to boil an egg?"

"Sure, especially if you were with a man who wanted a home cook meal everyday. But, I'm not that man."

"You are telling me that you won't ever wake up one morning desiring me to cook you a home cooked meal?"

"Baby, I've tasted some of your cooking before and you could rest assure that there will be no desire, whatsoever, for you to cook me a meal."

I tried to break his hysterical laughter by throwing a pillow at him. "Seriously Rocqui, if that's what I needed or wanted in my life, than I would have found that. I've met women before that can cook. But, so can I."

"What do you want me to do," I continued to probe?

"I want you to be the mother of my child. And I want you to wake up every morning next to me, for the rest of our lives," he stated seriously.

"How could I do that and keep my business in Richmond?"

"You could bring your business to Fayetteville," he suggested. "It's that simple."

"It sounds simple coming from you. But, it was really hard to get where I am with my business. I had little money and made a lot of pricey mistakes along the way. I even had to call my mother on several occasions to borrow money, because I couldn't afford to pay out some of my creditors. Besides, it makes me feel good to wake up every morning and know that I have my place in this world."

"You would have your place in this world with or without your business. It's not who you are. It's what you do....Look, I understand what you are saying. There have been some rough times in my business, as well. But, if you are waiting for me to say that I'm okay with you traveling back in forth to maintain your business and still be here for me and the baby, I don't think I am. I believe that you could be successful anywhere Rocqui, whether here in Fayetteville, or elsewhere. Because that's who you are. And I love that about you. But, I also love you enough to know that I want you here with me."

I pondered for a minute in silence. "Why do women have to be the one to make the sacrifices and give up everything? Why do I have to be that person? I deserve a career, just as much as you do," I emotionally belted out.

"You are exactly right. But, what I'm talking about is us. I want us," he strongly conveyed!

I had to take a deep breath and hold back any further irrational words, I was thinking. For a long moment, there was silence, until Avery rose up from his chair and sat beside me. He laid his arms tightly around me and muttered, "We are going to be fine. We just have to figure out a way to make it work."

But, I didn't necessarily feel fine. And I certainly didn't know any ways of making it work.

29

I was relieved when Ray called me to announce that we had sold our investment home. That was over one hundred thousand dollars that I could use right about now since it had been months since I've made commission off of anything. I anticipated Zoric and I house would sit on the market much longer, considering we were in the slowest period of the housing market season. I wasn't too in much of a hurry for it to be sold. Whenever I returned to Richmond, it was still my home. I still slept in my old bed and ate from the dishes of my own plates, like my life had been the same.

But nothing about this house was the same anymore. Zoric's things have been completely cleared out from our bedroom, except for a couple framed pictures of him and I that were left on top of his emptied dresser and night stand. The downstairs media room was emptied, as well. The L- shaped sofa and the mounted TV that Zoric bought with his own money were gone. The trace of imprinted carpet and the bracket drilled to the wall only indicated what was once here.

It was hard at times to dwell alone in what was once our shared space. Yet, I never for one moment long for him to walk through that front door. The solitude that surrounded me only convinced me even more so that I had no desire of spending the rest of my life alone. However, with the past few days of very few spoken exchanged between Avery and I, I was starting to feel that way.

"How are things going with the sale of my house?" Keisha and I were coordinating the details of my visit over the cell phone, while I prepared to pack my luggage for my trip to Richmond tomorrow. "Any interest yet?"

"There appears to be some interest. But no one has, of yet, dropped any figures before me," she replied.

With some concern, I voiced, "Alright Keisha. I'm entrusting you with my investment. I know that this is your first official sale, but you know the longer it sits on the market, the more money I may lose."

"I know what I'm doing. I've learned from the best, remember," she crooned?

I relaxed some and recounted, "The market is slow right now. I have a few clients and other realtors who may be interested in my house. I will pull those names for you so that you can send out a few emails or flyers when I get there on Wednesday.

"I thought you said you would be here tomorrow?"

"I will. But first, Avery and I are going to my doctor. And then I have an afternoon meeting with Ray. I may stop in for a minute, but I won't be there all day. I do, however, want you to set up a meeting with the staff for Wednesday afternoon. There are a few announcements I need to make."

"Yes, like the arrival of my Godchild," she gleefully echoed.

"Yes. That's one of the things."

"I'm just excited to finally meet Avery. I mean, he must be some hell of a man to have taken you away from a man like Zoric."

"Let's just say, Avery is more of a man than Zoric will ever be." The realization of my words reminded me why I loved him so.

The distance between us was widening. I didn't know how much longer I could pretend to hide my attention behind watching TV or typing on my laptop when he came home at night, just to avoid revisiting the discussion about us. And I didn't want to continue our morning dialogue, over coffee, to sound scripted and to feel like we were talking in circles around what we really wanted to say. I just needed him in my life, even if that meant compromising things that I've worked so hard to obtain.

Keisha and my conversation ended by the time Avery entered into the bedroom, holding his dry-cleaned clothes in his hand. He looked to be busy sorting out what he was attending to pack while I pretended too occupied with placing my clothes inside my luggage on the opposite side of the bed. Finally I interrupted the silence and said, "I love you Avery." I released an exasperated breath, like I've been holding it inside me these last few days and continued, "And not just because you love me. But because of who you are and how much you mean to me."

He stopped and stared for a minute, before he waltzed over towards me. I gazed up into his promising eyes and I listened wholeheartedly when he declared, "I've never doubted that for one second. And because I love you so much, I want you to be happy." A familiar comfort overcame my emotions as my arms tightly embraced the crease in his back. At that moment, he gave me sense of home that I had never imagined having with anyone other than my mother and father. I affectionately relayed, "I'm glad that I have you."

"Me too," he admitted. "That's why if we decide to live on the moon, it wouldn't matter to me as long as we are together." That was all I needed to hear. And once again I was in a good place with the world.

Bright and early the next day, we loaded the Escalade and headed north towards Richmond. A few hours later, we arrived at Dr Michael's office. When she entered into the room she looked liked a black Barbie, with her bouncy shoulder length hair wearing her white medical jacket over a dark slate wool gabardine dress. She was immediately taken aback by the presence of Avery. I quickly introduced her to him, as the father of my baby and the love of my life. After an exchange of 'hi' and handshake, she astoundingly replied, "Wow! Things surely move fast for you, Rocqui."

I couldn't have agreed with her more. I acknowledged her humorous gesture with a nod and a gracious smile.

"Well, are you two proud expectant parents ready to hear your baby's heartbeat," she asked in a more professional manner?

We listened astoundingly to the resonance of the Kentucky Derby echoing in my womb. Avery and I exchanged a surprisingly glance, at each other, as he stood next to me and held my hand. The waves of motion projected what looked to be the head. And, then, there were tiny fingers and legs all balled up inside of me. Dr Michaels then asked, "Do you want to know the sex of your baby?"

I glanced up at Avery and waited for his response. He could sense that I wanted his say-so, so he easily answered, "No. I just want a healthy baby with ten fingers and ten toes." And I agreed.

"Okay," Dr. Michaels passively replied. "The baby does looks healthy. Just know that if you change your mind, you could just give me a call and I would be more than happy to tell you," she said. After she had completed her medical examination and filled out my chart, she pleasantly implied, "It was really nice meeting you, Avery. Rocqui, when you are done with getting dress, could I talk with you for a minute in my office."

I understood she was cueing for us to talk alone. Once I had gotten myself together, Avery gave me a kiss and stated that he would be in the waiting area when I'm done. Her door was partly ajar for my entrance. I just slid right on in and took a seat in front of her grand desk. Her coffee painted walls and the dimly lit fountain that streamed a light flow of water provided a relaxing atmosphere in her office. Her white medical jacket neatly hung behind her desk chair, as she anxiously awaited me with a million and one questions. "Okay, Sister Girl... It's apparent that I've missed a few chapters in your book. Tell me, what is exactly going on?"

"Nothing really," I casually answered. "I met Avery traveling back and forth from here to Fayetteville, while I was caring for my mom. One thing led to another. We fell in love and now we are having a baby together."

"You got to be the only woman I know, that could track down a good man in any city," she comically implied. "I've lived in four different cities and I cannot find one to commit, let alone, have a baby by."

Over my laughter, I responded, "Trust me, I didn't plan any of this."

"That's the crazy part. Now, I have to forewarn you of something. And let me first say that I am very sorry."

My laughter quickly ceased by the seriousness in her tone. "What?"

"I kinda told Zoric, that you were pregnant," she regretfully admitted.

"What," I sharply retorted?

"Let me explain what happened. I was at a party and he was there. I had no idea that you two were no longer together. You kinda omitted that important piece of information from me. I asked him if you were still suffering from morning sickness. Because I was gonna suggest to him some ways to help you."

"And what did he say," I coolly asked?

"At first, he looked at me like I was crazy. Now, I know why. And then he said, 'she seems to be feeling a lot better, lately."

I shook my head in disbelief. I wasn't prepared for to deal with this type of news. What would I tell him if he saw me pregnant, just a month after our relationship ended? What would I say, I repeated again in my mind, cautiously thinking of my exact words. I would say that, without a hesitance in my voice, I hope he has found as much happiness in Julia, as I have found in Avery. With a quirky smile, I held my head up high and eyed Kandice securely, like I was envisioning Zoric sitting self-centeredly before me. "You know what, it doesn't matter," I determined. I arrogantly proclaimed, "It's not his baby. I don't care."

"That's right. That's my girl," she cheered. "But let me tell you this Rocqui. If you find yourself in another situation where another tall attractive man wants to talk to you, you give him my card." She pulled her business card from out of her desk and handed it to me. We shared another round of laughs, before we exchange a tight girlfriend hug. And I left with Avery's hand in mine.

After we had lunch, I was eager to show Avery my business. My intentions were to drop in for a brief moment to introduce Avery to Keisha, return a couple important phone calls and go through my mail before meeting Ray at four o'clock.

The receptionist desk, which once occupied Keisha's warm welcome, was now vacant. Since, she had obtained her real estate license, I proudly moved her to her own cubicle desk area.

Joddy was at her desk, meeting with a client, as I walked by. I half-way positioned myself inside the entrance of her office spaced. "Hello," I warmly spoke.

"Hello, Rocquelle", she pleasantly replied, as her headed tilted up, from her desk at the sound of my voice. She looked to be thoroughly reviewing some paperwork with a client. She had always been attentive to detail and one of my best realtors. Her long hair was clamped in a pony-tail that drew more emphasis on her oval-shaped face and strikingly white teeth.

"How long are you gonna be here today," she modestly whispered, trying uphold her tactfulness, in front of her client?

I returned, with subtleness, "Just for a moment, but we will talk tomorrow." Then, I continued in stride, with Avery next to me towards Keisha's desk.

"Hey Girl," I excitedly greeted, at the sight of Keisha sitting behind her desk, going over some paperwork.

"Hi Rocqui," she roared, filled with enthusiasm, from across her desk. She immediately leaped from her seat to embrace my neck with a cheerful hug before her eyes were captivated by Avery presence. "You must be Avery," she excitedly acknowledged.

"How are you," he modestly spoke?

"I'm great. I just can't believe that I am finally getting the chance to meet you." Keisha was so thrilled over his presence, that I don't think she was aware of the uncomfortable gaze she was causing him.

"Okay Keisha. You can stop staring at him. He is real."

Without any restraints she gregariously spoke. "I know that. I just didn't think that he would be this good looking."

"Anything interesting happening around here today," I asked trying to refocus her attention on something other than, Avery?

"No. Not really. I've only been here for about five minutes."

My eyes glared towards the back. Ray had supposed to be meeting me here today. Looks like he was a little early,

I gathered from the shadowy figure sitting comfortably in my guest chair facing my desk.

"Looks like Ray is here early. I will be back, baby, in a minute," I assured Avery. "I can't wait for you to meet him. You and him have a lot in common," I pointed out before gracing towards my office.

"Ray, I thought we agreed…" I'd began to confer, before my face became transfixed on the unwelcoming presence of Zoric, sitting poise, with his leg crossed and his black Prada shoes pointing swervingly towards my desk. Impetuously, I asked, "What are you doing here, Zoric?"

A devilish grin stretched for miles across his face. "Now, is that a way to greet the father of our baby."

His ludicrous admission, created a knot in the pit of my stomach. A nervous chuckled expelled from my lips before I retracted, "Our baby? And what makes you think you have anything to do with my baby?"

"It's true." His demeanor quickly changed, as he stood within a breath of my face, in complete sincerity. "Why didn't you tell me that you were pregnant, Rocqui?"

"Cause, I didn't feel like you needed to know," I bluntly answered, moving away from, trying to create distance between me and him.

"What kinda shit is that? You're pregnant with my baby, yet you don't think have the right to know… You are still pissed over that shit that happened, aren't you? Listen Rocqui, that thing is over…long over. She is just a memory. I have my own place, living by myself." His adverse tone became increasingly louder.

"I'm happy for you, Zoric, I condescendingly replied. "But this baby has nothing to do with you or her."

"You're just afraid, right now. That baby got you thinking irrational. But, Baby, everything between us is going to be just fine. I figure now that our old house is the market, we could get a bigger house. You know we are gonna need a lot of room now for Little Z" He gently charmed. He walked over towards me and cornered me like I was his prey. His arms tightly gripped my body and locked me into his hold.

My words were muffled by the imprint of my head pressed into his Brooks Brother tailored shirt. "Little Z? Who are you talking about? And you can cancel your wishful thinking and plans about another house, unless you are planning to live there by yourself. You are not the father of my baby," I coldly delivered.

His arms fell. And I looked intently into his eyes to read the anger that now overshadowed his ego. "Who is the father.... It's that 'joker' you were seeing in Fayetteville, isn't it?"

"Yes. It is," I admitted proudly. "And he is waiting for me out in the lobby? Would you like for me to introduce you to him," I spitefully implied.

Zoric head quickly turned, casing the office area. "Where is he? I would like to finally meet him, but I don't see him."

"What you mean? He is right there in the lobby." But even my search-filled eyes didn't see him, after my words left my mouth. Worriedly, I rushed out my office and nervously marched towards Keisha. "Where is Avery?"

"I don't know. We were talking for a minute and then I had to answer my phone. The next thing, I knew, I saw him walk out the door.

A riot of thoughts and feelings overwhelmed my rational tone. I yelled, "You just let him leave like that, without saying anything to me?"

In a calming and more composed matter, she answered, "Rocqui, I didn't know what to do. You and Zoric were talking so loud. And I was trying to keep his attention away from you two, as long as I could," she coaxed.

"Forget it," I upsettingly replied. I pushed opened the entrance door and proceeded hastily, to find him. I didn't know where to look. The Escalade was still parked in front of the building, but he wasn't there. The streets were bustling with people moving up and down the sidewalk, while I recklessly rushed, in heels, between them.

It wasn't until I stopped to catch my breath, that my eyes captured a full glimpse of him standing across the street in front of a vacant three story building. I could see from a distance that the window had a 'For Lease' sign reflecting through it and curiously wondered why Avery was marveled by its presence. I removed my heels from my feet and then slowly and very cautiously proceeded across the street to where he stood.

"What are you doing," I nervously asked, as I studied his bizarre disposition to the deteriorating building that encased tall period windows.

"Tell me, what do you think of this building," he asked never removing his eyes away from its obvious appeal.

Baffled and confused, I asked, "What do you mean?"

"I mean, do you think this would be a good site to open up a Georgia's restaurant here?"

Coming to a full understanding of what he was doing, I quickly responded, "No Baby."

"No," he repeated, this time parking his perplexed eyes upon my assured face?

"No, not at all. Because this is not Fayetteville. Fayetteville is the only place for Georgia's. And it will be the only place where we will live and be a family."

"What about your business, Rocquelle? Because, I don't want to have to kill that Motherfucker in your office, in order for you to have what you want." He stated angry and definitely, pointing sternly, in the direction of my office building.

Feeling admirably, I couldn't detain the full-right smile that emerged from my lips. Softly, I promised him, "You don't ever have to worry about him ever again or even my business, because I'm selling it. That's why I'm meeting with Ray this afternoon. We are gonna discuss our new business plans for Fayetteville. He is already ready and willing to open up this investment business that he had been singing about for a while now. I've decided to go ahead with it."

"You are going to do that for me," he unexpectantly wondered?

"No," I frankly answered. But then my smiled unfolded again. "I'm doing this for us."

Meeting with Ray exceeded my time limit that I had granted him. After a few hours of compromising ideas to bring forth this business proposition, I was ready to eat again and felt long overdue for a nap. But, even once we'd returned back to our hotel room and I'd laid comfortably in bed my restless eyes did not render to my tiresome body.

We stopped by my house earlier so that I could gather more things to take back with me. We even contemplated for a moment, staying here, instead of at a hotel. But then we agreed that this was apart of my past and didn't have any place in our future. We decided to get a hotel room, instead.

30

So soon. It was already Christmas Eve. I had hardly slept half of the night thinking about this would be my first Christmas without my mother. The thought of it scared me and even weakened my spirit for the holidays. But I had decided to try. I can do this, I reminded myself. I will not let the absence of my mother overwhelm me and keep me wallowing in tears, all day long. However, by the time the water from the shower sprinkle on my face, the tears had already begun to fall.

I got out the shower and dried off, only to crawl right back into bed, in a fetal position, with the covers tightly grasped around my body. I needed my mother. The more those words echoed through my head, the more my heart hurt. And I cried some more.

"Baby, I thought you were getting dressed," Avery canted, from a distance across the room, as he made his entrance into the bedroom.

My words trembled, as I tried to hold back my tears. "I was. I think I'm gonna lay down a little longer."

There was a short moment of silence that convinced me that Avery understood my intentions. But then his persistent words interrupted my moment of pity. "No love. You can't stay in the bed today. It's Christmas Eve. And I need you to help me."

"What do you need me to help you with," my off-cord words scrambled to leave my quivering lips?

"Aah…" his voice echoed with obvious hesitation. "I need you to help me at the restaurant. George called off today. Now I don't have anyone to stock inventory for me."

"Why would you have George stock inventory on Christmas Eve?"

"Because the first of the year is just a week away. We had planned to get started a little early this year, rather than wait until the last minute and end up spending New Year's together stuck inside the walk-in storage. Now that I have you, my holidays are devoted only to you."

His reason sounded rational but bared no motivation for me to move out of my solitude of self-pity. My eyes were lost through the stone finished vase that towered a tropical banana leaf plant, as I intently awaited his departure from the room. However, his presence wasted no more time hiding in the background as I quickly zoomed in to his subtle approaching denim pants legs taking a seat next to my lethargic body. I tried to sustain my eyes from closing, as he stated "I know you are having a hard time today. I'm gonna be right here for you all day. My job today is to make TODAY one of the best days of your life."

"And how are you gonna do that?"

"I don't know yet, but if you give me a chance I promise I will do my best."

Each passing breath allowed me to breathe deeper and deeper. I studied his face and understood his intentions, which merited a gently smile. I held my body up and slowly allowed my toes to graze across the carpeted floor.

I walked over to the walk-in closet and slipped on my increasingly becoming tighter jeans and pulled one of Avery's sweatshirt over my head. I walked into the bathroom and grabbed my brush to pull my hair into a ponytail. Once, the elastic was secured around my hair, I starred through the reflections of me in the mirror and replayed the memories of last Christmas Eve.

We were together at Tamra's house. Tamra had just received news that Diesel was gonna be deployed to Iraq four days before Christmas and I couldn't stand the thought of my baby sister being alone without her family being with her during the holiday. Immediately after Diesel's family left to return back to Fayetteville after seeing their son off, I booked three tickets for me, my mom and Zoric to fly out to Fort Hood where she lived. My mother never cared too much for flying, but I had arranged a direct flight for her from Fayetteville to Texas. I coordinated plans so that Zoric and I would arrive at Killeen Airport around the same time that her plane landed.

Within seconds of us meeting her at the terminal, she fussed continuously about the flight. Her seat was uncomfortable. She couldn't sleep because the man next to her was listening to music that was too loud. It was too cold on the plane. And the list went on and on. I listened on patiently, thinking she should have been glad that I didn't let her drive.

Once we arrived on post at Tamra's apartment, my mother immediately welcomed herself into the kitchen where she spent all day cooking and never batting an eyelash for help from anyone. Tamra and I did some last-minute shopping trying to beat the closing hours, while Zoric found him a nearby golf course to spend his afternoon. We ate big, as we always did and exchanged presents. We laughed and told of memories that was once of us. At that time, it was just another Christmas together, with my family. There was nothing significantly unique or magical about it, except that no one ever imagined hat she would not be here to see the next one.

Avery's sudden entrance into the bathroom faded my memory of last year's happiness to the daunting presence. It was right then that I knew that I wasn't ready to accept this day, as it was. I looked at him sadly and decided, "Avery I can't do this." A sustaining rush of tears flowed down my cheeks.

His arms immediately encased my frail body, like he was never letting go. "Shhh...It's okay." He softly whispered, next to my ear. "If you want to stay home, then I will stay with you. We don't have to do this."

While Avery's arms were consoling me, I could see my mother standing right next to me, probably disappointingly over my pathetic mess of a face. Even after my father died, I use to study her from a distance and could not fathom how she could remain so calm and cool. Naturally, she had a few quiet spell of tears, but never did I see her wallowing around in pure sorrow or self-pity. Everything suddenly became very real to me and I began to understand that this was the last thing she would want me to do.

My crying gradually ceased, long enough for me to listen to the words she would have spoken if she was here. 'Don't waste too many tears on me. *Live each day as if it is your last.* I could feel myself calmly breathing. Steadily, I was able to hold my head up and gaze into Avery's compassionate eyes. And declare "I'm gonna be okay."

When we arrived at Georgia's I was a little baffled by the empty parking lot on one the busiest days of the year. I immediately took note of every mom and pop shop that surrounded the restaurant. They were bustling with last minute shoppers rushing through their doors trying to beat the six o'clock closing time, except Georgia's.

"Baby, why didn't you open today, at least for lunch," I questioned. I thought he should take advantage of any opportunity to make money, especially during the holidays.

"I've rent the restaurant out for a private party for later tonight," he answered, as he led me through the back entrance of the kitchen. I was curious to see how the dining room was set up for this engagement, so I strolled through the double doors leaving Avery busy in the kitchen and entered into an array of Tiffany blue setting, with black and cream colored balloons streaming towards the ceiling. The tables were draped with satin blue linen and champagne bottles and crystal flutes were placed along the bar.

"The celebration looked promising. The decorations were beautiful." I thought as I waltzed back into the kitchen.

"You think so," he asked wondrously.

"Yeah, especially that Tiffany blue color accenting the room. Did you know that it is my favorite color?"

"Really. That's interesting", he replied, without any obvious interest this conversation.

He took note of me rubbing my hand on my stomach. I was feeling the motion of the baby moving inside of me. "Are you feeling hungry," he asked, walking over towards the walk-in refrigerator?

"I think your son is probably hungrier than I am," I implied after settling down at the prep table.

"My son, huh," he curiously repeated. "And how do you know it's a boy?" He grabbed a loaf of bread and sliced fresh deli meat for our sandwiches as we continued to talk.

"Because my mother told me it's going to be a boy."

"And what if it's a girl."

"As long as it's not twins, then I'm happy."

426 L L Alexander

From his laugh, I could tell that he thought I was being funny. But, in actuality, I was very serious. "If we had twins that would mean we wouldn't have to be in a rush to have our next child."

"Our next child," I surprisingly repeated.

"Yes. Wouldn't it be nice to have a house full of kids, running around tearing up the place?"

"No, that wouldn't be nice at all. I mean I could see two or three but, after that, I'm out of my league. How many children are you exactly hoping to have?"

"I would like three. But, I don't see anything wrong with four."

I was deep in thought, picturing me with three kids or maybe four. I would have never entertained such thought before. I probably would go insane trying to juggle a successful career along with raising three or four children.

"What are you thinking about," he asked, after finishing making me a perfect sandwich, along with chips and a sliced pickle on the side.

"I was just thinking how funny it would be to see me with three kids, or even two for that matter."

"I don't think it's funny. I think it would be the most incredible and beautiful thing ever to happen."

"Yeah, well you wouldn't be the one in the delivery room trying to squeeze them out, either."

In all sincerity he added, "You are so right. I wouldn't want that job for anything. But even if we have just our one child or even two, it honestly wouldn't matter to me Rocqui, as long as I had you." His intense words dwelled inside my mind and my heart for a minute that made time stand still. No other man that I had ever met before had such profound affect on me the way he did.

He pulled up a stool next to me and we enjoyed our lunch together tossing around ideas about our future together, like the names of our children, how big we wanted our next house to be and things like that until I was well satisfied over my hunger.

He grabbed a napkin and wiped away whatever evidence of food I may had left behind from my mouth and prompted, "Are we ready to get started on checking inventory?

Finishing off the last bite of my chips, I answered, "yes."

"The quicker we get this done, the quicker we can head out to my parent's house for dinner", he continued, in a more managerial tone.

"Okay. Where do I start," I answered feeling less enthused by committing to this task? I was quite certain that Avery's thoroughness to details will certainly keep my mind occupied for a few hours.

"You can start by counting how many sanitizing lotions I have," he pointed out, on the third level shelf, while he held a clipboard and pen in his hand.

A couple of hours passed and I was hands deep indexing condiments, paper cups, Styrofoam carry out trays, plastic forks and sauces "I tell you what, help me stock these paper towels and then we'll eat," he settled, opening a tall cardboard packaged box.

He took each roll of paper towels out of the box and placed them on the desk. I would then pick up the roll and stocked it high on the six feet wired shelf. It was beginning to seem like he had an endless supply of paper towel, until I looked down into the nearly empty box. I counted there were five left. Effortlessly and tiresomely, I placed the last five rolls on the shelf feeling relieved that our job for the day was finally done.

"You did good baby. Thank you for helping me," Avery stated after giving me a much appreciative hug.

"You're welcome. Just know that a much deserving foot rub is coming in your future,"

"Yes, indeed. You know it's my job to make you feel good and take some of the stress off of you," he added slyly.

"That's how we got ourselves in this situation, remember?"

"Yes my dear." He looked down at his watched. "It's getting late. We need to start getting ready to go."

"I'm gonna freshen up in your bathroom. It shouldn't take me long."

"Okay. I'm sure I will be ready for you."

I grabbed my bag and went through his office into his private bathroom. I brushed my teeth again, applied make-up to my face and got dressed in an off-the-shoulder charcoal cashmere sweater dress and laced my neck with a strand of pearls. When I returned to the kitchen, Avery was standing against the prep table wearing a black tie suit looking handsomely debonair like he was on his way to an exquisite ball. I, on the other hand, looked like I was about to go pick out china or something.

My forehead crinkled. "Did I miss something?"

He looked down at his glossy black shoes. "Oh this," he stated in a nonchalant manner. "This is nothing," he tried to unconvincingly down play.

"The way I'm dressed is nothing," I retorted. I could feel myself increasingly becoming disturbed. "Is there something that I should know Avery? Are we not attending the same party," I asked trying to maintain my cool?

"I wouldn't go anywhere without you," he answered confidently.

The tension in my brows began to relax a bit. "Why are you dressed like Prince Charming and I am standing here looking like Cinderella after the clock struck midnight?

He approached me slowly and reached out for my hands. "This is gonna be much better than Cinderella," he stated, holding my hand promisingly.

"Better than Cinderella?"

"Much better than Cinderella," he confirmed. "Better than anything, you've ever imagined."

I was so lost and confused that I didn't really know what to say. And then I noticed two champagne glasses on the prep table beside him half filled with sparkling cider. "What is exactly going on, Avery?"

He knelt down on one knee before me and pulled the black velvet box out of his pocket. It was then, I knew exactly what this was all about. I hung on patiently and happily to every word he proposed to me. "Rocquelle, will you make me the happiest man in the world and love me and marry me so that we may live happily ever after."

I gasped with excitement as my hands pressed nervously against my chest. It had always been discussed between us that some day we would get married. Surprisingly, I did not know that 'some day' would become this day, so fast and so soon. But then, I realized that there was nothing carefully rehearsed about our relationship and our love. Without any thought, I loved him. And nothing would make me happier than marrying him, today, tomorrow or even yesterday. With my heart filled with joy, I answered unquestionably, "Yes, Avery. I will marry you."

He gently slid the immaculate rock along my finger and I was overwhelmed by its sparkle. It was so big and breathtaking, it could have lit up an entire dark room.

"Wow. You must really love me."

"This ring is only a small part of how much I love you."

I didn't noticed the small CD player in the background, until he pushed play and the lyrics of Anthony Hamilton's *The Point of It All* harmonized from the background. And then we danced. We didn't need a marriage license or even a minister. It became official right then that Avery and I were gonna be together for the rest of our lives.

After the music stopped and our long kissed ended, I was still left wondering. "The champagne and music were all special, but you didn't have to get all dressed up in a tux to propose to me."

"I know. Your sister, however, insisted that I did. She was babbling something about it being fairy tale like and I should look like Prince Charming or something..."

"Prince Charming! I'm not in love with Prince Charming. I'm in love with you. I am marrying you. She had really lost her mind. I don't understand her at all. You just wait until I see her again."

"What are you going to say to her," he egged on?

"I'm gonna say, thank you for all that you've done in the past, helping us get back together, but we got this now. Her assistance is no longer needed. It's time that she takes a backseat to you and I. If you wanted to propose to me in boxers and house slippers, that would have been fine by me. I'm gonna make sure that she won't have any part in planning our wedding, besides holding my bouquet at the altar."

"You sure you want that? I mean, I think she is pretty smart and very darn helpful in helping me know what you want."

"She thinks she knows what I want, but, she really doesn't know anything. If I don't stop her now, it's gonna go on forever. "

I don't know, Baby. I think she would be pretty upset."

"So! She will get over it. Who does she think she is, anyway?"

"But look what else she had done for us," he announced, leading me by my hand through the kitchen doors, out into the dining area.

It was then that we entered on an awaiting crowd of gleaming eyes and joyous smiles. The emptiness that was once present was now filled with family and friends.

"She said yes," Avery announced. Floor to ceiling laughter, clapping and whistling, erupted from a sea of smiling faces. It was like I was having an outer body experience. Tamra and Diesel were the first to emerge out the crowd and glide up towards us with their arms open wide. Then, I spotted Ray's, iridescent smile. The cheering of my name drew my attention towards the presence of Keisha, who had little white man standing beside her. Avery's mother, father, his sister Angela and brothers Zeke and Chris were all there embracing us and happily cheering amongst the crowd. All of my aunts, in particular my Aunt Jennifer were apart of the overwhelming reception, that was surprisingly held in our honor.

My Aunt Jennifer finally made her way through the crowded parade of affection to welcome Avery into the family. Her hands extended around my neck as she whispered in my ear, "I guess you won't be spending your nights in bed by yourself, after all."

I beamed as I looked into her warm oval brown eyes and answered, "Not at all."

The celebration continued through the rest of the night, with a live band, plenty of food and lots of love. When Avery had a brief moment to be alone, I said to him, "so, this was your so-called dinner at moms?"

He replied cunningly, "Yes it was."

"This was pretty clever. Did you and Tamra plan this together?" My hands held on tight to his waistline, while everyone else casually indulged themselves in food and conversation.

"No. This was all her doing. She just instructed me to get you here and propose," he admitted. 'That's all I had to do."

"And what if I would have said 'no.'

"Baby, I don't think neither one of us thought for a second that you would say 'no.' I mean, we went through a lot of trouble thinking that there was a good possibility that you would say 'yes'.

I looked around the room at how detailed the Tiffany blue color mixed perfectly with the black and cream setting. My eyes returned towards his gleaming face. "You both were absolutely right."

Immediately, my hands fell to my side and I began darting off into Tamra's direction. But Avery's gentle tug pulled me back to his stance. "Where are you wondering off to," he asked?

"I wanted to tell Tamra 'Thank You' for making this day special."

"I thought you were going to give her a piece of you mind, like you said earlier?"

"That was before I realized how hard she worked to make this day perfect."

"Okay. But I just wanted to tell you that from the first time I saw you standing by that pool table, I thought to myself immediately that I was meeting my wife, for the first time. I am grateful also, that you have made this day perfect for me too. And not one moment that we've been together have I ever doubted that."

I smiled remembering some questionable moments between us and asked, "Are you sure you've never doubted it?"

"Maybe once or twice. But in the end, it was all worth it."

"I totally agree." For that moment, we sort of became lost in our own world and began kissing passionately and tenderly.

That was until Tamra interrupted our moment of intimacy and candidly stated, "You two may want to save all of that for your honeymoon. But then again, it really doesn't matter now. You're already pregnant."

"Yes, I am," I proudly admitted. "And even though you had nothing to do with that part of me, thank you for making everything else so special."

31

On Christmas Day, Avery and I were up bright and early heading down to the restaurant to open the doors for the homeless. Avery and his family cooked and sweated in the kitchen, all morning long, while I perfectly arranged the tables and the sitting area in the dining room. There was a huge Christmas tree with ornaments towering near the window with presents underneath. The presents under the tree weren't for Avery's family or friends but they were real gifts to be given to the homeless, along with a hot delicious dinner.

I was so busy with setting up for today and prepping the tables, that there was little time to waddle in sadness over my mother's absence. Avery's family was all in attendance at the restaurant, helping out and pitching in wherever they were needed. Tamra and Diesel even stopped by for a minute, but, only to witness my hands at work and not to lend a hand.

"Would you please stop taking pictures of me," I ordered Tamra as I tried to neatly arrange the paper plates neatly beside the plastic utensils.

"I'm sorry," she laughingly stated. "But, I've just never seen you with an apron on like someone who knows there way around the kitchen."

"You have seen it. Now leave. Or at least help out around here," I directed.

"That is okay. Diesel and I have dinner awaiting us at his parent's house. But, I would see you later on." Before, I could find too many more words to say, she turned and left out of the restaurant with Diesel beside her.

By one o'clock the restaurant was crowded with every nameless face from off the street imaginable. A line curved along the front of the building to the organized buffet tables where Avery, myself, and his family stood behind. We were all adorned in white aprons tied around our waist and big heavy spoons in our hands dipping inside metal pans. We robotically placed the food inside each person's plate, as people moved through the line. Some of the guest didn't look homeless, not even slightly, but, rather greedy. Their attire looked cleaner and pricier than mine. Avery whispered to me that every year there are always a few people who regularly attend just to get a free meal. Despite their selfishness, Avery family continues to feed them anyway. It is like he said, "You never really know what people need. So we feed them all." If I never loved this man before, I loved him a million times more just by his subtle kindness.

Around six, Avery and I were at home, cuddling and relaxing for a desperate moment before Tamra, Diesel, Angela and Ray visited for an evening of cocktails. "Are you ready to exchange gifts," he motioned?" With the events of last night and today, I almost had forgotten that today was really Christmas.

"Yes, I am. I need to go out to my car and get your gift," I stated before rising up from my spot and rushing out into the garage to grab his present from the car. About two weeks ago, Avery and I decided that instead of spending a ridiculous amount of money on a gift at the mall that we should try to be creative and find something special for one another at the Flea Market.

"The Flea Market," I exclaimed, when he first uttered those words! "I've never been to a Flea Market ever in my life," I admitted, still not enthused by his suggestion.

"I know, Honey. But, you'll be surprised by what you would find there."

"And if I don't find anything that I want you to have?"

"Then I would let you take me to the mall and you could lavish me with as many expensive gifts as you like," he proposed playfully.

When we pulled up into parking lot, I was already not feeling this idea, even though I had agreed. Yet, I held his hand and we entered inside together only to part our separate ways momentarily. At first, I was unimpressed by some of the second hand materials and things that looked years beyond wear and tear. But, then again, I was determined to meet Avery's challenged. So, I wavered towards the back and there I stumbled upon the most perfect gift ever.

Avery had already returned to his position on the sofa by the time I'd returned inside the house with his gift. I sat beside him and asked smilingly, "Are you ready?"

"Yes, I am ready," he smiled.

"Let me go first." I was so excited that I couldn't wait to see the expression on his face. I handed him a thin black box, about the size of a picture frame, with a red ribbon on it.

"So, you did find something from the Flea Market?

"Yes, I did."

"I told you, you would." He declared, without yet opening the box.

"Avery, just open the box. You could thank me later," I impatiently urged. He lifted the lid and carefully removed the layer of tissue paper to reveal several photos I'd taken. I gazed entertainingly at his forehead crinkle with questioning.

"Honey, take a closer look at the pictures," I insisted.

He held the four pictures up closer towards his stare. And I patiently waited for his facial expression to suddenly changed from puzzlingly to surprise. I got the reaction that I was hoping for. "Baby, this is mine? This is really for me," he joyfully asked? So, where is it? Where is my jukebox?" His eyes darted swiftly around the room like it was going to magically appear out of nowhere.

"It's at your parent's house in the garage. Your dad helped me pick it up and he put it in the garage until after Christmas." One picture was of the jukebox alone, with a big bow taped to the top of it. The other picture was of me leaning against its towering size that measured to my chest. The last two pictures were of his father, grinning widely like the jukebox was really intended for him. "I had to take pictures of it because I knew we wouldn't have time to get it over here before today. Do you like it?"

"Baby, I love it. It is fabulous." He was so busy laughing and smiling, in a boyish manner that he had almost forgotten about giving me my gift. "Oh, I'm sorry. This is for you."

He reached over from the side of the end table and handed me a heavy boxed presented with a pink ribbon on top. I knew that it wasn't jewelry or anything of that sort. The box was too heavy. I do not know why immediately I thought there was an actual rock inside. I kind of psyched myself up for a disappointment, before I removed the lid. No one had ever been correctly able to shop for me. The gifts that I've received in the past have never been about what I've wanted, but, usually about what the person who is giving the gift wanted for themselves. Like for instance, one year Zoric bought me a pair of golf shoes, knowing that I have never golfed in all of my life. However, because around Christmas time he needed a new pair of golf shoes, he thought it would be cute, if he got me a pair too. I did, however, appreciate his sentiment for buying the shoes with the idea that he would show me how to play golf, one day. Yet after a month of awaiting an invitation to go golfing with him, I searched for the receipt for those shoes and returned them, quickly.

So, I figured that Avery would follow suite like everyone else. I also, kept in mind, as I removed the top from the box that this gift did come from the Flea Market. There weren't too many options as I looked around, that I would have actually considered buying for myself. But, as I studied the top of the item, I became suddenly astounded by its beauty. It looked to be a porcelain antique jewelry box with intricate brass details and ancient painting inscribed on it. I took it out of the box and raised the lid slowly. The lining was of pink silk. Immediately I thought of royalty, from centuries ago, must have own this. It was so exquisite.

"You've been quiet for a long time," Avery spoke, breaking my captive moment of silence. I placed the jewelry box down to my side and kissed him. I almost started to cry. "I take this as, you like it."

"I do. It is beautiful. Tell me the truth," I questioned. "You did not get this from the Flea Market?"

"I promise you I did."

"Wow. We are going to have to go back next weekend then and find some more fabulous things."

We laughed.

Our expectant guests finally arrived and we all gathered around the kitchen and in the family room with plenty of alcohol for them and juice for me. Some of the food that was left over from the restaurant was reheated, served and eaten again. Tamra and Diesel rattled on, giving Avery and I their perspective on marriage, while Ray and Angela shared their pleasures of living the single life. At a certain point, I suspected that Ray and Angela's conversation was becoming more exclusive and intimate as oppose to being engaging and entertaining directed at the rest of us that were in their company.

When Avery finally got up to go the bathroom, I waited anxiously outside the door, for him to come out. Just when the door knob turned and an opening in the doorway was created, I jumped into his path, barely leaving room for him to enter out into the hallway. "Are you trying to sleep with Angela," I blurted out in a nervous whisper?

"What? Did she tell you she wants to," he answered like I was giving him an open invitation?

"No. But, I could tell by the subtle laughs and the girlish whisper that somebody wants to."

"What's it to you? She is single. I'm single. Why not?"

"Because she is Avery's sister."

"And a grown ass woman, who obviously wants me to personally deliver her a Christmas present tonight."

"I think I'm gonna be sick. You guys just met."

"So did you and Avery. And now you have a baby and wedding to look forward to."

"This is not about me..."

"You are absolutely right. This is not about you. So, if you would excuse me, I need to find a Santa's suit really fast. I got one more job to take care of, before I retire my sleigh."

He brushed right past me, leaving me speechless, but still puzzled over how to keep this situation from going down tonight. We all returned to the kitchen, circling one another with drink glasses in our hands.

"Well, I had a good Christmas, despite mom not being here," Tamra admitted. "Thank you Avery and Rocqui for having us over. I'm quite ready for some sleep now."

"I think I'm starting to feel kinda tired myself," Angela joined in. But her admittance sounded more like a cue rather than a confession.

"You don't have to go," I jumped in. "We have an extra bed upstairs," I offered trying to intercept her possible plan.

"Thanks, but I think I'm good." She relayed an eye signal towards Ray that could have been easily read by a blind person.

"Avery, it's been real. I had a great time, tonight. Merry Christmas to you. Merry Christmas, Rocqui."

"I'm glad you all came by. I think I'm starting to feel a little tired myself," Avery decided, merging in with the others.

"Honey, don't you think we should open our guestroom to Ray. I'm sure he doesn't want to spend the rest of Christmas night in a hotel by himself," I suggested.

"He won't be alone," Angela chimed in. "I'm gonna keep him company." Her forward admission left everyone else chuckling, except me. But, there wasn't more I could say.

Then Tamra joined in, "There goes Rocqui, thinking that she had to be everybody's mother. Would you just leave grown folks alone?"

Avery tightly snug his arm around me, as a signal that maybe I should. So, I was left with nothing further to say.

Avery and I walked our guest to the door and watched them drive off. Angela, of course, left her car parked next to mine in the driveway as she drove away with Ray horny ass.

When Avery and I settled along the sofa, next to each other, I was dieing to bring up the situation. I stated,

"Wasn't that kinda odd that Ray and Angela hooked up, tonight?"

"What was odd about? They have been eyeballing one another all night. I'm glad they did."

"Yeah, but that's your sister. And Ray is like my brother."

"They are also adults, right. How would you have felt if someone interfered with you and I being together?"

"Well, I did have that problem."

"How could I forget. But, we are together now. And that's all that matters. Who knows, we might be responsible for another wedding in the future."

"I guess it would be kind of interesting if Ray and Angela falls in love. This may lead to her moving back to Fayetteville."

"That story is sounding all too familiar to me."

We laughed.

The next morning I had found myself awakening on the sofa wearing the very same clothes from last night. I looked over at Avery, who also shared my position on the sofa. We were obvious exhausted. I shook him awake and we went upstairs for a more deserving rest.

32

Today, I tried to convince myself that my swollen stomach would have no hindrance on me sliding my body into a pair of jeans that use to compliment my flirty slim figure. Consequently, the word slim doesn't exist in this body anymore. The jeans barely made it up beyond my thighs before finally I realized that I was fooling myself. The relationship that I once had with these three hundred dollar jeans are now an evidence of what once was. My body five months ago once was sexy and slim and curvaceously defined. Now, my stomach is looking rounder and thicker than my behind. For the first time, during the course of nearly five months, I was starting to look pregnant.

Avery thinks all of this added weight is sexy. His words of flattery and compliments only translated to me feelings of insult and insecurity. He had now taken an interest in noticing my ass more by patting it every time he is near me. Sometimes, I have to take a look around at my own ass to see what is really going on back there that apparently did not exist before. Yet, there were other times his gentleness embraces me from behind and lovingly caresses my belly while he softly kisses my neck.

My aunts insist that I could eat as much as I want, whenever I want it. "You're pregnant," they encourage. "You have that right." I trust very little of what they say. They are, of course, big women and frown on such words as diet, fat free and low caloric intake. In their ideology, dieting is just a manipulative tactic used by the food industry to convince consumers that they could starve themselves to death in order to be happy. "Even 'diet' food can make you fat, if you eat enough of it", they argued. They lived to cook. And when they cooked, it pleased them to see everyone eats.

What did they know? They were too darn busy running up high blood pressure and cholesterol in our family. For my Aunt Myrna, it could have been apart of her devious plan to slowly kill off poor Uncle Jerry. Every morning he would swallow up three different prescription pills to stay alive, only to sit down every night to eat up Aunt Myrna's poisonous, greasy, fatty food.

I was never a big eater, despite the way they would insist on loading my plate up with food. And there was simply nothing good about the food they cooked. Just the sight of all that grease saturating over everything that once contained nutritional value piled on my plate would not allow me to stomach a taste of it. And to add to my misery, they treated water as if it was a luxury, not a necessity. Even a small glass of tap water was off limits in their house. Only if you've eaten up most of the food on your plate would you be allowed to recover from the dehydration caused by all that salt that you'd swallowed down your dry throat. "All that water does is fills you up," they preached.

Thinking back on those thirst-full days of suffering, I do not think my aunts took too kindly to me sitting there at their tables, twirling my fork around in my plate, on the verge of revulsion by their presentation of 'good food'. Everyone else merrily ate up everything they fixed them and did not complain. Some even asked for seconds. But not me. I was different and seemed odd, to them. They called me 'skinny girl', a nickname that began playfully only to eventually feel hurtful. Their implication led me to believe that I was some sort of misfit from a family of big women.

"You think you too good to it eat my cooking or sum' ting," My Aunt Myrna snarled, with her eyes gawking, at the sight of me dancing my fork around my uneaten plate.

"I don't think I'm too good for anything. I just don't wanna eat all of this stupid food," I answered in a very sassy manner to cause immediate silence to have fallen on a once disturbingly loud dining room table. All faces suddenly stared at my small presence as if I had been transformed into some sort of alien. No one under Aunt Myrna's roof would dare to talk to her in that manner.

Before a second past, she reached her mammoth-sized hand from across the table and threw my plate onto the floor just below my black patent leather buckled shoes. My horrified eyes fell on the sight of the broken dish filled with okra and fields pees running over into the blackberry cobbler, while the overly salted pig-feet hung from the side of the plate, onto the linoleum floor.

"Now, you get down there and pick it up," she ordered, with eyes burning of fiery.

"I aint getting nothing up," I boldly returned. At first, I didn't realize what I had said until after I had said it. However, it was too late. I knew then that I had three seconds left of my young life breathing inside of me before she leaped across that table and knock my head off my shoulder. But, I had no where to run and no where to hide. I was in her house where respect wasn't earned. It was assumed.

Just as I predicted, she was one leap away from whooping my little ass. But, Aunt Jerry reached out and grabbed her arm, with his callous hardworking hand and defended me. "Leave her be, Myr." He was the only person on earth that called her that. This was the only time that I ever saw him take a position against her. "She aint hungry right now. Just leave her be," he cautiously added.

"She aint gonna sit her lil' prissy self at my table and disrespect me, after I've slaved in this hot kitchen all day," she barked.

Calmly he added, "We all know you worked hard in this kitchen. Everything is delicious too, right kids?"

Aunt Myrna's four children were too afraid of her not to agree. They all chorused, 'Yes,' and 'it's delicious.' That was just enough echoing of appreciation to settle her back down into her seat, but that did not remove the threatening gaze she remained on me. I remained still in my chair frightened by the unknown of what was next to come until she ordered "Get up from my table, with your grown mouth." Without a second thought, I did just that and marched myself into one of the bedrooms to hide away from the rest of the night.

The next day, by the time my mother had come to pick me up Aunt Myrna had downplayed the whole incident as a simple misunderstanding between us. I didn't argue with her differently. My mother knew her younger sister and understood me well enough to know that something more than a misunderstanding had occurred between her and me. The case rested and my aunt never forced me to eat any of her food ever again. And I never backtalk her again either...even though she continued to relish over calling me 'Skinny Girl' from time to time.

There are some days I wake up and still cannot believe that I've found myself living in Fayetteville once again. Even though being with Avery had made me the happiest I've ever been, I still hold onto the memory of me not so long ago, living in Richmond. Downtown Richmond was the center of my life. I could walk to places I needed to go. Shopping, entertainment and fine dining were just blocks away from home. Now, my life had been quietly tucked far away in the suburbs, where you could hear birds chirping during the early mornings, and trees rustling with the slightest breeze. And the existence of a gas station within every mile reminded you that you had to drive somewhere in order to do anything.

My cousins were now just a few miles away from my address, rather than the hundreds of miles that I had once created between us. The reaquainces have been strangely odd. After many years, I have found myself to be nothing more than a visitor amongst the gathering of my kinfolks. There were so many new and younger cousins that I had never met before. Then they were others that I once knew like the back of my hand. We grew up together, shared each other's clothes and stayed over one another's houses on the weekend. Yet, I found it surprisingly odd that I looked at them more like strangers than my family. It was challenging to find a common ground from who we once were to who we have become.

I had gone off to college in DC, earned a graduate's degree and have strolled casually down the Champs Elysees on a few occasions while others had never even been beyond the city limits. Despite our obvious differences, in our own way, we were still family. Yet, it was only with a handful of them that felt more like old friends.

Ray had followed faithfully through on his plans. As soon as he finished trekking through the white sands of some deserted island and watching the sunset while sipping on some Hennessey, he immediately returned to

Fayetteville anxiously eager to start our new business. I didn't bring up any questions to Ray about his current status with Angela even though I was anxious to find out. It appeared however, whatever happened in that hotel room on Christmas Night remained there. Whenever they were in the same room together, they continued on with their lives, like the interest they had in each other was only for one night.

I was reluctant at first to take another leap of faith out into the business world and make it happen all over again. However, Avery reminded me that business was very much apart of who I am. He added, "If it's what you want to do, then I'll support you one hundred percent to do it." To add to the pressure, Matt randomly came by one day and laid an offer on the table that I could not refuse.

I was in Richmond, just for a few days for my prenatal checkup and to catch up on some work at the office when Matt casually dropped by without an appointment.

"I see you've run off and found yourself a new husband," Matt cunningly pointed out.

"Is it Wednesday," I asked?

"Yes, of course. Why do you ask," he responded in a proper manner?

"Because I'd forgotten what an asshole you could be on Wednesdays. Wait a minute. That is not true, because everyday you are an asshole, right Matt?"

"Now, now. I did not come here to fight," he replied, trying to ease me over.

"Then why are you here?"

"Rumor is that Dream House Realty is on the market," he slyly mentioned?

"Yes it is," I casually answered, not quite certain what his interest was in all of this. I continued to scan over some documents on my desk, ignoring direct eye contact with him.

"I want to buy it," he undoubtedly stated.

I was thrown off by his assertive interest. "Are you serious," I verified? I dropped my pen down and sternly looked across my desk at his pierced eyes.

"Completely," he conceited.

"What are you going to do with it, fire all of my dedicated agents and bring in your own top sellers to reconstruct the business?"

"I like the way you think. But, actually no. My plans are to maintain it exactly as it is and to keep your agents on board, if they choose."

"It sounds too good to be true. I don't know if I trust you, Matt."

"You do trust me Rocquelle." His voice had tightened with intensity. "That is exactly why you are always running to me for financial advice or help of some kind. Because you know like I know that I make dollars and cents."

He had me there. I was without words. "Look," he continued to propose. "I am doing you a favor. You now live in Fayetteville and I know you are not going to keep driving up here everyday to try to hold down this business. The commute itself is insane. Let me take this off your hand now, so that you could move on with your new life."

For a minute into our conversation, he actually sounded like a real person and not the asshole that I've known him to be. I took in a breather and asked, "What numbers do you have in mind?"

He looked into his briefcase and slid a manila folder across my desk that contained pages of my net income from my business last year and showed me the possible growth net in the next five years, with a colorful scaled graph. I was astounded by what I saw in front of me. I wasn't even fully aware of these figures myself. The numbers were so high that they just leaped from the pages of the document. I was almost tempted to pull my business off the table and began trying to map out a plan so that I could maintain it and reap the financial possibilities.

But no matter how tempting and how large the figures were, I couldn't, even though I really wanted to, badly. "Okay," I mumbled. "It's yours." It nearly hurt me deeply to utter those words, but something bigger and deeper inside of me spoke for me. Signing my name on the bottom line was literally like I had signed my life away. What I've worked so hard for and dedicated all of my time and money towards was gone with just a scribble of my name. A couple days later, it became official. Matt became the proprietor of Dream House Reality. And I was paid substantially more than what I was asking for.

With the money from the sale of my business, I plan to use it to kick off this next business venture with Ray. "Are we gonna do this or not," Ray readily prepared, as he awaited my confirmation?

"Yes," I firmly agreed. I signed off on the new partnership agreement next to his signature and we officially formed 'R & R Property Investment'. We are designed to appraise homes and property and buy and sale property as well as serve as a rental contractor. Initially, I would work from home, because in the beginning it would take us some time to make our place in this market, here in Fayetteville. But, Ray and I anticipated opening an office within the next year, at the latest. For the time being, Ray had headed back up to Richmond to find another deal on a house for us to flip and foresees moving to Fayetteville in the next couple of months.

On top of all the business negotiating, Keisha called me and finally announced that Zoric and my house had been sold. A bittersweet feeling had fallen on me with the news. I was happy to finally sovereign ties of the past that Zoric and I shared. But, yet, the life that I once held in Richmond was officially coming to a close. All of sudden, I was a little timid about my future. All of my life, I have maintain a level of control over what I wanted to do and who I wanted to be. Yet, now I've become like a leaf falling from a tree that had no clear idea of where the wind may take me.

Sometimes, if I stopped and thought too hard about how I've lost control over the things that once held importance to me I would endure a bit of sadness. But then the voice of my mother would be heard and she would make me realize that I never really had any control in the first place. God was always in control. As I slowly embrace life changing and unpredictable events, I finally began to see her words to be true.

"Rocqui, you cannot find a wedding dress inside a magazine," Tamra voiced, becoming increasingly irritated watching me skim through the pages of a bridal magazine. Tamra and Avery's mom and sister have taken upon themselves to plan my so-called 'fairy tale' wedding. All they have given me is the time-six o'clock and the date-February fifteenth. Every other detailed imaginable had been left in their hands to coordinate, from the flowers down to the bridesmaid dresses. The only one responsibility that I have been given for my very own wedding is to choose a wedding dress, which is becoming an even increasingly harder task than when I was going to marry Zoric.

At every page turned, I was at awe at the flattering snug fit of the skinny waist models, showcasing these perfectly sculpted flowy or ruffled filled wedding gowns. Nothing that I had came across thus far seemed hopeful for a pregnant woman like me who cannot imagine how big I will be exactly a month from now, when I walk down the aisle.

"What do you expect me to do Tamra," I questioned slamming the magazine on the table?

"You need to get up off your ass and actually try one on," she commanded.

"I'm sure that would make me feel so much better, seemingly I may have trouble squeezing into a dress."

"Girl, you are much harder on yourself than necessary. And you're not even that big. I don't know why you are even wearing maternity clothes. Trying to make yourself look like you are more pregnant than what you really are."

"Have you seen my stomach lately?"

"What stomach? That little pouch you are carrying around. Seriously Rocqui, lets go to a bridal shop."

"You mean a maternity shop."

"Get over yourself," she ordered! She grabbed my car keys off the table and I reluctantly trailed behind her hopelessly, as we headed off to a couple bridal stores.

"What do you think of this dress," Tamra pulled from the rack and held it up in front of her?

"I think... what the hell is it? That is the ugliest thing I've ever seen. It looks like something mom got married in."

"Don't you want to stay true to tradition," Tamra relayed, attempting to be humorous?

"I'm gonna leave in a minute. You think this is some kind of joke," I snapped.

"Okay, okay." She returned to the overstock rack of white bridal dresses and pulled two more dresses that were equally displeasing to me, as I sat and watched her try to model the dresses.

"Well, maybe you should get up and find your own dress. I don't know what you have in mind, anyhow."

"What I should have done was have my dress designed just for me, like I wanted to before. But, some people think that Avery and I have to get married so quickly rather than being patient like him and I."

"Everyone had waited long enough. It is time that you and he finally get married. And it's gonna happen on February fifteenth whether you like it or not."

"Long enough? We just got engaged last month. Hell, we just met five months ago."

"Are you having doubts about marrying him?"

"No. It just that Avery and I have talked about just simply going down to the justice of the peace and getting married. We don't need all the frills and shrills in order for us to be married. All of this other stuff really isn't necessary."

"Well, his mother and I agreed that there would be a wedding, come hail or high-water. We are not gonna let another person go to some courtroom in the middle of the week to finalize the rest of their life together. So pick a damn dress, Rocqui."

There was no sense in further arguing with her. I arose from the comfy chaise and reached my arms through the stuffed frilly continuous row of dresses. I pulled off the rack, one distinctive eye catching dress and immediately felt a rush of energy flow through me.

"Look at this dress," I voiced to Tamra in a child-like manner.

"Oh yes. That is one beautiful dress, Suga" an older silver-head white lady interjected, catching a glimpse at my dress in passing.

"It is very pretty," Tamra agreed. "You should try it on," she advised.

"I can't wear this. This is a size six. I use to be a size weeks ago, remember?"

"What's the matter Suga? Are you pregnant," the silver-head woman returned once again butting in on my conversation between my sister and me without any formal introduction. She was obviously a sales associate here. But, something about her led me to believe that she bared a warm caring spirit, like she had known me all of my life. This time she stood and waited on my answer.

"Yes, I am. And I would love to wear this dress, but I don't think I would be able to fit into it," I openly admitted in a humble manner.

"Suga, Ms. Campbell had been in this situation lot of times, before. Don't you worry. If this is the dress you want, then this will be the dress you will have," she encouragingly relayed. "Follow me and lets see what we have for you." Tamra and I followed her, gleefully like we anticipated her to wave a magic wand and make the dress suddenly appear on my body perfectly fitted, like Cinderella.

"You hardly even look pregnant," she continued, studying my physique.

Modestly I answered, "Well, I am five months."

"And how many months would you be at the time of your wedding?"

"Six months."

"That's perfect then. Here," she handed me an identical dress but looked to be in a larger size. "Go try this on and I will get my seamstress to alter it to your growing figure.

I was smiling so intensely, I didn't know what to do with myself. I hurried off into the dressing room and nearly jumped out of my clothes anxious to try it on. I stared at the dress for a moment as it hung on the latch on the back of the door and was amazingly impressed by its design. It was a pure white lace sheath with a ruffled bodice. The wide spaghetti straps were intricately beaded with sparkling crystals. A silk banding tapered the bodice from the slightly loose empire waist. And more detailed crystals trailed all the way along the train that seemed to go on forever. When I tried it on and looked into the mirror, the dress seemed to have made me sparkle. It was perfect, except, for one noticeable fact...it was a little too big. The straps dropped off of my shoulders and I had too much room in the waistline, even for a pregnant woman like myself.

But that didn't stop me from entering the showroom and standing on the platform surrounded by mirrors to show all angles of my dress. Tamra's mouth dropped open at the sight of me. It was everything and more than what I've ever envisioned my wedding dress to be.

"Oh Suga. That dress is perfectly suiting for you," Ms Campbell admired. She was standing in front of me with another sales associate beside her. "This is Rachel and she is gonna adjust you okay? And I've already told Rachel to leave room for that baby too." Ms Campbell was so sweet and pleasant, you could tell that she must have been the grandmother of a lot of happy children.

After we had left the bridal shop, I was still smiling enormously. When I dropped Tamra off, at her apartment, she had her last words to say, "Now aren't you glad we went and tried on dresses?"

I was able to break through my smile to answer back. "Yes, I am very glad."

"Rocqui, where are you?" I heard Avery summoning my name from the top of the stairs.

"I'm in here," I answered. I knew if he heard the sound of my voice, it would lead him into the bathroom where I was.

He appeared all gorgeously handsome towering over my soaking body. "Don't you look tempting sitting in that tub with all those bubbles everywhere?"

I smiled teasingly. "Tempting to do what?"

"To join you. Can I," he asked seemingly knowing the answer?

"There may not be that much room for you in here anymore Baby. I'm not the size that I use to be."

He dropped his clothes to the floor, to reveal his nakedness. Slowly, he stepped into the tub facing me baring a sensual smile. "That is okay. There is just a little bit more for me to love, that's all."

My lips tighten. I replied, "I don't think that's funny."

The bubbles now engulfed his body, as we both were surrounded in warm soothing water. "Would you rather

I say that I wish you were slim again, like the way you were when I first met you?

My hand slapped through the bubbles and splashed water up into the air. "No," I angered.

His forehead instantly creased. "I was forewarned about these hormonal changes that you were going to go through, but not for one second did I believed it. I said, 'not by Baby. She is always calm and cool about everything."

I suddenly felt childish and silly. I mumbled, "I'm sorry. It's just that I'm struggling a bit today. One minute I'm up and happy and the next minute, I'm crying over a toilet tissue commercial."

"That's okay. I got something that would take your mine off of everything." His hands sunk into the deep water and elevated my foot out of the water as he began massaging it. My head fell back into a subdued state. Before long, he placed my feet into his mouth and began to gently massage his tongue around every single toe, leading into gentle bites around the bottom of my foot.

Instantaneously, I felt my nerves run from leg and into my inner core. I smiled overpoweringly at his artful arousal. "I know what you are after," I slyly stated.

"Who me," he answered in a surprised manner? "I just want to massage your feet. That's all." He continued to toy with me.

I was truly enjoying every bit of his seduction, until I heard my cell phone ring. Apart of me instinctively wanted to jump up out the tub to see who it was. But then, I didn't want to suddenly interrupt Avery's attentive service to my feet, either. He noticed the perplexed look on my face and insisted that I go see who it was that text me.

My intentions were to read the text real quick and jump back into the tub. But that was before I saw that the text was written by Zoric. It read, *See you at closing on February the 1ˢᵗ. Can't wait to see you. I've really missed you.* I froze. I suddenly lost a sense of where I was.

"Is everything okay," Avery asked?

"Aah," I stuttered, at first. But then I turned in full view of everything that was good about my life. And that was Avery. He was so handsomely cute, all covered in bubbles. I had no qualms about telling him that the text was from Zoric. "Yes, everything is okay."

"What did he say," he asked unmoved by the mentioning of his name?

"He said 'closing on the house is February the first and that he couldn't wait to see me there."

Avery stared through the tempered glass of the separate shower, reflecting his own image of contemplation for a second, before he avowed, and "Little does he know that I can't wait to see him either."

33

"**A**very is really coming with you to closing," Keisha asked with obvious skepticism in her voice? We were discussing details of the closing over the phone.

"Of course. He is my fiancé" I answered full of confidence.

"Well…so was Zoric. Aren't you worried that they may exchange a few words and start fighting or something?" Keisha voiced more weariness over the situation than I held.

"Keisha, these are two grown men, we are talking about. What reason would they have to fight? Zoric and I are no longer together. I'm quite sure he is with Julia and I'm with Avery.

"Okay. All I know is that, this day is going to be quite interesting. I'm going to be standing from a distant, but close enough so that I could see everything just in case someone starts swinging."

"There will be no fight. I could guarantee you that. And if they were to behave like little boys, it would be nothing more than just a one punch show. And then it would be all over."

"By Zoric?"

"Girlfriend, I don't think so. Zoric may be from the hood. But Avery has hood in him."

"I know right. Poor Zoric may get his ass kicked tomorrow and he doesn't even know it."

We laughed.

"I will see you tomorrow," I began to wrap up this conversation.

"Yes ma'am. And I will bring the popcorn," she comically added.

We both said our 'goodbyes'. Suddenly, I began feel a tinge of nervousness sparked by the conversation Keisha and me, just held. I wanted to rest on the idea that nothing but good would present itself when I finally close off my life with Zoric tomorrow. But I no longer could hold that thought realistically. Even though Zoric is quite composed and instinctively wise, his actions have proven lately to be rather unpredictable. Avery, on the other hand has a peaceful soul and a rational mind. However, I could tell from the first day I met him that it would be nothing for him to protect what's rightfully his. The coming of the two would be like thunder and lightning.

I paused for a moment and silently prayed to God. 'Lord, please let me know right now, if I am making a smart decision by agreeing to let Avery accompany me at this closing. I am pregnant God and there is only so much a pregnant girl could handle. I know you would not allow anything to happen to me and Avery that we could not handle. And I don't think I could handle Avery going to jail over choking the life out Zoric. You chose him for me, God. I trust you. Please God, keep our world at peace. Amen.'

On our way up to Richmond the following day, Avery asked me if I was nervous. I lied and said 'no', because I had really no reason to explain why I was. I sat with my fingers tightly crossed throughout the three and a half hour drive just hoping everything would go smoothly. Zoric would sign the papers without wasting too much time trying to read between the legal jargons and asking wasteful questions. I hoped that he wouldn't ignite an argument over who deserves what share of the money. Knowing Zoric, he would try to prove that he deserves more than his half, just to keep shit going even though, I am the one that put down the twenty percent down payment. At this point, I was willing to give him whatever he wanted just as long as we got down to business and departed civilly without any harsh words between him and me or Avery.

When we arrived downtown at the law office, Keisha waited for me outside the building, with a knee length wide collard coat on with a thick scarf wrapped around her neck and tall black boots. It was as cold as ice when I step out of the Escalade, but the rush of blood flowing through my body made me warm. I was relieved with joy to see her there. I ran up to her to embrace her tightly like it wasn't two weeks ago that we last seen each other.

"I'm glad to see you too," she spoke after we released our arms from around each other.

She looked onto Avery and pleasantly smiled. "Hi Avery."

"Hi Keisha," he spoke.

"Well..." She took a deep breath. "Are we all ready to go in and get this over with?"

"Yes. Finally," I gladly admitted.

When we entered through the solid mahogany wood doors, there awaited us Zoric sitting very debonair and distinguish in one the finely designed wing back chairs that was positioned in the lobby. Keisha went ahead of us into one of the conference rooms, while Avery and I stood tentatively uncertain of what to do next. Zoric eyes were filled with surprised as he noted me standing with Avery. I suspected that he was alone and he probably assumed that I would be too. Something sparked my brain to reactivate once again and I opened my mouth to speak to Zoric. "Hi Zoric." My words sounded faint, as I tried to find a neutral ground of dialogue between us. "This is Avery. Avery this is Zoric." Zoric rose from his seat, securely and swaggered over to shake Avery's hand. I wasn't expecting that.

"Nice meeting you," Avery coolly exchanged. "I've heard so much about you," Avery continued after they exchanged handshakes.

"Really? I haven't heard really anything about you," Zoric arrogantly replied. It was at that moment the air became suddenly thick. Whatever coolness Avery held moments ago had now vanished. His face harden with intensity and his eyes pierced through Zoric's core. "There aint really much you need to know about me besides the fact that I'm her fiancé," he returned callously.

Zoric shot this furious glare at me. "That's quite interesting, since just three months ago, I was saying those very same words, myself. Isn't that some serious shit, Rocqui," he disgustingly tried to swallow?

"Look, she doesn't need to confirm with you what she is doing with her life now. You are what once-was," Avery defended.

"I'm not even talking to you 'homeboy'," Zoric bravely tossed back, maintaining his pretentious mannerism.

It was then that I became frighten and timid of what may happen next. "Baby, please just let it go," I pleaded to Avery. But, by then Avery had already sliced right between the narrow space that stood between Zoric and

I. He professed in a very forward threatening manner, "I'm not your fucking 'homeboy'. I don't know what rock you crawled from under but let me remind you of something. You don't know shit about me, like you said...remember? But it's starting to get real personal just between me and you."

At that moment, Avery's already muscular physique seemed to swell. I grabbed his constricting arm in fear at anytime he might swing. Zoric eased back carefully, widening the distance between Avery's fist and his face. I tried to calmly pace myself to breathe easily, as I tightly held onto him. Suddenly, Keisha emerged out of nowhere happily and grinning, totally unaware of the potential display of violence that almost occurred. "Are we ready to make this sale final," she announced cheerfully? When I was able to calmly rationalize this situation I spoke with Avery privately while Zoric followed behind Keisha into the conference room. "I know that this is a trying situation that I put you in..."

"Rocqui, I'm fine," he hurriedly responded trying to avoid my eyes.

"I know you are. But, I am not. I don't want today to be about this between you and him. After I go in and sign these papers, he is forever no more. Please for me, don't go there with him. Please."

He deliberated intensely for minute. Then he replied, "Yeah okay. But if that nigga steps up to you like that again, I just hope you'll forgive me later."

"I know you're my man. And you got my back. I love that. As a matter of fact, I can't wait till this is all over. Because it's me and you Boy...at the Marriot." I had a sly grin on my face. "Don't you remember what happened the last time we were at the Marriot?"

Finally, I provoked a smile. He kissed me and said "Go handle your business. It's all good."

"Oh so you do remember," I teased, implying the words 'it's all good' to what I had in store for him later on. I continued to hold my smile until I entered through the conference doors where everyone had already positioned around the long conference table.

Signing and skimming through all the stack documents amounted to no more than an hour's time. I was happy and relieved when I handed over the keys to my once own townhouse to the new owners. Zoric, went through the process maintaining a quiet disposition, occasionally stealing glances at me. As soon as everything was legally bound, I strutted quickly over towards the closed door, with my hand tightly grasping the knob ready to join Avery on the other side. But that was before Zoric's hand laid gently over mind. My face was full of surprise when I gazed up into his mild face. Just like I thought, he was not interested in making this day simple. I waited for his hand to release my grip from the doorknob before I disclosed any interest in what he had to say.

"You look beautiful pregnant," he released like he had been waiting to say something the entire time we were closed off in this conference room. "I always knew you would, though."

"Thank you." I exhaled.

"Not a day goes by that I don't think of you, Rocqui. We could have had it all."

"You did have it all. I just wasn't enough."

"I know I've said it before, but I'm sorry."

"And I've said it before too. It really doesn't matter." My gripped returned to the doorknob and I freed myself from Zoric's past. I entered out into the lobby where Avery remained seated casually. He stood up and we proceeded to exit out the doors hand and hand.

"Hey...wait up," Keisha shouted, strutting hurriedly behind us. "I know you were not rushing to leave without saying goodbye." That was exactly what I was trying to do. I wanted to avoid Zoric saying something stupid before he ended up getting his ass kicked, today. But it was too late. He exited right behind Keisha into the front lawn. "I know your wedding is just two weeks ago, but Andrew and I wanted to invite you two out to dinner to celebrate," Keisha proceeded.

"Sure. That sounds like a plan," I agreed.

"Let's say around seven tonight."

"Let's make it six thirty. You know I am feeding for two."

"Six thirty it is. I am so excited. We have much to celebrate…the wedding, the baby and the closing on your house."

"We sure do."

"I will call you with the details, a little later. Can't wait to see you'll then."

As Avery was opening the car door for me, Zoric's voice arose from a short distance. He was a few cars ahead us. He repeated, "Eating for two, Rocqui? Are you sure that isn't my baby that you are eating for?"

I answered definitely, "Oh I am very sure, Zoric."

"Hey Avery, I hope for your sake that this baby doesn't come out light-skinned with curly hair."

Avery turned and slyly replied, "Nah, man. You got it all wrong. I hope for your sake that he doesn't, because he is going to be calling me 'daddy', regardless.

Without any further exchange of words, Zoric got inside of his Land Rover and drove off. Avery and I made a u-turn in the middle of the street and headed towards the Marriot.

The week of the wedding had arrived. I really didn't believe that it was finally happening. Tamra had left little details for me to know about my wedding besides, their bridesmaid dresses are Tiffany blue and Aunt Jennifer was making my wedding cake. But, I had already assumed that much. And of course, we were getting married at our family church. It is the same church where we sat restlessly, as kids, on those long hot Sundays morning observing everyone else worshipping and praying, except for us. In addition, it is also the church where my parent's memorial service of their lives were held.

The first thing that I needed to get done before Saturday was the last fitting of my dress.

"Hi Ms Campbell," I spoke after entering the bridal shop. She was already trekking towards me with open arms.

"Hi Suga," she sweetly returned. This time her hugged included a short peck on my cheek, like I was one her children or something. She took a few steps back and noticed, "Boy, haven't you grown since the last time I saw you." She noted my increasing ballooning stomach.

"Yes he has," I laughingly agreed.

"I knew it was a boy," she relayed, as we followed her into the fitting area. "I could tell by the way you are carrying it...up high and all," she continued.

Even though I wasn't certain what I was having, I led her to believe that she was right. "Here is your beautiful dress." She handed it to me and I went into the dressing room while Tamra and Ms. Campbell waited patiently for my emergence.

When I step out of the dressing room, wearing my wedding dress Tamra rose to her feet and immediately rushed to my side for an enduring hug. "Isn't she beautiful," she turned to Ms Campbell and asked?

"Perfect," Ms Campbell smiled and complimented.

I turned and looked at Tamra whose eyes were now flooded with tears. "Why are you crying," I puzzled?

"Because you are my sister. And I am so proud of you," she barely mumbled.

"Okay Tamra. If you are doing all of this crying now, what are you gonna do at the wedding?"

"Everybody will have their tissue on hand. Trust me, because we have already planned that there would not be a dry eye at the church."

I wrapped my arms around her and told her once again how thankful I am for all that she had done for me. Then, I stood on the platform for my last altering. "Your dress is perfectly fitted," Ms Campbell noted. "We probably just need to take a in an inch around the bust, but other than that I'll say that someone is ready to get married."

"Yes I am," I proudly shouted.

As Ms Campbell pinned the last inch of my dress, she advised, "Make sure you use this hidden button along your dress to gather your train, because we don't want all of that snow trapping underneath your beautiful gown and making it dirty."

"Snow," I repeated surprisingly. "What snow?"

"Suga, the weatherman is calling for snow on Saturday. You didn't know that?"

I looked sternly over at Tamra, whose face was doing an obvious poor job trying to conceal her knowledge of the matter. "No, I did not know they were calling for snow on my wedding day," I retorted, without a hint of humor on my face. "Did you know about this snow, Tamra?"

"Sort of, kinda," she timidly answered.

"Why didn't you tell me?" I was flustered.

"Because, we live in Fayetteville. When was the last time it snowed in Fayetteville? Probably, a half of a century ago...It is not going to snow on your wedding day, trust me," she assured me all-knowingly.

When I woke up Saturday, after a long night of dancing and laughing hysterically with my eight bridesmaids, the sun had graced a clear sky. I was relieved. No snow was going to happen today. Not on my wedding day. Keisha, Tamra, Candice and Joddy have camped out at my house for the past few days, while Avery had remained at his parent's house, like a captive prisoner. I was so glad that today was finally here, because I've been in absence of him every since they all arrived. Those dreadful wenches, who are so-called my friends, refused to let me see him, even for a minute. The only form of communication that Avery and I have been allowed is through the usage of the phone.

Last night, however, while I thought I could steal a moment alone, Tamra abruptly walked into my bedroom and caught me eye-chatting to Avery on my laptop and took my computer away. "Do you understand how much I hate you right now," I yelled, as I sneered at the view of my laptop being carried under her arm to an undisclosed location!

Once we all were awake and dressed, a limo arrived at my house and chauffeured us to the restaurant for a cozy intimate brunch. Avery's mother and my other bridesmaids joined us there and we all ate and continued the vibe of this joyous occasion. The entire time, however, Avery kept texting me, trying to plot a way so that we could see each other, before the wedding. But, once again my sister intercepted that idea and confiscated my cell phone. She smirked and replied, "You won't be needing this today," before taking it from me, like I was a child.

I was at the point of having a tantrum until, my soon to be mother-in-law called me to the center of the room. After giving a short, but deeply touching speech, she called Tamra to join me at my side. I eyed Tamra approaching me carrying a small present. She announced, "This is your 'something new." She handed me the present and I opened it anxiously. There, twinkling like glitter was a solitaire diamond pendant. I peeled my eyes away from its beauty and gaze at Tamra with a questionable face. "This is from Avery," she responded. Then, she fastened it around my neck. I was speechless.

Avery's mother returned from out of the kitchen with a garment bag in her hand. She walked up to me smilingly and announced, "This is your 'something borrowed'... and I do mean borrowed." Tamra helped me unzip the bag to behold inside, a white genuine waist-length mink coat. I thought my eyes had fallen out of my head at that point. She urged, "Try it on to see if it fits." I did and it was perfect.

Okay, I thought to myself, I have my something new, something borrowed. The only thing that was missing was something blue. I remained patient waiting for a blue scarf, or a blue ribbon to be handed to me. But no one made any immediate effort like there was going to be any blue. Yet, I remained standing, waiting for something more to come. Tamra puzzled over my patience and asked, "What?"

"Did you all forget my 'something blue'," I questioned, darting my eyes between Avery's mom and Tamra?

"No, of course, not," they answered nonchalantly. "We already have blue as apart of the decorations and the bridesmaid dresses, remember," Tamra replied?

"Of course," I uttered remembering that was one of the few details they cared to share with me.

"But, I do have this for you," Tamra added. She reached into her purse and handed me a very small white box. Inside, there was a satin light blue garter inside. "This is from me," she announced.

"I love it. But Avery's gonna enjoy this even more so, at the reception," I joked. Laughter filled the room.

We were coming towards the end of the brunch and Avery's mom asked me if there was anything I would like to say. There was something I had been feeling passionate about that I needed everyone in this room to know. I walked up closer towards the tables and exhaled deeply. I stated sincerely to every smiling face that I looked at, "You people who sit here and surround me on one the happiest days of my life are mean evil-plotting people. I appreciate the gifts and the love that you all have given me. But what I don't appreciate is you'll keeping me away from the man I truly love. That is just plain evil and wrong." Their faces still retained smiles of affection "Despite that...I still love you all very dearly and I could not have done any of this without you."

The room echoed in "Aah", harmoniously. Everyone rose from their seat and surrounded me with a group hug. That was the beginning of the endless flow of tears, for the rest of the day.

As we were returning to our house to begin preparing for the wedding, the sun suddenly disappeared. The sky was gradually covered with thick gray clouds as I began to feel a wave of anxiety. I turned to Tamra for reassurance. "Tamra, you don't really think it's going to snow, do you," I asked disappointedly?

"No. Of course, not," she rushed to answer.

However, God had a different plan in mind. By the time we had arrived at the church, white powder began to sprinkle from the skies. It was now five o'clock. Like Tamra had said, *come hail, high water or even snow* there was going to be a wedding today. I just never imagined it would actually snow on my wedding day.

"Are you okay," Tamra asked, noticing me fidgeting with my train on my dress, once we had arrived at the church.

"I can't find the hidden button on my dress," I yelled, frantically. All of sudden everyone halted to a pure silence. My bridesmaids in the downstairs waiting room stopped what they were doing and stared at my mindless behavior. I almost started to cry, until Tamra calmly bent downward and found the button for me. She then demonstrated how she was going to button it up right after the ceremony so that it would not drag to the ground, during the reception.

"I don't want my dress to drag in the snow and get dirty," I stressed over, almost on the verge of crying.

She comfortingly reminded me, "All of us in this room have everything under control. There is nothing you have to worry about…okay?" For that instant, I held her assuring eyes I saw the exact resemblance of my mother in her. She even sounded like her. I could feel the tears forcing their way from my eyes. Yet I bit down on my bottom lip nervously and held them back.

"You are gonna be just fine," she reminded me.

"Okay," I humbly whispered.

As she embraced my waist with her comforting arms, my head rested gently on her shoulder only to be suddenly distracted by the presence of my little cousin Jalen, whose only job today was to carry our wedding rings down the idea. Much to my surprised, he arrived bravely in the room surrounded by all these women, alone, dressed in his tux holding a brown box that looked like it was just delivered from UPS.

"This is for you Rocqui," he conveyed in his childlike voice.

"Ahhh," the voices echoed behind me.

"Thank you," I exchanged with a sweet kiss on his cheek before he disappeared. I didn't think much of receiving the box, until my eyes read swiftly the insignia scribbled in black ink on top of the lid. 'Christian Louboutin. Paris.' I was quickly losing my breath as I swiftly tossed the lid off the box to reveal Swarovski crystals studded on four-inch glistening pumps. I could have fainted right there. But then Tamra was leaning intensely over my shoulder that helped me to maintain my balance. "There is a card inside," she stated overly excited.

I gathered my composure well enough to open the small envelope and pull out the small note. It read, 'To a Beautiful Shoe. ☺ Happy Wedding Day! Love, Avery.' I could have melted. Everyone rushed me over to the chair and threw off my other heels and gently placed my red sole glittery Loubotin's on my feet. I felt like the perfect bride.

"It's Showtime ladies," my wedding coordinator anxiously announced, as he suddenly appeared in the room. All of the beautiful sleeveless Tiffany blue gowns with big white bows tied at their waist trailed behind him, leaving me alone in my solitude. I didn't want to be left alone. Someone should be here with me. Someone like my daddy, I decided. This is the day that we talked about and planned. One time ago, it didn't really matter to me who I would one day marry, as long as I had my father with me. But he wasn't here, on the one day that I needed him the most. No one was here, as I glanced around the empty room. Suddenly, I felt like I couldn't breathe. I needed to sit down for a moment. But time was up.

My wedding coordinator returned. "Are you ready," he asked? "They are all waiting for you," he subtly announced. At that point, I felt like I had stop breathing, even though I gracefully followed him up the stairs. We had arrived in front of the closed doubled-doors leading into the sanctuary. The wedding coordinator moved to the side and cued for the ushers to take their place.

When the ushers pulled back the doors simultaneously, my entire world and life awaited me. The entire church was filled with people of our past, present and future. Right before I made my entrance, everyone rose to their feet to bare witness to me. At the end of each pew there were towering stands of thick fresh red roses surrounding a tall white lit candle. The white floor runner that was rolled out for me was covered with red rose petals sprinkled by the flower girl. My bridesmaids all stood evenly lined in their silk stunning Tiffany blue dresses with a handful of fresh red roses in their hands parallel to the raised alter. While, Avery and his groomsmen were all decked out in black tuxedos with soft blue ties and matching cummerbunds representing the most stunning and attractive men on earth.

I embraced the magical overpowering beauty that surrounded me. My feet carried me slowly down the aisle, occasionally catching a glimpse of a familiar face that smiled on me, as I walked by. Closer and closer towards the altar I moved, the more pain I began to feel inside. Until suddenly I stopped. My legs unexpectedly disconnected from my heart and I became planted like a tree.

At that moment, as I stood still, thoughts of my mother and my father overwhelmed me. Everything in my life seemed to have caught up with me at that instant as my lips began to tremble uncontrollably and I began to cry.

The music ceased and the church drew to an immediate silence. Everyone around me suddenly became irrelevant as the tears steadily streamed over my makeup. The only thing that mattered was the presence of Avery that appeared perched up on a hill, while I became frightened to climb up a few steps to reach him.

He maintained soft eyes along my statue figure. He didn't seem slightly disturbed by my senseless behavior, as he waited patiently for me to decide what's next. But, I didn't know that either. I tried to move hastily, but my legs would not allow me to. However, somehow deep within this moment of truth, his own thoughts and feelings allowed for an assuring smile to emerged on his face. It was so quaint and simple that it overpowered me to smile back too. Immediately, we connected more at that moment than any words we had ever conveyed. He seemed to have known that at this particular moment, when I appeared lost and frazzled to the rest of the world, that I was actually anxious and sad. He somehow understood that this questionable moment that I brought about wasn't about my love for him or whether I would marry him. Instead, it was all because I couldn't walk the rest of the way alone, without him.

He left his position as the groom and walked down to the bottom of the steps of the altar and then extended his hand out to me. Something inside of me reconnected with my limbs and allowed me to move closer towards him. I extended my arm out towards him and met the gentleness of his touch. Our fingers immediately intertwined and we walked up the steps of the altar together, hand and hand where the Bishop waited intently.

Before the Bishop proceeded with the formality of the ceremony, he motioned loudly, eyeing Avery and I powerfully, "Let the church say 'Amen'. The church roared, "Amen." There was a thunderous rupture of clapping and whistling throughout the sanctuary. Avery and I turned and graciously smiled at our guests and family. Everyone were then seated.

Throughout the entire ceremony, my eyes remained on Avery's loving face. I didn't comprehend every word the Bishop spoke. I just gladly followed along and repeated whenever I was prompted to. All I had anxiously awaited seemed like it was taking forever to become finally official. I just wanted to hear him say, "I now pronounce you husband and wife. You may now Avery kiss your beautiful bride." Even though, our lips touched, Avery and I couldn't really kiss the way we wanted to over all the cheering, whistling and clapping expelling from the entire church.

We exited down the center aisle hand and hand, staring endlessly into each other's eyes. When we reached the lobby, we shared a quick intimate moment.

"Can you believe it baby," I shouted with joy? "We are husband and wife."

"No, I can't believe it. Seems like I've waited all my life for this to happen" he answered pleasantly.

"I'm glad you came down the steps of the altar for me."

"I'm glad you waited for me to get here. You had me scared there for a moment."

"You thought I wasn't going to marry you?"

"I didn't know what to think, at first. Then, I sort of felt something when I looked at you. I really can't explain it. I just felt like I needed to reach out and grab you before you got away."

"I did need you. I will always need you."

"I'm never going anywhere. You are my wife now. You belong to me."

"I am glad to hear you say so."

"You better be because we have a long road ahead of us." We laughed.

After the exchange of many hugs and several kisses, from friends and family inside the sanctuary, the coordinator prompted Avery and I to follow him to the lobby. We knew that time was starting to carry over into the reception especially after all the pictures that were taken. We suspected that he was urging us to get to the reception site, immediately. However, when he cued for the ushers to wait next to the doors of the entrance of the church, we anticipated some sort of surprise about to emerge. But nothing like this.

"Mr. and Mrs. Smith, your carriage awaits you," he announced. The doors slowly opened wide and revealed an actual white Cinderella-inspired carriage drawn by two white horses, with a coachman...waiting in a pure bed of crystal white snow.

It was breathtaking. Someone unknowingly walked up behind me and layered Avery's mother's white mink coat over my wedding dress. Then Avery took me by my hand and led me down the steps and into the carriage. From that point, the horses trekked us through the snow covered streets as snow continued to trickle down from the nightly skies.

Once we arrived at the restaurant where the reception was held, we embarked on a standing ovation as we entered through the doors. There were so many amazing things to see at the reception that I could hardly focus my eyes on just one thing. The soft blue lighting that illuminated the white satin drapery hanging from the walls to the floor. Tall candelabra centered every table with romantic red roses, and soft white orchids. Even the wedding cake that Aunt Jennifer created was an exact replica of a big Tiffany blue box with a woven white edible bow on the two layered cake.

Tonight was a party and a celebration. It was into the early morning that we did just that. Cinderella could only dream of having a fairy tale wedding better than this, I proudly admitted.

19173692R00280

Made in the USA
Lexington, KY
09 December 2012